DARTMOOR'S ALLURING UPLANDS

Harold Fox's last book is a pioneering study of transhumance in a country where its existence has often been doubted. It explains how the grazing of livestock on Dartmoor was organised to meet the needs of the numerous peasant farmers who wished to use the land but lived many miles from the moor.

"His scholarship is meticulous; his knowledge of medieval documents, his skill in reading them (literally and in a deeper sense), and his understanding of context are skilfully deployed to answer a series of questions germane to his overall theme. This book is his masterwork; it is without question one of the most original contributions to the medieval history— and landscape history—of Dartmoor and Devon written in recent years. It is also an important contribution to the study of medieval transhumance in Britain."

Andrew Fleming, Emeritus Professor of Archaeology, University of Lampeter, Wales

The late **Harold Fox** was brought up in South Devon, and was Professor of Social and Landscape History at the Centre for English Local History, University of Leicester. He was a recognised authority on late-medieval landscape, agrarian and social history, particularly in the South-West and Midlands, and had served as president of the Medieval Settlement Research Group, chairman of the Society for Landscape Studies, vice-president of the English Place-Names Society and president of the Devon History Society.

Sadly he died before completing the final stages of this book, but two colleagues have brought it to the point of publication. **Matthew Tompkins** is Honorary Visiting Fellow at the Centre for English Local History, University of Leicester. **Christopher Dyer** is Emeritus Professor at the Centre for English Local History, University of Leicester.

Dartmoor's Alluring Uplands

Transhumance and Pastoral Management in the Middle Ages

HAROLD FOX

edited and introduced by
Matthew Tompkins and Christopher Dyer

UNIVERSITY
of
EXETER
PRESS

COVER IMAGES: *Front*: South Devon cattle at Combestone Tor, reproduced by kind permission of Elisabeth Stanbrook; *Back*: Sheep being gathered near Sheepstor, reproduced by kind permission of Tom Greeves, *and* pony drift at Merrivale, reproduced by kind permission of Andrew Fleming.

First published in 2012 by
University of Exeter Press
Reed Hall, Streatham Drive
Exeter EX4 4QR
UK
www.exeterpress.co.uk

British Library Cataloguing in Publication Data
A catalogue record for this book is available from the British Library.

Hardback ISBN 978 0 85989 864 5

Paperback ISBN 978 0 85989 865 2

Contents

Colour Plates

Figures

Tables

Editors' Acknowledgements

Professor Fox discussed the subject matter of this book, and received assistance in the collection of the data on which it is based, from a great many individuals over a lengthy period. The editors cannot know the full number of those to whom he owed a debt, and since any list they could produce would inevitably omit many deserving names, they have thought it better not to attempt such a list at all.

They themselves have received much invaluable assistance in completing Professor Fox's manuscript from Tom Greeves, Peter Herring, Andrew Fleming, Nat Alcock, Sam Turner, Graham Jones, Gillian Austen, Andy Isham, Malcolm Noble, Angela Doughty at Exeter Cathedral Archives and John Brunton, Susan Laithwaite and others at the Devon Record Office. Much is owed to Ken Smith, who designed many of the illustrative figures and carried out much of the research on which they are based. Tom Greeves, Peter Herring, Yoh Kawana, Frances Griffith, Sue Kilby and Ronan O'Donnell have generously given photographs from their own collections, four of which are included with the kind permission of Devon County Council (which has waived its reproduction fee in memory of all the work the author did for Devon) and English Heritage's National Monuments Record.

Encouragement and financial support was provided by Professor Fox's siblings, Jo Peters, Phoebe Kelly and Frank Meeres (who also prepared the index). Financial support has also been received from the Friends of the Centre for English Local History and Miss Eleanor Vollans.

Abbreviations

AHE&W III	E. Miller (ed.), *Agrarian History of England and Wales; III 1348–1500* (Cambridge, 1991)
AHR	*Agricultural History Review*
Cal Inq Misc	*Calendar of Inquisitions Miscellaneous (Chancery) preserved in the Public Record Office*
Cal InqPM	*Calendar of Inquisitions post Mortem and other analogous documents preserved in the Public Record Office*
CPR	*Calendar of the Patent Rolls*
CCR	*Calendar of the Close Rolls*
DB	C. Thorn and F. Thorn, *Domesday Book: Devon* (Chichester, 1985)
DCNQ	*Devon and Cornwall Notes and Queries*
DCRS	Devon and Cornwall Record Society
DNB	*Dictionary of National Biography*
DRO	Devon Record Office
ECRO	Exeter City Record Office (now subsumed in DRO)
EHR	*Economic History Review*
Exon DB	*Domesday Book*, vol. 4, *Libri Censualis Vocati Domesday Book, Additamenta ex Codic. Antiquiss.*, Record Commission (London, 1816), fols 83–494b
OED	*Oxford English Dictionary*
PDAS	*Devon Archaeological Society Proceedings*
PnD	J.E.B. Gover, A. Mawer and F.M. Stenton, *The Place-names of Devon*, 2 vols. (Cambridge, 1931–32)
Short History	S. Moore and P. Birkett, *A Short History of the Rights of Common upon the Forest of Dartmoor & the Commons of Devon* (Plymouth, 1890)
Trans. Devon Assoc.	*Reports and Transactions of the Devonshire Association for the Advancement of Science, Literature and Art*
VCH	*Victoria County History*

Introduction

The chapters of this book were written by Harold Fox, mainly between 2003 and 2007, but this introduction represents the work of the two editors, compiled after his untimely death, and we have also contributed a conclusion. We will begin with a brief account of how the book came to be written and completed, which necessarily includes a brief explanation of the author's life. Harold Fox who was born in 1945, grew up in south Devon and went to school near Brixham. Having been a geography student at University College London, he migrated to Cambridge with his supervisor, H.C. Darby, and there completed a thesis on the field systems of Devon and Cornwall.[1] After a brief episode as a lecturer in geography at Queens University Belfast he was appointed in 1976 to a post in the Department of English Local History at Leicester, and stayed there for the rest of his academic career. He was awarded a personal chair (in social and landscape history) in 2003, and retired in August 2007. He died a fortnight later.

His research was not confined to the South West: for example he wrote a series of innovative articles about the field systems of midland villages, and he defined the character of wold landscapes, taking his prime examples from the east Midlands.[2] Harold Fox constantly returned to his native region, however, from his early work on field systems, to the regional chapters in the third volume of the *Agrarian History of England Wales*, covering the period 1348 to 1500.[3] In the 1990s he wrote about labour: the young landless on the Glastonbury Abbey manors mostly in the early fourteenth century, and the tied cottages which he detected in fifteenth-century Devon.[4] His book on fishing villages was published in 2001.[5] Meanwhile he was writing a number of articles about many other dimensions of south-western history, including towns.[6]

He was drawn to study Dartmoor partly because in his youth 'the moor' had been a looming presence in south Devon, and like many others he was attracted by its grandeur and desolation. As a geographer and agrarian historian he realised that it provided a striking local example of the transhumance of livestock on to the high pastures in the summer, a widespread feature of traditional agriculture. As a topographer (a term he preferred to the more modern 'landscape historian') he showed how access was gained to the moor by herds of cattle driven along well-defined roads, and the way that the pasture was divided and managed, and partly enclosed. He combined analysis of documents with his own field work and reports on archaeological surveys and excavations, and also gained as much as possible from place names. Harold Fox showed that the documents enriched our understanding of a landscape already much studied by archaeologists.

The beginnings of his more closely focused study of Dartmoor can be traced in his writings through the 1990s, as he published articles on the manorial records which threw light on the profits gained from the moor, and he came to think and write more about transhumance. This was closely related to his work on fishing villages: both the sea and the moor were exploited in some periods from temporary dwellings occupied in the appropriate seasons, when the fish shoals arrived in the case of the coastal 'cellars', and in the time of summer grazing on the moor. He contributed a general essay on transhumance to a slim volume of essays on seasonal settlement (published in 1994). He also discovered and analysed the attachment to lowland manors of parcels of pasture at some distance on the edge of the moor.[7] He had already noted a great deal of documentary and topographical evidence for Dartmoor in the course of his research into Devon's agrarian history, beginning with his doctoral thesis. He was aware, however, that he needed to collect transcripts of documents systematically, and he had to find the time both for work in the archives and for analysis and writing. He applied successfully to the British Academy for a Research Readership which he held in 2001–02, and in the succeeding years was aiming to complete the writing.

The book's themes

Had Harold Fox been writing this introduction, he would not have wished for it to be solely concerned with Dartmoor and Devon, but would have indicated (with a typical lightness of touch) that this local research was related to more general, even universal historical and geographical questions. This is apparent in the text of the chapters, with its parallels and analogies from, for example, early medieval Warwickshire, nineteenth-century Ireland and late medieval Spain.

The first question relates to the importance of pastoral agriculture in the medieval economy. The great weight of scholarship which accumulated through the twentieth century gave arable cultivation an overwhelming importance in any assessment of farming in the Middle Ages, and especially in the period before the Black Death, 1250–1348. The expansion of rural society was judged by the quantity of land that was brought under the plough, and special attention was given to the 'great clearances' or 'internal colonisation' by which thousands of acres all over Europe were cleared and cultivated in the twelfth and thirteenth centuries. No better measure of the late medieval contraction was available than the abandonment of ploughed fields and the conversion of grain-growing land to grass. Archaeologists and landscape historians could demonstrate the importance of the arable fields because villages were surrounded even in modern times by the physical evidence of medieval cultivation. Agricultural productivity was judged primarily by the yields of crops, by calculating the numbers of bushels per acre, or the number of bushels harvested compared with the number sown. Technology was mainly a matter of crop rotation and ploughing. Estate studies gave the organisation of animal husbandry some prominence, such as Page's account of the management of sheep on the Crowland manors, and everyone was aware of the large income derived from the export of wool from the late thirteenth century.[8] Beasts of burden and manuring were clearly necessary for the efficient cultivation of grain, but there was a widespread belief in the small size of the pastoral sector. Postan argued in a famous article that in the thirteenth century the small numbers of peasant animals and the limited contribution of manure to soil fertility held back production and damaged the whole economy.[9]

The emphasis on grain production had some justification, as bread, ale and pottage based on cereals provided the bulk of the diet of the mass of the population. The received wisdom flowed naturally from a bias in the evidence, as surveys calculated the acreage of arable land, but were less precise about the extent of pasture if it was a share of a common. Sheep were sometimes omitted from manorial accounts because they were managed centrally (as at Crowland). There is a much greater wealth of documents from the corn-producing East, South and Midlands, with relatively thin coverage of the pastoral West and far North. The written evidence is reduced in quantity and detail in the fifteenth century, when pastures and livestock were expanding. And a sweep of pasture left no physical traces comparable with the ploughed corrugations of a landscape of ridge and furrow.

Gradually the balance is being redressed. Biddick has examined the pastoral management of a great estate, Peterborough Abbey, while Stephenson has calculated changes in fleece weights, one of the main clues to the productivity of pastoral husbandry.[10] The management of livestock is now seen (by Page and Stone, for example) in terms of the care taken over their welfare, which varied according to market circumstances, and the complex arrangements for securing their grazing throughout the year have been revealed by Winchester.[11] Harold Fox's own re-evaluation of the origin and development of the midland field systems showed how vital a role grazing played in the organisation of the village lands. Archaeology has revealed a great deal about the size, breed and lifecycle from animal bones, and sheep housing is now better understood.[12] We are not so sure that peasant holdings in *c.*1300 really were deprived of manure;

more attention is now given to the fifteenth century; and we appreciate that the switch from arable to pasture was not necessarily a symptom of economic distress.[13] In the 1990s in particular the Middle Ages were reinterpreted as a period of commercial growth, and while a high proportion of grain was produced for subsistence, most pastoral products were sold, and therefore made a great contribution to the expanding market.[14] A recent calculation, based on the value of produce, has suggested that pastoral output in c.1300 exceeded that derived from arable.[15]

It was in the context of this swing in historical opinion, which was part of a more positive view of the medieval economy, that Harold Fox decided that the time was right for him to embark on an investigation of one of the largest pasture resources of the period, in the midst of a county and a region which of necessity, in view of its hilly topography, depended on livestock husbandry for its living.

The second question on which this study sheds light is the nature and character of regions. Old-fashioned approaches to regional differences would identify Dartmoor as part of the 'highland zone' and therefore likely to be slow to change or receive outside influences. Another, more negative view, would be to see it as a periphery of limited significance, remote from the centre of things in London, or even in nearby Exeter. Harold Fox's approach, influenced by the Leicester school's idea of *pays*, was to avoid value judgements about remoteness and innate conservatism, but rather to aim to understand a local landscape, economy and way of life which was both distinctive in itself, but also closely connected to the surrounding lowlands.[16] He appreciated that there were many other comparable pastoral *pays*, like the Weald of Kent or the Arden of Warwickshire, with which comparison can be made. Indeed such wastes, forests and uplands can be found across Europe, and a study of one may discover features that can throw light on all of them.

The third question concerns property rights—when did private land develop on a waste shared by many communities? Central Dartmoor for a long period was operated as a great common, under the management of the Crown. The earliest records show that parts of the moor—its lower slopes mainly—belonged to the manors and villages that ringed the central moor. Much of the history of the moor consists of shifting relations between common and private interests, with many people competing for access, including turf cutters and tin miners as well as those wishing to graze animals. There was even a recreational interest, as now, because the moor was also a hunting reserve, a royal forest. The emergence of private property is of course a crucial influence on economic development. New trends in economic history for the study of institutions (which could include a common pasture) argue that people gain incentives to improve their lands and resources if they can establish their rights of ownership, and can enjoy the profits without fear of others claiming a share.[17]

Plate 1. Harold Fox at Hound Tor, 'on safari' with Hiroe Kawana from Tokyo (p. 8). (Yoh Kawana)

Plate 2. Cattle, including red Devons, on Cosdon Hill in South Tawton Common, north-east Dartmoor. This was a private manorial common in the outer moors, belonging in the thirteenth century to the de Tosny family and in the fourteenth and fifteenth centuries to the Beauchamp earls of Warwick. (Peter Herring)

Plate 3. Cattle on Cosdon Hill in South Tawton Common. In 1439 a survey of the manor of South Tawton mentioned 100 acres of hilly pasture (*pastura montanea*), worth 2d. an acre (p. 82). (Peter Herring)

Plate 4. *opposite top* Cattle at Merrivale, with Great Mis Tor in the background, in June 1995. They are being driven from Taviton Farm, near Tavistock, to their summer pasture at Powder Mills, in the central moor. Taviton, part of Tavistock Abbey's manor of Hurdwick, was a venville settlement, so summer pasturing on the moor is a centuries-old tradition. (Tom Greeves)

Plate 5. *opposite* Cattle being driven in Drift Lane, Postbridge, one of the great drift routes to the north moor, in October 1997. (Tom Greeves)

Plate 6. *above* The red tide: red Devon cattle passing through Holne, on the south-east edge of Dartmoor, in February 1997 (Tom Greeves)

Plate 7. *above* A moor-edge settlement in the outer moors: Widecombe in the Moor, looking westward from Bonehill Down (one of the detached areas of outer moor) towards Dunstone Down (part of the inner area of contiguous moorland but lying in the manors of Widecombe and Dunstone, not in the royal central moor) (p. 18). (Sue Kilby)

Plate 8. *opposite top* Lettaford, a small venville hamlet in the parish of North Bovey, surrounded by ancient enclosures but only 300 yards from the north-eastern edge of the open moor. The view is eastwards. Sanders, the medieval longhouse in Plate 9, is on the left of the open space on the further or eastern edge of the hamlet. A droveway leading to the moor runs between the two large fields in the bottom of the photograph (pp. 18, 53, 125). (Frances Griffith, Devon County Council, 10 December 1986, copyright DCC)

Plate 9. *opposite* Sanders in Lettaford, a classic Dartmoor longhouse (p. 14). Built in the early sixteenth century, the present structure dates mostly from the seventeenth century. Its subsequent use as a farmworker's house ensured its survival virtually unaltered until the 1970s, when it was restored by the Landmark Trust. Seen from the south, the entrance porch marks the division between the house, upslope to the left, and the livestock byre, downhill to the right. (N.W. Alcock, P. Child and M. Laithwaite, 'Sanders, Lettaford: a Devon long-house', *PDAS.*, xxx (1972), pp. 227–33.)

Plate 10. *opposite top* Hound Tor House 1, under which were found traces of three small transhumant huts (p. 141 and Fig. 5.1). (Ronan O'Donnell)

Plate 11. *opposite* Hound Tor, a deserted Dartmoor hamlet which began as a transhumant settlement of seasonally occupied shielings, had become a permanently occupied farming hamlet by the thirteenth century, and was finally abandoned in the late fourteenth century. Its longhouses, field boundaries and some hints of ridge-and-furrow can be seen in the snow (pp. 22, 140). The view is south-westwards. (Frances Griffith, Devon County Council, 17 March 1985, copyright DCC)

Plate 12. *above* Hound Tor House 3, a medieval longhouse. The opposed entrances can just be made out, halfway along its length where the grass has been worn bare; in the lower, further half, where the livestock were sheltered, the drain which removed their liquid waste can be seen (pp. 14, 141). (Sue Kilby)

Plate 13.   Two herdsmen's huts at Brownwilly on Bodmin Moor, sited to give panoramic views over the adjacent pastures. Three similar huts can be seen on Dartmoor, on Dean Moor (p. 79). (Peter Herring)

Plate 14.   *opposite top* A gully or openwork left by tin-mining at Gobbett, near Swincombe. In 1314 it was alleged that 300 acres of pasture on Dartmoor were destroyed by such means every year (p. 101). (Tom Greeves)

Plate 15.   *opposite* The Dartmoor end of a droveway from Cornwall. Having crossed the Tamar on the Greystone Bridge, it is seen here passing south of Brent Tor and about to enter the Moor at Gibbet Hill (p. 55). Andrew Fleming is standing at a spot where two conjoined triangular swellings were created, probably to contain and check livestock. (Peter Herring)

Plate 16. Denbury Green, an overnight stop on the droveway from Cockington to Dartmoor (pp. 200, 202). The Union Inn can be seen on the far side. (Paul Hutchinson)

Plate 17. Woolston Green, an overnight stop on the droveway from Paignton to Dartmoor (p. 200). (Yoh Kawana)

Plate 18. Denbury Down Lane, leading from Denbury Hill towards Dartmoor, visible on the skyline (p. 199).

Plate 19. Wide verges below Landscove church on the Paignton to Ashburton droveway (p. 200). (Yoh Kawana)

Plate 20. *above* Buckland Common, on the eastern flank of the outer moors, seen from Chuley Hill, south of Ashburton, near the end of the droveway from Paignton (p. 200). (Yoh Kawana)

Plate 21. *opposite* Lane running down Chuley Hill, south of Ashburton, on the droveway from Paignton, looking north towards Ausewell Common (p. 200). (Yoh Kawana)

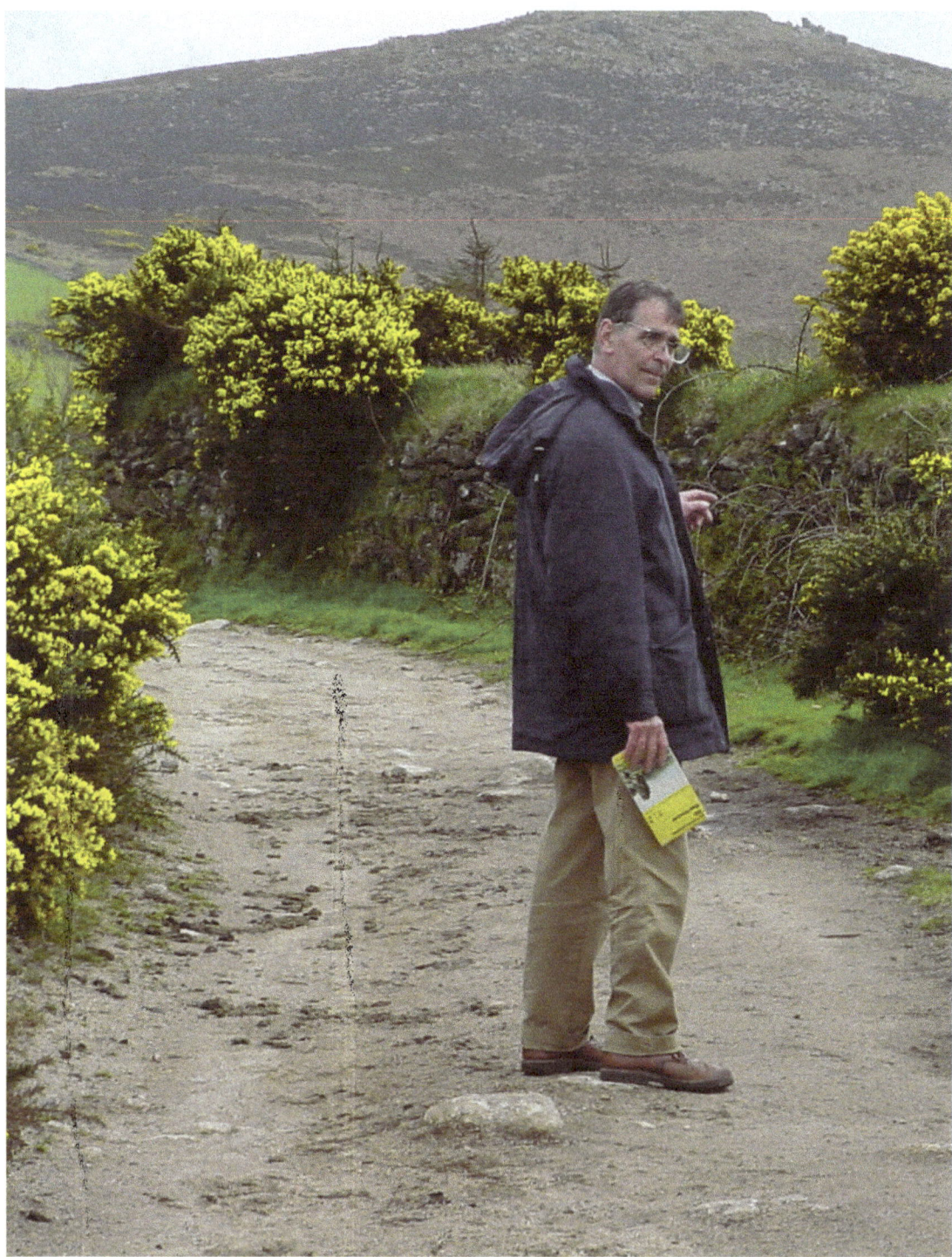

Plate 22. Harold Fox on a Dartmoor droveway. (Yoh Kawana)

With these general questions before him, and with other lesser historical problems in mind as well, Harold Fox set out to write a book which defines the moor and its various characteristics, both positive and negative. Dartmoor is shown to have served the county of Devon and parts of Cornwall as a pastoral resource in the late medieval and early modern periods, by means of a system of transhumance described by Peter Herring as 'transhumance by proxy' and by Harold Fox as 'impersonal transhumance'. This means that the cattle owners delivered their beasts into the hands of herdsmen and paid a modest sum for their services. He shows how the edges of the moor was held in manors, the lords of which controlled the grazing, and some parcels of pasture were attached to more remote manors for their livestock. These detachments are recorded or can be detected in the pre-Conquest period, and take us back to a period of 'personal transhumance', when the herdsmen and perhaps dairy maids travelled with the animals and lived on the pastures. We can still trace on the ground the droveways by which, under both systems of transhumance, cattle were taken on to the moor.

Preparing the book

The manuscript from which this book was edited came into our hands in varying states of completeness. The earlier chapters had gone through several drafts and were largely finished (though lacking footnotes), but the later ones were in a much less polished state. Parts of chapters 6 and 7 existed only as hand-written first drafts, with a number of *lacunae*, while the third and final section of chapter 7 consisted only of a bullet point outline and a few fragmentary paragraphs. We have linked the fragments into a coherent account consistent with the outline, though inevitably not one as full or detailed as Harold Fox intended.

The manuscript had few footnotes, as Harold Fox always wrote his footnotes last, after the text was complete. This is a great loss, as he took them very seriously, indeed had elevated them to an art-form, providing not merely his sources but also short and pithy reviews of the relevant literature and illuminating, often amusing, asides.[18] Some of the footnotes which appear in the following chapters are his own—some found in two of his recent journal articles which were based closely on sections of the manuscript, others in various of his earlier publications which were based on the same sources as the manuscript—but most have had to be worked up by Matthew Tompkins (with assistance from Tom Greeves and Peter Herring—but sole responsibility for any errors rests with Matthew Tompkins). It is never easy to identify the sources for someone else's work, and it has not proved any easier on this particular occasion—indeed, in a few cases we have had to admit defeat and have left the reference un-noted. Errors have undoubtedly occurred, and any

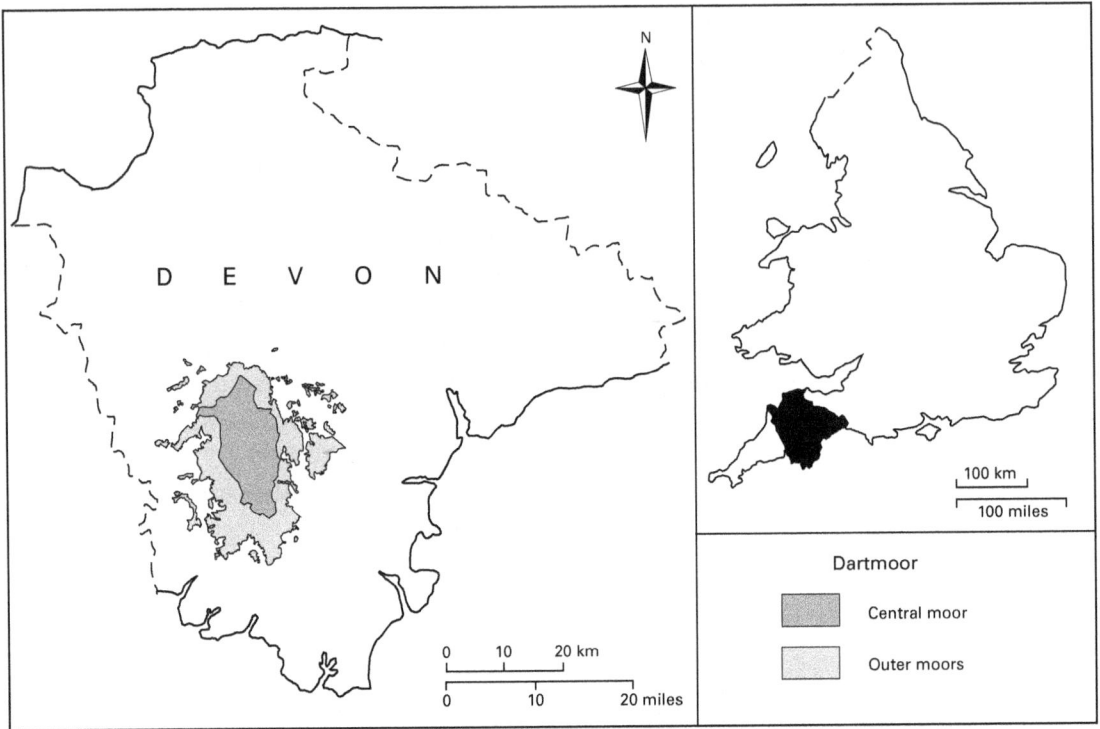

0.1 **Dartmoor:
location map.**

reader who spots one is invited to send the details to the Centre for English Local History at the University of Leicester.

The original manuscript referred to about 45 illustrative figures and eight tables. Professor Fox had produced drawings or rough drafts of about half of them (with much assistance from Ken Smith), and a few more had appeared in those of his recent articles which were closely based on the manuscript; the Figures and Tables appearing in the following chapters are based on these existing drawings and drafts, though where only a rough or partial draft was available the editors have had to fill the gaps, and the results may not be exactly as Professor Fox envisaged them (these are Figs 7.2, 7.3 and 7.5 and Tabs 3.1 and 3.2). Some of the other Figures and Tables mentioned in the manuscript were clearly references to existing maps from other publications, and with one exception were not difficult to identify (the exception was replaced by a new map based on data kindly provided by Nat Alcock—Fig. 1.2). Others it seems Harold Fox had not found the time to draw, or at least they could not be found among his papers. Some of these the editors have produced themselves, so far as they were able, usually based on his own research notes (Fig. 7.3 and Tabs 6.1, 6.2 and 7.1–3), but others, based on research for which no notes could be found, have had to be omitted (see notes 9 in chapter 5 and 15 in chapter 7). Four more have been added by the editors, where it seemed some illustration of the points made in the text might be useful (Figs 0.1, 1.4, 2.1 and 6.4).

CHAPTER ONE

Definitions and limitations

'Before my pen has gleaned my teeming brain'

Defining Dartmoor's resources

It is tempting to begin a book on an aspect of Dartmoor's past with romantic references to the region's folklore, some of it imposed from outside, to the picturesque qualities of the region's hills and valleys and to literary associations, not least the wild and lusting hound of the Baskervilles. An alternative way to begin is with the voices of insiders and others who knew Dartmoor well, especially their views on the potential of the region for the grazing of livestock, which is the main theme of this book. The latter track is adopted here.

In 1627, William Pellowe, inhabitant of Lydford, testified before an Exchequer court during one of an interminable series of lawsuits about tithe arising from Dartmoor's prime agricultural product, its grazing land. Where rough pasture had been converted into enclosed fields, he said, there was 'good land ... inhabited by rich inhabitants and tilled with oats and rye and with manurance ... with barley', this land being 'prized or esteemed the better by reason of the commons'. The other face of Dartmoor, beyond the improved farms, he continued, comprised 'wild wastes' and 'hilly grounds ... dangerous in the winter to be travelled through by reason of waters, rocks and mires'. These last words echo an injunction of Bishop Bronescombe—written in 1260 and relating to the distance which certain inhabitants of Dartmoor had to travel to their mother church—when he wrote of the 'tempests and floods' which hindered journeys within the region. From a few generations after William Pellowe's time we have a description of a land surveyor who, after inspecting farms in the parish of Manaton and speaking to their inhabitants, described the land as 'very poor, cold and hungry ground full of rocks and naturally heathy but [which] by the extraordinary pains and costs of its owners produces good rye, some wheat but more oats and barley'. Like Pellowe he went on to comment on the value of the rough pastures: 'their comons ... are heathy downs which are large'.[1]

In the summer and winter of 1791 the ever-observant agricultural writer William Marshall, always keen to speak to local inhabitants wherever he went, was staying at Buckland Abbey, home of the Drake family, and frequently set out to study Dartmoor. The great extent of the rough grazings drew from him a most enthusiastic description: 'herbage!' he exclaimed, 'greensward! even of the highest, bleakest hills, frequently intermixed however with heath which indeed chiefly occupies the worst-soiled parts of the mountain; while on the lower grounds the furze [gorse], particularly of the trailing sort, is prevalent.' Five summers later, William Simpson, a surveyor for the Duchy of Cornwall, toured extensively on Dartmoor. He tasted 'mutton . . . uncommonly fine and sweet so as to become proverbial', the 'very well flavoured' meat of another writer at about the same time, and he watched the turf-diggers working at their seams. He made careful observations of the region's grazing potential, noting 'how well both the cattle and sheep look upon such a poor, barren soil' and explaining this by the presence, 'among the rocks and loose stones . . . of a sweet grass called sheep's fescue'. In conclusion Simpson noted that some parts of the moorlands might be enclosed and then planted with trees to provide timber sales or drained to provide better herbage, but he considered that the isolation of the region from markets was an obstacle to improvement—a point also made by William Marshall and by other near contemporaries. The point made by Simpson about the health of animals grazing upon Dartmoor was repeated in the nineteenth century by Henry Tanner: he wrote that cattle rapidly improved when they came to the summer pastures, largely from the fresh breezes and the fact that there were fewer insects to infect them than in drowsy, warm and windless south Devon.[2]

These voices give an accurate picture of small islands of cultivation in a wide sea of rough, often rocky grazing ground and they introduce some of the main products to be had by the harvesters of the hills. The island farms and their occupiers are frequently mentioned in this book, but its main concerns are the open seas of pasture and their management, especially through the practice of transhumance by which livestock were brought to the region from outside (discussed in more detail in the next section). Visitors today can still see the sheep, cattle and ponies of commoners, some from outside the region, browsing on the moorlands and crossing the unfenced roads. (A Japanese lady to whom I introduced the region described her journey through it as 'a great safari'—Plate 1.) This ancient grazing system is now the subject of controversy as ecological studies by distant academics voice disapproval while Dartmoor farmers, wise ecologists through experience, defend customs developed over many generations. The livestock are feeding upon several species of moorland grasses, especially flying bent, bog cotton grass and *molinia*, and upon heather and gorse, all discussed in a little more detail later in this section.

The grazings are of great extent. The central moor (the parish of Lydford), defined more closely later in this chapter, covers about 54,000 acres and has a circuit of about 42 miles; beyond it, the outer moors belonging to the surrounding parishes, taken together, today cover an area which is even greater than that. The highest ridge, from High Willhays to Yes Tor in northern Dartmoor ('the roof of Devon'), reaches to 2,039 feet, while the heights of the summits of the principal hills in the south range from about 1,200 to about 1,600 feet. Westerly winds hit these hills and discharge rain which keeps the ground moist and suitable for growth of grass. Dartmoor is wet: 'The only thing that is certain in this world,' said Charles Stuart, 'is that it is raining in Tavistock.'[3] Princetown, situated in the west of Dartmoor, receives 81 inches of rain, compared with Plymouth, on the coast to the south of the region, which receives only 38 inches. Rain nurtures the grazing, but for only part of the year, because in winter cold weather stops plant growth. In April the number of days with ground frost on high Dartmoor can be as many as ten to fifteen, but later there is improvement.

Let us begin in winter. Then the relatively small number of livestock on the moorlands feed on the rank remains of the previous season's growth of grass and on the evergreen heather and gorse. After the long, lorn winter a new cycle commences, at first slowly, then triumphantly, 12 May being the traditional date for moor-edge farmers to increase stocking rates on the rough grazings near their farms. Now the grasses begin to lose rankness, shooting at rates which vary according to species, and increased numbers of animals, by their grazing, help to force the new bright growth. We can begin to observe a lovely ripple as the wind bows and bends the fresh green blades. As we move further into the year the volume of feed for livestock greatly increases and the moorlands are at their fullest and most productive: both William Marshall and William Simpson, whose enthusiastic remarks about grazing potential have been quoted earlier, were observers of the bright summer scene on Dartmoor. And so is set in motion that annual cycle of movements of livestock towards the hills which is the main subject of this book as, unfailingly, the pastures offer up their riches. Summer grazing on Dartmoor was especially attractive in those years when grassland elsewhere in Devon, but particularly in the warm south, became parched. A modern farmer and historian, Freda Wilkinson, explains that, because of high rainfall and the moisture-retaining properties of a peaty soil, moorland grass 'can still provide grazing when many of the "down-country" pastures are brown and bare', and William Marshall made the same point at the end of the eighteenth century—especially large numbers of animals were sent to Dartmoor 'in a dry season when the cultivated ... leys [elsewhere] are burnt up'. Later, Sabine Baring-Gould wrote: 'in the abnormally dry summers of 1893 and 1897 Dartmoor proved of incalculable advantage ... [so that] the starving cattle were driven there in thousands and tens of thousands.'[4]

It should not be thought that the grasses of Dartmoor were everywhere simply grazed by the livestock, for they were also mown as upland hay which was taken down to moor-side farms for winter feed. This practice has not received any notice in the huge literature on the region, but it was commonplace and important. Its importance lies in the fact that many of the manors around Dartmoor had very little valley-bottom meadowland, the valleys being so relatively narrow. This is quite clear from Domesday Book which, for example, gives 200 acres of demesne meadow to Ottery St Mary in the wide, lush valley of the Otter in east Devon but only 10 acres to the southerly moor-edge manor of Dean (Prior) and 8 acres to Throwleigh in the north-east of the region. So these slender resources were supplemented by hay mown on the moors, mentioned, for example, in medieval charters relating to the farms and hamlets of Bullhornstone, Ash, Beara and Hurburnford, all in South Brent parish. There are also medieval references to men who attempted to cheat by going up to cut the upland hay before the accustomed time. Presumably the hay was protected in some way from roaming livestock, and this may possibly explain some of the low-banked enclosures still to be seen on the moors today.[5]

We have introduced the grazings of Dartmoor with reference to grass, but two other plants, abundant in the region, provided food for livestock, namely gorse (always called furze in Devon) and heather. Animal mouths are more tolerant of gorse and other prickly species than we might think: holly was once an important source of animal feed in parts of England, while as long ago as 1379 John de Brie (in a treatise on flock management written for Charles V of France) noticed how sheep fed with relish on thistles growing in their pastures. Gorse can be bruised to make it slightly more edible and on Dartmoor I have seen horses doing this with their hooves (in relatively modern times a bruising machine was invented, though I have been told by a Dartmoor farmer that it was never introduced into the region). At the beginning of the twentieth century John French of Middle Merripit (near Postbridge) cut low-growing gorse, known as 'dell-vuzz', in winter and put it through a chaff-cutter before feeding it to his horses. Gorse is deep-rooted, taking up minerals and trace elements which are not found in the grasses and which prevent certain types of sickness in animals. The plant grows high, so when snow lies, covering the grass, it is an especially valuable source of feed for over-wintering livestock. It was also widely used as a fuel. For all of these reasons, the poet's line—'With blossom'd furze unprofitably gay', cited by Hoskins—is not entirely accurate: gorse was profitable, being valued in medieval surveys at four times as much per acre as rough pasture (for example, at Okehampton in 1292).[6]

The gathering of gorse from the lord's waste was a common right on most of the moor-edge manors and there are frequent references, in charters to free tenants, of grants of this right; for example, a medieval charter from Lutton (Cornwood) gives the tenant gorse in 'reasonable' quantity and 'sufficient for his own use', that is, not to be sold on. A document of 1382 refers to rights of gorse gathering 'from time immemorial'. As well as growing wild it was a cultivated plant in the Middle Ages, a fifteenth-century survey of Milton Abbot referring to the 'cultivation' of the plant (while there is a reference in a 1347 deed for Brixham, way beyond Dartmoor, to a strip in an open field which was cultivated with gorse). Presumably medieval farmers or their daughters gathered the seed and then sowed it in enclosed or protected places where it was safe from browsing animals and could be cut when needed and given to stall-fed animals during the winter. Later on, the seed was sold commercially, William Marshall in the eighteenth century noting how Tavistock had 'long been a market for furze seed'. A local farmer tells me that gorse was cultivated on Dartmoor up to 100 years ago.[7]

The charter for Lutton mentioned above also gives the grantee right to cut heather on the lord's moors. This was another useful moorland plant, also deep-rooted and therefore, like gorse, taking up minerals. Heather is browsed by livestock and in the past was also gathered for winter feed, litter and other uses. It too is mentioned as having been taken 'from time immemorial' in the same document of 1382 quoted above for its reference to gorse.

The natural resources of Dartmoor have been introduced here through plants which were edible to the livestock of people involved with transhumance, the subject which is the main theme of this book. The region provided medieval people with many other resources. The very bedrock of most of Dartmoor, the granite, was gathered and hewn. Granite is the first feature which strangers visiting Dartmoor notice, even before the grazing animals, because in many places it outcrops in the strange shapes of the tors, famously in one case in the form of a crouching hound which much influenced Conan Doyle's mind. The names of the tors tell much of local legend and folklore and association—the hound, kite, crow, fox, hart, the goat, the vixen, mist and wind and laughter, a bell, a cromlech, a seat. Granite is also visible where it appears to spill down the slopes of hills in blocks of various sizes detached from the tors themselves in ancient geological time. The blocks are known locally as clitters, an Old-English word meaning 'loose stones', and Clitters is the name of a farm to the south of the rock-strewn slopes of Sheeps Tor (also of a settlement on the north-east flank of Bodmin Moor, likewise a granitic upland; Clithers, perched on the moorland edge in Chagford parish, may be another such name). There are rather few medieval references to the exploitation of granite, the best coming from the manor of Shaugh Prior, to be mentioned in chapter 3. Tin is another of Dartmoor's inanimate resources, possibly exploited in the Bronze Age, possibly in the sub-Roman period and certainly from the twelfth century onwards. Its exploitation gave employment to many, enriched a few, and has left striking traces in the landscape. Associated with tin working was the seasonal occupation of turf-cutting, undertaken by *carbonarii*, for turves, after having been turned into peat charcoal, were used to smelt the metal: in her *Home Scenes* (1846) Rachel Evans described, near Whitchurch, 'the hills in the distance glowing with the conflagration of the turf cutters'. Turf was also the common fuel of Dartmoor farms and households. Dartmoor was distinctive in its many other resources, including bracken and rushes (both mentioned in medieval grants of rights of common), deer, for sanctioned and illegal hunting, and rabbits—possibly introduced quite soon after the Norman Conquest—for which Dartmoor provided an excellent home, far from the temptation of munching arable crops. There were other resources which we might today call 'minor', although they were not thus to the people who used them, such as the partridges of the moors of Sampford Courtenay.[8]

Dartmoor and its parts

How to delimit Dartmoor? One could select a contour line, because height influences temperature and rainfall, and both affect the growth of grass and therefore pastoral management. But which contour? One could use a geological criterion, but to select simply the granite, Dartmoor's main rock, would be to discard many tracts of country, such as Roborough Down, which insiders and outsiders regard as part of the moorland landscape. The present-day boundary between improved land (crops and good pasture) and rough pasture, that is 'moor', is clearly inappropriate as a marker for the past, because tides of cultivation have ebbed and flowed in prehistoric and historic times. To define Dartmoor as including all parishes which have a slice of the rough pastures would be to include large tracts of, say, southern Ugborough or northern Okehampton in which elevation and geology give human landscapes which have no resemblance at all to the common image of Dartmoor. 'There is difficulty in defining the limits of Dartmoor,' wrote the region's great luminary, R. Hansford Worth, in the 1920s and the problem is no easier today. Some complicated combination of all of the measures mentioned above might solve our problem, but that is not attempted here. Instead we shall discuss some distinctive aspects of the material culture of Dartmoor's people in the past, thereby evading the question of boundaries, for the evidence for those topics is sparse and sporadic.[9]

In the Middle Ages, families which farmed at high altitudes, many well above 900 feet, lived according to rhythms much influenced by the relatively late arrival of spring, and therefore of milking, cheese making and the sowing of oats, by the late date of harvest, by other moorland tasks which had their seasons, such as swaling (burning the pastures) and turf-cutting; as well as by the influx, rounding-up and departure of livestock brought from afar by outsiders. Crops grown by the tenants of South Teign manor in the early fifteenth century were rye and pillcorn or pillas, both highly tolerant, the latter being a tough variety of oats with a very small grain. We know this because there is a record of what they took to the manorial mill to be ground and, although similar information does not survive for other Dartmoor manors, the fare at South Teign appears to be typical to judge from crops grown on lords' demesnes, where cropping practice was dictated by local custom and by the knowledge of the manorial reeve, always a tenant of the manor and therefore familiar with the most reliable practices of the country. At Lustleigh in February 1393, part of Sir John Daumarle's demesne had been set down to rye the previous autumn, but the oats remained to be sown. Court rolls, which often contain references to crop types, usually in the context of pleas resulting from trespass and trampling by animals, reveal that rye (especially) and oats were grown on tenants' holdings throughout the region. Medieval Dartmoor farmers grew these crops for sale in a small way at the market towns on the borders of the region, though not with great profit because neither commanded high prices. Most of the produce, however, went to their own tables and taverns, the rye for loaves, described as 'black' at Tavistock in the early sixteenth century and at Chagford in the late fifteenth. The oats went towards cakes, like the 'halfpenny cake' doled out to the men who assisted at the annual rounding-up of livestock on central Dartmoor; and also towards ale said to be 'lyke wash as pygges had wrestled in' which, according to one sixteenth-century observer, caused vomiting in strangers, 'notwithstandinge the people ... [round about] doe endure the same very well'. There are very few medieval references from Dartmoor to cider or orchards. The fact that some of the local produce was taken to markets indicates that not only local farmers but also local non-producers of grains such as townspeople and tinners enjoyed a similar diet: we know from a document of 1220 that in the town of Chagford bakers sold bread, presumably made from local crops, to a 'gathering' of buyers on market day.[10]

Dartmoor farmers had special privileges of grazing animals on the moorlands, and the occupiers of even the smallest farms could make additional profits in cash from acting as middlemen, taking in the livestock of outsiders for the summer season, as described in chapters 2 and 3. A farming family's diet could therefore be enlivened by meat in some plenty—fresh, or salted after immersion in a granite vat—with no great drain upon a farm's resources, and those without land could buy this abundant commodity cheaply at local markets (recorded, again, at Chagford as early as 1220). On special occasions the farmer might have upon his table something like the veritable meat mountain which Robert Herrick saw in his lonely moor-edge parish of Dean Prior:

> ... first the large and cheefe
> Foundation of your feast, fat beef:
> With upper stories, mutton, veal
> And bacon (which makes full the meale).[11]

Tastes and smells and warmth add to the quality of everyday life. The medieval Dartmoor farmer had access to plentiful supplies of peat for heating and cooking, and usually it came free if it was 'for his own hearth' to use the terminology of a thirteenth-century deed. Bacon cooked on a turf fire has its own special flavour, to be enjoyed along with the half sweet, half acid scent of smoke from the peat. It was believed in the past that the mutton from sheep grazed upon Dartmoor's pastures was especially sweet and fine because of some special qualities of the grassland there and because of the heather and gorse browse, just as it was thought that Cheshire cheese or Stilton could not be made outside its regions of origin, for the same kind of reasons. In the Middle Ages many Dartmoor farmers lived in longhouses (a technical term for a house in which humans and animals lived in inter-connecting compartments under one roof, often without a roof-high partition between them) where the warm smell of cattle was ever-present at night-time, as well as the danger of tuberculosis caught from them. We first know of longhouses on Dartmoor from excavations of thirteenth-century structures such as those in Okehampton Park, on Sourton Down, at Hutholes, Dinna Clerks and Hound Tor. They may still be seen today, with their gently sloping central drains in the livestock's end to carry out the liquid waste (Plates 9–12). The construction of longhouses, as part of the culture of the people of Dartmoor, persisted, remarkably, into the seventeenth century among farmers and minor landed families, unaffected by the 'great rebuilding' of more sophisticated (if that is the right term) dwellings which took place in some other parts of England. It is probable that medieval Dartmoor people used a distinctive breed of pony. Finally, the Dartmoor farmer and his sons had opportunities for employment in a variety of occupations either in sequence (sometimes as part of the life cycle) or in combination (as by-employments): hewing stones, poaching rabbits and deer, getting tin and cutting turf, for example. This made them distinctive for the variety of skills they possessed which would not have been found, for example, among the medieval people of the South Hams to the south of Dartmoor, except in the region's coastal fringe where there were also opportunities for men to enter into a great variety of maritime occupations.[12]

Such features of everyday life made Dartmoor people distinctive, and this would not have gone unnoticed in the Middle Ages when they visited the market places which ringed the region or when countrymen from the surroundings went to the moorland farms in order to hand over livestock for the summer grazing season and returned in autumn to reclaim them. In Ashburton parish the youths of the 'upland', as it was termed, from isolated moor-edge farms and hamlets such as Ausewell and Welstor, had their own store and fraternity in the fifteenth and early sixteenth centuries and may well have been regarded as just a little rough by the 'sophisticated' dwellers of the grand borough of Ashburton, who boasted their communality and common seal. If a Dartmoor man moved away from the region to take up a farm relatively close by, he might be given the surname Moorman because of his distinctiveness as seen by outsiders. This at least is one explanation for the name which is found in several Devon parishes among lists of those who paid the royal taxes of 1524 and 1525, but most notably in places in the vicinity of Dartmoor and Exmoor. Later on the description of 'moorman' became more closely defined, being used for a herdsman employed to guard livestock or for a dweller in the central moor.[13]

The people of medieval Dartmoor certainly saw themselves as distinct and this is reflected in the terms which they used for people from beyond the bounds of the region. To Nicholas Knight of Mary Tavy, speaking in 1699, people living beyond the ring of parishes which surround central Dartmoor, of which his was one, were known as 'countrymen', 'country' being used here in the sense of 'a tract or district ... inhabited by people of the same race, dialect of occupation': the countrymen had life-styles which differed significantly from the moorman's. In the seventeenth century and later, local people described those who lived beyond the ring of Dartmoor parishes as 'foreigners' or 'strangers' or 'strange men'. The same words seem to have been in the minds of the local people who testified before an inquisition of 1382 held at Lydford and touching rights of turf-cutting on central Dartmoor, and in the minds of the local lord and men from the neighbourhood who drew up and witnessed a deed of 1331 which mentioned grazing rights on the moor belonging to the manor of Shapley Helion: *extraneii*, 'foreigners', is the term used in both documents. 'Foreigner' in the past had connotations of 'otherness' and was used also by dwellers in the Forest of Dean to describe outsiders.[14]

All of these terms for outsiders give a hint of a notion among Dartmoor people, of belonging to a district, of what Alan Everitt has described as consciousness of region in the past, of a region 'with a sense of its own identity'. And it is easy to understand how such a sense might develop on Dartmoor. Farmers living on and near Dartmoor had special rights of grazing which, although they did not exclude the commoning 'foreigners' or 'strangers', set their owners in a particularly privileged position. An inner group, the most privileged of them all in terms of grazing rights, had special duties when livestock on the central moor were rounded up and counted; although they lived in isolated farms and hamlets, they came together to cooperate on these occasions. The same group cooperated as a syndicate in renting the mill at Babeny where they ground their rye and oats. In a sixteenth-century document there is a fascinating hint of inter-manorial cooperation over the dates which moor-edge manors set for their yearly drifts. Moreover, from 1317 there is good evidence of a small-scale regional 'revolt' over the illegal killing of deer. A certain amount of 'background' poaching always

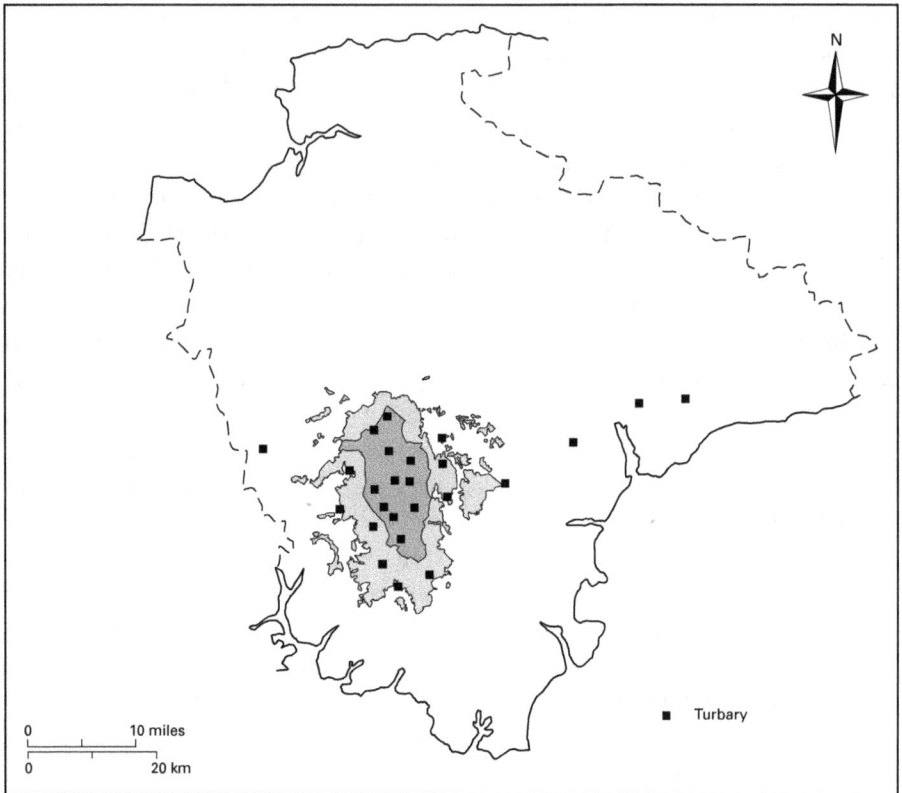

existed on Dartmoor, but in the high summer of 1317 matters seem to have got out of hand, large raiding parties were involved, assaults were made on herdsmen and the head of one of the local religious houses, Thomas, abbot of Buckland, appears to have high-handedly thrown a hunt protester into his private gaol. The region found all of this too much and a group of 30 men complained to Edward II: analysis of their names, some of a locative type and some which may be matched to rentals of the early fourteenth century, shows that this was a truly regional protest involving men from a good number of Dartmoor parishes. Under all of the circumstances mentioned in this paragraph something of a sense of belonging to a region emerged. And it is, of course, highly developed still today.[15]

Aspects of culture such as diet or housing or a sense of belonging are difficult, if not impossible, to define precisely on the ground for any moment in the past. Nevertheless, two attempts are made here. Fig. 1.1 shows medieval and sixteenth-century references, from throughout Devon, to the use of turf in heating and cooking, many of them from grants which allow the grantee rights of turbary (turf-digging), although other sources, such as valuations of turbaries in medieval inquisitions and other surveys, have also been used. Fig. 1.2 shows recorded longhouses, most of which date from the seventeenth

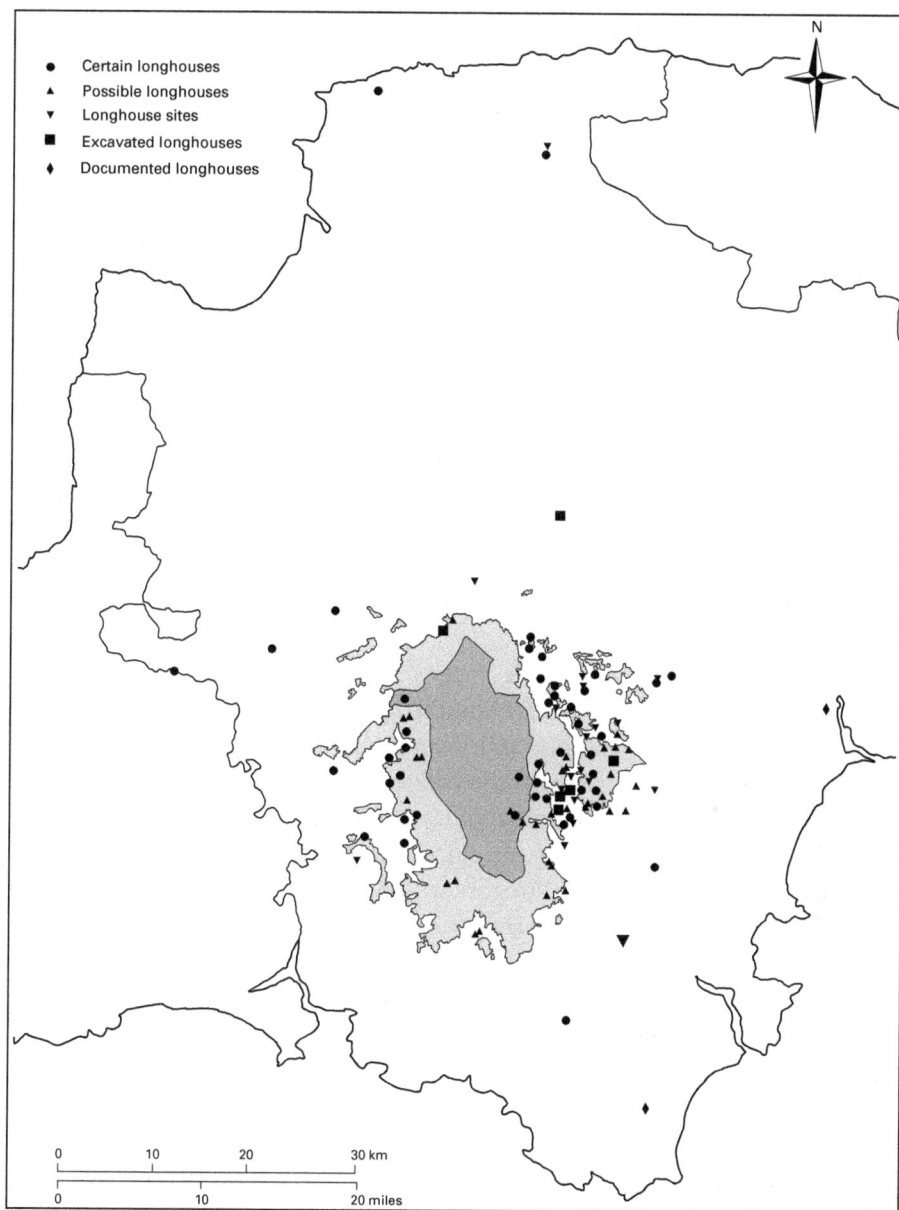

1.2 The Dartmoor region: longhouses.

All known sites of longhouses in Devon, whether still surviving, ruined or known only through excavation or documentary sources (there are none in east Devon).

Based on data supplied by Nat Alcock, whose kind assistance the editors gratefully acknowledge. Professor Fox's manuscript referred to a map of longhouses and longhouse sites in Devon and Cornwall compiled by Nat Alcock in the 1970s, based on information provided by local field-workers. For the present publication, that has been updated to a limited extent. The 'Documented Longhouses' are taken from sources used in N. Alcock and C. Carson, *West Country Farms: House-and-Estate Surveys, 1598–1764* (Oxford, 2007).

century or earlier; they range from those which have been excavated, as at Hound Tor and in Okehampton Park, to buildings still occupied today, and to ruinous structures or ruins recorded but now destroyed.

The concept of Dartmoor as a distinctive region was certainly in local minds and in local speech during the Middle Ages. When local assessors, supervising the royal tax in 1332, came to Buckland next to Ashburton, they returned the place as *Bocland in the Mor*; *Bokeland in Le More* is the rather grand spelling used in the record of an inquisition into the property made in 1378. Widecombe is given as *Whithecombe in the More* in the records of an assize court held in 1362, the form of the name finding its way into the royal record because it was presented as such by local jurors (Plate 7). These two names, meaning 'land granted by charter' and 'wide or withy coomb', are common ones in Devon, repeated in many parts of the county, so the tag or affix was highly convenient as a means of distinguishing places from one another, for taxation or judicial officials, as well as for the people of a locality. But we also find the affix attached to place-names which are less common, for example to Scobitor (*in le Mor* in the fifteenth century) and to Blackaton (*in themore* in the early fourteenth).[16]

It is noteworthy that all of the places mentioned in the last paragraph lie close to the heart of Dartmoor. By contrast, perhaps, Lettaford was described as *Luttreford by Dertemore* (not '*in*') in an inquisition of 1389, and the hamlet lies, together with others, towards the fringes of the region in a relatively large area of reclaimed land in the gentle valleys of the upper Bovey tributaries. In 1219, Henry III commanded the sheriff of Devon to convoke his county and elect two worthy and discreet knights to look after Dartmoor; they were to be 'of the neighbourhood of Dartmoor', in a position to know the region and its customs well. Both references perhaps imply a popular concept of a blurred border zone. Beyond the borderlands themselves were the 'further places more remote', as they were described by a Dartmoor man in the seventeenth century, truly, to use words coined in another context, beyond the pale.[17]

Place-names with the affix 'in the Moor', including the definite article, are reflected in present-day usage. Dartmoor is known simply as 'The Moor'—this was current usage when, as a boy, I first became aware of the lure of the region and still is for a considerable circuit around. Because of the vast extent of the region and because its hills and tors dominate skylines in so many directions, from 15 miles and more in some cases, the question 'which moor?' is never asked.

Extent of the moorland

Although it is not easy to define Dartmoor as a cultural region because it has no boundary which can be shown as a firm line on a map, it is in fact crossed and re-crossed by boundaries of a variety of kinds, those for example which

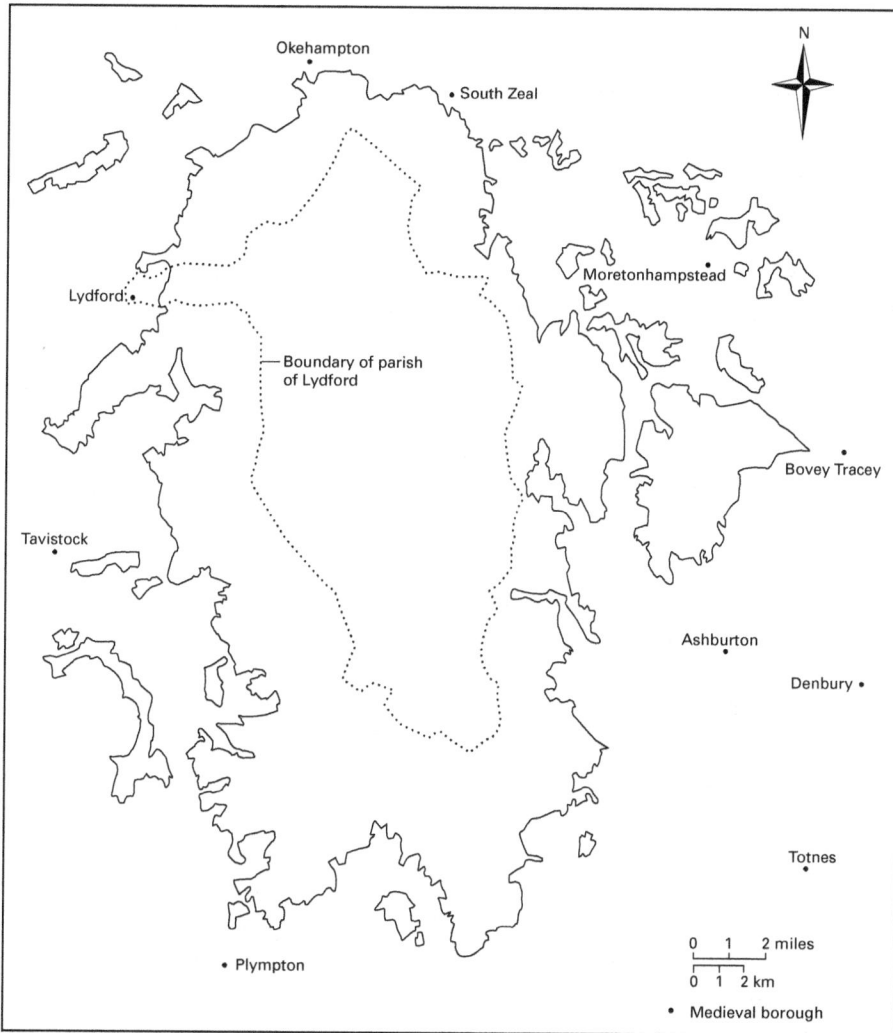

1.3 Modern Dartmoor.

The extent of the moorland shown on twentieth-century Ordnance Survey One Inch maps.

divide one type of land-use from another and others drawn for purposes of administration of manors, parishes, stannaries (jurisdictions for tinworkers) and of pastoral management (the bailiwicks of the herdsmen). Of these the most difficult for the historian to trace are the boundaries between, on the one hand, moorland itself—rough grazing ground, including unimproved grassland, heather, gorse and peat bog—and improved farmland on the other. My attempt, from recent Ordnance Survey 1-inch maps, is shown as Fig. 1.3, which portrays a continuous area of moorland in the centre and, around that area, detached fragments of moor, some of them quite large. Woodland is not shown, for example the famous small acreage of dwarf oaks called Wistman's Wood in Lydford parish or the oak woods mixed with holly in the valley of the Dart in Holne parish, a place-name which means 'at the hollies'. Many

Dartmoor rivers have valleys which are densely wooded and woodland history, elsewhere much studied, has been neglected here.

The *continuous area of moorland* as shown on Fig. 1.3 covers the large, central, ovoid parish of Lydford and spills over into adjoining parishes. By 1300 there were a few reclamations (not shown on Fig. 1.3) within Lydford parish but we know that they had a limited impact on the extent of moorland because a survey of 1345 made by William de Cusancia and Hugh de Berewyk lists them and their acreage, a total of about 1,020 acres at that time (out of 54,000 acres for the whole of the parish of Lydford). Most of these reclamations were in the east, hard up against the eastern boundary of Lydford parish, and were the improved lands of the group of farms and hamlets later known as the 'ancient tenements' (see Fig. 6.4). Further small reclamations in the later fourteenth century and the fifteenth reduced the area of rough grazing within the central moor, though to no considerable extent, and it was not until the eighteenth and nineteenth centuries that enclosures here had any large-scale impact upon the landscape. These latest enclosures were of three types (again, not shown on the map). There were large additions to the lands of the ancient tenements, reclaimed on the basis of a supposed right to enclose such as those around Prince Hall developed by Justice Francis Buller in the 1780s. There were entirely new estates obtained under grants of moorland from the Duchy of Cornwall, such as the grant of land around Postbridge to Thomas and John Hullett, on which a village was founded, or the Tor Royal and Princetown estates developed by Thomas Tyrwhitt, the latter becoming, after the building of the prison (1806–10), a new small planted town complete with a formally established market and a railway. The walker or driver through the central moorlands today, especially on the road from Princetown to Postbridge, still experiences the sense of loss of the vastness of Dartmoor which elsewhere is the first impression of the visitor to the region. Finally, at a number of places there were enclosures associated with farms which started off as smallholdings, such as Nuns Cross near the western boundary of the central moor or, in the east, Snaily House, formerly Whiteslade, eventually lived in by two spinster sisters who lived off slugs and snails. Enclosed fields in Lydford parish were described as 'detested depradations' in 1786 and in the 1880s the Dartmoor Preservation Association was formed in order to safeguard the prehistoric antiquities of the moorlands and rights of common grazing.[18]

Fragments of moorland encircle the once almost continuous area of moorland in the centre (see Fig. 1.3), giving the land-use boundary that ragged appearance which makes a precise delimitation of Dartmoor so difficult. To invert an analogy used earlier in this chapter, the vast island of moor at the centre is surrounded by an archipelago of smaller moors which have become separated at some time from the central block as if by a rising tide, for example Lustleigh Cleave in Lustleigh parish, Brent Hill in South Brent and Whitchurch Down in

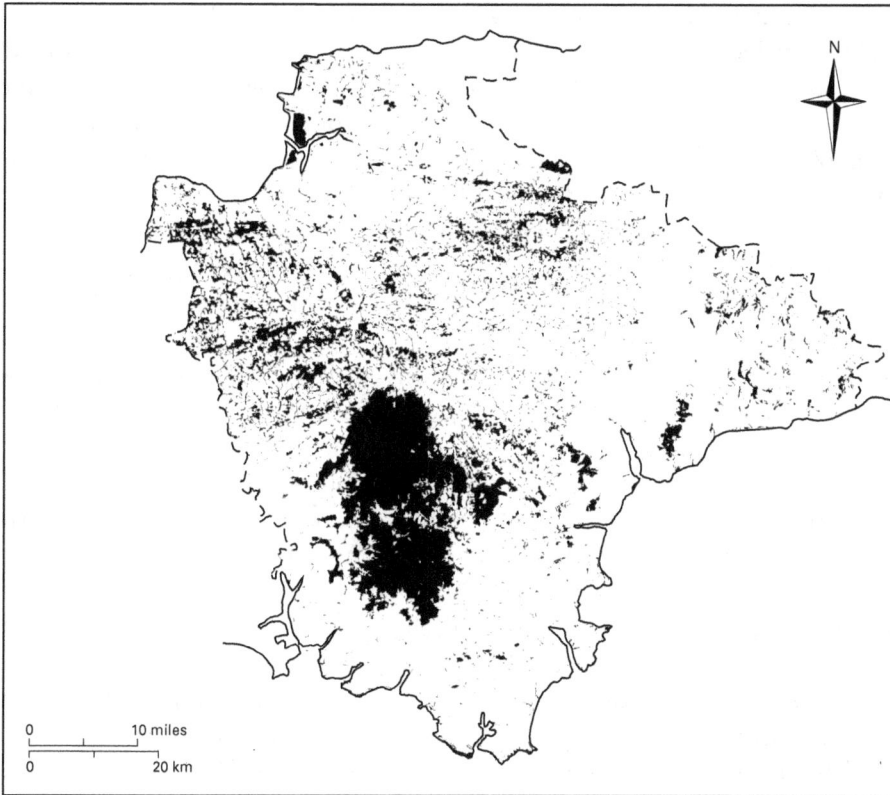

1.4 Rough ground in Devon, c. 1890.

Note that Exmoor is not shown on this map—its Devonian half is the blank area in the north, next to the county boundary.

Based on S. Turner, *Ancient Country: The Historic Character of Rural Devon*, Devon Archaeological Society Occasional Paper 20 (2007), Fig. 91.

Whitchurch. A recent historic landscape analysis of Devon and Cornwall has revealed that small islands of moorland formerly existed in most parts of both counties, not just the peripheries of Dartmoor, Exmoor and Bodmin Moor, as shown in Fig. 1.4.[19]

The boundaries of the once more or less continuous central moorland and of the fragmented portions have rarely remained static for any long period of time. At times reclamations have been made, at other times rough pasture has triumphed again. Reduction of the area of moorland was almost certainly taking place through establishment of new farms and hamlets in the tenth and eleventh centuries, to judge from the evidence of place-names, to be discussed in detail in chapter 6. It may have been at this time, for example, that the fragment of moorland represented by Lustleigh Cleave became separated from the central moor to the west, because by 1086 Domesday Book records several manors lying in the intervening area, still largely farmland today, with a total recorded population of 25 heads of households and with a fair number of ploughteams, implying cultivation; at that time there may have been other people farming in this area but not attributed to it in Domesday Book. Further reductions of moorland continued into the twelfth and thirteenth centuries, a period of noted growth in population; these further pushed back the boundary of the continuous moor, they also caused some fragments to break away from it and they reduced the areas of the fragments. Excavated settlements—at Hound Tor, Hutholes and Sourton Down, for example—are now dated to this period on the basis of pottery sequences and, in the case of the first, by pollen analysis; each of these, and other similar sites not excavated, was associated with moorland reclamation. The fourteenth and fifteenth centuries saw a reversal in the process of reclamation now that population pressure was relaxed. At Hound Tor the medieval arable field system reverted to rough pasture, though probably not suddenly, at some time in the late fourteenth century (Plate 11) and near Venford in Holne parish part of one large arable field was allowed to revert to moorland, its boundary deliberately broken down in several places to give access for livestock grazing on adjacent rough pasture.[20]

A scheme of active colonisation and contraction of the moorland boundaries before the beginning of the fourteenth century, followed by retreat of improved land (together with expansion of the area of moorland) in the later fourteenth century and the fifteenth is in fact far too simplistic. There is, for example, evidence of small reclamations being made during the century after the Black Death of 1348, a period of population decline, perhaps encouraged by demand for foodstuffs from workers in the tin fields which were booming at that time. There are also many local examples of both retreat and expansion of moorland in more recent times. Examples of the former are the 'ruthless' enclosing in the late nineteenth century by South Zeal's mining inhabitants of the flanks of Cosdon, where their small, rectangular fields may still be seen today; and the newtakes of stone quarriers at Hillside near the Merivale quarry. Reversion to moorland of formerly enclosed fields is represented, for example, on an eighteenth-century estate map which shows the farm of Twist in Peter Tavy parish, for which the surveyor used a special symbol for decayed walls around fields, and on the tithe map of Harford parish, where the surveyor treats the field boundaries of the farm called Piles in the same way. Moreover, the widespread local custom of temporarily enclosing relatively small patches, of ploughing and cropping them for a few years and then allowing them to return to rough pasture, as at Aish Ridge in South Brent parish, where there is excellent documentary and visual evidence for this, would complicate an estimate of the acreage of moorland at any one time, even if the historian had the data with which to make one.[21]

Parochial, manorial and other boundaries

Cutting across the moorlands and former moorlands is a pattern of boundaries of great complexity and intriguing structure. Fig. 1.5 shows parish boundaries as they are recorded on recent 1-inch Ordnance Survey maps. Inspection of the early nineteenth-century O.S. maps in the series called 'Index to the tithe survey', and selective scrutiny of tithe maps from the 1840s, show that

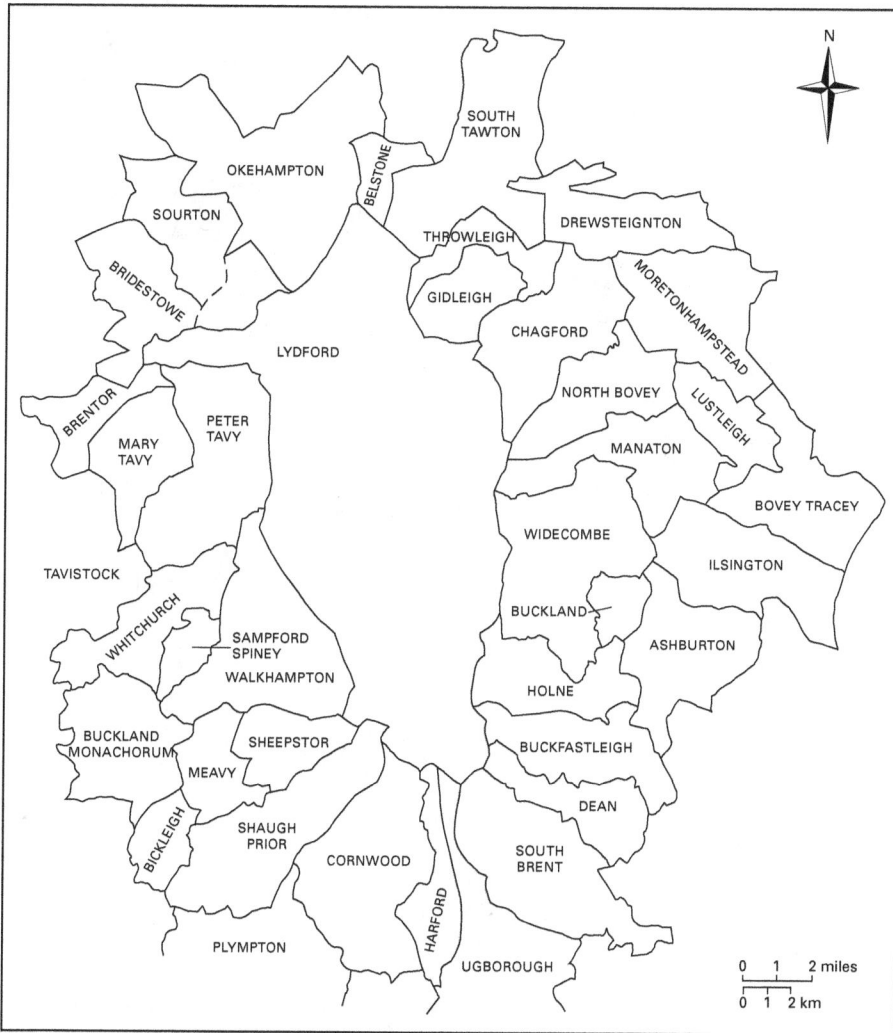

1.5 Parish boundaries around Dartmoor.

The boundaries of the parishes which include portions of Dartmoor, as shown on twentieth-century Ordnance Survey One Inch maps.

relatively few changes have taken place. Nothing as comprehensive exists for earlier centuries although there are written records of perambulations of some Dartmoor parishes within the collection of glebe terriers for the See of Exeter, some of them dating from the seventeenth century. Perambulation of these boundaries, especially where they cross open moorland, is still sometimes practised today and in William Crossing's time, in the late nineteenth century, few Dartmoor parishes 'fail to recognise its necessity'. A crucial point to make about these boundaries is that where they cross open moorland (Fig. 1.6) they are not hedged or fenced in any way: they are in the mind's eye and are marked by boundary stones which were remembered by punishments in perambulations.[22]

Many other types of boundary cut across the moorlands. The central moor

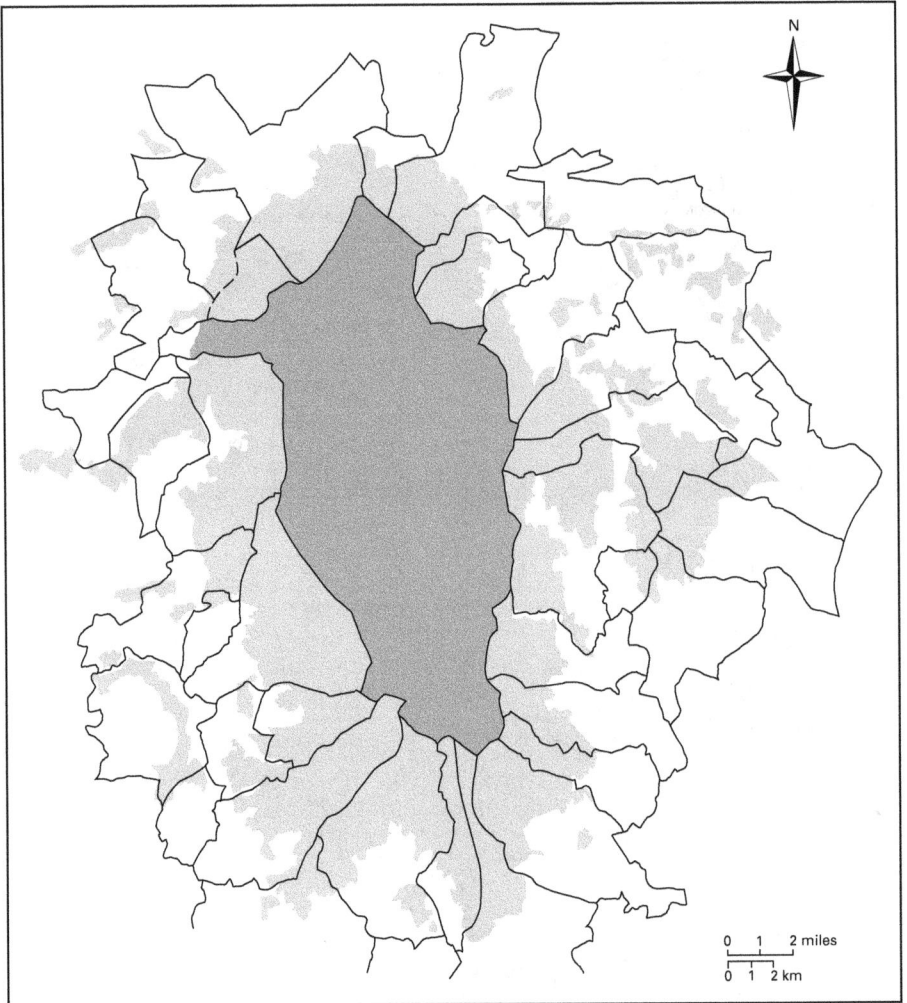

1.6 Parish
boundaries
crossing open
moorland.

was divided into four quarters, each in the charge of a master herdsman
responsible for guarding livestock brought to Dartmoor through transhumance,
for counting diggers of turf and for apprehending offenders; and there were
also boundaries, beginning on the central moor and extending far into the
enclosed country around Dartmoor, which delimited the jurisdiction of the
four stannary courts where cases involving tinworkers were heard. Moreover,
in some of the parishes which surround the central moor, there were several
manors, each one having its own boundaries which in many cases stretched
onto open moorland. No comprehensive record of these manorial boundaries
exists. In some localities they have been mapped by local historians, such as
Elizabeth Gawne, who established the bounds of the seven manors which lie
within Widecombe in the Moor parish (Fig. 1.7), where Seven Lords' Lands is
a place still recorded on Ordnance Survey maps; or Dave Brewer, who, with

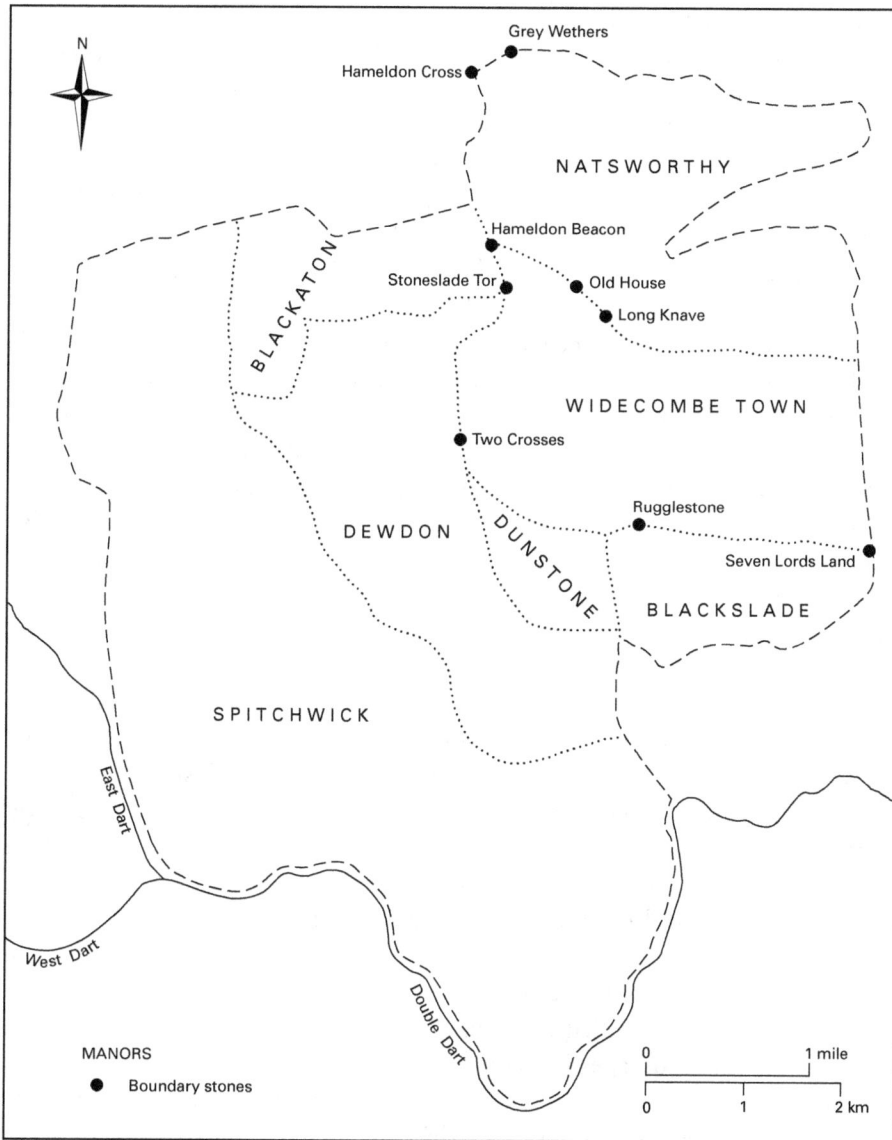

1.7 The seven manors in the parish of Widecombe in the Moor.

Based on E. Gawne, 'Field patterns in Widecombe Parish and the Forest of Dartmoor', *Trans. Devon. Assoc.* 102 (1970), pp. 49–69, Fig. 1.

great expertise, has identified manorial boundaries and boundary markers— natural stones and set stones—within the same parish and has carried out much other research into other manorial boundaries and their marks, for example at Willsworthy. Manorial boundaries may be reconstructed through use of written descriptions which have survived from the past, themselves set down in some cases after a perambulation on the ground made in order to prevent and resolve disputes. The custom of manorial perambulation is dealt with in some detail in chapter 3, so only two examples need be given here, first, the detailed record from 1566 of a perambulation on Haytor Down, probably made on the testimony of tenants, which is included in a manorial survey book of lands formerly belonging to the Dinham family. The second example concerns the moorland boundary between Harford manor and Langford Lestre manor. This was not carried out by tenants but by two men, presumably surveyors, acting on behalf of one of the manorial lords. They were not locals, because they made very heavy going of their task. They employed a local guide, Richard Willis, and noted at one point 'a bog . . . and another, seemingly dangerous, further north'. Beginning in August 1799 they were still at it (though not working every day) in October of that year when they packed up their instruments and notebooks because of inclement weather. They resumed on 3 June 1800, working through to 23 September. Never was a boundary of about five miles so thoroughly surveyed. The earliest known post-Conquest written record of a manorial boundary which runs through moorland dates from 1291 and there are three from before the Norman Conquest, discussed in chapter 6.[23]

Where we know something of manorial boundaries in the vicinity of parish boundaries the two almost always coincide, as in the case of South Brent, where we have written perambulations, discussed in more detail in chapter 3. The same is also the case where we have maps showing manorial boundaries, such as one of Spitchwick whose western boundary follows the western edge of Widecombe in the Moor parish, and one of Halstock whose eastern boundary follows the eastern limits of Okehampton parish. This is simply to say that parishes, when they were formed, fitted on top of an existing pattern of manors. Sometimes a single parish contained within it a single ancient manor, as at South Brent, and in those cases, Fig. 1.5 provides a fairly accurate picture of manorial boundaries. Where there were several manors within a parish, the map provides a record only of the outer manorial boundaries.[24]

Always remembering that Fig. 1.5 is a map of only a small proportion of all of the boundaries which crossed the moorlands, we can make two basic points about the pattern that it shows. First, the moorlands have clearly been highly contested landscapes in the past. They have been important in the lives of many people who have staked out their interests and laid claim to tracts of moor, making them their own by setting out boundary stones and drawing lines to be remembered in the mind's eye and perpetuated by perambulation. Part of the purpose of this book is to ask about when the lines were drawn and about what they tell us about moorland management in the past. Second, the pattern is made up of a large hub (the parish of Lydford) at the centre and a number of spokes converging upon it and dividing up the outer moors into slices. Lydford has over twenty parishes touching it, 'a condition probably unique' as R.H. Worth correctly put it in 1944.[25] The pattern provides a very special kind of historical record, if only we have enough patience and affection to learn how to read it correctly. The contrast in boundary pattern between the central and outer areas may reflect some important aspects of moorland management in the past, and we should question the topographical record with that possibility in mind. But will it yield its answers?

The 'central moor', 'outer moors', 'moor-edge' and 'down-country'

Now to turn to some of the terms which are employed in this book, to distinctions which I hope will give clarity to the chapters which follow. I try usually to avoid 'The Moor' (see above p. 18), despite the affection which local people have for that description, because I feel that it would confuse those outsiders who may wish to use my book. For that central area of once almost continuous moorland (see above p. 20) in the parish of Lydford I use the term 'central moor', again contrary to local usage in which the area is usually known as 'The Forest'. My reasons are that it was a separate royal forest for only a very limited period of time, that even then it was not administered in a special way as most other royal forests were, and that the pastoral management of Dartmoor was only in small ways, if at all, affected by the short-lived forest status. 'The Forest' is a term widely used by those who live in it and its surroundings and though, for the sake of clarity, I do not use it, I sincerely hope that I do not in this way offend a body of people who may possibly be readers of this book. The central moor belonged to a member of the royal family for most of the period covered by this book; to the king and, after 1337, to the Duke of Cornwall, when there was one, though both might lease it from time to time; and when I refer to ownership I usually use the word 'Crown' in order to escape the complications of see-saw changes in lordship after 1337 and of the leases by king or duke. The term 'outer moors' is used for moorland beyond the central moor, including the fragmented parts, the plural indicating that these moors were divided between many parishes and manors; this implies a view from the centre outwards, perhaps not so much a Devonian's view as one which would have been in the minds of Dartmoor dwellers. 'Moor-side' or 'moor-edge' is a term used here for those manors, parishes or farms with rights on one of the outer moors. Finally, the 'down-country', a word used locally by people living in and around the region, is a convenient expression for land beyond the moor-side parishes, the 'places further remote' according to a seventeenth-century description, to which so many tracks and lanes and ways lead away from the high hills, determined and impatient in direction and very much *down*hill.

Transhumance and its types

In the past the British landscape was peppered with sites and structures of a great variety of kinds which were not permanent habitations throughout the year. They included the cabins and lodges of the 'lookers' of Romney Marsh; the lone beehive-shaped herdsmen's daytime shelters on Bodmin Moor, 'in positions offering impressive panoramic views of pasture'; groups of corbelled stone huts, also of beehive form, in the seasonally used pastures of the Dingle peninsula in Ireland and on the Hebridean islands of Harris and Lewis; and the *summerhus* of a Wealden den or swine pasture, apparently a lodging for a lord and his officials while they exercised jurisdiction on a remote woodland property. Trades and activities other than pastoralism also generated seasonally used sites. The word shieling, a northern term, is normally used of seasonally used pastoral sites, but we hear of the 'shielings of the fishermen' near Paisley in an early medieval source and of miners' shielings on Alston Moor, Cumberland. Both fishing and mining were often seasonal occupations. Fishing generated the cellar settlements of Devon which gave the name Coombe Cellars, still on the map today, and the 'cabins and a common dining room', used by fishermen, on the shore near Lydd in Kent.[26] Mining generated the 'many little houses built for the stannary men to shroud them in near the works', as noted by the ever-observant John Norden in the sixteenth century in the Cornish tin-fields, and there is also a reference to a common dining room for these workers. Nor must we forget that some masons' lodges were located at quarries, used for the storing of tools and for accommodation, perhaps at certain times of the year only, for quarrying could be a seasonal occupation.[27] Cultural activities gave seasonally used features to the landscape: John Thoresby, in his tours of Leicestershire at the end of the eighteenth century, noted 'little eminences called shepherds' tables . . . for shepherds to have a day of festivities at certain seasons of the year'.[28]

Undoubtedly the majority of seasonally used sites were connected with transhumance, the subject of this book, so something should be said by way of introduction about the custom and its variants. The *Oxford English Dictionary* defines transhumance as 'the seasonal transfer of grazing animals to different pastures often over substantial distances'. It cites the work of the geographer Marion Newbiggen for the first use of the term in an English publication, in 1911, to describe Spanish practices of 'periodic and alternating displacement of flocks and herds between two regions of different climates'. The dictionary's earliest citation of an English historian's use of the word is from Maurice Beresford's *Lost Villages of England* (1954) where he wrote of 'sheep which knew transhumance' within the Parts of Lindsey, animals which were moved periodically between the drier grasslands of the Lincolnshire Wolds, some of which occupied the territories of deserted villages, and, say, the damper grazings of the Marsh region. Earlier than these two citations, in the nineteenth century, the term was used by French agricultural writers, topographers and geographers, mostly in the context of southern France. It comes from a Spanish word (*transhumancia*) ultimately derived from Latin *trans* (across) and *humus* (the ground).[29]

At a seminar on seasonal settlement convened at Leicester just before Christmas in 1993, some members of the audience were, according to Mick

Aston, 'sceptical about the existence of transhumance in the British Isles during the Middle Ages'. When editing the proceedings of the conference I therefore set out formally to counter that view by collecting together some of the evidence in an Introduction to the conference publication (*Seasonal Settlement*). The volume was relatively well received and a review by Aston ended with an exclamation: 'I was wrong to be sceptical of the existence of seasonal settlements!' Since the early 1990s, my further research on Dartmoor and further reading more generally has caused me to realise that some of the arguments which I used in that Introduction were not always too clear. What follows here is, I hope, a revision and refinement, with some new detail added.

At the outset of a discussion of the historic practice of transhumance in the British Isles, it is wise to bear in mind two principal types—'lesser' and 'greater' transhumance—noted by those who have studied livestock movements past and present in continental Europe. One must also bear in mind that some scholars have invented more complex classes where the two basic types branch out into a variety of sub-types and combinations, although Fernand Braudel has the wisest words on this subject: 'it is impossible to do justice to this complex phenomenon by rigid classification.'[30]

Lesser transhumance

Lesser transhumance is so called because the individual flocks and herds on the move are relatively small and because the distances traversed are relatively short. The rationale of the system according to E. Davies, writing with the Alps in mind, is as follows: 'transhumance ... is closely related to cultivation, and the movements of livestock to mountain pastures arise from the need for clearing the lower-lying land for cultivation, especially of fodder crops and hay.'[31] This may be to lay too great an emphasis on the character of the lower lands as a driving force. In reality, the lesser transhumance has two purposes, which are neatly inter-related. The first of these largely concerns crops: in summer the narrow Alpine valleys and their steep lower slopes are the only lands which may be cultivated for bread grains and fodder and it therefore becomes essential to clear them of animals as far as is possible, both to make space and also to minimise the risk of damage to crops by livestock. The second purpose largely concerns livestock: in summer the upper slopes, too cold to allow growth of grass in winter, become verdant again and are able to receive animals displaced from below; moreover, use of the upper slopes allows the farmer to keep more head of stock then he would be able to do if he used the lower lands for both summer pasture and growth of enough fodder to keep animals alive in winter.

Practices very similar to these were the custom in northern England, in the uplands of the Pennines, the hills of the Lake District and the Cheviot Hills. The most vivid descriptions date from the sixteenth and seventeenth centuries (when the practice in the North had almost run its course) and three must suffice. The survey of debatable and border lands made in 1604 records that in Redesdale (Northumberland) 'each man knoweth his sheildinge steed [summer settlement] and they sheylde together by surnames' in the small, sheltered tributary valleys a few miles from the 'wintersteeds' lower down the dale. In 1588 it was ordained by the manorial court of Middleton (Yorkshire, NR) that 'the lodgers ... shall goe to there shelings three weikes and three daies next after St Hellen daye [27 May] without anye longer tarryinge and shall not retorne backe againe before the first Ladies Eaven [14 Aug.] according to the auncient custome and usages'. William Camden's observations, written after his visit to the Roman wall at the end of the sixteenth century, is the most vivid: 'every way around in the wasts ... you may see as it were the ancient nomades, a martiall kinde of men, who from the moneth of Aprill unto August lye out scattering and summering, as they tearme it, with their cattell in little cottages here and there which they call sheales and shealings.' 'Summering' was the English word for transhumance, used by Camden and his local informants, by Carew in his *Survey of Cornwall* (1602), by a seventeenth-century Cornish poem and by the anonymous commentator on Risdon's *Survey of Devon* in the early nineteenth century.[32]

The descriptions given above make it clear that movement of people and their livestock to summer pastures in the uplands of the north of England was a custom very similar to the 'lesser' transhumance of, say, the Alps, although the altitudes traversed were less. The rationale of summering was similar in the two regions. After surveying the northern evidence in court rolls, surveys and other documents, Angus Winchester concludes that 'going "a-summering" not only enabled distant pastures to be exploited but also freed the growing crops of corn and hay from the otherwise perennial danger of damage by straying livestock, and allowed pastures closer to home to recuperate'; while to Gordon Elliott, transhumance in the North allowed 'the better ... lands around settlements ... [to be] cropped for hay and oats'. The whole system was set in motion not only by the 'first flush of plant growth' in the hills but also by 'bigg seed time', the sowing of the barley crop, soon after which it was considered unsafe to have many animals close to the growing grain.[33]

In the north of England transhumance of this type may be traced backwards in time through medieval documentary references, although most of them are not as graphic as those given above. In Longsleddale (Westmorland) a 'scaling' (seasonally used site) was granted in 1246; in North Tynedale (Northumberland) there were 22 'scalings' each valued at 16s. in the early fourteenth century; in upper Redesdale (also Northumberland) plots of pasture, moor and waste mentioned in the early fourteenth century may be matched up topographically to shieling grounds surveyed in 1604. Earlier than the thirteenth century, transhumance in the north of England has a documentary pedigree which could hardly be more distinguished, for Bede, in his life of St Cuthbert, portrays the saint seeking shelter one winter in some 'shepherds' huts . . . which had been roughly built during the summer and were then lying open and deserted'. Moreover, in the northern English counties there are hundreds of place-names containing elements which speak to us clearly of the use of uplands for summer grazing, principally Old English *scela* and its Middle English derivatives and Old Scandinavian *skali*, *saetr* and *erg*. They give names such as Allenshiel (Durham, a personal name plus *sceala*), Gatesgill (Cumberland, *geit*, 'goat', plus *skali*), Summerseat (Lancashire, *sumor*, 'summer', plus *saetr*) and Argam (Yorkshire, ER, *erg* as a simplex). These place-name elements for the most part tell of the seasonal use of built structures—huts and booths—usually by people looking after animals in summer pastures, although a very few of the names containing them take us to other occupations such as fishing, mining and the drying of turves, all likewise seasonal, while some may refer to seasonally used pastures rather than to the buildings which were constructed on them. We now have a distribution map of place-names containing some of these elements for English counties north of (and including) Yorkshire. The names occur in impressive numbers, are testimony to the widespread practice of transhumance in the North and some of them take the evidence for the custom back before the Norman Conquest.[34]

Elsewhere in the British Isles, movements of livestock, with their keepers, which illustrate lesser transhumance are well known from Scotland, for which there is now a detailed full-length study, *The Shieling* (1990) by Albert Bil, largely on highland Perthshire but with sidelights on other parts of the country; from Wales, Ireland and the Isle of Man. In some of these countries the custom of transhumance survived until quite recent times. Commentators on transhumance in all of these countries have noted the efficiency of the practice in removing livestock from the vicinity of the arable fields and their valuable grain crops during the growing season, a key feature of lesser transhumance. Finally, to move to south-western England, on Bodmin Moor and on other smaller Cornish uplands, place-names, field archaeology and (generally late) documentary evidence provide excellent evidence for the lesser transhumance.[35]

Greater transhumance

Greater transhumance is the second type recognised by those who have studied continental European practices. Classifications and delimitations are never entirely satisfactory so there is some overlapping of the two types, in both space and practice, and the second type has several variants. Its classic territory is Castile where flocks and their shepherds hailed from the north, higher and colder in winter than the south, and where the shepherds took their charges often for many hundreds of miles southwards to the warm winter grazings of, for example, Estremadura and Andalusia (the plains of the rivers Guadiana and

Guadalquivir). Much is known about these movements thanks to Klein's classic work, *The Mesta*, dealing with the corporate body which with royal support (on account of taxes on wool) regulated and protected the wide *canadas* along which ebbed and flowed the wealth of the country, from plateaux to plains and back to plateaux again. Much has been written about these movements; about the inevitable clashes between the shepherds and the landowners through whose lands the flocks were driven; about the master-shepherds who moved with their charges and underlings, with horses and mules to carry cooking-pots and presumably tents; about their material and mental culture, their carved crooks, flutes and pipes, their music-making, saints and nonconformity.[36]

The greater transhumance often involved long distances; ultimately it generated great wealth—wool, writes Robert Lopez, meant more to the Iberian economy 'than ... olives, grapes, copper, or even the treasures of Peru'. From an ecological standpoint it was a movement driven by the different seasonal qualities of grassland in different regions with differing climates: in Castile the upper lands in summer are hospitable and their grazings relatively lush, while the southern lands with a Mediterranean climate are parched and useless as pastures; in winter the upper lands become inhospitable and the herbage of the lower lands revives. From an ecological standpoint the greater transhumance differed from the lesser in that it was driven entirely by the needs of pastoral farming, by inter-regional differences in the quality of pastures, and was not closely associated with the requirements of the arable.[37]

Transhumance in England

Needless to say, nothing quite on the scale of Castilian transhumance existed in medieval England. Climate here has less violence and there was never that absolute necessity of moving livestock which resulted in Castile from the existence of settlements at high and, in winter, inhospitable altitudes and from the desiccation of Mediterranean grasslands in summer. Nevertheless, in England there are significant spatial variations in the qualities of grassland, the results of variations in climate and in the moisture-retentiveness of soils, and these led to a muted form of greater transhumance. When livestock were moved to fresh pastures beyond the boundaries of a manor the practice required command over land and for this reason—and because of the nature of the documentation—we know most about it as practised by the landlords of medieval England. Landlords were, in fact, instructed to move their livestock between pastures of differing types by the most widely circulated agricultural treatise of the thirteenth century, Walter de Henley's 'Husbandry'. In a passage which seems not to have been noticed before in the literature of rural history, de Henley wrote of landlords who might 'wish to send oxen or cows or calves ... away from open-field countryside [*hors du pays de chaumpaynge*] into wooded countryside [*en pays du boscage*]'. Later in the same passage he refers to 'woodland herbage' (*herbes du boyes*, what a later age would call 'wood-pasture'), so clearly he had in mind the seasonal removal of livestock from open-field land—where good grazing was in short supply and where much of the feed comprised the poor grasses, weeds and stubble of fallows—to countrysides where there was permanent pasture with stands of trees which themselves provided additional browse for animals. I have translated his *pays* as 'countryside', but he probably had in mind *regional* variation in types of pasture; perhaps we should render the word as 'region' or keep it as *pays*, as used by the French (Pays de Beauce, Pays de Brie, for example) and recently by some English historians.[38]

Thirteenth-century statutes also provide indisputable evidence for transhumance (of both types, it should be said, but probably they were aimed largely at the greater which was at that time probably more widespread). Two important texts here are a statute of Alexander, Bishop of Coventry and Lichfield (*c.*1240) and a section in the Synodal Statutes of Winchester (1295). The former, first noted by a foremost expert on the medieval wool trade, Eileen Power, in her discussion of transhumance in medieval Europe at large, runs: 'if sheep are fed in one place in winter and in another place [i.e. another parish] in summer the tithes shall be divided.' The latter is more elaborate. 'Since by the driving of flocks to different pastures contentions sometimes arise between rectors concerning tithes, we, in order to make peace, decide that the tithe of wool shall be paid to the churches of those parishes in which the sheep are fed and folded from their shearing-time until Easter, even if afterwards they are removed and shorn elsewhere.' The medieval sheep yielded two major products on which greater tithes were levied: lambs, born in early spring, of which one in ten went to the tithe owner, or the price of one-tenth of the lambs if they numbered nine or fewer; and wool, from shearing around the month of June (tithe on cheeses made wholly or partly from the milk of ewes were normally reckoned to be small tithes). Locally, parishes might come to their own form of agreement which differed slightly from the injunctions cited above, as did Knowstone, Molland and North Molton (with its chapelry of Twitchen) near Exmoor where the incumbents in 1345 asked two canons of Exeter Cathedral to draw up an arbitration which went into great detail about the destination of tithes of livestock moved from one place to another. This local document and the two more general ecclesiastical injunctions, as well as Walter de Henley's advice, show how normal 'the driving of flocks to different pastures' (and herds too) was in medieval England.[39]

Tudor church reform, especially Henry VIII's canons of 1535, introduced more elaborate guidance.

Furthermore, we decree that the tithes of wool, milk and cheese in its season shall be paid in full to the churches in whose parishes the sheep graze and sleep right through from shearing time [June] until the feast of St Martin [11 November] in the winter, even if afterwards they are taken away from that parish and sheared elsewhere, and in order to prevent fraud in the case of the foregoing, we decree that before the sheep are removed from the pastures and even sold, there must be guarantee to pay tithe to the rectors of the churches. But if within the aforesaid time they are transferred to pasture in different parishes, each church shall receive a tithe in proportion to the time [spent in them], not counting any period which is less than the space of thirty days. But if during the whole of the aforesaid time they sleep in one parish and normally graze in another, the tithe shall be divided between those churches.

There were different rules for cows, calves and kids. Calves and kids were to be tithed in the parish where they were born unless the local custom decreed otherwise, an interesting reference to regional variation in tithing customs. The canons of 1535 make allowance for *daily* movements of livestock (not strictly transhumance): the offspring of sheep (see above), cows and goats which slept in one parish and grazed by day in another were to be tithed equally in both places.[40]

There are many examples of greater transhumance in medieval England (although it is rarely called this in the literature), and a few cases only need be mentioned here. Christopher Dyer has made an expert regional study of flock movements, and the sheepcotes associated with them, in the Cotswolds and their surroundings. There landlords with command over manors in both the vales and wolds sent ewes with their lambs to the latter in May, presumably to pastures which were fresh and shooting, and thus highly suitable for mothers in milk and for their offspring, the latter inexperienced (as my observations on Dartmoor show me) at nipping short herbage. Wethers (castrated males) were in some cases sent to the pastures of the wolds in winter or were transferred to them permanently: these are animals hardier and of less value than ewes. It could have been (although there is no proof of this) that ewes were fed on the better wold pastures, often the former village fields of settlements deserted in the latter half of the fourteenth century and later, while wethers made do with the older Cotswolds pastures on inferior land which had never been ploughed. These complex movements were not generated by the needs of arable farming but entirely by the suitability of different grasslands to various types of stock at different times of the year.[41]

An excellent example of inter-manorial transhumance at the level of the great estate is the discussion on animal transfers in Kathy Biddick's monograph on Peterborough Abbey's lands, entitled *The Other Economy* (1989). Central to livestock transfers—for which the old Roman roads converging on Castor (near Peterborough) were probably used—were the home manors, close to the

abbey, of Eye and Glinton with land stretching into the fens. As the fens began to dry out in early spring, ewes in lamb and therefore needing the best care were sent to these manors with their extensive and valuable pastures; they were also breeding manors for cattle, later transferred to other places on the estate; and they received crones (elderly ewes) coming home for a final journey to be fattened for the market. Hoggs (yearling sheep) were not so pampered for, not yet breeders or great wool producers, they tended to be dispersed from the fen-edge to those of the abbey's manors which had pastures less lush.[42]

Many other studies of great estates have revealed that medieval landlords, their managers and their councils had sophisticated knowledge and perception of local variations in the quality of grazings and reactions to those differences which were as complex as those on the estate of Peterborough Abbey. Perhaps the first English medieval historian to touch upon movements of animals was Frances Page, who wrote of inter-manorial transfers of sheep on the estate of Crowland Abbey, watery lands on which some of the transit was by raft with 'obstreperous sheep confined in crates' (as the abbey's account rolls show). The Cistercians, studied by the late Robin Donkin, regularly moved their flocks from place to place and for that reason, and as owners of tithes, the monks of Vale Royal copied the injunctions of the Bishop of Coventry and Lichfield, discussed above, into their Ledger Book. The estate managers of Oseney Abbey, studied by Dave Postles, set aside some of their manors for breeding ewes and others for wethers, a practice which naturally generated inter-manorial movements of animals. A study of large lay estates in Wiltshire gives a picture of 'lanes thronged with stock moving from manor to manor'. Finally, a recent analysis by Mary Atkin of the cattle-rearing estate of the de Lacy family in Blackburnshire—a study which is highly sensitive to differences between manors in the qualities and growing season of grass—concludes that early in May there was always 'an enormous amount of ... movement ... as stock were shifted ... according to their ages and classification'.[43]

For landlords to move livestock between different pastures was easy and natural, because they had command over land, many owning a large number of manors. Did medieval peasant farmers, those living outside the upland regions where the lesser transhumance was practised, also transfer stock from one type of pasture to another? This question is not easy to answer because the evidence is far more patchy than it is for landlords and it is best to look briefly at later periods first before returning to the Middle Ages. The evidence indicates quite clearly that England in, say, the seventeenth century and later was criss-crossed by a myriad of lines and routes taken by animals, of a great variety of types and breeds, belonging to tenant farmers. There were four main practices, each distinct in itself: selling on livestock; purchase of additional pasture at a remove; renting of additional pasture at a remove; and exercise of common rights at a remove. Selling on meant sales by the breeders of one district to graziers in another, for example by farmers who bred Cheshire cattle to graziers in the Home Counties, a trade described by the topographers William Smith and William Camden. Some farmers purchased additional pasture at a remove, those of Romney Marsh, for example, owning pastures elsewhere in Kent to which sheep were sent in winter in order to prevent death through exposure to the bleak, and generally hedgeless marshland grazings. Finally, the inhabitants of some townships in the seventeenth century had rights of common in tracts of pasture beyond the township boundary. Thus in the Fenlands of Lincolnshire some fen pastures were not reckoned to belong to any parish in the seventeenth century and were inter-commoned by people from adjacent or nearby places when the fens dried out in the summer months. Similarly, in the Somerset Levels, the inhabitants of some townships at some distance away—for example, those along the coast north of the mouth of the Parret—inter-commoned during the summer. It should be noted here that Somerton, on the edge of the Levels, means 'place used only in summer' and, for some obscure reason, has given its name to the whole county.[44]

It is unlikely that these strategies among tenant farmers for gaining access to pastures at a remove were novel in the seventeenth century. And, indeed, medieval examples may be found despite relatively poor survival of evidence relating to such subjects. If we return to Dyer's Cotswolds, it is found that villagers at West Littleton and Tormarton in the 1490s passed by-laws which attempted to prevent some of their number from taking in the sheep and cattle of outsiders and allowing them to feed on the common pastures, a clear reference to a ban on renting pasture at a remove. In the vicinity of Lutterworth (Leicestershire) in the early sixteenth century, farmers supplemented their common-field farming with grazing on rented pastures which were in some cases the permanent grass territories of deserted villages; and it is very probable that this symbiotic relationship goes back to the previous century when desertion of settlements and conversion from arable to grass took place. At a court at Great Horwood (Buckinghamshire) in 1521 it was 'ordained by the assent of all the tenants there that no one henceforth shall bring in any shepherd with a flock of sheep from any outsider under pain of 40s.'. On the north Cornish coastlands in 1371, William Brugge of the hamlet of Trevia, near the coast, supplemented his holding there by renting large quantities of rough grazing at the deserted upland site of Goosehill, three miles away on Bodmin Moor; what could have been better practice for a farmer with soils derived from coastal slates, notorious for their parching in dry summers, than to lease additional acres in a moister, more verdant location?[45]

There is also good medieval documentary evidence (thirteenth to fifteenth centuries) for transhumance towards pastures which were inter-commoned by the people of surrounding and more distant vills, the case of the Weald of Kent and Sussex being the best-known example. Records of small payments for the use of these formerly inter-commoned wood-pastures show that peasants took their pigs to the Weald along with those of the lord. Payments for pannage (feeding of pigs) do indeed dominate the sources, but livestock other than swine were involved, and Du Boulay was correct in arguing that transhumance to the Weald, over a distance of 20 miles or more in some cases, was not simply for the feeding of pigs on acorns and beech mast when these became available in the short autumn season (October and a few weeks before and after that month): other animals and other kinds of feed were involved and the name of one of the Wealden hundreds is Somerden, indicating a grazing season which began in summer, not autumn. The labour of driving livestock to the wood-pastures may originally have been organised communally and there is plenty of evidence in place-names for the huts, sheds and folds which housed and secured man and beast upon their arrival. From some marshland regions, too, there is good evidence from the thirteenth century onwards for inter-commoning by the people of nearby and more distant vills: the Somerset Levels and, in Lincolnshire, West Fen (south of Bolingbroke) and Eight Hundred Fen provide good examples where relative (not absolute) desiccation was the propelling force behind transhumance. Perhaps the very best evidence for the sharing of pasture by people from a distance comes from medieval Dartmoor where almost all the people of Devon had common rights, as discussed in chapter 2.[46]

In our backwards travel through time, if only we were able to observe in detail English landscapes of the period between the sixth and eleventh centuries, we should almost certainly find a good deal of the type of transhumance which is being discussed here—the type driven by inter-regional differences in the quality of pastures—and that most levels of society took part in it, lords and tenants alike. The reason for this is that densities of settlement and population were less then than they became later, pressure on the land was relatively relaxed and the landscape less 'crowded and complicated' to use Christopher Dyer's words: there were more fresh pastures to beckon and entice. There are some indications of the custom of transhumance among peoples living in vales of the great valleys of the east Midlands who used the wolds (lightly wooded pastures) which fringe some of them as summer grazings—the Lincolnshire Wolds, for example, the Wolds of the Leicestershire–Nottinghamshire border and the rolling and empty green pastures of 'High Leicestershire' which begin beyond my study window and the red-brick garden wall as I write these pages. In these regions the practice of taking livestock to fresh grazings in the summer had largely died out by the time of the Norman Conquest but it existed in the Scandinavian period (ninth and tenth centuries) if not earlier, as testified by the place-name Somerby (this time a Scandinavian place-name formation possibly or probably meaning 'summer-settlement') and others containing *skali* (also Scandinavian, meaning, as already discussed, 'a hut or shed not permanently occupied'), an element more commonly associated with the uplands of the north of England. These were the sites of seasonally used settlements associated with transhumance. Downlands formed another *genre* of region which was attractive to people practising transhumance.[47]

More densely wooded regions, as well as wolds and downs, are environments where we should look for transhumance in these early centuries well before the Norman Conquest. In one of his most evocative passages, Marc Bloch made the point that in the early Middle Ages pasture was available where in our days of more controlled woodland management we might least expect to find it: *par ses feuilles fraîches, ses jeunes pousses, l'herbe de ses sous-bois, ses glands et ses faînes, elle [la forêt] servait, avant tout, de terrain de pâture* ('through its fresh leaves, its young shoots, the grass of its under-woods, its acorns and beech mast, woodland served, above all, as pasture land') Wood-pastures were highly attractive as grazing grounds: they had grassy well-sheltered glades while the stands of trees provided further shelter and the browse of low branches and saplings, freshly shooting in spring, was especially valuable for livestock which had been confined to stall-feeding or the meagre fallows during the winter months. A few semi-wooded tracts of country in England are still used as pastures and here one may observe what must have been a very common sight in the past—variations in the 'browse line', beyond which livestock cannot reach, the height depending on the type of animals kept, whether cattle or sheep for example.

For the Weald of Kent and Sussex there is excellent evidence for transhumance from before the Norman Conquest. The 'Forest' of Arden is another woodland region which was alluring to livestock and their keepers in these early centuries. In a seminal paper published in 1976 and based upon a Leicester thesis, W.J. Ford found many examples of manors in the Feldon, 'open-field land', of Warwickshire, for example, the valley of the Avon, which were linked (to use his term) with outlying dependent territories in the Arden woodlands, the linkages leap-frogging many other manors in between. This methodology, the discovery of linked territories, is much used in chapter 4 of this book, so full discussion of it is reserved until later. Ford concluded that the linkages point to transhumance, adding that the nature of the movements along the links was 'undoubtedly complex and it would be optimistic to think that at this stage they can be fully clarified'. Warwickshire has also been studied by Della Hooke who likewise concluded that the purpose of the links to Arden 'may have been initially one of transhumance'; she also perceptively noted that the direction of the links is paralleled by trackways of determined direction, namely droveways, although she did not develop a methodology for identifying these (that we do in chapter 7). The heyday of transhumance between Avon and Arden must have been in the early and middle Anglo-Saxon periods because, later on, we have the first signs of colonisation in the Arden woodlands, and this would have resulted in a degree of conflict between permanent and seasonal settlers and also a diminution of woodland grazing.[48]

Transhumance between the Avon valley and Arden was clearly to the benefit of the livestock which undertook these movements: the pasture of the Arden greens, virtually untouched in winter, would have provided them with a welcome change of feed, the more so because they had been confined to stubble grazing and stall-feeding during the winter. But, bearing in mind the comments cited already about the relationship between transhumance and arable husbandry in other places and periods, it is worth speculating about the benefits of these movements to grain farming in the Avon lands. In the early and middle Anglo-Saxon periods, when transhumance to Arden was at its height, 'Midland' field systems, with their great, secure, fallow field specifically set aside for livestock did not yet exist. One must probably envisage small patches of land under crops set among patches of pasture and fallow, with many risky boundaries which livestock might cross in summer, damaging crops to the detriment of the harvest later on. The distant Arden grazings would therefore have acted as a kind of safety valve, for they allowed people to remove some of their livestock from the vicinity of the crops when they were most vulnerable. The corollary to this argument might be that when the Avon–Arden links began to break down in the later Anglo-Saxon period, this acted as one catalyst for the people of Avon to adopt 'safer' Midland field systems with great spaces, the fallow fields, set aside for the accommodation of livestock, safely separated from growing crops in summer. In addition, when the links diminished and transhumance came to an end, Feldon communities had less command over pasture at a remove; this, as well as pressure on pasture at home, was another catalyst for the introduction of the Midland system under which the great fallow field came to be the principal, or only, grazing land for livestock. A further extension of this argument is that in regions where transhumance continued as a custom, this was one reason for failure to adopt field systems similar to the Midland system. That argument would apply well to Cornwall and to Devon, where transhumance continued on Dartmoor and Exmoor, and to Kent, with its Weald. This is explored further in chapter 7.

In drawing this general discussion of transhumance and its types to a close, we shall develop two general themes, one about distance and another about livestock movements and the history of settlement. The *Oxford English Dictionary*, in its definition of transhumance cited above (p. 28), includes the words 'often over substantial distances' and is undoubtedly influenced by the practices of the greater transhumance in Mediterranean countries. Regional variations in the British Isles are more muted than in, say, Spain or Italy, and regions are on a small scale here. As a consequence, movements of livestock to different pastures can be over relatively short distances when measured on a map, although they may have appeared to be long in terms of the emotional separation of people from within communities which followed the custom. Albert Bil's study of Perthshire shows that distances between wintertowns and summer shielings in that county were 12 miles in a few cases, only 2 in others. On the estate of Peterborough Abbey some transfers of livestock were over a distance of about 12 miles, others over about four miles.[49] Clearly there was much variation within the British Isles, but the relatively short distances compared with some on the Continent they encompass does not disqualify these movements from being described as transhumance.

One can go too far, of course, and definitions can become too precise. Most readers will agree that transhumance does not include routine transfers of animals from one type of land to another *within* the boundaries of townships. In the Midlands of England, over a long period of time lasting in some places from the tenth century to the eighteenth, livestock were moved from one of the two or three great fields to another when harvesting was over, but this was not transhumance. Where field systems were enclosed, farmers moved their livestock from close to close to encourage growth of grass and to give livestock a change of feed. In Devon they were moved frequently in this way, Hooker, in the sixteenth century, writing that the practice meant that animals always fed upon 'a new springing grass'. There was a local saying here that sheep did not hear Sunday's church bells twice from the same field. If there was woodland within a township, and if it was commonable, a peasant's livestock were taken to feed from its pasture and its browse at certain seasons: in Buckinghamshire at Newton Longville, a village by-law of 1545 allows us to see the common herdsman and his charges 'coming from the [local] woods', presumably at the end of the day, and at Great Horwood, according to an extent of 1320, any tenant summoned to do the lord's ploughing was allowed three days notice in case his oxen were 'depasturing in the woods where he may not be able to find them when he wants to' (the length of time seems excessive).[50] The practices described in this paragraph differed from movements properly described as transhumance in two respects: first, township boundaries were not crossed and, second, the guardians of the livestock did not generally stay with them overnight. Finally, sending livestock, often over long distances, to a point of sale is not usually included in discussions of transhumance. Such movements have always been described as 'droving', on which there is a large literature because of the adventurous and arduous nature of the trade. There are specialist monographs on droving to London meat markets from Scotland and Wales. The South West, however, is under-represented in the literature: there, early-modern topographical writers noted large numbers of cattle which 'the graziers or feeders drive fat to London' from Dorset, and how great herds from Somerset were sent to the pastures of north Cornwall before finally being driven to easterly markets.[51]

Transhumant settlement patterns

The connections between transhumance and the history of rural settlements are complex ones. Some types of transhumance were associated with the establishment of seasonally occupied settlements. This was the case with the lesser transhumance of mountainous and upland regions, each of the higher summer sites being linked—by known trackways, long usage and division of labour within the family or wider group—to a valley settlement: *hafod* and *hendref* in Wales, *havos* and *hendre* in Cornwall, shielings and wintersteads in Northumberland.[52]

The classic greater transhumance of Mediterranean regions did not usually create settlements, for the shepherds who took part in what Ladurie called 'the great migrations' to winter pastures on the warmer plains usually made do with lodgings (or perhaps tents?) when away from their home base. The same probably applies, after, say, 1100, to most of the English medieval types of transhumance away from the uplands: 'selling on' animals clearly did not usually involve the setting up of new settlements, nor in most cases did the transfer of animals between manors on the estates of landlords. To this general rule there were a few exceptions: for example, on some of the pastures of the Cotswolds which were used by landlords as seasonal pastures for sheep, large and impressive sheepcotes were built, sometimes with an ancillary building for a shepherd or shepherds (as evidenced by hearths and the discovery of pottery at excavated sites); the Cotswold place-name Hilmancot may be relevant here, for it means 'the cottage of the hill-man'. Such practices lingered on, for in the seventeenth century the typical deserted village was described as 'nothing but a wilderness for sheep, with a cote, a pastorall boy and his dog', a clear reference to how former arable village fields became great sheepwalks after desertion. The further back in time we go, into a less crowded and contested landscape, the more likely are we to find seasonally used settlement sites away from the Highland Zone, in the wolds of the eastern Midlands, for example, as evidenced by the place-names mentioned above.[53]

Transhumance and settlement history are linked, also, because some seasonally used settlements became permanently occupied farms or hamlets, usually under conditions of population pressure and because the sequence could, in places, be reversed if population declined. Some of the dens, originally swine pastures, of the Weald became colonised in the last years of Anglo-Saxon England; in highland Perthshire some shielings are converted into permanent settlements in the eighteenth century as a result of pressure of population; in Cornwall some places with names in *havos* (summer settlement) had become permanently occupied by 1066, for they are named in Domesday Book with their fixed populations and their ploughlands. Reversal of the trend from seasonal to permanent occupation is probably indicated by the quotation in the previous paragraph about the 'cote, a pastoral boy and his dog': a village with a permanent population and arable land has become a cottage inhabited only by a youth, perhaps on a seasonal basis if his flock was moved around as, for example, in the Cotswolds, described above.

We may illustrate the points made in the last paragraph with a series of snapshots of the small lost Yorkshire vill of Argam, just inland from Filey Bay where Wolds meet sea: a spot which is hot and dry in summer and suffers isolation through snow-drifts in winter. The name is from the dative plural of *erg,* a term which means a seasonally used pastoral site of some kind. So Argam began as a place 'at the shielings', perhaps in the tenth century or the early eleventh. By the time of Domesday Book it had a settled population with ploughlands, plough teams and arable fields (these are mentioned in charters between the twelfth century and the early fourteenth) and became a village community with a church of its own. Seasonal use was therefore followed by permanent occupation as English population figures began to approach their medieval peak. Subsequently, either in the late fourteenth century or the fifteenth—when pressure of population was reduced and more relaxed systems of land-use became possible—Argam reverted to being a pastoral settlement occupied by a shepherd and his wife, perhaps on a seasonal basis, the village deserted and the arable fields now a sheepwalk. The only other visitor to the site was, as Maurice Beresford vividly relates, the incumbent who occasionally fulfilled his canonical obligations by saying a few prayers on the spot where the church had once stood. The fluctuating, see-saw history of Argam shows how the changing fortunes of seasonally used settlements were closely associated with demographic and economic trends.[54]

Personal and impersonal transhumance

The conversion of seasonal settlements to permanently occupied ones did not necessarily end the seasonal movement of livestock, though it must often have resulted in a change in the nature of the transhumance practised, from what in this book will be called *personal transhumance,* in which the livestock's owners lived with their animals while they were on the summer pastures, to *impersonal transhumance,* in which they handed their livestock over to the pasture's permanent residents for the duration of the summer. This is what happened on Dartmoor, and chapter 6 of this book is concerned with the transition in the Anglo-Saxon period from settlements used in the summer season to permanently occupied hamlets. Chapters 2 and 3 will discuss the later, impersonal phase of transhumance on the Moor, and chapters 4 and 5 its earlier, personal phase.

Limitations of this book

My book has limitations in both time and topic. It hardly touches on prehistory, although Mesolithic men and women (around 10,000 BC to 4000 BC) visited the region studied in this book—which cannot yet be called Dart*moor* because it was then largely tree-covered—in order to hunt. Their movements may well have been seasonal, with people following wild animals; no doubt the distant ancestors of these animals had moved to the new, fresh pastures of the shady glades during summers long before men and women had evolved. Mesolithic people left behind numerous flint tools such as microliths (tiny blades) for arrows used in hunting and for scrapers to clean leather and other animal skins, such as those found at East Week. Of all prehistoric peoples, those of the Bronze Age (around 2300 BC to 700 BC) made the greatest impact on the landscape of Dartmoor. The Saxon and medieval people with which this book is concerned could hardly have been unaware of monuments from the Bronze Age. For example, they named Soussons in Manaton and Zeaston in Ugborough (Soueston in 1330) from 'seven stones', almost certainly Bronze Age ritual stone circles; the former name is first recorded in the eleventh century. They would have used single standing stones as points of reference in the landscape as they watched over livestock, and there is more than one farm called Langstone on Dartmoor today. They incorporated the standing remains of Bronze Age huts into their farmhouses, as at the ruined isolated medieval farm site about 350 yards north-west of the deserted hamlet of Hound Tor. It would be strange if herdsmen and shepherds guarding their livestock did not shelter in Bronze Age huts. An exciting book has been written about the Bronze Age in the region—*The Dartmoor Reaves* by Andrew Fleming—with much material on pastoral management and boundaries (the Bronze Age reaves), both topics dealt with at length in my book, but for another period.[55]

The centuries following the withdrawal of Roman armies from Devon is an obscure period and failure to explore it properly here is another limitation of this book. One thing is certain about those centuries: that Celtic people knew the hills of Dartmoor, and in greater numbers than might be guessed from the list of Celtic place-names in *The Place-names of Devon*. In the Introduction to that survey, in what appears to be intended to be a discussion of all purely Celtic names in Devon, several Dartmoor names are missed, for example Laughter Tor in Lydford and Leather Tor in Walkhampton, even though they are classified, correctly, as Celtic in the entries which form the main body of the book. The derivation of these names from Celtic *lether*, 'steep slope', has been accepted by the Cornish place-name expert Oliver Padel. The Introduction also misses Gavrick, from Celtic *gaver*, 'goat', also in Ilsington, even though that too is in the main body of the text. In its discussion of names in *walh*, 'a foreigner, a Welshman, a serf', the Introduction mentions only one of the

Dartmoor streams with the name Walla Brook, whereas in fact three exist. Celtic river names are also ignored in the Introduction, even though Dartmoor takes its name from a river with a Celtic word meaning 'oak', while others of the region's river and stream names are also pre-English, for example Avon, Erme, Glaze and Okement, to mention but a few. Scattered quite liberally throughout *The Place-names of Devon* are possible Celtic or hybrid place-names which, since the editors had some doubts, they did not include in their Introduction. Dartmoor examples include Glendon in Okehampton parish, Cornwood parish and Coarsewell in Ugborough. I have given examples where modern scholarship on Cornish place-names allows one to identify the first elements in these hybrids, *glynn* ('large valley'), *corn* ('horn or corner') and *cors* ('reeds, fen'). The name Was Tor in Brentor, a parish where possible Dark Age structures have been identified, contains the Celtic personal name Wassa, akin to that of Wasso, a recorded slave freed in the Bodmin manumissions.[56]

Whether or not these names were coined by people engaged in transhumance we shall never know. But two observations may be made. Firstly, Bodmin Moor in Cornwall, another granitic upland very similar to Dartmoor, was the scene of transhumance in the seventh century and almost certainly earlier, because the farm name Hendra is found on the moor. This is the Cornish word for a winter settlement, *hendre*, literally 'old farmstead' (*hen*, 'old', plus *tre*, 'farmstead') which 'must be early, since it is shared by Welsh and Cornish'; that is, the first element is not what we should expect although 'perhaps it came about through the sense "original homestead"'. The fact that the word is shared by the Welsh and the West Welsh (Cornish) means that it originated before these people were split asunder by the coming of Saxon influence to Devon in the seventh century. A second reason for suspecting transhumance to Dartmoor in the period between the fifth and seventh centuries is, according to Susan Pearce, the presence of inscribed stones of this date, some not in churchyards but near the edge of the moorland and on tracks leading up to the summer pastures, as at Sourton, Fardel (in Ivybridge in Cornwall), and Roborough. The names on these stones, for example, Audetus *princeps* (a title of authority) on the Sourton stone, may recall the lords or administrators who controlled or led livestock movements; interestingly we shall find, later on, evidence for lords who gave their names to certain droveways and fords much used by them and their people. The names on the stones seem to declare 'this is the end of my trackway, although others may use it'. They may also declare 'this is the edge of my moorland'; there is no problem about the Fardel stone having been sited (before its removal to the British Museum) away from the edge of rough grazing as it is today, because the field patterns to the east towards Hanger Down are clearly of late Saxon or medieval type, later than the stone which was once therefore on the moorland edge. A recently discovered stone near a trackway leading to the open moor is in Ilsington parish. The dating of these stones is probably not as problematic as has been claimed. All (except perhaps the one at Ilsington) are certainly of pre-Saxon date, the personal names on them being Celtic or Romano-British.[57]

Supervision of grazing and pastoral management occupied a large part of the lives of many people living on or near medieval Dartmoor, and those topics are at the centre of this book. Study of them draws the historian into many other fields, such as the history of boundaries and of trackways. But the book is not intended to be a total history of medieval Dartmoor: it has limitations in terms of topics as well as in terms of time. But let this pen first glean a brain teeming with ideas about transhumance before, perhaps, moving to other things, such as place-names denoting various types of vegetation on the borders of the region, which might allow us to reconstruct an earlier Dartmoor and its borders. Dartmoor farmers grew grain crops for their own consumption and for animal feed, and field systems are touched on here but not studied in detail. To include pastoral farming and exclude arable cultivation is a highly artificial division, I realise, although it does help to redress a degree of emphasis on the latter which has been a little apparent in studies of agrarian history since the publication of H.L. Gray's *English Field Systems* in 1915.[58] Some of the people who looked after livestock were also tin workers for part of the year or part of their lives and nobody living on or visiting medieval Dartmoor could have been unaware of the activities, sounds, smells and landscapes of this industry. In the Middle Ages tin working was unique to the South West of England and for this reason it has been relatively closely studied. It will be touched upon in this book only in the context of interactions between tinners and pastoralists. Exploitation of the many other resources of Dartmoor, already mentioned in this chapter, will not be studied in depth but will be mentioned from time to time; for example, turf-cutting and the production of peat charcoal, associated with tin production, feature in my discussion in chapter 2, of moorland buildings which could have been used by workers in those industries and in the paragraphs on contested landscapes in chapter 3.

CHAPTER TWO

The red tides

Impersonal transhumance and the central moor

In this chapter and the next we discuss transhumance to Dartmoor in its largely 'impersonal' phase, when most of the cattle taken to the moorlands were looked after there not by their owners but by guardian herdsmen. This is what Peter Herring, writing about Bodmin Moor in Cornwall, has cleverly called 'transhumance by proxy'. In that region, latterly, livestock were moved to the uplands in the summer to be looked after by supervisors, and their owners did not reside there. The practice, as it existed in the seventeenth century, was described by Richard Carew and by an anonymous poet, but at some time before then it had replaced what I call 'personal transhumance', in which the owners of the livestock resided with their animals for the duration of the summer. There is excellent evidence for early personal transhumance on Bodmin Moor in the groups of huts for summer dwelling which Peter Herring has discovered on the open pastures there. Dartmoor was very similar: personal transhumance there, described in chapters 4 and 5, gave way to the impersonal type in the late Saxon period.[1]

The period covered by this chapter starts in the late thirteenth century, not because impersonal transhumance began then, but because detailed documentation for it first becomes available in that period. Each year over many centuries the first flush of spring grass was inviting and alluring to the herds and flocks. Along deep lanes linking the down-country to the moors,[2] cattle and other livestock began to move, with their owners, or family members or delegates appointed by them, for the duration of the journey, to fan out as the constricting trackways gave way to open moorland. In autumn these tides of livestock began to ebb. There were daily flows and counter-flows too, as moor-edge farmers lucky enough to live close to the rough grazing sent up some of their stock and brought them home again—according to the sun's rhythms, as a sixteenth-century document put it.[3]

The total value of the cattle grazing on Dartmoor during the period covered by this chapter was probably greater than that of any other type of livestock, and many of them were red: hence its title, which is taken from the writings of Freda Wilkinson, Dartmoor farmer, historian, poet and friend. There are references to red cattle in medieval sources from throughout Devon, for example, in court rolls of Ashprington for 1440 (a cow), of Werrington in 1366 (a bull) and of Holsworthy in 1399 (an ox). The court rolls of Dartmoor itself reveal other examples. It should be added that there is some difficulty in reconciling this good medieval evidence with what other writers have said about the colours of post-medieval livestock types in Devon.[4]

The central moor: ownership and commoners

In the documented history of the central moor—now the parish of Lydford, the hub of the centre of Dartmoor—which begins after the Norman Conquest, two dominant strands are royal ownership and common rights belonging to all the people of Devon. The common rights are the main subjects of this section, for they were complicated and intricate, but royal ownership is a more straightforward topic and will be dealt with first.

There are direct references to royal ownership of Dartmoor in the reigns of Richard I (1189–99) and John (1199–1216) and in the early years of the reign of Henry III (1216–72). The first of these references is not as early as we might wish, but nevertheless provides a respectable pedigree. There was a brief severance of the direct link with the Crown in the thirteenth century and the early fourteenth, as a result of Henry III's grant of the central moor to his brother, Richard, Earl of Cornwall (and Poitou), and his heirs in 1239. The last Earl of Cornwall, Edmund, was unlucky in marriage, dying childless in 1300, so his estate, including the central moor of Dartmoor, reverted to the Crown. Between 1300 and 1337 the ownership of the moor oscillated greatly, determined partly by intimacies, factions and intrigues surrounding the Crown, especially during the reign of Edward II. It was probably this unsettled ownership which led Edward III to create, in full Parliament, a permanent indisputable institution for the ownership and management of Edmund's former estate—the Duchy of Cornwall (including Dartmoor). By the Great Charter of the Duchy, issued in 1337, Edward III's eldest son was made Duke of Cornwall and the Duchy was constituted as the property of all future eldest sons of the Crown down to this day, or the Crown itself at such times when there was no son. The Duchy, centred on Cornish manors and jurisdictions but including the central moor of Dartmoor and other properties in Devon and beyond, thereby remained indisputably royal throughout the rest of the Middle Ages and down to the present day—although the stern provisions of the charter were sometimes broken by grants of the whole of it or parts, including Dartmoor, through royal favours.[5]

From before the Norman Conquest there is no direct evidence for royal ownership of Dartmoor. We should hardly expect any. However, Chris Wickham has made the point that, in Europe at large in the post-Roman period, uncultivated tracts of land tended to become 'public', to be used by rulers who, as protectors of the people, permitted them to have rights of common. Nothing at all is known about the ownership of Dartmoor in the Roman period, but in the post-Roman centuries the developments outlined by Wickham almost certainly applied there. These would explain the strong strand of royal ownership, apparent as soon as documents begin to survive, in the twelfth century, and the equally strong emphasis on common rights, first explicitly mentioned in 1204.[6]

There is, in fact, an earlier, indirect and oblique suggestion of common rights on Dartmoor. According to a seventeenth-century deposition concerning tithe payments from the region, common rights belonged to all of the people of Devon 'except Barnstaple and Totnes'. It must be admitted that this reference is late. But if this late mention refers to ancient custom, why is there this odd exclusion, never adequately explained in the huge literature which a special region has generated? What these two places have in common is that they were both urban defended places, *burh* fortresses, the former created by Alfred at the end of the ninth century, the latter a subsequent creation, probably by Edward the Elder in the early tenth century.[7] At a time of constant Viking threat when the *burh* fortresses of Devon served a very real purpose as seats of the army (*fyrd*) and places from which armies were provisioned, there was a need to prevent some of their people from being far away on the moorland grazings and beyond easy recall when danger suddenly threatened; these would have been the resident shepherds mentioned later in this chapter, exercising their common rights. It is not too difficult to explain why the other two *burh* fortresses of Devon, Lydford and Exeter, are not mentioned in this exclusion. Lydford, which suffered a Viking assault in 997, was perched on the edge of Dartmoor and it would have been easy to recall its people in times of danger, while the people of Exeter perhaps did not take their livestock to the summer pastures because the wide River Exe, almost certainly un-bridged in the Saxon period, and often high and raging in spring and autumn, deterred them. Evidence presented later in this chapter shows that the people of east Devon, the region in which Exeter lies, did not send animals to Dartmoor in the Middle Ages, even after the construction of Exe Bridge in the twelfth century, though the reasons for this are obscure. However, the important point to make is that, if the main argument of this paragraph is correct—that the exclusion of Barnstaple and Totnes was to prevent fighting men from being beyond recall—we have evidence to show that common rights were being exercised on Dartmoor in the early tenth century. It would be difficult to understand any mechanisms by which such rights could be taken away from these two towns after the tenth century.

Because of the strong thread of royal ownership on the central moor, and also because of equally strong rights of common there, the medieval evidence about those classes of people who could graze their animals upon it is extremely abundant and very clear for the most part, with a few ambiguities here and there. There was a hierarchy comprising three classes:

a) all people from the down-country, beyond the ring of moor-side manors;

b) some occupiers of land in the moor-side manors (who might also act as middlemen for down-country people);

c) all occupiers of the farms within the central moor called the 'ancient tenements' (who, likewise, could also be middlemen).

The down-country's rights of common

We shall deal with each of these three classes in turn, *first* with those people who lived at the greatest distance and for whom transhumance was an inescapable necessity if their animals were to benefit from the summer pastures. There are many statements from the sixteenth century and later about the rights of common enjoyed by down-country people and, with a few small exceptions, they are all in agreement. From the seventeenth century we have statements about their 'common of pasture *sans number* for sheep and cattle ... time out of mind'; their 'right to feed and depasture their cattle' on the central moor; about 'three sorts of commoners', of whom the down-countrymen were one; about 'every inhabitant of the county of Devon, except Totnes and Barnstaple', having 'a right to turn out their cattle' on the central moor.[8] From the fourteenth century the statements which we have are equally emphatic: an inquisition of 1388 states that 'outsiders' dwelling beyond the central moor and certain adjacent manors had common for livestock grazing on the central moor, and details about this arrangement, given in the inquisition, allow us to equate these outsiders with the down-country commoners of later documents. Tracing the evidence further backwards, the Hundred Rolls of 1275, results of an enquiry into royal rights instituted by Edward I, speak of the custom (*consuetudo*) of common rights on Dartmoor, and a charter of John, in 1204, refers to 'all Devon and the men dwelling in it' as having 'customs' on Dartmoor which we may reasonably equate with the common grazing rights of the later evidence.[9]

Witnesses and deponents who spoke so clearly about the rights of the down-country people in the seventeenth and eighteenth centuries also spoke, unanimously, of the guardianship of their animals by the Crown's herdsmen and of a fee paid by the owners (or keepers) of the animals for each head of cattle summering on the central moor. It was a payment of 1½d. per head and the reason why they spoke about it apparently without any complaint, as ancient practice and custom, was that it was then a paltry sum compared to the value of the animal: the national average price of an ox was about 12s., of which the fee of 1½d. per head is a minute fraction. Devon's oxen commanded a lower price than the national average, presumably because of their small size, and many of the animals grazing on Dartmoor in the Middle Ages and later were immature cattle, commanding lower prices than adults, but even in their case the payment was a minimal one. In any case, a down-country farmer would probably have not made mental calculations of this kind; rather he would have set the benefit of summer grazing for his beast at 1½d. per head against what he might have paid in the hire of grassland in the down-country, and he would have been aware of the number of extra animals he could keep by his own pastures during the summer through the practice of transhumance—an advantage to which we return in chapter 7. There is no real contradiction between common rights on the one hand and a fee on the other. At 1½d. per head of cattle it was probably regarded by the commoners in the seventeenth century, and indeed in the Middle Ages, as good value for the guardianship of their livestock provided by the Crown's herdsmen and their underlings and not as an unwelcome impost. The fee was not a rent for the pasture of Dartmoor, which would have been higher than 1½d., and may be compared to payments, 'protection money', made to the lord of Nether Gorddwr in the Welsh borders for providing a cattle guardian armed with a staff, 'because the country was wild and disordered'. There is every reason to suppose that the fee on Dartmoor was of some antiquity, although admittedly the evidence is comparative and comes from other places. Domesday Book occasionally mentions such fees, for example the 32d. received by the lord of Balsham (Cambridgeshire) 'from the pasture'. For Devon we have a very explicit mention in Domesday Book, the entry for Molland near Exmoor stating that the lord could take 'every third animal pastured on the moor', which could presumably be commuted to cash if he wished. Normally the lord's fee paid by men whose animals grazed on his pasture was presumably included in Domesday in the total value of the manor and that this assumption is correct is shown by the unique entry for Woodbury: the manor was worth 30s. 'with the common pasture'.[10]

The fee paid by the down-country men in association with their right of common on the central moor was a long established one. According to the inquisition of 1388, it was 'an ancient custom', although in the summer of that year the chief herdsman who looked after the animals on behalf of the Crown attempted to increase the payment. He decided that more money could be made from the ancient custom of transhumance and by his 'connivance . . . for his own advantage and emolument' he increased the fee to 3d. Much trouble followed. Unfortunately we do not know what part the commoners played in the complaint because the wholly royal documentation, which is all we have to go on, portrays John Dabernoun, locally the Crown's steward, as the worried party; he officially complained about 'the damage and disherison' which the

Crown might sustain in the future if the increase in fee was continued. Read in one way, this is a strange statement for, given the large number of animals involved, the extra 1½d. represented significant new income for the Crown and should have been supported by its steward. Probably, therefore, we can see behind Dabernoun's complaint a minor revolt among the commoners who were aggrieved partly at a change to what they regarded as their privilege and custom, because a doubling of the grazing fee from 1½d. to 3d. represented a significant, though still relatively small, increase in their costs. In addition, Dabernoun himself would have been worried for it would have been quite clear to him that, faced with a doubling of the guardianship fee on the central moor, down-country farmers might take their livestock to the outer moors, where fees were lower: in other words they could vote with their feet and the hooves of their cattle, to the 'damage and disherison' of the Crown. Richard II was clearly worried and ordered an inquisition to be held, not at the royal stronghold and administrative centre of Lydford but at the moor-side town of Chagford, from which the verdict might be seen to be more impartial, and to take place on 23 September 1388, after the commoners had removed many of their animals from the central moor, in order to prevent further trouble. The inquisition found for the 'old' rate of 1½d.[11]

'Old' is a relative term, for in the thirteenth century the rate per head of cattle had been lower. It had apparently been ½d. around the middle of the thirteenth century but then, during the tenure of the central moor by the earls of Cornwall, their bailiffs took to charging 1d. (before 1275) and by 1296 they had increased the fee to 1½d. As for the first increase, the commoners complained bitterly to the royal enquiries of 1275 which have given us the documents which we now know as the Hundred Rolls. The down-countrymen of the Hundred of Plympton rose up and expressed their discontent, through their representatives, and so did the burgesses of the town of Okehampton. Plympton Hundred stretched from the coast around Down Thomas and Plymstock, through enclosed countryside, then to the moors of Shaugh Moor, and touched the boundary of the central moor at Plym Head. It was a tract of countryside containing many settlements whose people were involved in transhumance. The complaint of the burgesses of Okehampton is perfectly understandable, because we know from other evidence that townspeople enhanced their livelihoods by sending livestock to the moors in summer. The complaints were not upheld, however, probably because of the great power and influence of the Earl of Cornwall and because the Crown had no prerogative in the matter at this time. A trebling of the fee during the later thirteenth century coincided with the non-royal interlude in the ownership of the central moor. Later on, the Crown and the Duchy, on the other hand, appear as more benevolent lords and under them the fee of 1½d. remained unchanged, save for the short interlude in 1388, down to relatively recent times.[12]

Venville rights

The *second* group in the hierarchy of people with common rights on the central moor comprised the occupiers of certain moor-side farms, those with 'venville' rights (in Fig. 2.1 the parishes containing farms with these rights are marked 'V'—the proportion of such farms in each parish varied). These moor-side farmers, being closer to the central moor than the down-country men, enjoyed greater rights of common, principally the option of sending their livestock to the pastures of the central moor by day and bringing them back to their enclosed farms at night. There are many statements about their right to this practice, some coming from the farmers themselves, some from the Crown or Duchy: the borderers could go into the central moor 'by sonne and goo home by sonne' (sixteenth century); they were accustomed to pasture their animals 'between the rising and the setting of the sun, and not remaining . . . by night' (1388); they had done so 'from time immemorial' (1382). There is a statement about the practice in 1345, but many of the words are missing because the document is badly damaged, and the earliest, oblique, reference to it is in 1297; before that, detail disappears from the documentation. The practice resulted in short lanes, technically called drift lanes, such as the one which I have walked leading from Babeny to Riddon Ridge, or that from the hamlet of Halstock to Okehampton Common and the central moor beyond. The occupiers of the moor-side farms might also wish to leave some of their livestock overnight on the central moor (perhaps applying this practice to bullocks and steers while cows and calves were brought home in the evening) and they claimed and exercised this right too: 'night rest' and 'staying over night' are mentioned in some documents while in the damaged statement of 1345 the beginning of a truncated sentence seems to indicate that the practice was being recorded then.[13]

The greater freedoms enjoyed by occupiers of the moor-edge properties were curtailed in two small respects. In the first place, they were permitted to send to the central moor only as many animals as could be wintered upon their farms, a restriction described several times in the early seventeenth century (for example, 'common . . . for as many cattle as their tenements will keep in winter') and also in the early fourteenth century. The reason for this stipulation is clear and concerns the important role of middleman, discussed in more detail in the next section, assumed by many moor-edge farmers. The occupiers of many farms situated close to the central moor took in, for a fee, livestock from down-countrymen, perhaps a little earlier in spring than the formal opening of the grazings, then sent them, along with their own livestock, to the central moor. Had these livestock been given the same privileged status as the stock of the moor-edge farmers, a loophole would have been created and the down-countrymen could have avoided the 1½d. fee paid to the Crown. Hence the stipulation that the privileges enjoyed by the moor-side farmers applied only

2.1 Parishes containing Venville farms.

Based on J. Somers Cocks, 'Saxon and early medieval times', in C. Gill (ed.), *Dartmoor: A New Study* (Newton Abbot, 1970), Fig. 11.

to their own animals which had over-wintered on their farms: they did not apply to livestock taken in by the moor-side farmers acting as middlemen.[14]

A second restriction on farmers from the moor-edge properties was that they paid fees for their right of common, though these were nominal—for example, the hamlet of Lettaford (Plate 8), in which there were three farms in the Middle Ages, paid 4d. collectively and a little extra for night rest if needs be; from the whole of the parish of Sourton the fee was only 4½d., a sum which might have been paid collectively by about 40 farmers, if we can make an estimate of their number from the lay subsidy return of 1525.[15]

What has been said above about the rights of common belonging to moor-edge farmers can be stated with some confidence. In addition, there are some obscure features about these rights and their codification by the Crown. The farmers who owned them were called venville men and the fees were known as venville payments, or sometimes wengefeild or vengefeild payments. There has been much speculation about the English term which has in some cases, to put it frankly, thrown discussions of common rights on Dartmoor rather wildly off course. We can discount the views of the romantic widow Mrs Bray, in her Dartmoor letters written to Robert Southey, where she speculates etymologically that the payments were rewards paid to the moor-side farmers for destruction of the wolves which once lived in the region. R.H. Worth's explanation seems at first sight to be more acceptable—venville was simply a local and 'more suent and acceptable' rendering of *fines villarum*, 'payments of the vills'). The latter is not, however, accepted by the *Oxford English Dictionary* which points out that the earliest English forms of the word are unlikely to derive from the Latin; it can be added that, since this is a localised custom, it would have had an *English* name. Whatever the term may mean, there are other obscure features about these payments. The distribution of the farms on which they fell is highly irregular and seems to us, at this remove, to be rather eccentric. A few of the parishes with boundaries touching the central moor, e.g. Cornwood for example, were not 'in venville', so presumably their inhabitants did not have the rights and privileges described above; a large vill such as Ugborough paid 5d. whereas a small one such as Throwleigh paid 2s. 6d.; in some cases the payment was a collective one by vill (or parish coinciding with vill) yet in others, individual farms and hamlets paid, for example Lettaford, Hookney and Kendon in the vill of North Bovey. These distinctions are not easy to understand. It is possible that parishes and farms which were 'in venville' were those at which important droveways terminated, and that their tenants had a privileged status because they were in charge of receiving the livestock of the down-countrymen as they approached the moor-edge and handing them over to the Crown's herdsmen. Certainly local people were proud of their privileged status if they were 'in venville'; Buckfastleigh was called Fynfield (a corruption of venville) in the sixteenth century to distinguish it from nearby South Brent and Cornwood which did not have this status. In addition, they may have guarded the gates which, in the years before the cattle grid, prevented stock from roaming off the moor and down lanes to the down-country.[16]

The ancient tenements' rights of common

The *third* class of commoner using the central moor for the grazing of animals comprised those people whose farms actually lay within the centre (see Fig. 6.4). Closest of all to the pastures of the central moor, their privileges were the greatest, for they paid nothing for grazing their animals there, so long as those animals could be over-wintered upon their tenements, and in return for this preferential treatment they assisted in the rounding up of the cattle of other commoners, the drifts which are described in more detail later in this chapter.

If they acted as middlemen, which most of them did, taking in the livestock of the down-countrymen, they paid 1½d. per head of cattle taken in, the normal rate. This third class was a small one comprising the occupiers of just over thirty farms, according to lists made in the eighteenth and nineteenth centuries; shortly before the Black Death of 1348 there were just over 40 farms. Latterly these farms were always called the 'ancient tenements' although the term does not seem to have had a medieval pedigree. The origins of these farms are discussed in chapter 6; later in this present chapter their role in the systems of transhumance, through the drifts, is discussed.[17]

Distances travelled and the middlemen

At the end of the eighteenth century William Marshall wrote of 'distant townships' from which livestock were driven to the central moor, and a century previously various residents of moor-side parishes, in dispute with the rector of Lydford over tithes, described farmers who brought animals from 'places more remote' throughout the county of Devon to enjoy the summer pastures of the moors. In this section we examine the medieval evidence (thirteenth to fifteenth centuries) for the distances over which animals were driven to Dartmoor and we discuss the role of middlemen in transhumance.[18]

The evidence must be sought in two types of sources, emanating from the destinations at both ends of the two-way journey to Dartmoor, first from the down-country manors whose herdsmen sent animals up to the hills and second from the Crown's central moor whose officials were in charge of them over the summer. Discovery of references in the former type of source has taken over twenty years of searching, but a number have been found. In September 1473 the bailiff of the Abbot of Tavistock's home demesne of Hurdwick, five miles from the central moor, accounted for 4s. 8d. which he had spent on the grazing fee for forty bullocks sent there (strictly this should have been 5s. so perhaps a small reduction had been negotiated); the bailiff's account of 1480 records a payment 'for the pasture of fourteen beasts staying in the moor of the lord king called Dartmoor in the summer time'. Another manorial account which refers to movement of livestock towards Dartmoor is one for the manor of Halsford, about three miles from Exeter; dated 1342–43, it records the manorial reeve sending livestock to Dartmoor. A rarer type of document is an account, dated 1364–65, of the expenses of the warden of the store of the chapel of Mary which served the formidable castle of Trematon in eastern Cornwall. He was in charge of livestock donated in piety to provide an income for the chapel, and in the summer of 1364 he sent several cattle across the Tamar and accounted for 'driving them to Dertmor ... and their pasture there' (Plate 15).[19]

From manorial and other accounts we turn to more miscellaneous types of records of down-country manors from which transhumance to Dartmoor was practised. In 1388 at Holloway (in Northlew parish), five miles to the north of Dartmoor, the escheator of Devon and other commissioners were in charge of a royal inquisition into the possessions of Sir John Cary who, with many others, had been found guilty by the Merciless Parliament over an attempt to usurp the power of Richard II. They saw that the wine cellar at Holloway had been wisely emptied in advance of their visit and they then set about valuing Sir John's livestock. Here they ran into difficulties. Some of the animals, so they said, had become wild, while four mares with their foals were far away and had to be 'brought to Holway out of Dertmore at the great labour and expense of the commissioners'. From 1276 we have a reference to demesne livestock from Bickleigh being driven by their reeve through the manor of Shaugh Prior, upwards to or homewards from the moors. In 1369–70 the reeve of the north Devon manor of Monkleigh spent the relatively large sum of 2s. 6d. and five days of toil regaining cattle which had been seized somewhere near Tavistock (30 miles to the south) and, although the source does not say so, these were probably animals which had been sent to the moors and had then strayed through neglect to that vicinity. In a deed of 1341 relating to Parswell, west of Tavistock, it is stated that if the rent from a property were to fall into arrears, the grantee's animals could be seized 'anywhere . . . within the county of Devon', and this may well be a reference to the possibility that some of them might be on the summer pastures of Dartmoor.[20]

Fig. 2.2 shows the distribution of the places from which references have been found to transhumance towards Dartmoor in sources relating to down-country manors. Some of the distances travelled are quite great; for example, livestock came from Monkleigh, 18 miles away and from Halsford at 15 miles. It must be stressed that the map shows only a sample of movements, those which happen to be recorded in documents which happen to have survived. It is only by chance that the map does not show movements from manors in parishes directly bordering the central moor, but their involvement with transhumance is supported by other kinds of evidence, namely documentation coming from the administration of the centre, to which we now turn.

The rolls of the court of the manor of central Dartmoor have frequent references to people who pastured animals within its jurisdiction, usually in the context of fines levied on commoners who attempted to avoid paying the fees mentioned in the previous section. Thus the earliest surviving record of this court (summaries of proceedings for 1296–97) shows that the parson of the parish of Belstone and Elya de Cristinestow (Christow) had animals grazing illegally on the central moor. From the earliest surviving file of full records of this court, a broken series from 1366 to 1377, we can recover the names of William and John Clerk of Greenaway (Gidleigh parish), John *atte* Yeoldelande (probably from Yelland in North Tawton parish), John Codelip (from the place now called Cudlipptown, now in Peter Tavy parish), Walter

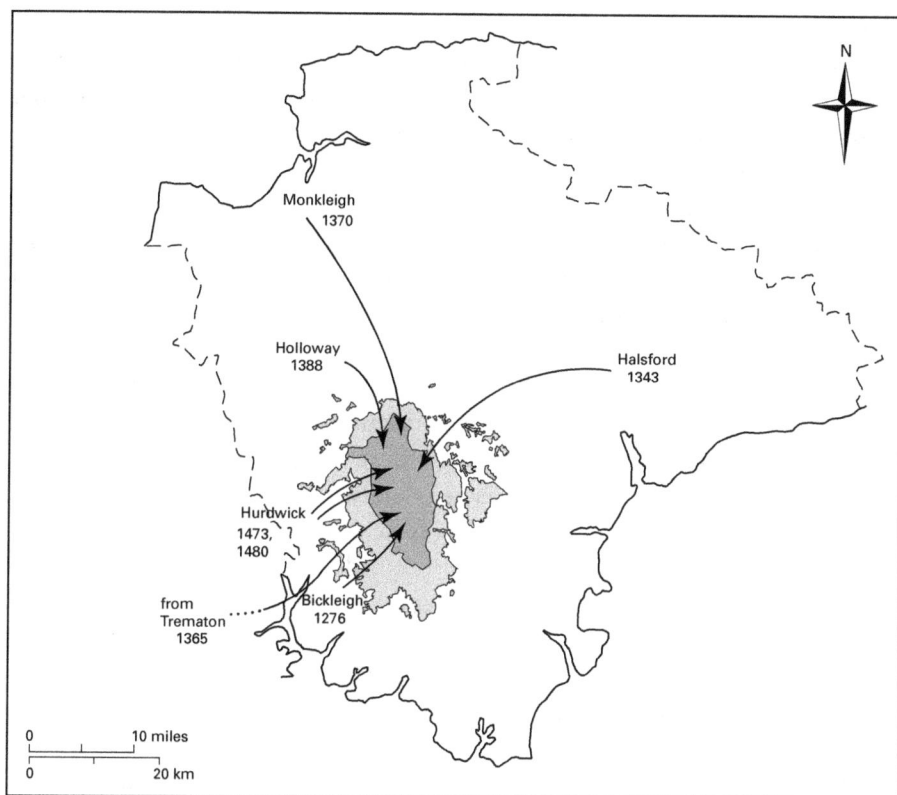

2.2 Some documented cases of livestock sent to Dartmoor from down-country manors.

Sources: see text.

Smyth from Sampford Courtenay parish, William Allynggistone (from Allison, once *Allingeston*, in South Tawton parish) and John Gnattorr (from Nattor in Peter Tavy parish) and many others from moor-side parishes who were unlucky enough to be apprehended for not paying their grazing fees.[21]

A more formal approach to the topic of distances over which cattle were driven to the central moor is to use the lists which were drawn up yearly to record the names of those who paid fees at 1½d. per head of cattle, the making of which is described in a following section. The purpose of the lists was financial and legal. Any of the officials in charge of the central moor might be called to account and might be questioned about the sums which they rendered, so they were therefore wise to keep lists of the people who paid fees. The commoners would not have objected to the lists, for any of them charged at the court of the central moor for illegally grazing their animals there might reasonably expect the documents to be produced for inspection if they wished to escape being fined. This dual purpose of the lists explains why some are found among the financial accounts of the moor and others among the court proceedings. The surviving series is by no means continuous and it may well be that lists were discarded except when there was occasion to use them for the purposes described above.

2.3 The
parishes of
residence of
some individuals
agisting on the
central moor in
1496.

The location
of residences
within parishes
is approximate
only; arrows
indicate farms
lying beyond the
frame of the map

Based on
H.S.A. Fox,
'Medieval
Dartmoor as
seen through the
account rolls',
PDAS 52 (1994),
Fig. 2.

Most of the people in the lists are identified by a combination of forename and surname, so it was not usually necessary for the toiling clerks who made them to add parish or place of residence. But occasionally they did so, and especially in the case of a common combination of forename and surname. For example, the list of 1414 shows that John Cole, a common combination, is tagged as 'of Peter Tavy' and in 1493 John Manna, with a surname which occurs many times in the lists, is said to be 'of Sheril' (in Widecombe in the Moor). The clerks also recorded place of residence if a man's surname was of the locative type but did not relate to his residence: thus, in the list of 1443, we find 'John Catru atte Chappel', *Catru* or the like being the usual early spelling for Cator in the parish of Widecombe, yet this man lived at Chapel in the moor-side parish of South Brent. Such instances, quite rare in these listings, bring us face to face with the farmsteads from which these men drove their animals onto the central moor. But there is another approach, to try to link the personal names in the lists with names in some other source which gives parish of residence; some limited success has been had with this method as applied to the especially well preserved list of 1496 and the subsidy returns for 1524 and 1525, the latter providing a relatively complete coverage, parish by parish, of the names of those who contributed to royal taxation in those years. This exercise is fraught with problems, it must be admitted, and it works best with uncommon surnames; indeed, with the most common combinations of names, for example John Smith, there is absolutely no means of linking the man so named as having animals grazing on the central moor in 1496 with any one of the several people with that name in the subsidy list. So the first proviso to be made about the map (Fig. 2.3), which is a result of this research exercise, is that it picks up only a very small sample of the people who used the central moor in 1496. A second proviso should be made: the subsidy is arranged by parish, not by manor or farm, so that, within the parishes shown in Fig. 2.3, the location of the symbols, each one representing a grazier, is conjectural.[22]

Fig. 2.3 is of very great interest. The occupiers of the 'ancient tenements' within the central moor are well represented, as is to be expected for they lived closest to, indeed surrounded by, pastures which could be grazed for the minimal fee of 1½d. per head of cattle. Many of the circle of parishes with boundaries touching the central hub, the moor-edge parishes, are shown as involved with transhumance to the central moor. It will be remembered from the previous section that some of the inhabitants of these moor-edge parishes did not pay, for their own animals, the 1½d. grazing fee with which the list of 1496 was concerned, but rather a small lump sum. This may explain the absence of symbols in a few of these parishes on Fig 2.3. If we work outwards from the centre, we find that the next rank of parishes, beyond the moor-edge ones, is well represented on the map—Bovey Tracey, for example, Drewsteignton, Brentor, Whitchurch, Plympton and Ermington. Beyond them, the list of

1496 reveals transhumance from even greater distances, from Staverton (6 miles away), for example, and from St Giles on the Heath (12 miles away, and particularly interesting because, as its name implies, there were extensive blocks of rough ground here in the Middle Ages).

Comparison of Fig. 2.3 (based on a list of fee payers) and Fig. 2.2 (based on manorial accounts and other sources) does, however, reveal an apparent anomaly, for the latter source records transhumance of cattle over quite long distances whereas on the former only a small proportion are long-distance movements. The explanation is quite simple, because some of the men named in the lists of fee payers were 'middlemen', living on or close to Dartmoor, who took in the cattle of farmers from a greater distance for a fee which went into their own pockets, and were responsible for paying the official 1½d. fee for each of those animals.

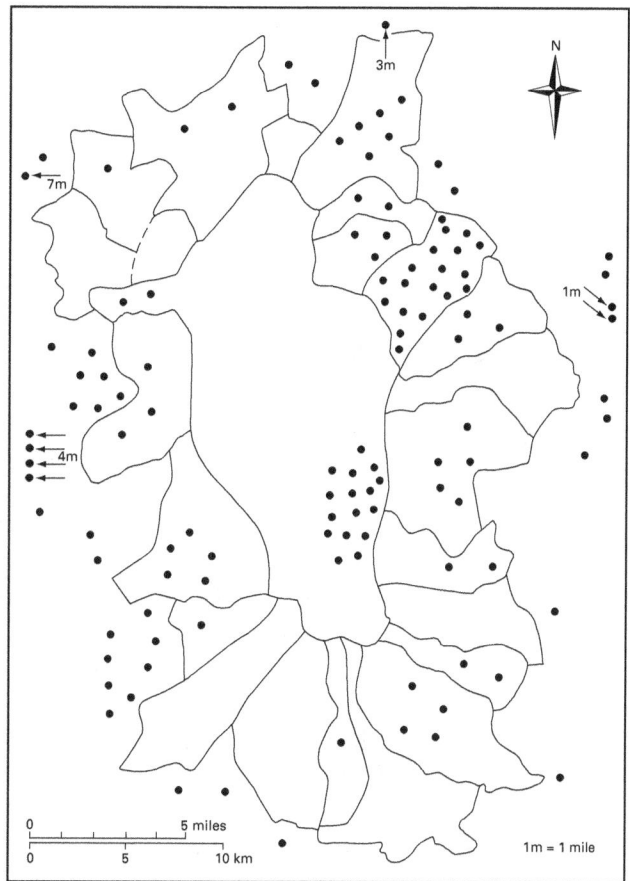

In such cases, the distant farmers who were the real owners of the cattle never appear in the lists of fee payers by name; they lie behind the screen of the middlemen, their names and places of residence lost to us for ever. The evidence for this practice is quite straightforward, for example a statement in 1627 from William Torre of Widecombe in the Moor who noted that there were farmers living near Dartmoor who were accustomed to 'take other men's cattle . . . and are paid for their pains in keeping them and they pay to the king's majesty for cattle so taken in 1½d. for every bullock' or from John Clement who in 1702 spoke of his 'oversight and care' of bullocks and sheep 'committed to him this last summer'; Torre went on to say that the inhabitants of the ancient tenements 'receive hire for herding of other men's cattle'. Middlemen are also apparent in medieval sources, for example in pleas of debt as when Roger Palmer in 1367 tried to recover before the court of Dartmoor 22d. from John Sladd, a sum which the latter should have paid for the custody of some cattle. We have a reference from 1331 to a Dartmoor farmer who had 'cattle . . . of outsiders being in his own custody'. Another indication of the activities of the middlemen is provided by the very large numbers of beasts which appear against some names in the lists of fee payers, far in excess of the livestock which could be kept on a Devon farm with a typical acreage of 32 acres.[23]

Many of the occupiers of the 'ancient tenements' within the central moor can be confidently identified as middlemen, for they too are credited with numbers of cattle greater than their farms' winter capacity. In the list for 1347 the 'ancient tenements' lying within the central moor are given their own sub-section and some of their occupiers are recorded as paying fees for huge numbers of cattle, 272 in the case of John Renwych, no doubt the occupier of Runnage, spelled Renewych in 1317, 178 for John Soper and 69 for the occupier of one of the tenements at Dunnabridge. We have a record of the acreage of these farms in 1345, so that we can be certain that there was no way in which they could have over-wintered so many animals. In the list for 1496, William Manna of Babeny and eight other occupants of 'ancient tenements' paid for over 100 cattle each. Among the farmers of the 'ancient tenements', well positioned to know all the habits of Dartmoor, pastoralists of renown with knowledge of their craft passed down from father to son, there was clearly a long-established tradition of acting as middlemen, extending from 1347 through 1496 and on into the seventeenth and eighteenth centuries, as witnessed by the words of William Torre and John Clement quoted above, and indeed into recent times.[24]

Other farmers living close to but not actually within the central moor also plied the trade of middleman, as shown for example by the large number of men in the list of 1496 who paid fees on between 50 and 100 head of cattle and who had names of types which show that they were tenant farmers not manorial lords. The Crown's herdsmen who had charge of the grazing animals were also in an excellent position to act as middlemen, as discussed more fully in the next section on the herdsman's year, and there is very good evidence for this practice. Farmers living at some distance from Dartmoor must have been greatly reassured to have the service of experienced middlemen but one might ask: why were middlemen necessary? The most obvious answer is that the Crown's herdsmen were concerned with major matters of pastoral management, such as discovering rustlers, apprehending the 'delinquent men' who failed to pay fees and with the movement of cattle, but there were too few of them to exercise minor pastoral care. A young, weaned, calf or a sick bullock owned by a distant farmer would have to be cared for by somebody living close to the central moor (or actually on it, in the case of 'ancient tenements') and this was the middleman's role: he could take the animal back to his farmstead for remedy.

Our picture of the distances over which transhumance to Dartmoor was practised (in its impersonal phase) is sometimes not quite as focused as we might like, but is probably as good as we should expect for such a transient activity—the type which is always the most difficult for the local historian to recreate. Livestock were driven from Halsford near Exeter, from Monkleigh, and St Giles on the Heath to the north and from Staverton to the south, to mention just four of the places referred to above; from Modbury and from Elburton in the parish of Plymstock on the south coast they came; people from parishes nearer to Dartmoor naturally sent animals in large numbers. During the period covered in this chapter some down-country farmers no doubt sent their livestock to the moors out of long-established custom—it was an important part of the farming year in the localities where they lived, already old by the thirteenth century, with misty origins almost lost. In addition, the practice of transhumance was sound and full of wisdom, bestowing economic advantages to the down-country farms from which the livestock were sent. The connection between transhumance and farm economies is a topic which will be taken up in chapter 7.

Pastoral management: the herdsman's year

Small though the fee for each head of livestock grazing the central moor may have been, the total sum collected yearly by the moor's owner, the Crown, was considerable. In 1346 it was around £60, from which must be deducted under £3 for the wages of the Crown's herdsmen.[25] It was necessary, in order to minimise loss of profits, for this income to be accounted for. Moreover, management of the summer grazings required some expenditure and it was necessary to keep track of that too. Luckily for the historian, the medieval accounts of income and expenditure on central Dartmoor have survived in very large numbers and these provide many insights into the management of the grazing system. There exist, in the Public Record Office and among the records of the Duchy of Cornwall, high-piled account rolls and court rolls relating to pastoralism on Dartmoor (Fig. 2.6), daunting at first sight, but alluring too, so that as a young man, over many a summer vacation, I forsook the bright blue skies above Chancery Lane, the birthday-cake towers of the Public Record Office silhouetted against them, and with a mixture of resentment at loss of July days, and excitement, and diffidence, entered through that building's doors to create another world far away:

> Then thought I, Virgil, how from Mantua reft,
> Shy as a peasant in the courts of Rome,
> You took the waxen tablets in your hand,
> And out of anger cut calm tales of home.[26]

The Crown's officials

The size of central Dartmoor was huge, around 54,000 acres, almost all of this being rough pasture, and the length of its boundary, not generally fenced but open to the adjacent outer moors, was long, around 42 miles. Moreover, the number of livestock pasturing there was very great, over 10,000 head of cattle at its height in the Middle Ages, together with unnumbered sheep and horses. It was therefore necessary for the Crown to invest in a good number of herdsmen whose job was to maximise profits and provide good order. During the fifteenth century, a period for which it is easiest to fit all of the types of evidence together, the hierarchy of officials was headed by an elevated 'riding or master forester', the term 'forester' being a survival from the short interval long before when the central moor had been a royal forest. This was an important position and the royal grants of appointments to it state that it could be 'discharged by a deputy', so it is probable that most of those who occupied it did so as a sinecure, paying another man to carry out the duties on the ground. Many of these elevated officials may never have visited Dartmoor, for example Thomas Staunton the younger, appointed in 1433, who also held, though not simultaneously, the constableship of the castle of Melbourne (Derbyshire) and that of Dryslwyn in South Wales. He was described as one of the marshals of the royal household, clearly a man in favour whose post on Dartmoor was one of a number of sinecures received for good and loyal service. In 1484 the post went to Sir John Dinham, a Devon knight and prominent Yorkist who had aided the escape of leading men of the cause after the battle of Ludlow (1459), hiding them in his coastal castle at Nutwell until a balinger could be found to take them across to Calais. He was a national and local figure of importance throughout the reigns of Edward IV and Henry VII. He held many offices, both local and national and, although his estate included two moor-edge manors, Natsworthy and Ilsington, it is unlikely that he had time personally to carry out his duties on the central moor.[27]

The brunt of the task of managing livestock brought to Dartmoor through transhumance was borne by herdsmen on the spot, who numbered eight in the fifteenth century. Their position was a responsible one, yet their yearly pay was 6s. 8d., far less than the £4 or so which might be earned by skilled craftsmen such as carpenters and masons, varying with the workers' inclination, the weather and availability of employment. The reason must be that there were considerable benefits or perquisites to the occupation of herdsmen, principally the opportunity to act as a middleman, taking in the cattle of outsiders and charging them a fee in addition to the 1½d. which was paid to the Crown. They were in a very good position to do this and that they did so we know from lists of those who put out cattle on the central moor. In addition, it is possible that they were permitted to graze their own animals on the moor without paying the 1½d. fee: such a perquisite would be similar to that of the medieval shepherd of Radbourne in Warwickshire who was allowed forty sheep on the pasture, in addition to his pay. The herdsmen were rangers on horseback. Their conditions were arduous in summer because of the long distances which had to be ridden in order to trace straying animals, to apprehend men who tried to use the pastures without payment and to catch rustlers and rustling gangs. During the long winter season there was less to do, because transhumance removed many, though not all, of the livestock, but even so, a journey across the central moor and its swollen rivers could be highly dangerous on account of the frequent 'tempests and floods' as a thirteenth-century document put it. The herdsmen could not have performed their duties without horses, the upkeep of which was a small charge to set against their wages, although their pasture was, of course, free; there is some evidence to show that they employed a servant. Those conditions did not, however, deter applicants: some men continued in this employment for many years, such as William Martyn who was in post in 1461 and still a herdsman, by now weathered and ruddy no doubt, in 1484; it is possible that the job attracted men from beyond the region, for some of their names, as recorded in their accounts, often do not seem to have been those of Dartmoor stock. Part of the reason for this may have been that the appointment of a herdsman was in the gift of the master forester, as the latter's royal letters of commission tell us, and that these masters, often outsiders, chose men who were known to them and who, also, would be less likely than locals to grant favours to the commoners.[28]

Below the herdsmen, in the hierarchy of men managing the herds during the fifteenth century, were seasonally employed under-herdsmen (*prehurdarii*) and a clerk. Some accounts describe the four under-herdsmen as 'keepers of livestock' at their favoured grazing spots, so we can see them less as rangers on horseback, more as guardian herdsmen, sitting in a lodge or the shelter of some tor while their charges spread gently out on the green hillslope below under the scudding skies. The clerk wrote down the names of the owners of the grazing cattle, and of the middlemen graziers, and recorded a number of animals against each name. In one account roll (for 1415–16) he is described as 'the clerk writing the roll ... and helping in the drifts throughout the whole moor this year at diverse times', for pay of 10s., a high sum considering that he worked relatively few days, but appropriate to a lettered man. Without this un-named clerk, and his predecessors and successors over the years, we as historians would not have the valuable listings of owners and numbers of animals, so useful as sources for this chapter.[29]

The picture given above is drawn from financial accounts from the late fifteenth century. Earlier, the personnel involved in the management of the central moor varied slightly from this. During the thirteenth century and for much of the fourteenth there were fewer herdsmen, six in all. On the other hand, the under-herdsmen, called 'custodians of the beasts' were more numerous, twelve in 1296–97, employed between the feast of the Invention of the Holy Cross (3 May) until the Assumption of the Blessed Mary (15 August). Over the years the composition of the personnel changed slowly. The seasonally employed under-herdsmen were reduced in number from twelve to four while numbers of herdsmen in permanent employment were increased from six to eight. The latter strategy, adopted in the early fifteenth century when animal numbers were very high, was part of a move to increase the efficiency of pastoral management through an increase in the number of more committed, permanently employed herdsmen. At the same time, the number of territories into which the central moor was divided for policing the grazing animals was increased from three to four, a formal change of strategy which must have originated with the master forester and the council of the Duchy of Cornwall. Henceforth each of the four quarters or bailiwicks, as they were variously called, was under the management of two herdsmen and one under-herdsman.[30]

The yearly cycle

The herdsman's year began in that very pastoral month of May, with their announcement of the impending 'opening' of the central moor for the summer grazing session: the financial account for 1346–47 records the expenses of 'making a proclamation at six markets for the grazing'. This is a tantalising reference because—although it clearly shows that the Crown took the annual opening of the central moor very seriously, in order to maximise the grazing fees which it collected and to prevent livestock from being slipped in earlier—it does not give the names of the markets. There were several borough towns, as well as one town which was never a borough, in the ring of moor-side parishes abutting the central moor and in the next ring of parishes, one removed from the centre. If we can judge by the criteria of size, antiquity and roughly equal spacing around the circuit of Dartmoor, we might guess that Tavistock, Lydford, Okehampton, Chagford (or Moretonhampstead), Ashburton and Plympton were the places at which the proclamations were made. Size was important, because the greater the number of countrymen who visited a market, the greater would be the number who, by word of mouth, heard of the date of the opening of the central moor. As for the date itself, the fact that a proclamation was necessary means that it must have been variable, presumably according to the state of growth, advanced or retarded, of the grassland.[31]

On and after the set date in May, the red streams began to move towards Dartmoor along the droveways which linked the region to other parts of Devon. Post-medieval evidence suggests that then the Crown's herdsmen were on occasion responsible for collecting the livestock at selected points in the down-country, but earlier sources contain no hint of this and it is probable that in the Middle Ages numbers of livestock engaged in transhumance were so great that the movement of the animals was the responsibility of their owners or delegates. The delegates might be sons or servants. But there is also evidence of professionals, such as Richard Frende, who lived at Ermington, about half way between moor and coast, in the 1460s; or Robert Hurder of South Pool on the south coast and Walter Herdhead of Woodleigh or Moreleigh, who were taxed in those places in the 1332 subsidy. Moreleigh, another half-way place, is certainly close to a droveway.[32]

Once on the central moor the animals were taken by the Crown's herdsmen to one of several favoured places, such as the wide and sheltered valley of the West Dart near Dunnabridge, the slopes of Crow Tor above the infant Dart, spots south of Steeperton Tor in the marshy top reaches of the Taw and on the moist slopes near Erme Head. These favoured places, called *prede* in medieval documents and lairs or lears later on, were the homes for the livestock's night rest during the summer months and there they were supervised by the herdsmen and under-herdsmen and encouraged to wander onto surrounding visible hillslopes in daytime. According to the oral evidence from moormen collected by William Crossing at the end of the nineteenth century, 'beasts seldom stray very far from the spot at which they are first depastured', a point confirmed to me by farmers today; Crossing recounts a tale of a bullock which wandered many miles because instinct told it to revisit the lair at which it had spent the previous summer. The *Oxford English Dictionary* defines a lair as 'a place for animals to lie down in', citing John Clare's 'low of distant cattle . . . dropping down to lair'.[33]

During the early summer the herdsmen carried out the first of their drifts of the moor's new intake, when the names of owners of the cattle were noted and a number attributed to each name. The date of these early summer drifts was variable, just as the date of the opening of the central pastures was: in different years we hear, for example, of drifts at the feast of St Barnabas, at Peter and Paul's day and at the Translation of St Thomas the Martyr (11 June, 29 June and 7 July). The long list of those who paid grazing fees in 1496, used earlier in this chapter, bears the date 8 July. The purpose of these midsummer drifts was to ascertain the names of the owners of the cattle and of the middlemen. At what time in the year the payments of 1½d. were made in the Middle Ages is not known; in more recent times this was done at the final drift at the beginning of autumn. Nor is it precisely known how the names were ascertained, although the most likely explanation is that the owners and middlemen travelled to Dartmoor in order to attend the midsummer drift, in which case they must have been all the more animated occasions. This was another event which added to the comings and goings to Dartmoor by people with livestock there.

As the days lengthened the herdsmen's tasks grew more varied and they received a bonus payment of 2s. each. In some financial accounts for the central moor (e.g. that for 1415–16) the bonus is described as 'for the time of calving, for four weeks' and this has led some commentators to conclude that the calving of cows is implied. Such an interpretation must be ruled out because under the system of impersonal transhumance practised during the period when the financial accounts are most numerous (thirteenth to fifteenth centuries) most

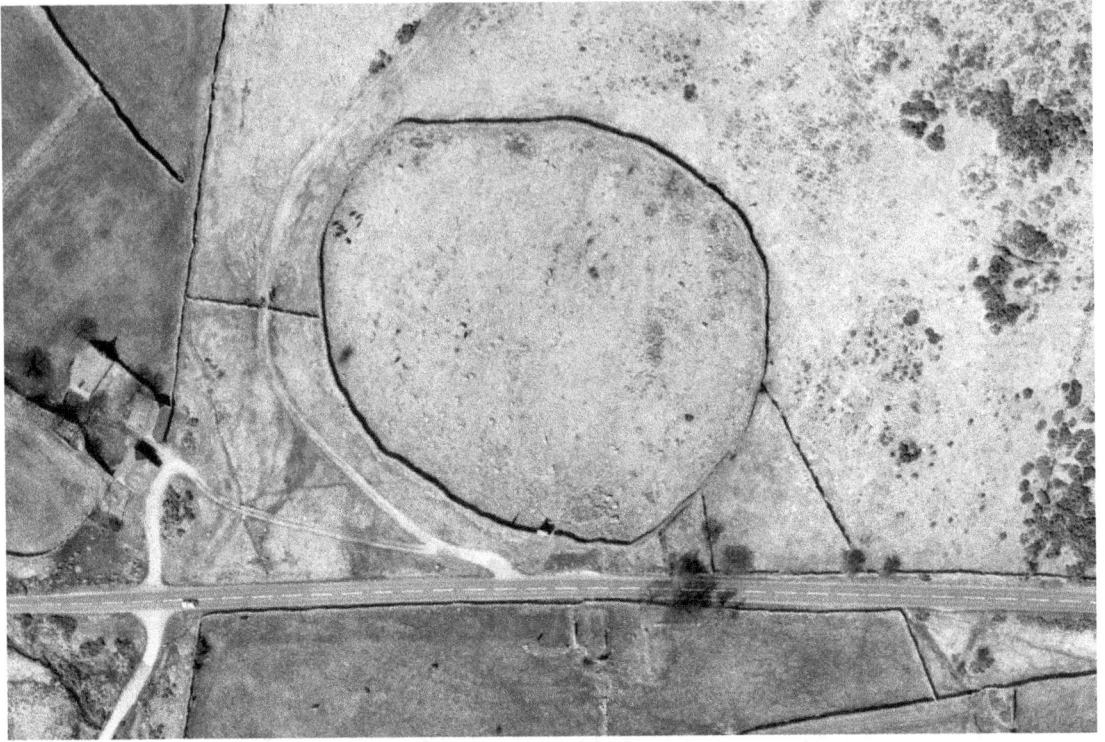

bovines summering on the central moor were immature males and females, breeding cows being left on their home farms. The Latin word for calving can refer to calves of any kind and that deer calves were the concern is confirmed by the occasional financial account which states that the herdsmen's bonus payment was made for the 'time of fawning' (*tempore venetionis*). This is the fence month which, according to the thorough researches of Jean Birrell on the management of deer during the Middle Ages, was 'traditionally the fortnight on either side of midsummer day', a period which is 'notoriously accompanied by high mortality if adequate cover and fodder are lacking'. In 1354 the Council of the Black Prince explicitly mentioned these concerns, ordering its Dartmoor herdsmen to take care 'while the does are fawning and the fawns are tender' and also 'to stay more continually on the moor and to construct lodges'; if these were not shelters for the herdsmen themselves then they may have been make-shift shelters of some kind for the does, perhaps constructed of gorse stems and roofed with heather or rushes. Another task for each herdsman towards midsummer was to count and collect fees from the charcoal-makers working on the central moor, the cutting of turves to make charcoal being a summertime occupation because good weather was needed in order for them to dry.[34]

The beginning of autumn saw the herdsmen undertaking their most important drift, that at which a final reckoning of numbers was made and the grazing fees were paid. Cattle grazing in the northern bailiwick of the central moor were driven to Creaber Green, formerly a funnel-shaped termination of a droveway; those from the other bailiwicks to Dunnabridge Pound, possibly a Bronze Age circular corral, possibly a purpose-built Saxon or medieval enclosure (Fig. 2.4). To these places their owners came and proved ownership, which was done through a system of marks or brands. That some kind of marking was practised in the Middle Ages we know from chance references: in 1478 an armed gang stole an immature bovine (*bovettus*) from the central moor and 'made a sign [*signa*] on its hide', presumably changing the mark in order to disguise the animal's ownership, and a stray on the manor of Christow in the early sixteenth century was described as *sine signo*, 'without a mark', as if this was unusual.[35] The autumn drift was probably the occasion when money

2.4 Dunnabridge pound and Grimspound from the air.

Dunnabridge pound (*opposite top*) is a corral of unknown date (possibly medieval, possibly Bronze Age) to which livestock found on the three southern quarters of the central moor were driven during the great drifts conducted several times a year by the Crown's officials, assisted by the tenants of the Ancient Tenements (p. 67). Grimspound (*opposite*) is a prehistoric corral lying in the private moor of the lord of the manor of Kenton, a coastal manor with a detached territory at Heatree in the parish of Manaton (p. 117). It lay immediately adjacent to the boundary with another private moor, that of the manor of Shapley/Hookney in the parish of North Bovey, and may perhaps have been used as the collection point for livestock rounded up during drifts of one or both of these private moors. The view is eastwards. (Photo credits: Dunnabridge, National Monument Record, Crown Copyright; Grimspound, Frances Griffith, Devon County Council, 14 June 1986, copyright DCC).

changed hands. Each owner of cattle, or the middleman whom he employed, paid over the guardianship fee for his stock, and for each of the bailiwicks a financial account was drawn up by the clerk, to be sent to the Duchy's administrative centre at Lostwithiel in Cornwall, where it was enrolled with the accounts of other Duchy properties to be audited at Michaelmas. Owners were now free to remove their animals, and for them, as the cattle were driven down the deep lanes towards their home farms, another pastoral year drew towards its accustomed close. It is probable that this exodus was carried out in stages, the hardiest animals being left longest on the moors. I am told by local people that in mild autumns there is still good feed on Dartmoor in November. There was another, very good, reason for tarrying, namely that in those years when royal taxation fell, the collectors often made their assessment in September and October and so it was wise for farmers to keep their livestock well out of view on Dartmoor at that time. The collectors for Lifton Hundred, in which the central moor lay, would have been familiar with Dartmoor but to have separated out and assessed the animals of each farmer would have been an impossible task and might incur hostility. The wily practice among Devon farmers of keeping their livestock, usually their principal possessions, on Dartmoor during the period of tax assessment may explain, in part, the miserably low tax yield of the county, although there were other reasons connected with concerted resistance by Devonians to state authority, which I have explored elsewhere.[36]

For the herdsmen, the year was not over. Some animals (sheep and horses) were over-wintered on the central moor and it was therefore necessary for the herdsmen to continue to be vigilant and to apprehend rustlers and deer-stalkers. Their tasks were, however, lighter in winter, coming to an end with a drift on the feast of the Invention of the Holy Cross (3 May), clearly a stock-taking before the busy summer season began. It was for the safety and comfort of the herdsmen in winter that the Council of the Black Prince, meeting at Waltham, probably at the royal abbey there, three days after Christmas in 1360, in deep mid-winter, ordered that a 'suitable lodge' be built on Dartmoor for their 'reception' and for the master forester should he or his delegate occasionally visit. Where it was we do not know.[37]

The ancient tenements' duty to assist at drifts

In this section we have discussed the working lives, in so far as they are known, of the Crown's paid officials whose principal task was to manage the pastures of the central moor. Of all their duties, the most responsible and arduous occurred at the time of the drifts and in these they were assisted by the occupiers of the 'ancient tenements', just over forty in number in the early fourteenth century, which formed islands in the sea of rough pasture, their farmhouses being the only permanent settlements within the central moor. Whereas customary

tenants in many parts of England had to assist in ploughing and harvesting the
lord's demesne, on Dartmoor, where there was no arable demesne, the occupiers
of the ancient tenements were obliged to help out with pastoral management.
There are plenty of post-medieval references to these duties. For example, in
1702, defendants in a case about tithe stated that the occupiers of the ancient
tenements 'assist in the drives . . ., each finding a man, horse and servant at
their own costs, save only a halfpenny cake each . . . driver hath according to
custom'. They are also referred to in the medieval documentation, as in 1478–79
when a court roll records that several tenants failed to appear at a drift 'with
one man', and were fined for this offence against the lord and against ancient
custom. Given the size of the central moor and the number of animals pastured
there, these men were very necessary helpers at the time of the drifts and it is
possible that the very foundation of some of their tenements, almost certainly
before the Norman Conquest, was closely associated with the beginnings of
the Crown's control over the central grazings.[38]

Drift days were no pastoral idyll. The presence of the mounted occupiers of
the ancient tenements, each with his servant, meant that the total number of
participants (including the herdsmen) must have exceeded eighty in the early
fourteenth century. Horns were blown from the tops of the tors to flush out the
stock; there was 'plenty of galloping to do . . . much shouting, men and horses
and dogs all being in a state of great excitement'. A very vivid description is
that of Sabine Baring-Gould, written in the late nineteenth century, although
it should be noted that he was sometimes prone to exaggeration: 'A drift is an
animated and striking scene . . . drivers and dogs sending the frightened beasts
plunging, galloping in one direction towards the place of gathering.' Drifts are
still noisy occasions and I witnessed one in autumn 2002 near Runnage, for
ponies, when there was much shouting, as in the past, but also the modern
roar of quad bikes on which the rangers rode over rough moorland to round
up the animals. At the drifts livestock were on the move, and fast, and this
may have been too much for some: a court roll of 1367 mentions a 'foal dead in
the drift' in May, presumably crushed to death by the rushing animals. These
were male occasions. Of all the names of occupiers of the ancient tenements
recorded in medieval rentals and court rolls not a single female is mentioned,
and that fact is probably connected with their dangerous duties at the drifts:
either the Crown or custom among the occupiers, or both, saw to it that this
was a male preserve.[39]

Livestock: numbers and types

Cattle

The historian who wishes to quantify trends in the numbers of livestock
pastured on central Dartmoor is restricted to dealing with cattle, and only

those cattle which were sent to the summer pastures by the people of the down-country. To a degree he is fortunate because, thanks to the hard work of the herdsmen and their clerk, the counts of those cattle survive in some numbers for the central moor. To a degree he is less lucky for, as we have seen, other classes besides the down-country people had common rights on Dartmoor (the venville men of the moor-side parishes and the occupiers of the 'ancient tenements') while there are no means to count livestock other than bovines. It is best, therefore, to begin with trends in those animals which may be quantified, leaving to the end a discussion of other types.

In the previous section we have seen how an important point in the herdsmen's year was the drift at which the cattle were counted and the names of owners or middlemen entered on a parchment roll by a clerk. We have excellent records, therefore, of cattle numbers and only two minor reservations need be made about them. First, it is natural for the reader to ask if there might not have been evasion of fee-paying on a scale large enough to make the figures unreliable. The retort is that this is unlikely. We have shown that the Crown took its income from fees very seriously. It invested in the wages of many officials in order to maximise income and it enrolled the services of its tenants to assist at the drifts. There was system and order. Although fees paid were small in relation to the value of the animals, instinct no doubt encouraged some owners and middlemen to try to evade them, the easiest way of doing this being to remove livestock before the date of the early autumn drift. These animals would have been noted at earlier drifts and their owners could have been apprehended on their holdings in the down-country during the winter months, though not without much toil on the part of the herdsmen. That they were apprehended in some cases is shown by separate lists and sums for 'men behaving badly' (*homines delinquentes*) which the herdsmen appended to their financial accounts. These delinquent men had been caught and made to pay, and there are other records of offenders in the rolls of the manorial court of Dartmoor, held at frequent intervals at Lydford. These men are sometimes described in the documents as *non scripti*, that is, their names were not written down in the lists of graziers. It would be unrealistic to expect that no owners managed to evade vigilance of this kind, but their numbers were not great.

Bearing these points in mind we can turn to Fig. 2.5 which shows trends over time in numbers of cattle pastured on the central moor during the summer and paying the 1½d. grazing fee. The numbers are impressive at all times but they are especially large during the fifteenth century when they reached a height of over 10,000, a reflection of the social and economic conditions of that period. By 1400 the population of England was around half of its size at its medieval peak in the late thirteenth century or early fourteenth. It had been cut back by the Black Death of 1348, by subsequent epidemics such as that of 1369 for which we have good evidence at Werrington, a few miles away from Dartmoor,

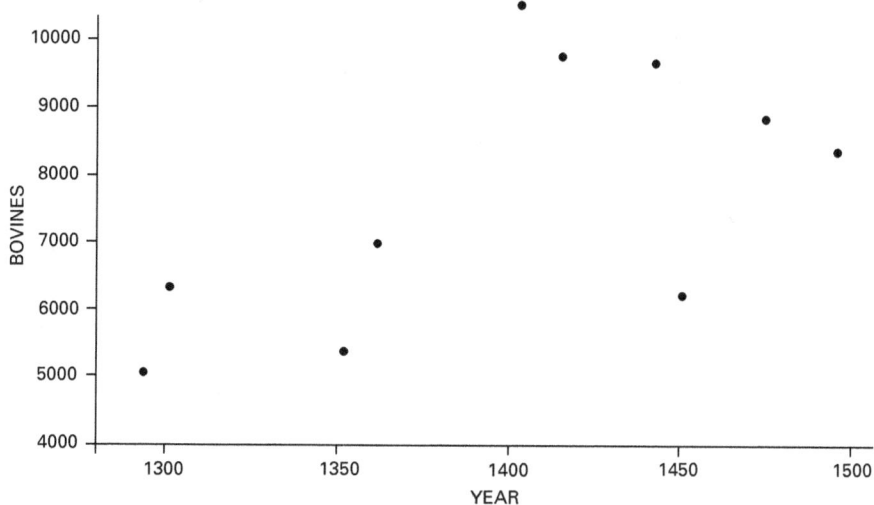

2.5 Numbers of cattle pastured on the Central Moor during the fourteenth and fifteenth centuries.

Calculated from the agistment fees, paid at the rate of 1½d. per head, recorded in the accounts of the Forest of Dartmoor.

Based on H.S.A. Fox, 'Medieval Dartmoor as seen through the account rolls', *PDAS* 52 (1994), Fig. 3.

and by other factors affecting family size. A reduced population meant a rise in living standards, because there was 'more to go round', and higher demand per head for meat, clothing and leather, all the products of pastoral farming. As a consequence, the proportion of the land given over to pasture, rather than arable, increased, for example in the countryside north of Dartmoor from 30% in 1300 to about 50% in 1500. Slowly some landlords and many tenant farmers came to own large numbers of animals and although these grazed for part of the year on the now greater acreage of grassland in the down-country, the attraction of the high summer pastures of Dartmoor persisted, for here supervised and generally safe grazing could be had for a nominal fee while custom and tradition ensured that transhumance continued. The large number of bovines for which the 1½d. fee was paid during the fifteenth century thus neatly reflects the pastoral trend of that period. Conversely, relatively smaller (though still impressive) numbers during the late thirteenth century and early fourteenth tell of smaller farms and fewer livestock on those farms during a time when levels of population were high and a good proportion of the land was necessarily devoted to arable farming to provide basic bread grains.[40]

The relatively low figure for 1351 (Fig. 2.5) is a direct result of the Black Death of 1348. The plague's impact on Dartmoor was no less severe than in other parts of Devon. Long ago some historians would have supposed that it would have been minimal, but we now know that Dartmoor was visited by large numbers of people –owners of livestock, tin workers, stannary officials, Cornish and other turf cutters, fetchers of millstones, hunters, poachers, vagabonds and others— and plague would have spread through contacts between these. In one of the last surviving financial accounts from before the Black Death, nothing unusual is recorded, unless the 'great inundation of rain' which stopped the annual fair at Lydford on St Bartholomew's Day (24 August) was an omen of some kind. The first surviving account after the Black Death is quite different, and full of doom. The mill at Lydford borough, which was used by the occupiers of a small number of agricultural tenements as well as the townspeople suffered a loss of income after 1348 because, laments its accountant, 'most of the tenants who should grind . . . are dead through pestilence'; the *censarii* of Dartmoor— probably sons and male servants living on the 'ancient tenements'—declined sharply in number; there was severe mortality also among the tenants of those tenements and sometimes a rapid succession of occupiers as one after another succumbed. In the accounting year 1350–51 rapidly changing circumstances rendered the account obsolete even as it was being drawn up. There is also a rental, much annotated as tenant after tenant on the 'ancient tenements' of the central moor died from the plague, and several lists of vacant farms made in order to monitor the changing tenurial situation. Drifts would have been badly organised immediately after the Black Death, and on the down-country farms there would have been general disruption caused by pestilence and a lack of labour to take animals on their annual trek to the hills. However, the fact that a fair number of cattle were depastured in 1351 shows the strength of the custom of transhumance despite the calamity of three years earlier.[41]

There is no doubt that Fig. 2.5 correctly presents *trends* for cattle on the central moor, but the *total* figures are too low. Absent from the figures are cattle belonging to moor-edge properties 'in venville' (see earlier), and to the 'ancient tenements', whose occupiers were permitted to use the central moor for a nominal fee or free provided that they did not send up more stock than could be over-wintered on their farms. Their privileges were very great and they no doubt used them to the full, thereby adding a roughly estimated additional 2,000 or so cattle to the figures at their medieval height, giving a total of around 11,000.

A final point to emphasise about cattle brought to Dartmoor through transhumance is that, during the period covered by this chapter (late thirteenth century to around 1550), mature dairy cows were excluded from these movements. This must have been so for the simple practical reasons that the cattle were so numerous and the herdsmen too few to milk them and that there were no facilities on Dartmoor to process the milk into cheese and butter in this phase of impersonal transhumance. This observation is borne out by the sources, for example the court rolls of the central moor, in which there are hardly any references to straying cows. The types of cattle most frequently mentioned as strays are two-year olds and three-year olds, described in the documents as *boviculi* and *bovetti*, words usually translated as bullocks or steers, meaning castrated male animals, not dairy cows (Fig. 2.6). There are also references to calves, showing that, after weaning in the down-country (for which there is medieval documentary evidence), the moorland pastures

2.6 A Dartmoor court roll.

Part of a roll recording a court of the manor and forest of Dartmoor held at Lydford on 4 August 1479. The marginal annotations on the photocopy are Harold Fox's, drawing attention, *inter alia*, to an entry recording three strayed cattle rounded up at the last drift, a castrated adult bull, a bullock and a young steer (a *gale*, a *boviculus* and a *juvencus*). (p. 72). TNA:PRO, SC 2/166/48).

were thought to be suitable for the very young. Transhumance to Dartmoor did not, therefore, contribute directly to Devonshire dairy farming, although there were indirect effects, of course, because movement of immature animals to the moors allowed greater numbers of dairy cows to be kept on the pastures of the down-country farms. To this there is one exception: occupiers of those moor-edge farms (and the ancient tenements) which were close enough to the central moor might send up cows between the morning and evening milkings, a practice which we find at Halstock in a sixteenth-century by-law.[42]

Horses

We now pass from the excellent evidence about cattle to other types of livestock. Here we must not be disappointed, but we cannot be precise. For horses there are two good, early references: first, the will of Bishop Ælfwold of Crediton, dated from the evidence of its witnesses between 1008 and 1012, mentions 'wild horses', the personal possessions of the bishop, running on his manor of Ashburton; second, the Exon Domesday Book refers to 'unbroken mares' at Cornwood, a moor-edge manor, and these are likely to have been Dartmoor ponies, just as the very large number recorded for Brendon in the same source were presumably the Exmoor breed. Later references to horses or ponies on Dartmoor are very frequent, for example, among records of strays in the court rolls: thus in the surviving rolls for the reign of Edward IV (1468–74 and 1479–81) we find 'castrated horses', 'mares', 'bay horses', 'horses with foals', or simply 'horses' (taking the most likely translations of the Latin words used in these records, which are not always unambiguous).

When we turn from the court rolls of the central moor to the account rolls we encounter a problem, for although these do sometimes give numbers of horses for which a grazing fee was paid, the figures are unrealistically small, for example only 50 in 1496. The explanation for the relatively small recorded numbers is probably as follows: few tamed horses were put under the special care of the herdsmen because most farmers in the down-country needed their horses for daily use. The more wild and roaming animals went free by ancient custom, some turning out to have no known owners and hence their description as strays in the court rolls. Dartmoor ponies were in demand, for in the fifteenth century we find the reeve of Bishop's Clyst in east Devon sending all the way to Ashburton for one.[43]

Goats and pigs

There is no mention of goats or pigs in the lists of those paying fees for guardianship of livestock on the central moor. Goats are found in place-names such as Buctor in Tavistock and Bucktor in Buckland Monachorum (Old English *bucca*, 'he-goat'), Gutter Tor in Sheepstor (Old English *gat*, 'goat'), and Gavrick in Ilsington (Celtic *gaver*, 'goat'). They are also found in entries for moor-side manors in Domesday Book (for example eleven belonging to the Count of Mortain at Harford and twenty-three belonging to the same lord in the adjacent manor of Cornwood), and are much more common there than in the coastal manors of the South Hams, south of Dartmoor. Thereafter they appear to fade from the documentary record of the borders of Dartmoor, although we occasionally find them elsewhere in Devon, as in 1388 on the demesne of Sir John Cary at Highampton, and in 1472 when a tenant was allowed to pasture one goat, or one cow with calf, and one pig on the rough pasture of Nymet Tracy. There is a remarkable charter from Shapley Hellion in Chagford parish, dated 1331, by which Lord John de Proutz granted land to Richard de la Lane, which is very specific about which animals should pasture on the moors there: 'all his own beasts [*averia*] and those of outsiders being in his custody and especially [*maxime*] goats and pigs'. A similar charter, undated but probably from the late thirteenth century, was granted by the lord of the manor of Spitchwick (in Widecombe in the Moor parish), permitting 'all kinds of animals ... and especially pigs and goats'. These grants are most unusual, and nothing quite like them exists elsewhere in Devon or in England, because it is quite clear that goats and pigs are being *encouraged* in order to clear heather and gorse. They were usually banned once they had done their job because they spoiled the pasture which they had created: there are medieval charters, including some from Devon, which forbid tenants to put goats onto common pasture. Occasionally a moor-edge farmer would attempt to introduce pigs to the central moor but it was stated in 1608 that they 'subverted and spoyled the soyle' and that their owners were 'presented at Lidford and ... fyned by the steward there'. We have good evidence that pigs were driven to the woods at Spitchwick in a much earlier period as this was the *wic*, 'seasonally used settlement', which produced *spic*, 'fat bacon'. It was a detached part of the manor of Littlehempston, from which pigs must have been sent to the borders of Dartmoor, but we have no means of knowing how widespread this custom was in Devon. That the custom dated from before the Norman Conquest is certain, because Spitchwick is named in Domesday Book. We hear nothing about it later, save for the two charters just mentioned, so perhaps pigs were banned, as goats were, because they spoiled the pasture.[44]

Sheep

Finally, we turn to sheep, and here it is best to approach the evidence retrospectively. The editors of Risdon's *Survey of the County of Devon* reported on an enquiry, made in the last decade of the eighteenth century, to ascertain the number of sheep kept on Dartmoor, which found that the figure fluctuated annually between 80,000 and 120,000, perhaps according to the goodness of the season. These figures probably relate to the central moor alone, because other observers—Burt in his introduction to Carrington's *Dartmoor*, Arthur Young in his *Annals of Agriculture* and Charles Vancouver, writing of Widecombe in the Moor, which had 14,000 sheep on its commons—reported flocks of many thousands more on the outer moors. In the 1760s, Edmund Gibson, the editor of Camden's *Britannia*, was told that the central moor was expected to feed 100,000 sheep, and Risdon himself, in the seventeenth century, wrote of 'great flocks' on Dartmoor. Given this evidence, it is likely that in the Middle Ages, also, Dartmoor was used as a great sheep pasture. Sheep, by their nimbleness, can reach spots which bovines cannot, they can nip the shorter blades and they help improve growth: a Dartmoor farmer explained in the seventeenth century that 'pasture is just as good when there are many sheep [as when there are few] because the lower the sedge and grass is eaten in spring, the sweeter the pasture all the year after'. Some of these animals, moreover, could be over-wintered on Dartmoor. The pastures of Dartmoor, in other words, were highly valuable as grazings for sheep, and sheep added value to them. It is unlikely that medieval farmers failed to take advantage of these benefits, but in making that claim we run into a problem with the evidence, because the annual financial accounts of grazing fees, analysed above for cattle, do not mention sheep, or mention them only in very small numbers.[45]

It is possible to reconcile the two strands in the evidence—flocks of very large size mentioned in post-medieval sources and no (or very small) flocks numbered in medieval financial accounts—by suggesting that sheep *were* pastured on Dartmoor during the Middle Ages but generally went free, unpaid for and therefore not appearing in financial documents. This suggestion is strongly supported by the legal evidence, for sheep are frequently mentioned in the court rolls of the central moor. For example, around Christmas 1376 the Crown's herdsmen found two male sheep (aged two years) on the central moor, clearly over-wintering; on another occasion 12 sheep worth 12d each were reported to have been slaughtered there in March; the early summer drift in 1479 found seven sheep whose owners could not be traced. This is only a very small sample of evidence from the court rolls which shows that in the Middle Ages sheep were grazed on Dartmoor in some numbers, although we shall never be able to give precise figures. It is possible to expand this argument by suggesting, speculatively, that flocks may have been too numerous for them to have been drawn into the system under which the Crown collected fees from the owners of animals grazing on the central moor, a system which was only applied to cattle: to pay large numbers of shepherds to look after them would have been too expensive. In the post-medieval period some owners of sheep, though only in small numbers, did put their stock in the charge of the Crown's herdsmen, but the option seems to have been entirely theirs and there was no compulsion.[46]

It is likely that only certain types of sheep were grazed on Dartmoor during the Middle Ages, as in the case of cattle. Ewes were valued for their milk at this time and were kept at home in the down-country to be milked along with the dairy herds, their combined yield going towards the making of cheese. Moreover, the lambing of ewes would have been difficult on the high moors which were too exposed and cold in March. The types of sheep kept on the rough pastures of Dartmoor were probably yearlings and the male components of a flock (except rams). We know nothing about arrangements for shearing them, something normally done in June, but it is probable that they were removed from Dartmoor at this time to be shorn on their home farms, when they could also benefit from a change of pasture, always relished by livestock, in the down-country for a short period. Some, but not all, of these animals were over-wintered on the moors, as is made clear by references in medieval court rolls and by the later evidence. Transhumance of sheep to Dartmoor thus involved many comings and goings. Selected animals were taken to the hills in spring, perhaps a little earlier than the cattle, in order to force the growth of herbage; they were then removed for a short time for shearing and returned again; part of a flock then returned in autumn, leaving the hardiest males to over-winter.

The care of sheep while they were on Dartmoor is an obscure topic, though an important one. Sheep, like cattle, when 'turned upon a good spot (called a lear or lair) ... will not leave it to range over other places' and, as Vancouver explained in the nineteenth century, particular flocks had their own special grazing grounds. This territoriality required some overseeing, if only of a limited kind, and there were always the problems of infirmity and theft, but supervision of sheep did not fall within the duties of the Crown's herdsmen.

A crucial reference, from the Register of the Black Prince in 1354, mentions 'shepherds who must necessarily be on the [central] moor in order to keep their beasts', and this is echoed in much later sources: William Simpson, surveyor to the Duchy of Cornwall, wrote in 1786 of farmers who had their own shepherds on Dartmoor, and Charles Vancouver, in 1808, described 'attendants' with their dogs who helped to keep the flocks in their accustomed places, as did the 'boys and shepherds in attendance' which he saw on rough pastures elsewhere in Devon. How these males sheltered so far away from the home farms in the down-country can only be a matter for conjecture. We may not be dealing with people in very large numbers, for it is likely that down-country parishes employed a common shepherd on the moors, as communities in Midland England did for the care of sheep roaming on the fallows of the open fields. The remains of prehistoric dwellings, some of which are very small, could have been adapted for summer use, and hides and fleeces could have been used to provide make-shift shelters under the rocks of the tors.[47]

Shepherds' huts

There is also the question of purpose-built huts for shepherds. Experts on the field archaeology of Dartmoor have frequently noted huts on open moorland, some of which may have had a pastoral purpose. Brian Le Messurier, in the 1970s, made an expert survey of 'ruined huts and shelters which can be found beside the infant rivers or on the wind-blasted ridge tops', counting 57 for the central moor. Phil Newman has recently made another survey (between 1993 and 1996) of the central moor, for the Royal Commission on Historical Monuments, discovering no less than 94. Jeremy Butler, in work for his remarkable *Atlas of Dartmoor Antiquities* has found even more. William Crossing, writing of Dartmoor in general in 1901, described how he had noticed on his tramps many structures 'of an altogether different type from the prehistoric remains so numerous on the moor ... in some instances ... sheltered under the rocks of a tor' and perhaps used by shepherds.[48]

It is not possible to prove an association between these structures and shepherds, because the face of Dartmoor was a hive of activity on which worked several occupational groups besides the herdsmen. If marked on the Ordnance Survey maps, and this is by no means always the case, the structures are sometimes called 'tinners' huts' and Brian Le Messurier writes of tin workers as 'living near their work by the rivers ... and travelling home on Saturdays until Monday morning'. There are many assumptions here: for example, in the medieval period we know in which parishes tin workers lived, because we have royal lists of them in connection with exemption from taxation, but we do not know whether they were generally householders or lodgers; nor do we know for certain if they travelled to work daily, or whether they occasionally, perhaps seasonally, slept near their workings. Certainly some lived in the countryside, in parishes such as Throwleigh parish where young men from the farms and hamlets of Combe, Wonson and Forder are recorded as having 'left the stannary' in the late fourteenth century; they were probably life-cycle workers in the industry who, having saved some money, invested in a farm. There were also tin-workers who lived in urban places, such as Tavistock where John Taillor and Richard Crocker, to take but two examples on the exemptions list, combined tin-working with the crafts of tailor and seller of pottery in the late 1330s. Chagford was another urban place where tinners resided, and was an especially unruly town according to a court roll of 1431 which records a long list of men who hit one another with their fists and wielded knives. Many were still fighting in 1432 when daggers and knives were drawn.[49]

Comparative evidence suggests that we might expect some of the 'tinners' huts' of Dartmoor to have been just that, similar to the shielings (seasonally occupied buildings) of lead-miners on Alston Moor in Cumberland or to the 'many little houses built for the stannary men to shroud them in near the works' which were observed by John Norden in Cornwall in about 1600 — in both cases we are dealing with the dwellings of metal-workers, perhaps used on a temporary or seasonal basis. Tinners built structures which had other purposes, caches in which tools were stowed away and shelters for eating and for escaping from rain or snow — the 'litle lodges' for use at mealtimes which were observed by Beare writing of the Cornish stannaries in the sixteenth century. Tin-working was closely associated with the cutting of turf, which supplied fuel, and some huts are claimed to have been built by turf-cutters: in the early nineteenth century Samuel Rowe described the structure with the jocular name of Mute's Inn as a 'rude hut which the turf-cutters have raised in this wild spot' and there are several other buildings whose location close to peat workings suggest an association between the two.[50]

Some of the Dartmoor huts could, of course, have been used sequentially by people in a number of different occupations, either during the course of the year or over a longer time-span, and shepherding may have been one of these occupations. William Crossing, who drew much upon local tradition and testimony, was convinced that some of them were used by shepherds. Newman queries use of the term 'tinners' huts' to describe all post-prehistoric structures on the moors and thinks that peat-cutters' or shepherds' shelters are more accurate descriptions for some of them. Jeremy Butler maps all post-prehistoric huts as 'tinners' huts' but he adds the following caution: 'there were others such as peat-cutters, shepherds and herdsmen who lived and worked on the moor for a considerable part of the year and who also built small dwellings for themselves.' All three verdicts are correct: the large numbers of sheep grazing on the central moor must have had keepers, as the reference from the Register of the Black Prince confirms, and those keepers, not necessarily in large numbers, must have had residences. So, despite the title of this chapter, 'Impersonal Transhumance', chosen because there is no doubt that the guardianship system for cattle did not involve residence on the central moor by their owners, care of sheep did. Shepherds lived on the central moor alongside the Crown's guardian herdsmen of cattle, and this was certainly personal transhumance. The word 'shelter' needs some qualification. Some of these structures may have been intended for the most part as temporary refuges to protect a herdsman from wind, driving rain and snow, like a number of the probably medieval beehive huts on Bodmin Moor, described by Peter Herring and Jacqueline Nowakowski as 'on open moorland ... in positions offering impressive panoramic views of pasture'; they were for the daytime use of 'lookers' (to employ a term from another part of England) and were not normally for sleeping in (Plate 13). On Dartmoor, good candidates for this role are three small rough huts, apparently of medieval date, lying on the hillside above the greatly more sophisticated house and byre belonging to Buckfast Abbey on the outer moor of Dean Prior and here one may surmise that the huts sheltered herdsmen looking out at their animals grazing the slopes in daytime. A beehive hut of unknown date at Lade Hill Brook on Dartmoor, illustrated by Butler, may be another example (this building tradition in the region is also represented by the nineteenth-century hut for quarry workers to shelter in at Holwell quarry).[51]

Shelters, either as day-time refuges or for sleeping in, were highly desirable when summer rains lashed the hillsides and when the snows of the spring came on unexpectedly, as I have witnessed on Dartmoor in April. Indeed, they were more than desirable, for they could save life. There are many local legends and true stories about violent death on account of the weather of Dartmoor, the former being represented by 'Childe of Plymstock' represented in the landscape today by the lonely moorland Childe's Tomb. Having lost his way on a freezing day, he killed his horse, disembowelled it and crept into its belly in an unsuccessful attempt to keep warm—apparently a much magnified and embellished version of an event in the life of Ordgar, a 7-foot giant who lived in the late-Saxon period, who freed slaves at many places near Dartmoor, such as Coryton and Churchford (in Meavy) and who helped in the foundation of Tavistock Abbey. His gigantic bones were found at Tavistock in the early eighteenth century when the foundations of what is now the Bedford Hotel, formerly a steward's house, were being built. Childe is a Dartmoor legend, 'an almost perfect specimen of folklore based on fact', according to Herbert Finberg. Of all of the local legends concerning violent death on Dartmoor, that most securely grounded is of a young servant in husbandry from a farm at Runnage in the central moor who, sent to search for straying sheep, was overcome by a snowstorm and could find no shelter. According to Carrington's poem, *Dartmoor*:

... the tide
Of life with him ebb'd slowly, inch by inch,
Endurance exquisite, till drowsy Death
Reluctant closed the scene and on the gale,
Unwept, unheard, he poured his parting groan![52]

Conclusion

In the late medieval period the central moor (the part owned by the Crown, comprised in the parish Lydford) was operating a complex system of impersonal transhumance. This saw livestock, most importantly cattle but also large numbers of sheep and some horses, brought to the moor every summer from a wide swathe of Devon (the entire county, less two towns, had the right to pasture unlimited livestock on the central moor for a small fee), and even from parts of Cornwall. These animals might be handed directly into the care of the Crown's herdsmen or might be placed with one of a number of Dartmoor farms which had special rights. These were the 30–40 'ancient tenements' lying within the central moor itself, and the larger number of 'venville' farms located in the ring of moor-edge parishes. The Crown managed the central moor through a permanent staff of herdsmen who kept watch on the livestock, probably from a number of small shelters scattered across the pastures. They kept detailed records of the animals permitted to be on the moor and conducted several drifts each year, in which the livestock were rounded up and checked.

CHAPTER THREE

The red tides

Impersonal transhumance and the outer moors

Lying in a circle around the central moor were the outer moors.[1] Their total acreage exceeded that of the central moor and they were lower and more accessible. Their pastoral management is a story of its own, although there are many similarities between it and practices in the central moor. In this section we deal principally with the outer moors, but in the last section, on order and disorder, we deal with the central moor as well because, for these topics, the moorlands are best treated together; indeed some disputes and trespasses concerned both categories.

Ownership and commoners

Manorial ownership of the outer moors

In the Middle Ages each of the outer moors was thought of as part of one of the moor-edge manors and there is little trace in the evidence of a Crown interest, despite what was to be claimed later. Vestiges of these manorial ties are still to be found on Ordnance Survey maps on which we can read, for example, the names of Dean Moor, Brent Moor, Ugborough Moor and Harford Moor towards the south, all incorporating the names of the manors to which they belonged; towards the north we find Belstone Common, South Tawton Common, Throwleigh Common and Gidleigh Common. All of these place-names were those of parishes as well as of manors. Where there was more than one manor in a parish we generally find that each had its own moor: thus in the parish of North Bovey, Shapleigh Common belonged to Shapleigh manor and in the parish of Widecombe, Blackslade Down belonged to Blackslade manor. Many individual farms and hamlets also had their own moors, for example Wapsworthy Common, Cudlipptown Down, Easdon Down and Heatree Down, all territories which we study in chapter 5.

While names are good evidence of perceptions of ownership in the thinking of the locality, more secure evidence comes from local documents. Thus in 1395–96 the Abbot of Buckfast's officials described Brent Moor as *moram domini*, 'the moor of the lord' and in 1489–90 the same words were used to describe the moor belonging to the manor of Plympton. Before the lord's court at Shaugh Prior in the 1340s, John Joel, a tenant of the manor, was charged with making a granite millstone from the lord's *terra* of Shaugh Moor: here *terra* ('land') describes the very fundament or bedrock of one of the outer moors as strictly seigneurial property. Medieval manorial surveys describe the outer moors as in the ownership of respective lords. On the manor of Battisford the moor (*mora*) was said in a survey of the 1240s to be worth 16s. to the lord; at Gidleigh in 1316 the moorland was valued at 6s. 8d.; in 1348, Sibyl Dauney, lady of Cornwood manor, was given as her dower one-third part of all the *vastum* (that is, moor) of Cornwood. Surveys of Bovey Tracey in 1326 and of South Tawton in 1439 describe the moors in these manors as their lord's 'hilly land' (*terra montanea*) or 'hilly pasture' (*pastura montanea*) and give a value to them (Plates 2, 3). Lying behind these valuations are the many profits which lords might make from their private shares of the outer moors, a topic dealt with in more detail later: profits from the herbage which was grazed and from other commodities such as turves, granite and gorse.[2]

Post-medieval references from local documentary sources are equally emphatic in stating that each of the outer moors belonged to a particular manorial lord. From court rolls we find, in May 1569 on Walkhampton Common near Pew Tor, that a man was accused of cutting turves without right and the court presentment described this act as destroying the very 'soil' (*terra*) of the lord of the manor. In 1562 the steward of the Petre family at South Brent read out the names of a number of men, outsiders, who had allowed their livestock to stray onto his moors and seemed especially concerned, in a laboured statement, to spell out his lord's ownership: the men had 'unjustly occupied the pasture of the lord of this manor at Brentmore ... with their animals where they have no grazing by right, to the grave damage of the lord of this manor'. Post-medieval manorial surveys paint the same picture: in 1566 Brent Moor was described as 'an entire common of pasture belonging to this manor ... in summer very fruitful and containeth by estimation 3,000 acres' while a survey of Ilsington in the same year ends with the statement that 'there belongeth to this manor the wast called Idetor doune [Haytor Down] whereupon certen tennants customery ... have comen of pasture'.[3]

Finally, the Crown (lord of the central moor and therefore near neighbour to the owners of the outer moors) can be seen from time to time confirming the private ownership of the outer manorial wastes which surrounded the inner royal core. A series of royal writs in the early years of the reign of Henry III, in the 1220s, command the sheriff of Devon, William Brewer, to permit the custodians of the manors of Plympton and Okehampton and the owner of South Tawton to have rights over their own moors as they had them in the time of King John 'before the war between him and his barons'. The wording of these writs is not always too clear, but they certainly refer to the outer moors and to rights of grazing livestock upon them, and they were sent out in April and May, at the beginning of the summer pasturing season. Nor is the reason for the writs clear, because it will be shown later, in chapter 6, that lords of moor-side manors were already claiming ownership of the outer moors before the Norman Conquest; but it may be suggested that these royal commands were requested by the surrounding lords to make them quite certain of their rights of ownership of moorland up to and as far as the boundary of the central moor. It could well have been that they feared that a new king might try to extend his jurisdiction into their lands and that they secured the writs to make doubly sure of their own rights. In 1359 the Council of the Black Prince, Prince of Wales and Duke of Cornwall, described Walkhampton's moors (property of Buckland Abbey) as 'the abbot's soil'. Later documents of royal provenance also confirm the outer moors to their respective lords, a commission ordered by the Privy Council of Henry VIII finding that South Holne Moor, Buckfast Moor and Brent Moor were integral parts of the manors after which they were named, the same king's Augmentation Office granting out to John Slanning and Anthony Butler the manor of Walkhampton (previously in monastic hands) together with 'all the furzes, heaths, moors, marshes, commons, ways and wastegrounds' belonging to it, a good description in common form of the area known today as Walkhampton Common.[4]

Statements about the ownership of the outer moors after the Norman Conquest have been given in some detail here because of their intrinsic interest and for two other reasons. First, ownership usually results in boundaries (even if drawn only in the mind's eye) and exploration of the boundary pattern of Dartmoor, and its age, is one theme of this book. Later we shall try to take this pattern of ownership and boundaries backwards in time. Second, and moving forwards, claims have been made from the sixteenth century onwards for Crown ownership of the soil of the outer moors. At their most blatant such claims contradicted both local knowledge and rights of lordship and also the Crown's own information and orders. In the reign of Henry VIII, as we have just seen, a royal commission found that certain of the moors were private manorial property, and his administrators were granting others (formerly monastic) into private hands. But just at the same time an advisor was urging that 'no lorde nor gentylman nor other' could have any right to or upon the outer moors. This claim is found nowhere else, it contradicts all other statements on ownership and is, put simply, wrong. For example, it was stated in the nineteenth century that if the Crown by mistake extended its drift of the central moor to some of the outer moors, severe violence followed. If the claim to Crown ownership is reduced very considerably to Crown *interest* in the outer moors, then there are good reasons to explain it (chapter 6).[5]

Manorial tenants' rights of common

Evidence for common rights on the outer moors is abundant and some of it is relatively early, from the thirteenth century. In 1277 the Abbot and Convent of Buckfast confirmed to Geoffrey de Bulehornston all the land which he held at Bullhornstone, a farm close to the swelling moorland slopes of Corringdon Ball, and a reclamation made in the previous generation by Geoffrey's father, confirming also 'common of pasture in the moor and waste of the monks for all of his animals'. In an early decade of the thirteenth century the lord of Cornwood, Guy de Bryttavilla, granted to Edryke Syward a holding at Cholwich, perched on the very edge of the moorland, together with 'common of pasture in all my moor and waste belonging to my demesne of Cornwood'. Extracts from a sample of other early grants to free tenants which contain information about the grazings of the outer moors, are given in Table 3.1. The table contains much further evidence on a topic discussed earlier, the private ownership of these moors: for example, 'the moor of Dartmoor belonging to that manor [of Ugborough]' in William Brewer's foundation gift of 1196 for Torre Abbey, or moorland 'towards ... the bounds of Dartmoor' (i.e. up to and as far as the boundary of the central moor) in Hugh Courtenay's grant of 1291 to his burgesses of Okehampton From the point of view of rights of common, the extracts in the table show that tenants had a considerable degree of freedom. Livestock were allowed to roam throughout the lord's moor, with

Table 3.1 Medieval grants of pasture rights on the outer moors

Date	Right granted	Location	Holding benefitted	Grantor	Grantee
early thirteenth century	common of pasture	in all my moor and waste belonging to my demesne of Cornwood	Cholwich in Cornwood	Guy de Brittavilla, lord of Cornwood	Edryke Syward of Cholwich
thirteenth century?	common of pasture with all animals	in my waste between *Throubrokes* and Hannaford and my waste west of *Leightone*	Hannaford in Spitchwick	William lord of Spitchwick	Hamelin Carpenter
1256	common pasture for their own animals of all kinds (except goats)	in the abbot's woods of Holne	Holne	Abbot of Buckfast	Tenants of Stephen Baucyn, lord of Holne

Date	Right granted	Location	Holding benefitted	Grantor	Grantee
1277	common pasture for all his animals	in the moor and waste of the abbey	probably Bullhornstone in S Brent	Buckfast Abbey	Geoffrey de Bullhornstone
1280	common pasture for all animals without agistment	in the abbey's moor and waste	Ash in S Brent	Buckfast Abbey	Alured de Ash
1291	pasture throughout the year for all his livestock which can be sustained in winter, without agistment	in the abbey's moor and waste	Harbourneford in S Brent	Buckfast Abbey	Robert *Faber* of Harbourneford
1291	common pasture for all their animals	throughout all my waste as far as the bounds of Dartmoor	Okehampton borough	Hugh Courtenay	Burgesses of Okehampton
1331	common of pasture for all his own beasts and those of outsiders in his keeping	throughout my moor and waste of Shapley	Cleave in N Bovey	John Proutz, lord of Shapley Hellion	Richard de la Lane
1339	common pasture	in my waste of Shapley	Wormhill in N Bovey	Hugh de Proutz, lord of Shapley Hellion	Richard atte Thorne
1342	common pasture throughout the year for all his animals belonging to the holding	all my land of Willsworthy	Redford in Willsworthy manor (Peter Tavy)	John Trenchard, lord of Willsworthy	Walter Broune
1342	pasture and right of common	on the moor of Dartmoor belonging to this manor of Ugborough	a ferling in Ugborough	William Brewer	Torre Abbey
1432	common of pasture for as many animals as can be kept there in winter	in my waste	'atte lepa' in Shapley Hellion	Thomas Stoneforde, lord of Shapley Hellion	Richard Sampson

Sources: Medieval charters and other miscellaneous documents, see n. 6
Compiled by the editors, based on a partial draft found in Professor Fox's papers and additional data from his research notes.

no restriction in terms of space; importantly, no fee was paid for them; they could graze throughout the year, a reference perhaps to sheep which were kept on the outer moors during the winter along with other types of livestock turned out on a daily basis if the weather was clement; and these privileges belonged to 'all the animals' of a tenant, usually with a certain proviso which is discussed a little later on. Tenants no doubt regarded the grants of common pasture recorded in these documents as confirmations of their long-established common rights and customs on the outer moors while lords, in issuing these charters, saw themselves both as confirming their basic right to the soil and herbage of the moors and at the same time exercising good lordship in allowing their tenants access to them.[6]

Because Table 3.1 is based largely upon medieval charters, the evidence which it contains relates to tenants who held by free tenures. Later sixteenth-century evidence shows that customary tenants and lessees shared the same generous privileges. On Brent Moor 'all the tennants as well ffree as custumarye have pasturage' without payment; 'tennants customery' of Ilsington manor had free common pasture for all of their stock on Haytor Down; a tenant at Scorriton had common of pasture on nearby Scoriaton Down, Challeford Marsh and Snowdon; a tenant in Buckland in the Moor had common on Uppedoun. A lease of 1551 for Meavy mentions a stint (restriction) on the number of animals, two cattle and twenty sheep, which could be put upon Yennadon, but this does not contradict our theme of liberal rights on the outer moors, for the lessee occupied a minute tenement—even the relatively poor were privileged. Only one formal agreement for a stint has been found, relating to Halstock (in Okehampton). There, in September 1590, the lord and tenants made a by-law (*ordinatio*) for 'the conserving and keeping of the stint in and upon Halstock ... Down forever hereafter'. Tenants were limited to a set number of kine each, cows only were to be pastured between the third week in June and the last day of August and they were to be brought home in the afternoon, presumably for milking; after the end of August any animals could be turned out. These measures were stringent by Dartmoor standards. They may perhaps be explained by the fact that the manor of Halstock was a very small one, with only a small share of the outer moorlands. Moreover, the by-laws were in force for only a few weeks—weeks when, given a little rain (which the west side of Dartmoor receives in abundance), the growth of grass is at its fastest. Farmers at Halstock clearly wished to ensure that the moorland was used to its best advantage at this season for dairying, at a time when there would have been good demand for butter and cheese at the nearby market town of Okehampton, and beyond.[7]

Manorial tenants as middlemen

We have begun with the tenants of the moor-edge manors. Who else made use of the grazing lands of the outer moors? As discussed in chapter 2, many down-country farmers sent their livestock to the central moor through a moor-edge middleman, a person who received the livestock for pay, perhaps accommodating them for a few days on his own farm and then passing them into the custody of the herdsmen of the central moor. These middlemen were farmers of the moor-edge manors and it would seem unlikely if they did not use also the outer moors for their operations—they were closer and they were extensive enough to support the livestock of outsiders. There is good evidence for the practice. First, several of the grants summarised in Table 3.1 allow the tenants of moor-side farms common of pasture on the outer moors for as many livestock as they could over-winter on their holdings; that is to say, pasture for their own animals was free, but if they took in the stock of others they must pay. Second, a grant of 1432 relating to Shapley Hellion confers common of pasture only 'for so many animals as can be kept there in winter-time', thus excluding livestock which were not the grantee's own property: these could use the moor belonging to Shapley, but not freely by common right. Third, as will be described a little later on, the lords of the moor-side manors regularly took fees for animals grazing on their moors: these cannot have been payments in respect of the stock of their own tenants, who were allowed to common freely, so they must be fees for the animals of men from the down-country.[8]

We do not know precisely how the fee-paying system worked. It may have been that the middlemen—both new colonists and the occupiers of the older moor-side farms—took a fee from each head of cattle belonging to down-country farmers and then split it, taking part for himself and handing part to a lord. Or it could have been that lords themselves acted as middlemen. Both systems probably existed side by side. The 'park books' of Okehampton Common and Park, which list fees, numbers of animals and names of owners, seem to suggest that both systems existed.[9]

A few post-medieval documentary statements claim that down-country people had rights of common on the outer moors. They may have regarded the outer moors as free for their use in some distant period well before the Norman Conquest; in fact this was almost certainly the case. But by the thirteenth century and later, almost all of the documentary evidence shows that they did not. The very few statements to the contrary are partial and incorrect, although they have coloured and confused a good deal of writing about Dartmoor over the last two centuries.

Pastoral management: drifts, structures, strays

Drifts of manorial moors

In the previous chapter we have seen how the financial accounts of the Crown are excellent sources for an understanding of pastoral management on the central moor. We would expect that accounts rendered by local reeves to lords of manors bordering the centre might contain similar information, and this is in fact the case. We can begin with the best of the accounts, those of the Courtenay family for their moor-side manors of Plympton, Okehampton and Cornwood. The earliest direct reference to Plympton's share of the outer moors comes in a survey of 1262/3, made after the death of Baldwin de Redvers, which has the simple statement that he was accustomed to draw yearly profits of 24s. from 'Dartmoor belonging to the castle', that is, his share of the outer moors administered from Plympton Castle. Some of these profits came from fees paid by diggers of turves and possibly from other kinds of revenue, but the lion's share was from grazing fees. A manorial account from 1422, when the Courtenay lands were in the hands of the Crown following the death of Sir Hugh, records 10s. 1d. as the profit made after a drift of Plympton's moor, but this sum would have been only part of the total which was collected, for the account is a partial one covering a few months only, not the normal twelve. A later account, from the end of the fifteenth century, gives more details of the drifts there—the expenses of 'diverse men driving animals and horses in the lord's moor this year ... [and] expenses of Richard Haydon, clerk, being at the said drifts for the convenience of the lord'.[10]

The moor belonging to the Courtenays' manor of Okehampton was very extensive indeed and probably included both the lord's deerpark (largely moorland, on which his tenants had rights of common) and a great slice of outer Dartmoor stretching up to the highest point at High Willhays. The account for 1424/5 is the most detailed, showing that there were four drifts for colts and 'beasts' (*averia*), on 4 December, 24 March, 3 July and 8 September. They were carried out by the manor's reeve (a tenant who acted as the lord's estate manager within the manor) and an estate official of higher status, assisted by other men of the manor, sixteen at the height of the summer grazing season. There are no clues, in the medieval accounts for Okehampton, about the places from which the large numbers of livestock came. But there survive later 'park books', from the eighteenth century, which show that livestock came to Okehampton commons not only, as might be expected, from moor-side parishes such as Throwleigh, Gidleigh, South Tawton, Manaton and Bridestowe, but also from greater distances, from Crediton (14 miles), Cheriton Bishop (12 miles), Kenton (24 miles) and Alphington (20 miles). We cannot be sure that these eighteenth-century patterns reflect the medieval ones, but customs are enduring and it is possible that this was so. On the smaller Courtenay manor of Cornwood in 1534/5, 26s. 8d. was accounted for as 'profit of the drifts of the moors'.[11]

Other families which owned moor-edge manors managed their moorlands in the same way, so that we find the Dynhams driving Hamel Down which was part of their manor of Natsworthy, and officials of abbots of Buckfast driving Brent Moor, part of their manor of South Brent. It was the same on Bodmin Moor, where we have a medieval reference to a drift at Harnatethy. Four general points may be made about these drifts. First, their purposes would have been to count the animals at several points in the year, to separate out those for which no fee was charged (livestock of the commoners of the manor) from those which were paid for (livestock of outsiders in the charge of middlemen) and to apprehend strays and animals of outsiders who attempted to evade fees. Second, there was clearly a degree of cooperation here among the lords of the moor-edge manors and between them and the Crown, lord of the central moor. This made very good practical sense, because if the lord of one manor carried out his drift on a particular day, without the co-operation of his neighbours, strays and livestock unpaid for would simply 'escape' across the unfenced manorial boundary. A concept of simultaneous drifts therefore developed, although occasionally it was not followed: for example, in 1588 three men (probably the reeves of three manors, or their herdsmen) were accused of making drifts on the three moors of Holne Common, Brent Common and Cornwood Common 'before the official of our Lady Queen did', that is, before the Crown's drift of the central moor. Did the lords of the outer moors develop the system in imitation of the Crown on the central moor? Or did the reverse happen? These are difficult questions but we shall attempt to answer them in chapter 6.[12]

A third general point to be made about the drifts is that they had a strongly manorial and financial character: they took place over the lord's soil, and were institutions initiated by lords for the profit of lords. The profits were large, £10 11s. 1d., if we take the largest which has been discovered in the documents, that of the four drifts on Okehampton manor's moors in 1424/5. The expenses of the drifts, 18s. 11½d. paid to herdsmen, must be set against the profits from the fees paid for the animals which were rounded up and these take the net profit to £9 12s. 9½d. In order to put this sum into perspective, we may compare it to income from other seigneurial rights; the rents paid by tenants, their payments for being excused from servile works, sale of the pasture of the lord's wood and the profits of the manor court (Table 3.2). Seen in this perspective, the profit which came (through drifts) to a lord who owned one of the outer moors was a highly significant item of income. Manorial owners of moor-side properties were privileged because they had access to resources which could be made to yield significant income without a great deal of expenditure or effort on their part. They profited from the location of their properties on the flanks of

Table 3.2 Okehampton manor, 1424–25: sources of income

Rents and aids from free, villein and conventionary tenants		£15 8s. 7d.		
less unpaid rents			(£1 3s. –)	£14 5s. 7d.
Rents from leases of barton (demesne) lands		£5 4s. 8d.		
less unpaid rents			(£1 5s. 2d.)	£3 19s. 6d.
Rents from leases of three mills				£5 4s. 8d.
(a 4th mill has just been leased for a further £5 p.a., but is rent-free for the first 4 years)				
Issues of lands in the lord's hands				7s. ¾d.
Payments from tenants in lieu of servile works				£1 2s. 11½d.
Agistment fees		£10 11s. 1d.		
less expenses of drifts	18s. 11½d.			
tithes of agisted animals	12s. 1½d.			
expenses of ditching, paling the park	36s. 10d.		(£3 7s. 11d.)	£6 3s. 2d.
Profits of woods and pastures				£1 – 7½d.
Pleas and profits of the fair in the park				4s. 4d.
Profits of courts		£3 11s. 6d.		
less steward's expenses			(£1 1½d.)	£2 11s. 4½d.
TOTAL income				£34 19s. 3¼d.

Source: BL Add. Ch. 64663, account of the reeve, Walter Brownyng, for the year to Michaelmas 1425. The account also lists 33s. 11d. spent on roofing the hall and stables in the castle and 6s. on sundry other expenses, plus a few minor expenses which have faded to illegibility.
Compiled by the editors from data contained in Professor Fox's research notes.

Dartmoor and they organised and managed them in a fashion entirely different from the management of their counterparts in parts of lowland England, where the arable fields of one manor jostled upon those of its neighbours, with no intervening rough pastures.[13]

A final point to be made about the drifts concerns the numbers of animals which were rounded up. We have written about imitation of the Crown by the surrounding lords, and if this applies to the 1½d. fee charged for each animal and an emphasis on cattle rather than other livestock, then the sum of £10 11s. 1d. received by the Courtenays at Okehampton in 1424/5 represents no less than 1,270 animals. The assumptions made here are reasonable ones, for had lords of Okehampton decided to levy a higher fee for each head of cattle, their owners would have voted with their feet, and the hooves of their cattle, and taken their animals to the central moor. Of course, Okehampton Park and Okehampton Common occupy a very large area, and some of the other moor-edge manors had much smaller moors. It would be dangerous, therefore, to try to extrapolate from this one figure to the total of fee-paying cattle on the outer moors, but we can conclude that this total must have been far higher than the 10,000 or so summering on the central moor in the early fifteenth century. We cannot escape moving towards the conclusion that Dartmoor as a whole might have supported well over 20,000 fee-paying cattle at this time, a figure which excludes the animals of several classes of tenant who did not pay the 1½d. fee (for example, the occupiers of the 'ancient tenements' of the central moor, the privileged venville tenants of some of the moor-side parishes and the manorial tenants who had common rights on an outer moor).

Strays will be discussed through evidence from the court rolls of Christow and Okehampton. There were significant differences between the two manors. Christow, the smaller of the two, is situated just beyond the edge of Dartmoor and had no moorland which adjoined the outer moors. Many of the strays here probably arrived along the dense network of narrow lanes which cross the manorial boundary and then 'came to the house' of a tenant as the court rolls put it (in other words, they were apprehended without a keeper before the tenant's door or farm gate); others were found in the lord's woodland which lay on the manor's boundary. But the total number of strays was not large and, in cases where the documents give the provenance of the owner of a reclaimed stray, they seem to have come from nearby manors: in 1500, William Stone of Bridford (a neighbouring parish) took back a stray horse, paying 1d. for its 'poundage' and Roger Thayccher of Holcombe Burnell (a nearby parish) reclaimed another, paying 3d. Okehampton, by contrast, was a much larger manor, adjoining many others and, moreover, some of its outer boundaries were drawn through the open moorland of Dartmoor. There were therefore many more entry points for strays and this is reflected in the large numbers recorded. Their total value was large, and the likelihood that they would all have been claimed was less than at Christow, the open moorland boundaries encouraging strays from some distance. Strays were another profitable source of income for a lord with jurisdiction over one of the outer moors.[14]

We can add some detail about the daily and seasonal management of livestock on the outer moors. Some of them, and parts of others, were close enough to the farms and hamlets of the moor-edge manors to allow farmers to bring home their livestock at night and we have already cited a by-law from Halstock which allows us to witness daily movements to that manor's moor. But many of the good pastures of the outer moors were relatively distant from the enclosed lands, three miles away in some cases, and on these night rest would have been usual. There are occasional, usually oblique, references to men employed to manage livestock on the outer moors, for example those assisting the lord of Okehampton in driving Okehampton Park and Common; the same men may have been guardians of livestock in periods between drifts, and paid by the community of commoners of a manor, in other words common herdsmen of a type known from other parts of medieval England.

Herdsmen's buildings

That there were structures on the outer moors for herdsmen and others looking after livestock is proven conclusively by the buildings on Dean Moor which were excavated in 1956 by Aileen Fox in advance of the construction of the Avon Dam. They were very remote, set on a south-facing slope above the infant River Avon, surrounded by a small enclosure of about four acres and beyond that by the vastness of heather and grass moor; they were about two miles from the limit of cultivation and one mile from the outer boundary of the central moor (Fig. 3.1). The site consists of a house and a byre parallel to one another and linked by an enclosed yard. The house was of two rooms, the lower one, with a hearth, being a kitchen and living room, the upper perhaps a bedroom. The byre was a large building with an exterior length of just under 100 feet, with a central drain running down its lower half and several interior pens. Finds from the excavation included pitchers of relatively high-status glazed ware (with decoration similar to that on wares found at Totnes Castle and Old Sarum), jugs and pots and jars for cooking and the storage of food.[15]

Lady Fox, who excavated these buildings, was almost certainly correct in linking them to a curious and highly unusual memorandum in the cartulary of Buckfast Abbey. The memorandum begins by stating that, before the first pestilence (1348) the abbot and convent of Buckfast had a house (*mansionis*) in their moor, in which lived a lay brother (*conversus*) with, under him, a shepherd (*pastor*); their task, the memorandum continues, was to look after livestock on the abbey's moors during daytime and drive them to the safety of the enclosure by night. The memorandum concludes with the statement that 'up to now the walls and enclosures of the said house are still visible'. To have a vivid description of this kind, matching excavated buildings, is very rare, especially for a relatively humble site, for this is no Troy. There are some topographical problems in the matching of the site to the memorandum, but these can probably be overcome, while the sources of information available to the writer, and his purpose, are not difficult to understand. The writer, at Buckfast Abbey, would have had access to manorial accounts (or other types of account) which recorded wages paid to the lay brother and shepherd and, possibly, the cost of food and drink taken up to the dwelling from the abbey. His purpose in copying the memorandum into the cartulary of Buckfast Abbey was almost certainly to reinforce the monks' claim to the moor on which the house was situated, for it occurs in the cartulary alongside boundary perambulations; moreover, it was dangerously close to the central moor and, as we shall see later in this chapter, this was constantly disputed territory.[16]

Both the house on Dean Moor, and its associated byre, were relatively

3.1
Buckfastleigh
Abbey's
herdsman's
house on Dean
Moor.

Based on A. Fox,
'A monastic
homestead on
Dean Moor,
S. Devon',
*Medieval
Archaeology* 2
(1958), pp. 141–
57, Fig. 39.

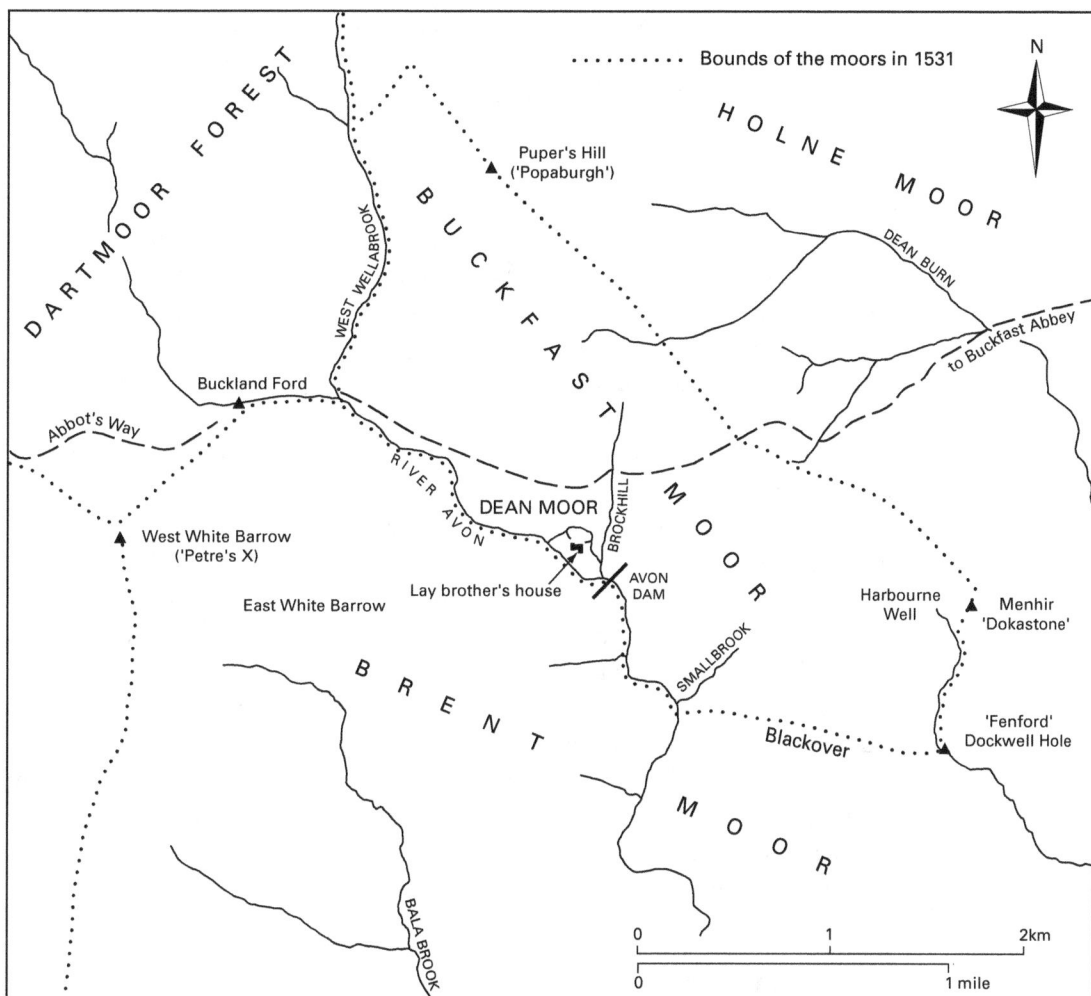

sophisticated buildings, as befits structures owned by a wealthy Benedictine abbey. On the basis of type and quantity of pottery and other artefacts found, Lady Fox concluded that there were no 'signs of women's work' and that the house was not in 'continuous or permanent occupation and ... was used seasonally'. So here we have a seasonally used dwelling on one of the outer moors, occupied by two males whose tasks were to guard the abbey's demesne livestock at their grazings during the summer season and used up until the time of the Black Death (a plausible date for the scaling down of demesne operations at the abbey). We are certainly dealing with transhumance here, although the distances involved are relatively short: three and four miles from the site of the house to Buckfast's demesne at South Brent and to Buckfast itself.

Given the evidence from Dean Moor, it is highly likely that other lords of the outer moors owned similar buildings, not necessarily as grand as Buckfast

Abbey's, and that tenants of the moor-edge manors likewise built structures for housing guardians of livestock on the particular moor where they commoned, each perhaps associated with a community of commoners.

Strays

One of the tasks of herdsmen who used shelters of the kinds discussed above was to prevent their charges from straying beyond the manorial boundaries of the outer moors and to apprehend strays coming in from other manors. A stray may be defined as an animal roaming from place to place and not obviously in charge of a keeper. In the Anglo-Saxon period strays were a concern of the court of the hundred and were dealt with quite explicitly in law codes, because animals without keepers encouraged theft and dispute. Later on they became a concern of manorial courts and were dealt with in a serious and systematic manner, partly for the same reasons and partly because, being found on the lord's soil, they became his property if not claimed, and therefore a source of profit. Swarms of bees which flew onto a manor were considered in the same light. There seems to have been a good deal of fairness in the treatment of strays: the animal was taken to the lord's pound or was put in the custody of a trustworthy tenant; the lord's steward proclaimed its existence at a session of the manor court, giving details of age and sex, the date and place at which it had been found and occasionally its colour; the proclamation was repeated in court after court and only after a year had passed was the lord allowed to claim it. The owner, if he appeared before the court, had to prove ownership and the lord benefited either way, by taking the animal if there was no claimant or by charging a fee to the owner ('for custody', as the documents put it).

Perambulation and dispute resolution

Inter-commoning

Two neighbouring lords, each with his own share of the outer moors, might come to an arrangement which permitted inter-commoning. Such an arrangement would reduce the complexity of moorland management because it cut down the mileage of boundary which had to be policed and perambulated. In all of the documentation from the moor-edge manors references to inter-commoning are rare and it is quite clear that most lords preferred to see their jurisdictions unfettered by reciprocal rights of common: despite the advantage mentioned above, to grant permission for the animals of a neighbouring manor to graze set a dangerous precedent, for the neighbour might then attempt to extend his claim to other products and profits of the waste, its turf and granite for example and, more valuable than those and than the profits from pasture, to mineral rights and profits from tin-working. By an agreement (*conventio*) probably dating to the late twelfth century, the lords of the neighbouring manors of

Ugborough and Wrangaton—William Brewer and Richard Peverel—came to a reciprocal understanding about rights on some of the moorland between the River Erme and the Glaze Brook. An abbot of Buckfast allowed the men of Dean Prior manor to pasture on Buckfastleigh Moor and there may have been a reciprocal arrangement on Dean's moors, and a survey of Spitchwick made in 1305 states that the manor's moors were commoned by people 'from the surroundings', that is, the surrounding manors. Finally, Ordnance Survey maps still show the following: 'Lands common to the parishes of Bridestowe and Sourton.'[17]

In sum, however, the evidence for inter-commoning on the outer moors is rather meagre. Far more abundant is evidence for the opposite—the vigorous affirmation by lords of their exclusive ownership of particular moors. This they achieved by several means: by charging grazing fees, by claiming rights to strays which trespassed on their soil, by taking charge of the drifts which swept across their properties, occasions which had both symbolic meaning and practical purpose, and by perambulating the outer boundaries of their moors.

Perambulation and recording of boundaries

The making of perambulations and boundary records for the outer moors was important for several reasons: the charging of grazing fees, the custom of drifts and administration of the system for declaring strays could not have operated without a precise knowledge of where one lord's jurisdiction ended and another's began and, moreover, rights to and profits from the other products of the rough pastures (and the soil and rocks below them) could only be apportioned by boundaries. It must be stressed here that by boundary we do not mean an impassable barrier—lines across the moor were in most cases in the mind's eye, though memory and accuracy were aided by reference to features in the physical landscape such as tors or rocks, to cultural features left by humans in remote prehistoric time and to bound-stones especially set up for that purpose. Many moorland boundaries, in the words of an abbot of Buckfast writing in the early sixteenth century, were 'only marks and bounds well noted and knowen ... by divers and many credyabell persons'. Records of some perambulations of the outer moors are respectably early. For example, when Isabella Countess of Devon, in 1291, ratified the gift of a compact block of three manors (Buckland, Bickleigh and Walkhampton) to Buckland Abbey, she made sure that the whole territory was thoroughly perambulated, including the outer boundary of Walkhampton's moors; so full are the details given in this charter that they must have been set down after inspection in the open air. The boundary points include prominent physical features like Mis Tor, a medieval cross, a droveway and 'bounds made of stones', this last being a possible reference to a prehistoric stone row. Another, more simple, record of the boundary of one of the outer moors occurs in an early thirteenth-century grant by which Guy de Brittevilla, lord of Cornwood, confirmed common of pasture to a free tenant, his grazing rights extending northwards as far as a line between *Toriz* headwater and *Yalumphauede*, that is the Tory Brook Head and Yealm Head of modern maps. There was no need for Guy to give any further elaboration, because the boundary of Cornwood's moor (followed by the parish bounds today) went in a straight line across the rough pastures between prominent inter-visible features, a pound from the Bronze Age, a rocky outcrop, two rounded hilltops and a cairn almost certainly of prehistoric origin. Later records of the perambulation of manorial boundaries through the outer moors are frequently found in collections of manorial documents, examples being a description of the 'metes and bounds of the lord's waste land called Shaghdowne' (i.e. Shaugh Moor) recorded in a court roll of 1548, a very full record of the limits of Widecombe manor agreed before the manorial court in 1659 and details of the bounds of Natsworthy and Ilsington included in a fine survey book made in 1566 of land once belonging to the Dinham family.[18]

We end this section with a case study of boundaries and their perambulation, from the southern flanks of Dartmoor where Holne Moor, Buckfastleigh Moor, and Brent Moor were all the possessions of the Abbey of Buckfast (Fig. 3.1). These moors had a vexed and troubled history of a kind likely to give rise to much documentation, and from as long ago as the fifteenth century there is an exciting reference to 'divers writings of perambulations of old time' relating to this area.[19] Documents described as 'of old time' inspire the spirit of the chase. Might they still exist? How old are they? The answers are 'yes, in part' and 'very old'.

One of the most detailed of all records of boundaries crossing the outer moors is that written down in August 1557 for Brent Moor. The general background to the making of this perambulation was uncertainty about rights and jurisdictions among the new post-Dissolution owners of Buckfast Abbey's manors, an awareness of claims made a few decades earlier for an extension of the Crown's interests in the outer moors, and awareness of dangerous disputes in earlier times. The manor of South Brent was, by 1557, in the hands of Sir William Petre and in that year he secured a royal commission to settle uncertainty over the true bounds of Brent Moor and to draw up a sealed certificate describing their course. The commissioners, including several nearby landowners who had been beneficiaries of the Dissolution, met at South Brent and took evidence from local tenant farmers whose names may be collated with those in a manorial survey made a few years later. The boundaries of the moor and the nature of Sir William's jurisdictions upon it were ascertained by three means: from the oral testimony of the tenants who spoke of bounds and rights which had existed 'beyond the memory of man' and which they had learned from their fathers before them; from medieval documentation which Sir William had acquired along with the manor; and from perambulation and inspection on the ground. We know that Sir William possessed a record of a medieval perambulation of Brent Moor and that this was used in 1557 is clear from similarity between its wording and the words (stripped of legal verbiage) of the certificate which was drawn up in that year. We know that this was not enough, and that the bounds were perambulated, because the document states that, along the way, the commissioners caused to be set up four crosses, 'christian signs' they called them, each inscribed with the words 'Bunda de Brentmore', one of which later came to be called Petre's Cross. The very landscape was inscribed with seigneurial and divine authority, inviting awe and the wrath of God in he who might attempt to alter or disrespect the boundary.[20]

Some of the tenants who helped in the perambulation of 1557 would have been alive in the early 1530s when rights on Brent Moor were in dispute, along with those on Holne Moor and Buckfastleigh Moor. This was in the time of Abbot John Rede, penultimate head of the house of Buckfast, who complained that officers of the Crown had 'come into the 3 moors ... taking ... [his] cattle and beasts' and forcing him to pay a fee 'contrary to right and good conscience and to the great hurt, damage and disherisance of the said monastry ... and of the ministering of God's divine service in the same place'. The abbot complained to the Privy Council which issued a commission to enquire into the ownership of the three moors and into who had rights of taking grazing fees for animals pasturing upon them. At dispute was the abbot's ownership of the moors and the extent of his jurisdiction, a matter easily disputable because, as he said, where his moors abutted onto the Crown's central moor there were 'no hegges ne other severaunces' but only boundary marks both natural and man-made. The abbot had everything on his side. He stated that his court rolls proved his jurisdiction: they would have recorded his control over strays and over animals illegally pastured on his moors. He referred to proof in his 'boks of accompt apperying', that is to his manorial accounts in his possession. Two accounts survive to this day and both refer to drifts of Brent Moor carried out by the abbey's servants, one in 1396 and another at some point in the fifteenth century (the heading of the second document is damaged, including its date). In the fifteenth-century account, beside the sentence which records the drift, has been added the word *nota*, possibly in the hand of abbot John himself. Finally, John could boast of 'divers writings of perambulations of old time' recording the boundaries of his three moors. With all of this evidence to hand he clearly won his case, the verdict of the jury of 1531 stating bluntly that 'the three mores ... be parcelle of the abbote's maners'.[21]

We do not know if a perambulation preceded the verdict of 1531 as was the case in 1557, but this is possible because towards the end of Buckfast Abbey's cartulary the bounds of the three moors have been inserted in a hand which could possibly belong to Abbot Rede's time. Nor can we be sure of the date

or whereabouts of the 'divers writings of perambulations' referred to by Rede:
he may have been referring to the records at the end of his cartulary, if these
could be said to be in a hand earlier than 1531 or, more likely, he may have had
in mind documents of far greater age, from seven centuries before his time,
which we come to soon.[22]

There were many other occasions on which disputes arose about these moors:
an abbot of Buckfast was accused of leaving his own moor and trespassing on
the Crown's central moor in 1335; there were troubles in the time of 'King
Harry the fyve' (1413–22) when the abbot's men impounded cattle which had
strayed off the central moor into the abbey's manors (the reverse of the events
of the 1530s); in 1541 the inhabitants of Buckfastleigh claimed that the new
post-Dissolution owner of the manor had deprived them of common rights
on Buckfastleigh Moor, resulting in another complaint to the Privy Council.
On several of these occasions boundaries were perambulated and records of
previous perambulations produced. During a dispute of 1446 inspection of
earlier records has given us knowledge of a perambulation dating from before
the Norman Conquest.[23]

In dispute in 1446 was the vexed question of boundaries and jurisdictions,
as in 1531 and 1557: that much is certain from the types of issues which are
referred to in a detailed memorandum compiled in 1446 or 1447. The original
memorandum has not survived and all that we have is a copy (to which later
evidence has been added), almost certainly drawn up in connection with
the dispute of 1557 discussed above. The copyist was hurried, and in places
uncertain, and the original scribe also faltered in some of his transcriptions.
Moreover, the paper sheets of the document have suffered from flaking and
words have been lost, despite the best efforts of modern conservators. Herbert
Finberg saw the memorandum in the late 1950s and concluded that it was
the work of John Fitz, a noted lawyer, a governor of Lincoln's Inn and a
representative of Tavistock in the parliaments of 1427 and 1431; but some of
the words which he read seem now to have perished, perhaps during the repair
of the document.[24]

Fitz went about his task of proving the abbey's title to its moors with great
thoroughness yet without any deviation which might detract from his case,
which was always direct and to the point. As Abbot Rede was to do later, he
searched the abbey's mundane administrative documents, records of their estate
management from year to year, and found, among court rolls and account rolls,
written evidence showing that the abbey's servants regularly took profit from
farmers who grazed their animals on the monastic moors. He searched the
abbey's cartularies and in those repositories of deeds of title he found plenty
of evidence which showed earlier abbots of Buckfast in full ownership of
their moors. His trump card was an epitome of two charters, which have not
survived, from the reign of Edgar (959–973), granting South Brent manor and

giving details of its boundaries, including those of Brent Moor, presumably made by perambulation. This is the earliest record we have—surviving only as a copy of a copy of a copy—of a perambulation relating to a landlord's share of the outer moorland. It takes the evidence for perambulation back to the tenth century.

The case of Buckfast Abbey's moors illustrates the crucial importance of perambulations, and records of them, in maintaining knowledge of the limits of jurisdictions over stretches of moorland. The practice was self-perpetuating in that possession of a written record of a boundary encouraged its checking and re-checking against the evidence of the landscape. Copies of older boundary records were taken into the field. A set of boundary descriptions included in the great volumes of surveys made of manors belonging to Glastonbury Abbey estate, on the instructions of Abbot Beere around 1516, include terms which suggest that they were expanded versions of Old English documents made many centuries earlier. It could well be that the record of the boundary of Brent Moor made in 1557 likewise has Anglo-Saxon roots: it was almost certainly compiled with the help of a medieval record, as suggested above, and *that* might have had the tenth-century charter seen by the lawyer John Fitz as its base, although we have no means of proving this. Clearly, it was useful to make a perambulation and keep a record of it when a property changed hands, that being the purpose of our earliest record, the South Brent grant from the tenth century. Perambulation and the exhibition of early boundary records were crucial, too, in the resolution of disputes about ownership and jurisdictions on the moors, as we have seen. Finally, the keeping of boundary records was also simply a matter of good estate management, which explains their inclusion in manorial surveys. They were all the more necessary for manors which included stretches of moorland: this was one reason why the practice of parochial perambulation in England at large tended to survive longest in unenclosed countrysides, another simply being, as David Underdown has explained, the ease of procession where there were no hedges to obstruct the journey. On open moorland it was easy to move a bound stone or dispute the course of an imaginary line.[25]

Order and disorder: outer moors *and* the central moor

This and the previous chapter have, perhaps, given an impression of transhumance to and from Dartmoor as a series of highly organised and orderly movements of livestock. In many senses this was the case, and we shall return to that theme formally at the end of this section. Disorder there certainly was, too, on medieval Dartmoor, and with that we begin, first discussing occupations other than those associated with pastoralism, then the opportunities for breaking rules within the system of transhumance itself.

The diverse occupations of medieval Dartmoor have already been mentioned, in chapter 1. We must not forget that those who guarded livestock on Dartmoor—the Crown's herdsmen, shepherds from the down-country and tenants of the moor-side manors, or their sons or servants—were working alongside many other people engaged in hunting and gathering. In the cases of stone-hewers, rabbit warreners and gatherers of gorse, heather, rushes and bracken, there was no conflict with pastoralism. In the cases of tinworkers, deer-hunters and turf-diggers, on the other hand, there were potential and actual contests for space, and opportunities for tension and disorder.

Deer hunting

Let us begin with the hunting of deer. In 1317 the abbot of Buckland and many others went to Dartmoor, 'hunted therein without licence, carried away ... deer' and assaulted the Crown's herdsmen. A complaint to the Crown followed, from one of the herdsmen, Walter Lybard, and twenty-nine other people including men from moor-side parishes such as Adam de Luwedon (from Lewdon in Moretonhampstead) and William de Wrey (Wrayland in Bovey Tracey) and many from 'the ancient tenements' situated in the central moor, Geoffrey de Babenay (Babeny), for example, John de Renewych (Runnage) and William Oldesbrom (Ollsbrim). The country was up in arms. Such a large hunting party would have caused consternation among pastoralists and their livestock because very numerous riders on horseback, and dogs, would have been present in 1317; there were so many animals on the moorlands in the Middle Ages, in so many places, that it is unlikely that the hunting party would not have disturbed some of them. The outrage and disorder took place in August, at the height of the summering season for cattle and was therefore all the more serious. The presence of moor-side farmers and occupiers of the 'ancient tenements' among those who were aggrieved is explained by the fact that both classes were allowed to take their livestock to the central moor without using the Crown's herdsmen. In this petition we can almost see them, or their servants, in charge of their livestock there.[26]

In this case we see competition between peace and quiet and noise and unrest, between the safety of domestic animals and pleasure to be had in chasing wild ones. The Crown on occasion licensed hunting on Dartmoor, for example in 1315 when Robert and David de Franketon, not local men, were required to go to Dartmoor with berners (hunt servants) and hunting dogs, and to take deer and salt the venison in barrels, presumably for the king's table or for royal gifts. The crucial point here concerns the number of dogs which, when in full chase, would have disturbed the grazing livestock. The licence was issued in July, again at the height of the grazing season. As well as licensed hunting there was also poaching, as in the wild event of 1317 described above. Lists of poachers who were apprehended confirm Jean Birrell's conclusion that the social composition of poaching parties was at the upper end of the social scale. Birrell points out, though, that the evidence is skewed, because people such as these hunted by day whereas more lowly people would have been surreptitious poachers by night.[27]

Tin mining

The sites of tinworks, as well as locations for hunting, were contested places. We have direct evidence of this. In 1361, John de Treeures, in Cornwall, complained that because of the presence of tinworkers on his soil 'nothing will remain of all ... [his] good land except great stones and gravel', while in 1314 the people of Devon complained, probably with some exaggeration, that 300 acres each year were destroyed by tin-working. Streamworks in valleys or on hillsides, where water was used to separate tin ore from soil and stones, were especially destructive, because the sides of valleys were cut back to expose more ore and hillslopes were dug up. Both valleys and hillslopes were prime grazing grounds. Tin workers also cut deep elongated gullies or quarries, technically called 'openworks' or, in the past, 'beamworks', which at a stroke destroyed pasture (Plate 14). These were contested landscapes, but those who were accustomed to graze them had no means of seeing off the tin-workers, who had authority granted by the Crown to enter any land whatsoever in order to work for tin. If we add together in the mind's eye the total area of streamworks on Dartmoor surveyed and mapped by Sandy Gerrard and others, and add an estimated 300 openworks, together with what must be thousands of spoil heaps dumped on pasture, we can begin to envisage a significant loss of grazing. Not all of these were present in the medieval landscape, of course, but their acreage was growing fast then because production of tin increased in a spectacular way between the 1370s (when we have the first post-Black Death figures) and the 1490s and indeed continued to boom thereafter.[28]

Turf-cutting

In a similar way, land required for turf-cutting was contested land, because it was generally on the flatter hilltops which were especially good, moist grazing land. Diana Woolner writes that 'large tracts of the higher parts of Dartmoor have been stripped completely of their covering of deep peat ... leaving bare rock', and although there is perhaps some exaggeration here, it is certainly true that much valuable grazing was destroyed in this way. A financial account for 1371 describes turf-cutters as men 'digging turves for [making] charcoal in order to sell it', the buyers being those who smelted tin in blowing houses. In the documents, these commercial turf-cutters are always called *carbonarii* and the sums collected from them are recorded in lists similar to the listings of those who paid for having their animals on Dartmoor: they are named and become real people.[29]

In 1347, for example, they included William Belstone and Margaret Mirifield, from the moor-edge parishes of Belstone and Buckfastleigh, where there is a farm named Merrifield. Margaret is interesting because of her gender, for she is one of the very few women in these lists, possibly discharging her work through a servant. People from all of the moor-edge parishes were involved in commercial turf-digging in the central moor, often as a by-employment, because we know, by matching the names of the *carbonarii* with those who paid guardianship fees for livestock that many of the former were farmers also, owners of livestock. There were also professional *carbonarii*, men who seemed to have owned no livestock. The professionals included the Cornish *carbonarii* who came to Dartmoor because, according to a petition of 1446, 'lands ... in their own county have been so devastated of turf ... that they cannot get enough to melt their tin'. As tin production boomed, in both Devon and Cornwall, so did the cutting of turves and the making of peat charcoal. There were around thirty *carbonarii* working on the central moor in the early fourteenth century and their numbers grew very steadily in that century and in the fifteenth as tin production increased, reaching just over 100 around 1450. This means that the environmental impact of turf-cutting and destruction of pasture must have proceeded apace during the Middle Ages. At the same time, there were in fact many more, and uncountable, turf-diggers on the central moor than these figures indicate. The *carbonarii* were defined as people who made charcoal for sale from the turves which they cut, but people who cut for domestic use did so for free. It was a customary right among all of the moor-edge parishes.[30]

Theft of livestock

As well as contests between those engaged in pastoralism, on the one hand, and other occupations on the other, there were conflicts and disorder within the system of pastoral management itself. This is not surprising, so numerous were the animals on the moorlands and so complex the jurisdictions on Dartmoor. Moreover, animals were not housed in any way on the central moor, although on the outer moorlands the name Stall Moor may indicate a pen of some kind, while on Dean Moor the Abbey of Buckfast had a byre and a yard.[31]

Court rolls from the late fourteenth century and the fifteenth show that theft of livestock was commonplace. At the lowest level was the theft of a single animal of small value as when Richard Collishull of South Zeal, 'with others unknown', stole a sheep from the central moor in 1366 and took it back to his home, presumably for consumption by this gang of thieves. If all of the parties came from South Zeal, this may have been a raid by tinners or labourers, for the place was not a farming settlement. Possibly they were working on the central moor, for South Zeal is some distance away from it; possibly it was a premeditated raid. Some of the animals stolen were of greater value than this unfortunate sheep: for example, Richard Wonston (probably from Wonson in Throwleigh parish) stole two oxen worth 24s., allegedly compounding his crime by being armed (it was done *vi et armis*) and by carrying out the raid under the cover of darkness. Then there were even more serious offences in the theft of livestock, as when three henchmen of William Bottreaux, lord of many manors in the South West, took away fourteen oxen and 'many' horses at Red Lake and other places on the central moor and 'delivered them to the use of the said William' in 1366. Disorder was especially rife at the time of the drifts when it was relatively easy to steal away an animal which had escaped from the galloping stock. This is what happened one year in the third quarter of the fourteenth century when several men, not named, stole over-wintering horses, with the connivance of one of the Crown's herdsmen, 'at the time of the drift at the Invention of the Holy Cross' (3 May). An especially cunning attempt at theft was the capture in 1478 of a bullock by several armed men who 'made a sign on its skin': the case was reported in an October court, so the crime of changing the mark in order to falsify ownership was probably conducted shortly before the autumn drift.[32]

Unlicensed grazing

Equally tempting as theft of animals was what in the Middle Ages was described as 'theft of grazing', that is, trespass. In some cases trespass on one of the moors was the result of negligence when a herdsman or shepherd allowed his stock to stray over one of Dartmoor's innumerable unfenced boundaries. In other cases, trespass was premeditated, although it is not always easy to separate out the two types in medieval documents which always describe acts of trespass in the strictest possible terms. On the central moor, as has been explained earlier in this book, trespassing animals were described as *non scripti*, that is 'not written down' in the lists of owners of stock or middlemen and the men who trespassed were described as 'the delinquent men'. Some of the lists of owners have a separate column for fines paid by these people: that for 1444, for example, includes Sir Thomas Wyse, John Wonston of Wonson in Throwleigh and John Standon of Standon in Peter Tavy. On the outer moors practices were similar and we find, for example, the Prior of Plympton's reeve of his manor of Shaugh being reprimanded and punished in the 1270s for not listing the names of men who had trespassed on the lord's moor and for not fining them, though he was successful in apprehending his colleague in administration, the reeve of Bickleigh, for trespass with his animals there. Three hundred years later, in 1562, Richard Skynner, John Howse, John Snowdon and five other men entered Brent Moor with their animals on 27 April, just when the herbage was beginning to invite, and were fined 3s. 4d. each because they 'had no common pasture by right' there. None of these men was listed in a detailed survey of the manor of South Brent made in 1566: they were outsiders, John Snawdon perhaps coming from Snowdon in Rattery, a parish adjoining Brent. Trespass must have been especially difficult to avoid at the times of the drifts when frightened animals galloped in advance of chasing men on horseback with their dogs: on these occasions, an animal might easily cross one of the moorland boundaries. There are no medieval references to trespass at a drift, but in the nineteenth century Sabine Baring-Gould wrote, perhaps with some exaggeration, that if it occurred 'farmers rise up ... and battles with clubs and horsewhips ensue ... [and] blows are given and returned'.[33]

Verbal insults, and worse, were exchanged between pastoralists because of trespass and competition for space. The Crown's herdsmen on the central moor were in a position to act high-handedly to communing shepherds and other herdsmen with whom they competed for space. This may be what lay behind an order made by the Black Prince in 1354, strictly instructing his herdsmen 'not to inflict any hardship or grievances' on shepherds and their charges on the central moor. The commoners, in their turn, had reason to distrust and dislike the Crown's herdsmen because of high-handed behaviour which they practised in the belief that they had royal authority for it. In 1276, Edward I instructed the coroner at Lydford to enquire into the killing of one of his herdsmen 'upon Dartmoor', presumably after some affray on the open moors, and in 1479 John Stone hit William Tybot, a servant of one of the Crown's herdsmen, perhaps in a dispute over competition for grazing grounds.[34]

Violence and insecurity

Disorder on medieval Dartmoor was encouraged by several circumstances. Firstly, isolated moor-edge farms encouraged raids and theft, as happened at Deancombe in Dean Prior parish, where in one of the dark days of November 1479, John Bounde came and hit a farmer, Robert Dert, then threatened him with a sword so that he despaired of his life, going on to steal a valuable pot and other items. The case illustrates something of the wealth which could be built up through owning and managing livestock on the moor-edge farms and also the fragility of possessions kept in a lonely farm at some distance from others along empty lanes.[35]

Under such circumstances some lords fortified their residences. The Prous family at Gidleigh constructed a tower-house of Irish character, with a first-floor solar reached by an external stair, a structure unusual in the South West, although there are others on the coast, as at Gomerock at the mouth of the Dart. The lord of Widecombe in the Moor dug a moat around his manor house, again an unusual feature in the South West, although there is said to be one around the rectory of Stokenham in south Devon, and there are a few in Cornwall, at Penhallam, Binhamy, Carminow and St Columb rectory. The tower-house at Gidleigh can still be seen, meeting the technical requirements of such a structure by having no windows to the ground floor; I have visited the remains of the moat at Widecombe, which are rather feeble. As for ordinary farmers, there are no examples on Dartmoor of fortified farms like those at Blegberry in north Devon or at Roscarrock in Cornwall. However, a few Dartmoor farms are of forbidding appearance, such as that at Cholwich in Cornwood, with a courtyard plan and minimal fenestration towards the outside to give the impression of closure and to prevent entry.[36]

A second reason for a degree of disorder on medieval Dartmoor was that it was an open, unenclosed vastness encouraging to wanderers and others intent on theft and disorder. Such wanderers, once on the open moorland, having passed through one of the many gates which separated open land from moor, had no more physical boundaries to cross. Whereas the most valuable assets of, say, a nucleated village could be carefully gathered together at night at the centre, in houses and yards and in close proximity to many people, the valuables of Dartmoor were dispersed and vulnerable. The region was attractive to lawbreakers because there were wild animals, plants and fuel and valuable tin ingots, as well as livestock, all of which could be hunted or taken surreptitiously, especially at night out of sight of the herdsmen of the Crown and of the men of the moor-edge manors. Destitute 'vagabonds' were recorded in 1318 'taking game and assaulting people passing through' for their possessions (a good reference to the well-peopled nature of Dartmoor in the Middle Ages). Piles of turves and peat-charcoal stacked on the open moors were tempting to poor people desperate to heat their homes and others such as Walter Smyth (probably a smith, or perhaps a tin-smelter) of Sampford Courtenay who stole charcoal in 1377 and was back again soon after when he was accused of armed theft at a 'turf pit' near Laughter Tor. An interesting case comes from 1519 when a tinworker was bribed to steal unsmelted tin from a tinworks near Cornwood, meeting his associate, Walter Langiford, at night on Cadover Bridge over the River Plym, where they recognised one another by calling out a secret password. Walter was also accused of assembling a gang of nineteen men in order to steal from a tin-work near Horrabridge and threaten the workers there. Some of these individuals were permanently settled in the moor-side parishes but others were transients, such as the vagabonds mentioned above, or young men who worked in tin-works for a time and then 'fled the stannary [jurisdiction of tinners]' as the documents put it. All took advantage of the open character of Dartmoor.[37]

A difficult decision to make was whether to begin this section with examples of disorder or to start with the relatively disciplined nature of pastoralism, turf-cutting and other activities on medieval Dartmoor. We took the former course not because disorder was dominant but because so much detail of orderly and highly regulated movements of livestock has been given already, in chapter 2 and in the first parts of this chapter. Our main sources in this section have been rolls recording court proceedings and these naturally have an emphasis

3.2 Schematic plan of seasonal livestock movements in and out of Dartmoor.

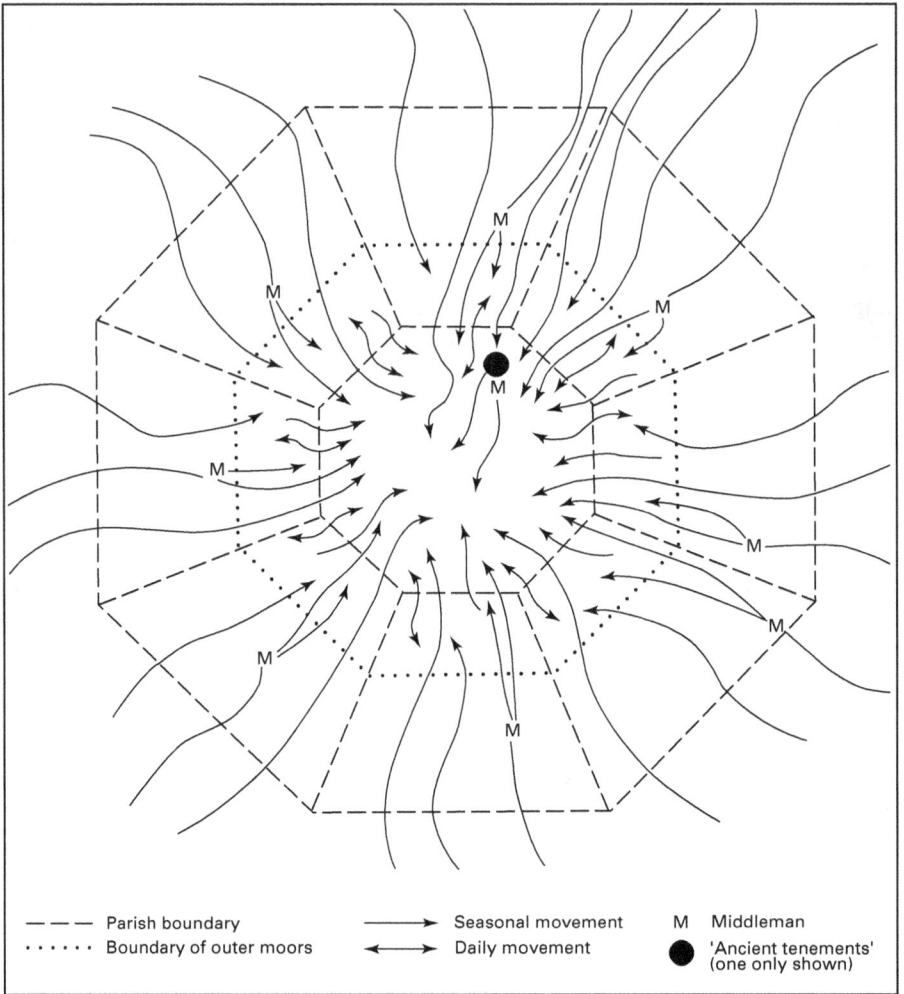

| ——— Parish boundary | ——→ Seasonal movement | M   Middleman |
| · · · · · Boundary of outer moors | ◄—→ Daily movement | ● 'Ancient tenements' (one only shown) |

on crime. Other documents present a picture of a far more orderly system of pastoral management, despite the great complexity of the movement of livestock to and from the central moor and the many outer moors. Fig. 3.2 is an attempt to show that complexity. It looks full and intricate even as it is, but in fact, for each of the moor-edge parishes, only one example of each of the several kinds of livestock movements is shown: reality was far more complicated. For the central moor commoners fell into what I have called, earlier in this book, a well-ordered hierarchy and, although they would not have used that word, each knew his place in that scheme. Order was imposed there by drifts at several times of the year, and this also applied to the outer moors.

Systems of pastoral management on medieval Dartmoor may not have worked exactly like clockwork: there were infringements and violations, not surprising given the large number of animals concerned, over 20,000 cattle around 1400. But work it did, as witnessed by the large profits which the Crown and local lords drew from it and by the benefits which the owners of the livestock derived from it. The medieval period was not one of chaos and primitive institutions, and this is as well illustrated by pastoral management on Dartmoor as it is, for example, by the operation of the complex and highly regulated 'Midland' two- and three-field system in some of the more arable regions of England in the Middle Ages.

Conclusion

In the late medieval period ownership of the outer moors was divided between the adjacent manors, each of which had its own slice of the moor where grazing was controlled by the manorial lord, not the Crown. The manor's tenants usually had rights of common over the manorial moorland but, like the Crown on the central moor, the manorial lords allowed down-country farmers to keep livestock in the summer on their moors for a fee. These might be placed directly with the manorial officials or with their tenants, acting as middlemen. The lords managed their private moors in the same way as the Crown did the central moor, employing herdsmen and conducting drifts and perambulations.

The resulting patchwork of ownerships and the many different interests competing to exploit the moor's resources—not only the various categories of pastoralists but also tin-miners, turf-diggers, quarrymen, huntsmen and others—created many opportunities for tension and disorder and disputes frequently arose.

CHAPTER FOUR

Personal transhumance

Distant detachments

On the flanks of Dartmoor there are examples of detached territories belonging to far-away manors, some of them as distant as the coast. Some have left only faint traces in records; often partially screened from our view, their shapes are the faintest layer in the palimpsest of Dartmoor boundaries, to be deciphered only after much effort. There can be little doubt that they represent toe-holds on Dartmoor for the people of down-country manors who used them for their summer settlements, in other words for personal transhumance. We shall elaborate on that argument later on, after first presenting the evidence for those detachments which are known about, almost certainly only a proportion of the number which once existed.

Cockington and Dewdon (Fig. 4.1)

Domesday Book makes a very clear and explicit reference to one of these detachments, though probably only by chance, others being hidden from us in the Norman record. Under the heading of manors held by the Norman William de Falaise are several which had formerly, before the Conquest, belonged to Alric, one of these being Cockington which paid tax on three hides. After the entry for Cockington, Domesday continues: 'Of this land Alric held 1 virgate of land in *Deptone*' which is *Dewdon* or the like in most later spellings, the 'p' of the Domesday scribe being a result of a misreading.[1] The two were 'held as one manor' but there is nothing unusual in that, Domesday being full of entries in which a main manor has a nearby subsidiary place associated with it, the two being regarded as a single unit.[2] What is unusual about the linking of Cockington and *Dewdon* is that the former is coastal, looking out over the blue bight of Tor Bay (and now, with its vernacular forge, very much part of the itinerary of visitors to this coast), while the latter lies 13 miles away on the flanks of Dartmoor, the 'dew-covered down' of the place-name being no doubt the hillside of open moorland just to the west of the present-day settlement (now called Jordan). Through Domesday, then, we are able to present our first example of a manor

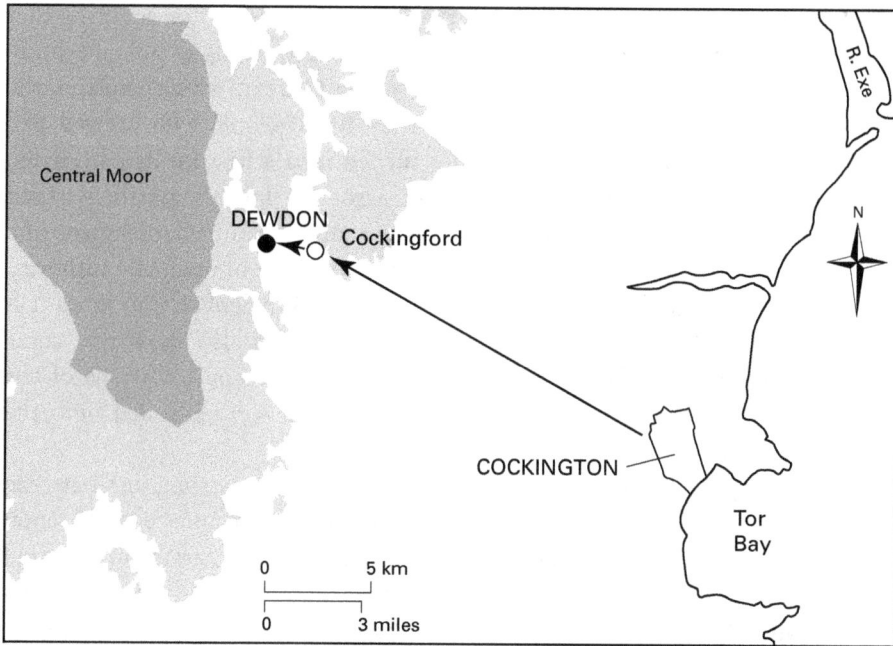

4.1 Detached territories: Cockington and Dewdon.

consisting of a parent core in the down-country with a distant detachment on Dartmoor.

The connection between Cockington and *Dewdon* continued until relatively recent times. It confused some local (and national) historians who, unaware of linkages, especially over so many miles, tended to search for the virgate *in Deptone* somewhere in the hinterland of Tor Bay. The connection between Cockington and *Dewdon* is mentioned many times in a well-researched paper of 1962 by Catherine Linehan who was, however, mainly interested in *Dewdon* itself and not in the link and others like it. Her paper has much excellent detail on manorial descent and on events and people at *Dewdon* in the seventeenth century and later; here we discuss the strength of the link as shown in the earliest surviving manorial documents of Cockington, which Mrs Linehan did not examine in detail. The manor's court rolls naturally contain much interesting detail about the coastal part of the manor but interspersed with this are entries referring to events taking place within the detached part on Dartmoor. Three examples from many must suffice: in 1434 the court heard that 'one black mare came as a stray at *Deudon*', perhaps wandering down a lane from Hamel Down; in 1490 'the tenants of *Deaundon* present that Robert Noseworthy is living with John Noseworthy outside the king's assize'; and in 1488 'the tenants of *Deaudon* present that John Noseworthy, tucker, and John Grey brew ale and thereby break the assize'. These entries show lords of Cockington busy in exercising manorial jurisdiction over their tenants at *Dewdon*. The lords made sure that strays were reported, because they stood to gain if the animal was not claimed; they were responsible for ensuring that all males over the age of twelve were placed within a tithing (a policing body answerable to the hundred and therefore to the Crown, which explains the 'king's assize' in the extract from 1490); they fined people who brewed bad ale, a type of jurisdiction which usually turned into a fine for any brewing, good or bad. These jurisdictions were not assumed lightly: control without right over brewing and over the tithing system might lead to punishment of a lord by the Crown while to control strays meant exercise of manorial authority over a given tract of land and would be disputed by neighbouring lords if it was assumed without right. Court rolls of Cockington also show that some of the tenants of *Dewdon* on occasion travelled to the court sessions of the parent manor on the coast and in 1491 two of them were enrolled onto the panel of jurors.[3]

Listings of people confirm, if that is necessary, the very strong link between Cockington and *Dewdon*. For example, an undated fifteenth-century rental of Cockington, headed 'Names of all the tenants', has a separate sub-heading which reads 'Names of the lord's tenants of *Dawdon*' while lists of landless males, made with the purpose of ensuring that they were sworn into a tithing, contain the names of the men of Cockington and *Dewdon* together. An unusual listing is that made for the royal Exchequer in the third decade of the fourteenth century in order to record the names of men who were exempt from taxes levied by the Crown because they were tinners and therefore free of royal burdens by custom. In this document 'the tithing of *Cokyngton*' occurs directly after other Dartmoor tithings, namely Buckland in the Moor, Spitchwick and Blackaton. For this reason, and because tinners are not to be expected near the coast, *Cockynton* here must be the detached part not the parent manor. In the eyes of the Crown, Cockington and *Dewdon* were one tithing with one name just as they were 'one manor' in Domesday Book; the detached part of the tithing was even given the same name as the parent part.[4]

We may take the link, with some certainty, beyond and before the time of the Domesday survey, good chronological depth being provided by the place-name Cockingford, just over 1 mile east of *Dewdon*. Today the ford has been replaced by a bridge, but the East Webburn River would formerly have been fordable at this point because it is relatively shallow and narrow here (though now altered by being channelled in a culvert) before becoming, downstream, the torrent from which it takes its name, 'the raging river'. Westwards of the ford a road ascends a steep hill, with gentle bends in order to reduce the slope, towards the open moorland and *Dewdon*. Eastwards this way ascends from the Webburn, again with gentle bends, is deflected from a straight course by a need to cross Ruddycleave Water at a suitable spot, passes the farm of Waye (taking its name after a significant road) and may then be traced for 11 miles along lanes which never deviate more than ¼ mile from a straight line drawn from *Dewdon* to Cockington (see Fig. 7.2). The way has all the characteristics of a droveway, as discussed in chapter 7. It is unlikely that the name Cockingford, situated as it is on this determined routeway, is of no significance, but unfortunately we do not have early spellings for it. It is not discussed by the editors of *The Place-names of Devon* because, like many minor names around Dartmoor, it does not appear on the first edition, or other early editions, of the 1-inch map.[5] Cockington means 'the estate of Cocca', the medial -*ing*- denoting association or ownership. Cockingford (again with the medial -*ing*-) is patently not 'Cockingtonford', that is 'the ford associated with, or leading to, Cockington'; rather it is 'the ford associated with Cocca', so one may reasonably suggest that it takes us back to the same person who once owned the estate based on coastal Cockington.[6] Cockingford was, perhaps, the most significant obstacle on this droveway and there his delegates and some of his tenants would have waited for the right moment to cross the river: one can almost see them there. The personal name must date from before the Norman Conquest because by that time the land at Cockington had passed to Alric. Some time after completing my research into the manorial documents of Cockington, I discovered that the parent manor's hundred, the Hundred of Kerswell (later renamed the Hundred of Haytor), had a detached portion on Dartmoor, containing *Dewdon*. Since hundreds were created in the Saxon period, that reinforces the antiquity of the link. The discovery also led me into research into other detached portions of hundreds, to be presented later in this chapter.

Through the place-name Cockingford, and through Domesday Book with which we began, this link between the people of the fertile coastlands of south Devon and their summer pastures of Dartmoor may be taken with some confidence to the period before the Norman Conquest.

Ipplepen and Abbotskerswell and their links (Fig. 4.2)

A characteristic of research into the Anglo-Saxon and medieval history of a chosen locality—though not if the emphasis is on themes of purely sociological or economic interest, when the researcher is able consciously to select the best sources—is that the historian who finds with excitement some especially telling and significant document relating to a particular place is then often let down with a sudden jolt because ancillary documentation fails him. Such moments of exhilaration and disappointment were a feature of much of the research lying behind this book. For Cockington's links the evidence is unusually good both before and after the Norman Conquest, but for Ipplepen, considered now, a pre-Conquest source is excellent, but the later topographical evidence is baffling.

The pre-Conquest source is a charter of 956 preserved in the Sherborne cartulary, by which King Eadwig gave to the 'noble woman' Æthelhild an

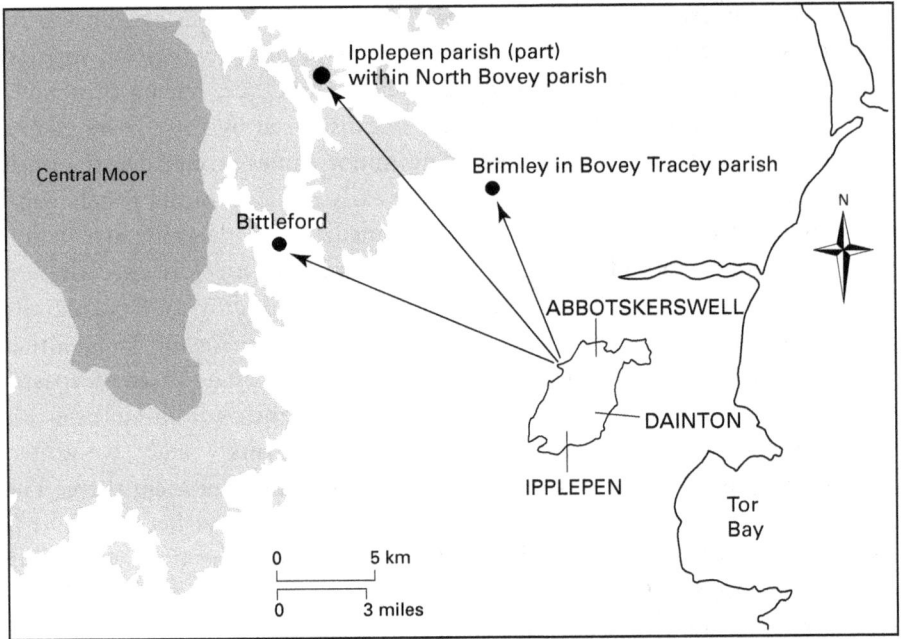

extensive estate lying a few miles inland from Tor Bay and Babbacombe Bay.
To this land belonged one hide *at Bitelanwyrthe* and another *at Bromleage*,
both of which lay detached towards Dartmoor and are named at the end of
the charter.[7] The charter states that the core of the estate comprised land at
the adjacent places, from west to east, of Ipplepen, Dainton and Kerswell,
later Abbotskerswell (Fig. 4.2). The charter has been claimed in the past to be
spurious, but the latest authorities find nothing doubtful about it, neither in
its preservation as a twelfth-century copy in the cartulary of Sherborne Abbey
nor in its diplomatic and list of witnesses. Eadwig's gift to Æthelhild may have
been made in order that she would give part of it to the endowment of Horton
Abbey in Dorset, a religious house whose early years have been described as
'obscure' and 'veiled'. Poverty and Viking damage gave it a faltering early
history and it was eventually, in the early twelfth century, merged with
Sherborne Priory, later to become an abbey.[8] Horton (later Sherborne) owned
only Abbotskerswell, according to Domesday, two papal privileges of 1126 and
1146, and later sources, but this is not strange: Mary O'Donovan, in her expert
treatment of Sherborne's charters, explains that 'perhaps the grant embodied
in the charter was divided before Horton received a portion' (an alternative
possibility being that Horton received the whole, but had lost some of it by
1066).[9] The charter, or a copy of it, was no doubt obtained by Sherborne from
Horton because it related, in part, to Abbotskerswell. It was once claimed
that the charter is unauthentic because it has, *mutatis mutandis*, the same
terminology, apart from the place-names and boundaries, as another diploma

by the same king to the same donee, of lands in Hampshire: the former, it was suggested, was copied from the latter. Thanks now to the work of Simon Keynes and Mary O'Donovan, we can say that there is nothing unusual or suspicious in this, for the duplication is simply the result of work by a single draughtsman at a single session of the royal court where the same group of witnesses was naturally present.[10]

Having cleared away these difficulties we may turn to our real interest, the detached parts of Ipplepen *at Bitelanwyrthe* and *at Bromleage*. Although the charter exists only in a post-956 copy, there is no reason at all to suggest that the statement about the detached parts was made by the copyist.[11] Taking the first place first, there is no suggestion at all in any of the later documentation that it lay *within* the parent manor, for there is no trace of the name in a variety of local sources containing information about field-names and boundaries. Tracing our way backwards through manorial sources, there may be a hint of a detached portion of upland belonging to Ipplepen in a survey made of the manor in 1310, which mentions, as well as arable and meadow, some acres of *terra montanea*, 'hilly or mountainous land'.[12] This is just what we would not expect within the smiling and fertile parent part of Ipplepen and it may be that here we have an oblique reference to a detached part on Dartmoor. In 1332, Hamelin de Byteleworthi was among the tax-payers of Ipplepen tithing who contributed to the royal tax levied in that year.[13] This is a highly significant reference for it shows that the place associated with Ipplepen in the tenth-century charter was still attached to it in 1332 and, moreover, the forename as well as the surname takes us towards Dartmoor, because Hamelin was a name abidingly popular in that region.

Place-name evidence suggests very strongly that Ipplepen's detached portion is Bittleford farm in Widecombe in the Moor parish, called *Bittelworthy* throughout the Middle Ages and later, until comparatively recent times: the earliest recorded post-Conquest spelling of the name (*Bittelworthi*) is very close to the form in the charter of 956; the place-name is not recorded elsewhere in Devon; the personal name only once; and we are coming to expect to look towards Dartmoor for these detached parts.[14] Bittleford today is a farm with fields abutting onto the rough moorland and gave its name to one of the gates which provided access to the summer pastures. It is in that segment of the outer moors where there were numerous detached portions of manors towards the coastlands. Moreover, Langworthy, a farm just over 1 mile to the north of Bittelford, was also a detached part of Ipplepen tithing.[15]

Although there are many positive reasons for an identification of the detached part of Ipplepen mentioned in 956 with Bittleford, formerly *Bittelworthy*, in Widecombe in the Moor, the later manorial affiliation of the outlier remains a problem, though not an insurmountable one.[16] A further problem is provided by another contender as an outlying part of Ipplepen, for a seventeenth-century survey of the manor of South Teign mentions a 'parcell of the mannor of Ippelpen within the parish of *North Bovie*' (see Fig. 4.2).[17] It is possible to locate this detached part, though only approximately, but unfortunately neither the tithe map, nor glebe terriers and other late documents reveal any names akin to *Bittelworthy* here. The evidence is baffling and no certain solution is possible.

The second detached part referred to in the charter of 956 is *at Bromleage*, a name which means 'broom clearing', often Brimley today, and which, as is to be expected, is fairly common in Devon. Some commentators on the charter have declared it to be unidentifiable,[18] but most of the places called Brimley within the county are unsuitable, if not improbable, locations for a detached part of Abbotskerswell. The most likely candidate is Brimley in Bovey Tracey parish, today just over 1 mile away from the moorland edge (Fig. 4.2).[19]

To take a summer walk through the tangle of lanes around Ipplepen, Dainton and Abbotskerswell is to wander in an ancient landscape, long cultivated, deeply arable, where warm loams feed lush grass and crops and nurture thick growths of luxuriant plants in the way-sides, where there is always a heady scent of flowers and a deep hum of bees drinking them under the sun. There are clues to former strip fields in documents and in the landscape, in well-developed lynchets and access roads to furlongs and flexed field boundaries, while the less fertile, pastoral outer moors seem very far away. But the two are not distinct and separate, for access to the moors by the people (only faintly seen at this stage) of the ancient lands helped them to protect their grain fields from livestock during the growing season, while animals, nurtured on the moors during the summer, could be kept in greater numbers, thereby benefiting the croplands.

Detached parts of the Hundreds of Exminster, Wonford and Kerswell (Fig. 4.3)

Domesday Book is very explicit about Cockington and *Dewdon*, the subjects of our first case-study—they were 'held as one manor'—and they continued to be a single manor and tithing right through the Middle Ages. Their story can therefore be told thoroughly. But Domesday contains other, less explicit, information on down-country manors with detachments on Dartmoor, revealed through the phenomenon of fragmented hundreds (administrative and judicial territories of late Saxon date). The hundreds of Devon at the time of the Norman Conquest may be reconstructed quite accurately from the order in which places are mentioned in Great Domesday's local predecessor, known as the Exon Domesday. Each estate's constituent places are listed together, ordered by the hundred to which they belong, the hundreds being always in the same order (there are some anomalies, though not too many, and they may sometimes be ironed out through the use of later sources). This information was worked

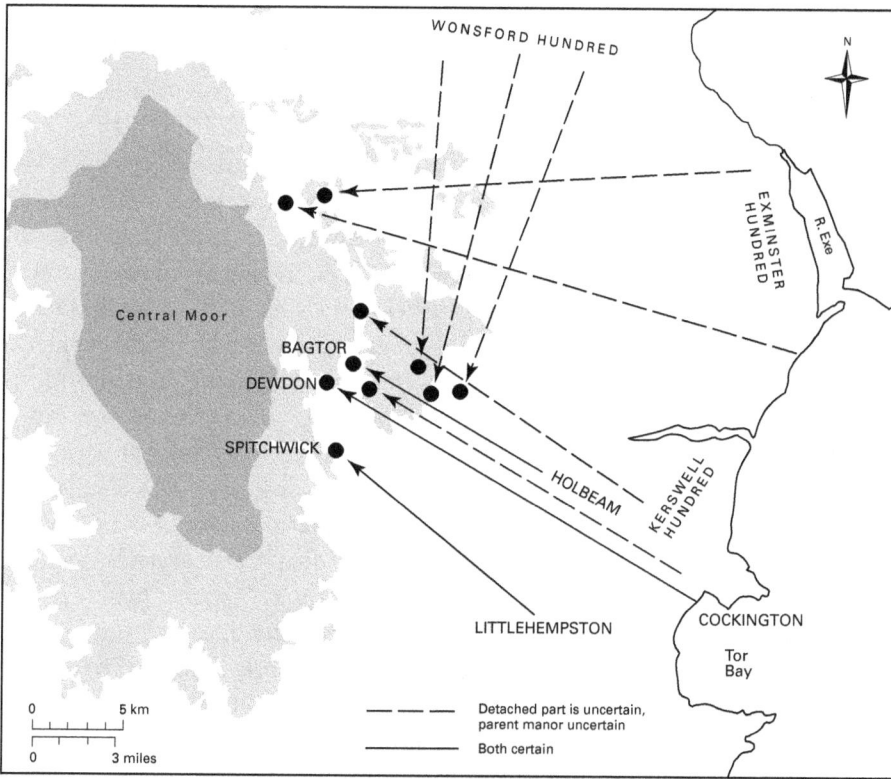

4.3 Detached
territories:
Exminster,
Wonford
and Kerswell
hundreds.

upon expertly by O.J. Reichel in the first part of the twentieth century and, more recently, it has come under the equally expert scrutiny of Caroline and Frank Thorn.[20] Fragmented hundreds with a detached part or parts came about in a variety of ways. In the seventeenth century the topographically minded historian William Dugdale noted that in some cases detached parts of hundreds originated through the desire of the owner and administrator of some great estate to have its scattered manors lying in as few hundreds as possible, for convenience when tax was collected or when pleas were taken to the hundred court.[21] Frank Thorn has given two other reasons for fragmented hundreds, the first being 'that several [Devon] hundreds had once been part of larger units' which were then split 'partly along territorial lines, so that isolated parts of one hundred are sometimes found within another'.[22] This is highly unlikely for those Devon hundreds with detached parts on Dartmoor because they were exceptionally large units. His second reason 'for some of the apparent complexity of the Devonshire hundreds' is that 'access to waste or moorland was important for the economies of many manors', and I am convinced that that is the explanation in the cases discussed below. In all of them manorial ties had been severed by 1066 (as was not the case with Cockington and *Dewdon*); through economic development the distant detachments, once pastoral, had become manors in their own right, with their own courts and arable ploughlands, so later documentation does not help.

Three Domesday hundreds in Devon have detached parts on the borders of Dartmoor—Exminster, inland from the River Exe, Wonford, a large territory west of Exeter, and Kerswell, west of Tor Bay (later called Haytor).[23] The detached parts contained ten properties all told by the time of Domesday Book and of those one may be reasonably confident in three cases, two in Kerswell Hundred and one in that of Wonford, of tracing the down-country parent manor to which the detached part belonged. One is *Dewdon*, linked to Cockington in Kerswell Hundred, a linkage which Domesday Book explicitly mentions: it is a special case, therefore, and for that reason has been dealt with separately above. Another is Spitchwick in Widecombe in the Moor parish, its name containing the element *wic* (discussed more fully at page 151), 'a temporary camp' according to the most recent discussion of this element; in this case the place-name strongly reinforces our interpretation of the detached parts of hundreds as summer camps when personal transhumance was the custom.[24] Ownership provides the clue as to Spitchwick's parent manor in the main part of Kerswell Hundred, because it was in the hands of the king in 1086 and the main part contained but two royal manors, Kingskerswell itself and Littlehempston. Of these two, the connection with Littlehempston is by far the stronger, because that manor is followed by Spitchwick in the order in which places are listed in Domesday Book.

The other place in a detached part of a hundred which may be linked quite confidently with a down-country manor is Bagtor in Ilsington parish. In 1086 it belonged to Nicholas *l'Arbalester* ('the bowman' or 'man in charge of siege engines'), almost all of whose lands had been held before the Norman Conquest by Ordric (so the link is not merely the result of a post-Conquest re-shuffling of manors).[25] The link we are suggesting is to Holbeam (in Ogwell parish, itself a detached portion of Wonford lying on the northern edge of Kerswell Hundred), because Bagtor occurs directly after Holbeam in Domesday Book, and both had been sub-infeudated by Nicholas to one Roger, whose sub-holding consisted of only these two manors. We have already reconstructed (in the previous section) a link between Ipplepen and a place in Bovey Tracey parish, and it may not be a coincidence that Ipplepen adjoins Ogwell while Bovey Tracey adjoins Ilsington, in which parish Bagtor lies.

There are insurmountable difficulties in attempts to elucidate the precise linkages of the remaining eight manors in the three detached parts of hundreds, and on Fig. 4.3 they have been shown as dotted lines to give a sense of this uncertainty. Our three successful links (for Spitchwick, Bagtor and *Dewdon*) make a strong case for the previous existence of the others, but time had already erased them by 1066.

Kenton with Heatree (Fig. 4.4)

Kenton manor stretches inland from the shore of the River Exe. Its settlement pattern contains a scatter of isolated farms and hamlets, as all Devon parishes do, together with the village of Kenton itself. There were links to a settlement on the shore of the Exe where certain of the manor's farmers occupied storage houses called cellars which were a convenience in the seasonal occupations of salt-making, early on, and the taking of oysters, salmon and other fish. The manor had a detached part which gave it access to the open sea, perhaps in order to allow tenants to fish for a greater variety of species than were available in the estuary.[26] Kenton was a complicated and fortunate manor, for there was also another link in another direction, inland towards the borders of Dartmoor, to a territory known in the documents as Heatree (after one of the farms within it) in the parish of Manaton.

The earliest record of a connection between Kenton and its detached part called Heatree on Dartmoor comes from 1296 when a financial account for the manor of Kenton records the toll of the mill at *Heuytru* and this is the first of a long series of references to the outlier in ministers' accounts, one from 1422, for example, mentioning 100s. rent from customary tenants and 15s. from two mills at *Hevetre*. In 1300 a survey describes *Hevittree* as a member of the manor of Kenton and a similar document of 1331–32 mentions the mill of *Hevetre* as belonging to the manor. Later surveys begin to add more detail and to bring the detachment to life, one of 1578 having the heading *Hamlet de Heaytree in parochia de Maneton parcella manerii de Kenton* ('Hamlet of Heatree in the parish of Manaton, part of the manor of Kenton') and telling us that some of the tenements there were very near to the central moor belonging to 'the Lady Queen', thereby being 'much burdened with wild beasts', that is, deer. The most emphatic statement about the unity of Kenton and Heatree is in a survey of around 1690 which states that the manor of Kenton 'is not bounded in one entire perifry but is in two parts', one in Kenton parish, the other 'near Dartmoore ... very poor, cold and hungry ground, full of rocks and naturally heathy'. Richard Polwhele, historian of Devonshire and rector of Kenton for a time, saw this survey and used it as a basis for his account of the manor of Kenton.[27]

The post-medieval documentation also allows us to see Kenton and Heatree as a single manor administered by a single manor court, as was the case of Cockington and *Dewdon*. The survey of around 1690 noted that 'according to the custom of the mannor ... the tenants of *Hartre* ... are to appear but by two men of the court'. Sure enough, court business from Heatree, largely concerning stray animals on the moors and the transmission of tenements there, is recorded in Kenton's surviving seventeenth-century court book. Two men from the moors made their 15-mile journey down to Kenton on the coast

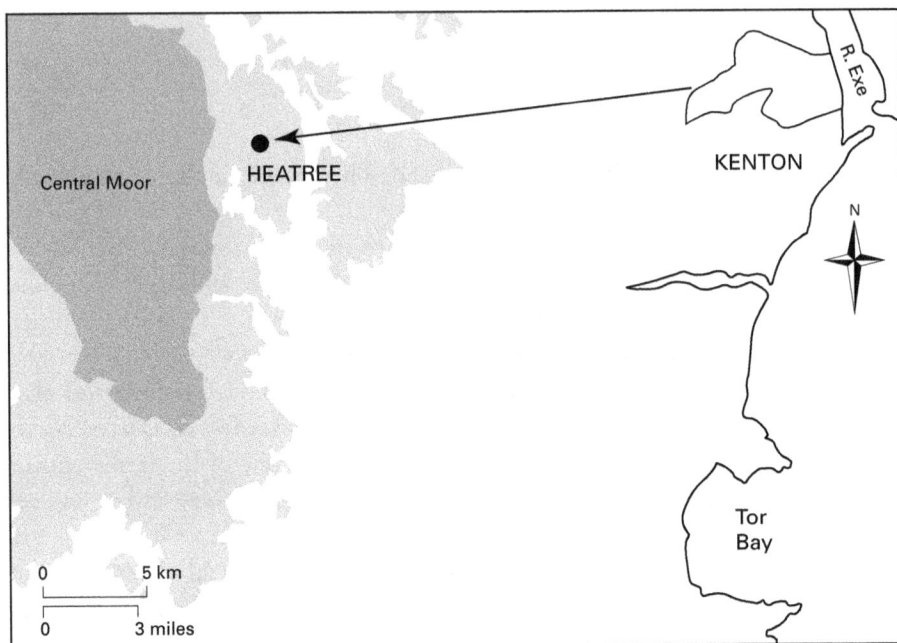

4.4 Detached
territories:
Kenton with
Heatree.

to attend the sessions of the manor court which, luckily, met with monotonous infrequency; it is the same custom that we have already noted on the manor of Cockington.[28]

Royal taxes were collected by tithing and, in the eyes of the Crown, Kenton and its detached portion on Dartmoor were a single tithing, as we found also at Cockington. Under the heading of Kenton tithing in the list of people who paid the royal tax of 1332 can be found William Canna and Floura de Hedercombe, while in the list for 1330 are the surnames Hedercomb and Bodecote: Canna, Heathercombe and Barracott are the names of tenements not in the coastal part of Kenton but in its distant outlier on Dartmoor.[29] More unusually, perhaps, is that in the thirteenth century the detached portion was seen to be part of the *parish* of Kenton, or at least tied to that parish in some way. The evidence for this is unequivocal and authoritative: in the list of churches and their values finished in 1291 and known as the Taxation of Pope Nicholas (for its purpose was a papal levy) is the statement that 'the rector of the church of Kenton takes tithes in the parish of Manaton', meaning that some of the tithes of Manaton—those of Heatree—formed part of the ecclesiastical income of Kenton church.[30] Precisely how this arrangement worked in the Middle Ages we shall never know. The incumbent of Manaton presumably had spiritual charge of, and duties towards, the people of Heatree because they were physically so close to him. A rector of Kenton, knowing that Heatree was in both the manor and tithing of Kenton, might be astute enough to begin to claim tithes on the grains grown there despite the distance, and perhaps an agreement was made to divide them. Alternatively, the Taxation may be referring to a division of the tithes from livestock wintering in one parish and summering in another, a division recommended by Bishop Alexander of Coventry in the middle of the thirteenth century (see page 33). Whatever was the case in the Middle Ages, the arrangement has left no trace in the later parish documentation.[31]

There were parochial links between Kenton and Heatree in the thirteenth century; in the early fourteenth century there were links through the tithing system, which was late Saxon in origin and later used for royal local administration of many kinds; manorial links are strongly in evidence for all centuries from the thirteenth to the eighteenth. No greater claims are made here than these. We may add, however, that it is reasonable to speculate that the links may be older than the thirteenth century and may date to the pre-Conquest period—given the evidence about the detached parts of Cockington and Ipplepen discussed earlier. We are certain that these links were for the purpose of personal transhumance, and a reconstruction of the seasonally used settlements in that phase is given later in this chapter.

Around 1690 Kenton's detached territory on Dartmoor contained one mill (successor to the two mentioned in 1422) and twenty-one tenanted farms with a mean size of 55 acres. Rye, oats and barley, but little wheat, were grown. Tenants were actively engaged in making profits from livestock farming: by 1690 they are reported to have adopted the practice of sowing clover grass in their leys, so these remote farms were not isolated backwaters from the point of view of farming innovation (close and frequent contact with the coastlands ensured this); it was specifically stated that the clover increased supplies of fodder and thereby the number of livestock which could be over-wintered, while in the summer the farmers around Heatree were especially well placed to act as middlemen, taking in animals from the down-country, as described earlier (chapters 2 and 3). The tenants heated their homes and cooked with turves gathered on the moors 'which are large' in the words of the survey of around 1690, providing plentiful rough grazing. The moors, indeed, occupied almost 2,000 acres, just under two-thirds of the total acreage of this detached part of Kenton (Fig. 2.4). The tenements were as islands in their sea of moorland, most of them single, isolated farmsteads such as Canna or in pairs such as Heathercombe, Heatree itself and Barracott; five were at the hamlet of Challacombe with its strange, archaic arable field system. Most were sold off during the eighteenth century, although those at Challacombe were still part of the Kenton estate in 1787, when they were included in a fine estate map of the manor and its parts. Set within a decorative cartouche showing a Dartmoor scene, is its title: 'A map of lands within the manor of Kenton in the parish of Mannaton.'[32]

Paignton and its parts (Fig. 4.5)

The link between Paignton (on the coast of Tor Bay, a near neighbour to Cockington) and Ashburton on the borders of Dartmoor was a very strong one and the evidence for it presents relatively few problems, despite claims to the contrary. Both places belonged to the See of Exeter and the evidence is best introduced through a map of ecclesiastical property in the tract of countryside between the coast and Dartmoor. Fig. 4.5 shows the area covered by what was later the bishop's manor of Ashburton, once part of Paignton, which was almost certainly contiguous with the parish of Ashburton; it also shows the great manor of Paignton, spread over several parishes (Bickington, Stoke Gabriel, Marldon and Paignton) and reconstructed from a detailed rental of 1567.[33] The map shows that the episcopal lands in this tract of countryside were in two parts, one towards coast and estuary, the other towards Dartmoor. Bickington looked both ways, being reckoned manorially as part of the coastal block and ecclesiastically as part of the moorland block. At some time it had been cut out of Ashburton, because the boundary between the two is jagged, going around farm boundaries, whereas Bickington's other boundaries are far smoother.

It is clear that, at one time and in some minds, all of the episcopal lands in this tract of country were regarded as one territory, called 'Paignton Land'[34] or the like, though a fragmented one; that, at least, is one interpretation of two crucial words which appear as a descriptive statement and endorsement on an eleventh-century document, words which have baffled previous scholars.[35] We shall encounter this document again (pages 174–79) in our discussion of the evolution of boundaries on the outer moors where it will be concluded that it is a record of the bounds of Ashburton, some already existing in the eleventh century, some staking a bold, projected claim to a segment of the moorland. We need not add any more detail here about Ashburton's claim, for it is the descriptive statement and endorsement which are now under the spotlight. The record of the boundary begins with the words *this is peading tunes landscario*, 'these are the boundaries of *peading tune*', and the endorsement, in the same hand as the front, reads *peding tunesland gemaere*, 'boundary of *peding tunesland*'. These words have bemused many. The most fanciful interpretation was that of J.B. Davidson who examined the document in the 1870s, concluding very speculatively, as he admitted, that it was 'a copy of an old Saxon perambulation made by John Padyngton' who was 'steward in about . . . 1310 to Bishop Stapledon, the great benefactor of Ashburton'—an impossible conclusion because the hand pre-dates John by over two centuries. The editors of *The Place-names of Devon* seemed baffled, stating that 'no trace of that name [*peadingtune*] has been found in later documents', others such as Rose-Troup, Finberg and Sawyer hazard no explanation and it has also been described as a 'place-name now lost'.[36]

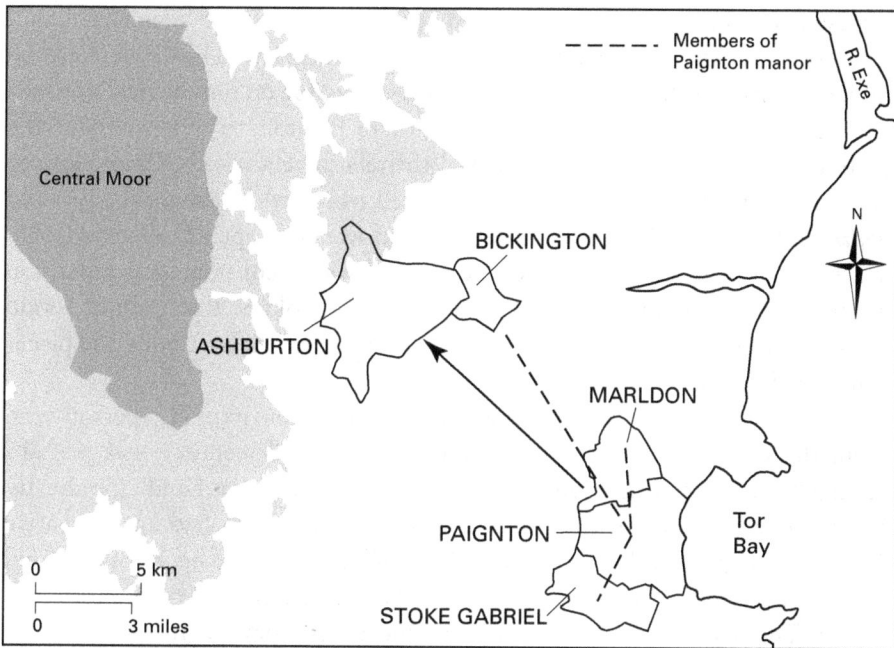

4.5 Detached territories: Paignton and its parts.

All of these problems may be removed at a single stroke if we interpret the endorsement as 'boundary of "Paignton Land"'. The scribe who wrote the endorsement in the first half of the eleventh century knew of a territory called Paignton Land comprising the coastal block centred on Paignton itself and the detached block, now Ashburton, towards Dartmoor (Fig. 4.5); possibly it may have been a somewhat archaic name then (for Ashburton was developing a life of its own) and perhaps those who drew up the record of the perambulation, with its bold claim to a segment of the outer moors, wished to add authority to it through this reference to the past. The boundaries do not include those of the coastal part, only the part towards Dartmoor, but readers of the document, which begins with references to the Dartmoor streams of the Ashburn, Dart and Webburn, would immediately realise what was meant: with this in mind we could expand the endorsement as meaning 'boundary of Paignton towards Dartmoor'—and, indeed, a hand much later than the eleventh century added a further endorsement, in Latin—*bunde per dart*—to make this absolutely clear.

Three points may be made in order to give further credibility to this interpretation. First, from the case studies of detached territories towards Dartmoor which we have already presented—those of Cockington, Ipplepen and Kenton (and there are more to follow)—it will be seen that the link between Paignton and Ashburton falls neatly into place as another example of a connection between the coastlands and the moorlands. This line of argument by no means proves the case for Paignton but it does greatly add to its plausibility. Second, the one-time unity of Paignton and Ashburton is suggested not only by the reference to the latter as part of 'Paignton Land' but also by Bickington's connections with both (Fig. 4.5). Third, there are no problems with the development of the place-name, for on philological grounds Peadingtun might easily develop into Peinton or Painton, to give two recurring spellings from the eleventh, twelfth and thirteenth centuries.[37] Quite close to Paignton is Dainton, a name which developed from (*æt*) *Doddintune* (956) and *Dodinton* (1249). In Gloucestershire, Doynton was once spelt *Didintone* (1086) or *Dedigtone* (1221).[38] In all cases we have, through constant oral repetition of a name, the dropping of the 'd' and the 'g'. Phonology, the study of sound change, can provide a respectable number of other examples among the place-names of England.

We should, briefly, trace the later history of Ashburton. The person who wrote the boundary description of the early eleventh century was perhaps looking backwards in time when he used the word 'Paignton Land', for already the territory bounded to the south by the River Ashburn had an alternative name, as is clear from the will of Bishop Ælfwold (drawn up between 1008 and 1012), for he left untamed horses, no doubt running on the moors, *æt æscburnan lande*.[39] The word 'land' here may simply mean 'territory' (as in Hartland and Climsland in the South West, and many other English examples) but Margaret Gelling has suggested that, in some cases, it had the sense of 'ground being newly brought into cultivation', which would fit here, allowing us to envisage the conversion of a detached pastoral dependency used for transhumance into more settled use.[40] We can only guess at how far this development had gone by the early eleventh century, but on Bodmin Moor seasonal settlements had become permanent well before the time of Domesday Book,[41] and the same source tells us that by 1086 Ashburton was already a relatively well-developed manor, having a recorded population of 34 villeins and 16 bordars, with 10 slaves working on the demesne. Significantly, however, the population density recorded in Domesday Book was less than at the parent manor of Paignton.[42] At this time Ashburton's population lived in dispersed farms and hamlets, some of them, such as Bowdley, Chuley, Dolbeare, Halshanger, Furzleigh and Pitleigh, with names having words for woodland, clearings or woods as their second elements: some of these came into being as separate places in the late Saxon period and two contain Old English personal names. Other place-names within the manor contain elements meaning moor and down and in these we can see moorland clearances, perhaps at about the same time, although by no means eliminating the rough pasture, some of which remained in 1086 and, indeed, to this day.

The way in which we perceive Ashburton and Paignton today is conditioned by far more recent changes connected with the development of transportation. The town of Ashburton, now a dominant nucleation in the parish, is a creation of the twelfth century or the thirteenth, strung out on the medieval roadway which skirts the southern flanks of Dartmoor. The awkward spelling of Paignton was (one would expect the 'n' before the 'g') was apparently introduced by the South Devon railway company in timetables and on the platform name board (by mistake, one wonders?).[43]

Lifton and Sourton (Fig. 4.6)

In our discussion and elucidation of manors with detached parts of moorland we turn now from the southern coastlands to the countryside west of Dartmoor. Lifton, the first western manor to be discussed, was a significant place in the pre-Conquest period. Here in 931, Athelstan held a witan attended by Welsh kings, by archbishops, bishops, earldormen, abbots and thegns;[44] before him, Alfred bequeathed Lifton in his will at the end of the ninth century.[45] Queen Edith owned the manor in 1066 and King William in 1086.[46] Thereafter, into the fourteenth century, it was often held by people with close royal connections, a queen, the foster mother of a queen, sons of kings. Attached to Lifton was a hundred of the same name, first mentioned in the geld roll of around 1084 although it is likely, because of the meeting of the witan in 931, that the place had had an earlier administrative importance.[47]

Lifton had many detached dependencies, two of which, manors of Cornwall, need not detain us for long here. Lifton's entry in Domesday Book says that 'two lands, Landinner and Trebeigh, belonged to this manor in the time of King Edward [i.e. 1066]', and there may be a hint of this or a similar arrangement in Alfred's will by which his younger son is given 'Lifton and the lands which belong to it, namely all that I have among the Welsh [i.e. the Cornish] except Trigg'.[48] Lifton's two dependencies in Cornwall are of great interest because they may take us back to a time when the boundary between Devon and Cornwall in these parts probably lay further west than at present, before it was set along the course of the Tamar, a measure which William of Malmesbury, citing an earlier source, thought to have been a gesture by Athelstan in the second quarter of the tenth century.[49] Detached dependencies which reveal something of political history are not our main concern here, for we are more interested in those which tell of economic arrangements, especially access to different types of land-use. Lifton had two such, both situated within its hundred. One was Westweek in the parish of Broadwoodwidger, a few miles from Lifton; it lay in a landscape which, though away from Dartmoor, had several small local moors on soils derived from the Culm Measures, and the second element in the place-name suggests a speciality, most likely for livestock, especially dairy cattle. The evidence for this detached part is ecclesiastical: in 1421 Richard Mileton and Emmota his wife were allowed by Bishop Lacy to have 'a chapel or oratory ... within their house at *Westwyke* in the parish of Lifton' and in 1438 William Mylaton, probably the son of Richard, was given a similar licence; this detached part is clearly drawn on the tithe map of Lifton.[50] About the antiquity of the detached parochial part one should not be dogmatic. If the formation of parishes and parish boundaries took place before the Norman Conquest (as most historians would argue),[51] then the link between Lifton and Westweek must be as old, for it seems very unlikely that the community, incumbent and patron associated with a church (in this case Broadwoodwidger) would have submitted to the loss of a portion of land to another parish *after* these boundary patterns had become established.

The earliest evidence for a link between Lifton and Dartmoor comes from 1330 when a survey of Lifton manor, made on the death of Edmund Earl of Kent, gives the total of the rents paid by free and customary tenants and adds that a smaller amount came from tenants somewhere in Sourton, a parish with a slice of the outer moors, nine miles from Lifton. A later financial account for Lifton mentions 8s. as an 'outside' rent from Sourton, which we can compare with just over £10 from the main part of the manor. The manor of Sourton had a history of ownership which was entirely different from that of Lifton; owners of Lifton did not own Sourton manor, but rather a detached part within it.[52]

In our exploration of Lifton we have found a link of a type which is now familiar from the other case studies presented earlier: a large manor, in this case not on the coastlands but in the upper valley of the Tamar and its tributaries, and a detached manorial outlier on the edge of Dartmoor for the convenience of its people. Unfortunately, despite expert research on land-ownership in Sourton by Peter Weddell (part of an archaeological project on a deserted medieval hamlet on Sourton Down)[53] the precise location of the outlier remains unknown: to judge from the rents which it paid to the main manor, it was probably small and is therefore difficult to identify, unlike Kenton's large segment of the outer moors in the parish of Manaton, as discussed above. Nor is it clear why Lifton's detached part in Sourton did not remain part of the parent parish as did that in Broadwoodwidger.

4.6 Detached territories: Lifton and Sourton.

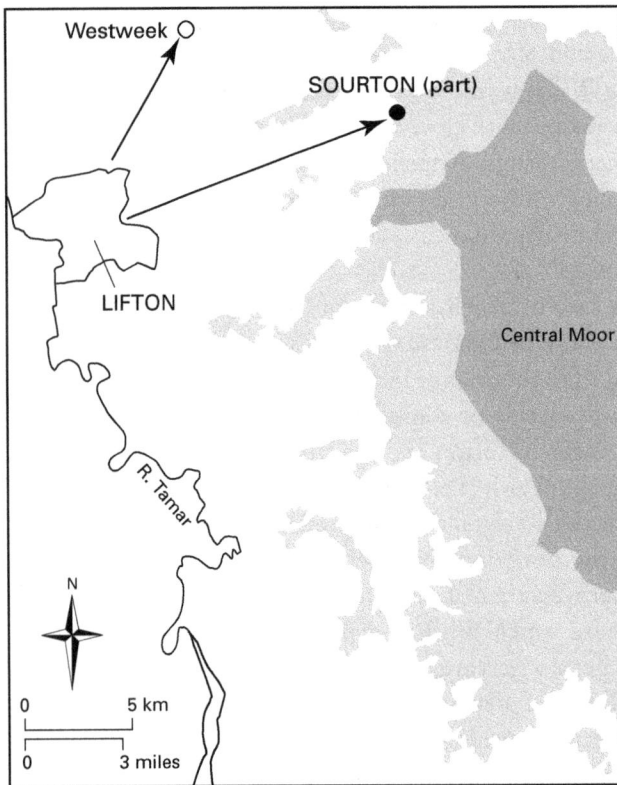

Northlew, Venn and Lettaford (Fig. 4.7)[54]

Northlew is a parish six miles north of Lifton and five miles from the skirts of Dartmoor, the bold silhouette of the hills being clearly visible on most days. The evidence for its detached part is very clear, though it comes rather late in the day: as recounted earlier in this book, in 1388 three commissioners—the escheator of Devon together with a clerk and a local knight—made an inquisition into the estate of Sir John Cary which had fallen to the Crown because of his treason.[55] They valued the goods and chattels at his residence and demesne of Holloway in Northlew parish (now a deserted site but easily located by reference to a bridge of the same name over the River Lew and to the tithe map) but had great difficulty in finding four mares with their foals, which were brought to them 'out of *Dertmore* with great labour and expense'. This was in early April, so the animals had been over-wintering on the outer moors. One can easily imagine the servants of the three commissioners searching the moors, identifying Sir John's animals, rounding them up in a wild chase because they were not used to being handled, then the procession led by the triumphant men wearing the escheator's colours with four tethered mares, each having her follower, trotting obediently now along one of the high, moory ridge-ways linking Northlew to Dartmoor. It is likely that the animals had not been placed in the hands of a Dartmoor middleman, but had rather

4.7 Detached territories: Northlew, Venn and Lettaford.

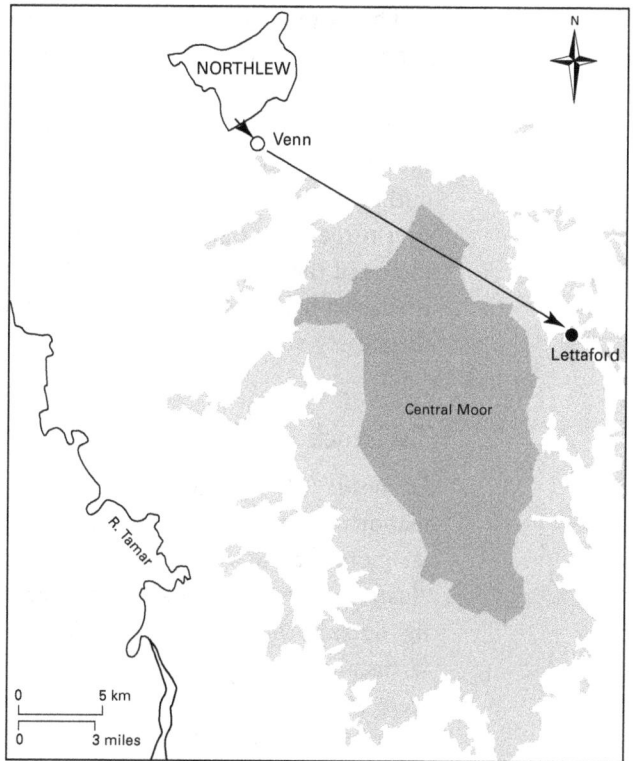

been sent to an outlying detachment of the manor, as the inquisition also reported that the manor's appurtenances included 'certain tenements at *Wrey* with a parcel of land near *Dertmore*, parcel of *Holway* and worth 40s. yearly'.

Wrey is Wreyland in Bovey Tracey, and a further inquisition into Cary's lands made the following year refers to the holding near *Dertmore* as 'lands at *Luttereforde by Dertemore* worth 40s', thus identifying it as Lettaford, a venville hamlet in North Bovey on the very edge of the open moor (Plate 8).[56] The identification is explicitly confirmed by two further inquisitions into Cary's Wreyland and Lettaford holdings held in 1390 and 1396.[57]

It must be a possibility that the link between Northlew and Lettaford in 1388 was not an ancient connection dating back to a period of personal transhumance, but was instead of recent creation, the result merely of the two properties having come into single ownership in the recent past. However the inquisition, in its list of several minor sub-manorial landholdings, carefully distinguished between those which were 'parcel of Holway' and those which were not, suggesting that the former's links to Holloway were based on something deeper than mere co-ownership. One early hint that Northlew had a Dartmoor outlier can be found in its Domesday Book entry, which mentions ten *eque silvestres*, woodland or wild mares, assets which Frank Thorn has suggested may identify manors with detached portions on the moors.[58]

The original 1388 inquisition also included in the list of Holloway manor's appurtenant tenements 'a rent at Melbury with certain lands in *Fenne*, parcel of *Holway*, worth 15s. yearly'. Two detailed rentals from around 1460 and later in the fifteenth century include a tenement 'at *le Fenne* in the parish of *Beworthy*', thus identifying the farm of Venn in Beaworthy parish as another detached outlier of Northlew. This farm, almost surrounded by small, local moors, is over three miles outside the border of a Dartmoor generously defined, but close to one of the ways leading from Northlew up to the summer pastures, so it was perhaps a half-way stopping place, giving livestock a first bite of fresh grass on their early summer journey.[59]

Tavistock and Cudlipp (Fig. 4.8)

Domesday Book's entry for the large manor of Tavistock (later to be called the manor of Hurdwick), like almost all manorial entries in that record, conceals far more than it tells us about settlement patterns.[60] It conceals whatever small cluster of dwellings belonging to artisans and traders may have already grown up outside the abbey's gate. Also missing is any mention of the scatter of farms and hamlets which, according to Finberg's imaginative reconstruction,[61] were already present in the landscape familiar to Geoffrey, the first abbot to be appointed after the Norman Conquest, some of them probably of ancient origin, others perhaps newborn or about to be born at that time, such as Rubbytown and Woodovis towards the western limits of the manor (the latter name meaning 'at the wood's edge'—*efes*—although that edge was soon to be removed to a distance by woodland clearance, as the present-day maps make clear). Domesday Book also conceals a detached outlier on the borders of Dartmoor—Cudlipp and other farms—separated from the parent manor by cultivated land in the valley of the Tavy.

The documentary evidence for this detached part is respectably early by any standards, referring back as it does to the time of the Saxon Abbot Wymund who ruled at Tavistock Abbey in the last decade of the eleventh century, some of whose monks would have been present on the spot when Domesday Book was compiled. In 1116 Henry I issued a writ commending the restoration of Cudlipp to Tavistock because they had been 'unjustly' disposed of by Wymund. Finberg, who examined the background to these transactions, concluded that Cudlipp had been relinquished by Wymund in order to settle it upon a knight who would increase the numbers of fighting men called upon when the abbey was required to provide a quota for war service, and that Henry I disapproved of such increases, requiring that the house's quota should be restored to its number in the time of King William.[62] This is very probable, but our main concern is not with motives but with the status of Cudlipp as part of the manor of Tavistock.

The connection is clear from most medieval and post-medieval manorial sources. For example, a detailed survey of 1387, headed *Extenta manerii de Hurdwyke* ('Survey of the manor of Hurdwick') shows that tenants living on the detached block around Cudlipp were fully integrated into the abbey's great manor of Hurdwick, owing suit of court and doing light services on the demesne.[63] Cudlipp and adjacent tenements never formed a truly independent manor although the military tenant who held them briefly at the end of the eleventh century may have had designs to make them into one; they were Tavistock's toehold on the outer moors, used by the manor's people for seasonal settlements which we reconstruct topographically in the following chapter. The names of three of the farms in the territory of Cudlipp are very significant: Butterberry (two) and Smeardon both contain Anglo-Saxon words telling of dairying and in chapter 5 we shall argue that this type of economy was typical of the seasonal settlements in the phase of personal transhumance.

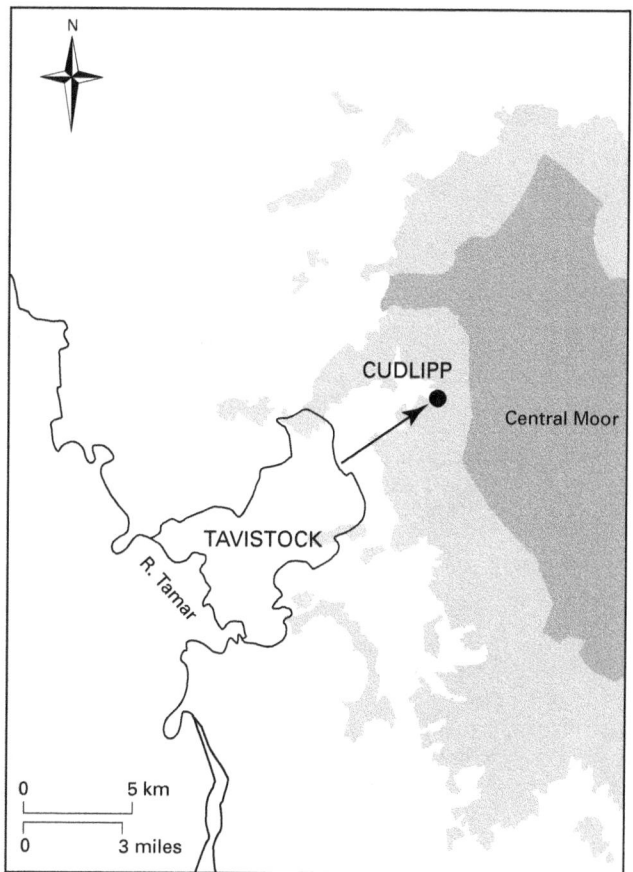

4.8 Detached territories: Tavistock and Cudlipp.

Bickleigh and Sheepstor (Fig. 4.9)

The manor of Bickleigh was part of the original endowment of the Cistercian abbey of Buckland. Together with Buckland itself, it belonged to William de Poilley in 1086, but that family lost it, probably through forfeiture to the Crown. Both manors came into the hands of the de Redvers family (later earls of Devon) and may have been given to them by Henry I (king from 1100 to 1135) because of the loyalty and long service of Richard de Redvers. Walkhampton, another nearby manor, and an important one, for it was head of a hundred and a property of the Crown in 1086, also came to de Redvers, probably through a grant from the same king. And so, by the early thirteenth century, the family was in possession of a compact block of three manors stretching from Bickleigh (bordered in the west by the still tidal Tavy, with its valuable fishery, recorded in 1086 and again at the end of the twelfth century) up to Walkhampton with its sizeable slice of the outer moors, as well as much land elsewhere in Devon and in Hampshire and the Isle of Wight. The block of land was highly suitable as a convenient endowment for a small religious house and this was its destiny when, in 1278, Amice, Countess of Devon and Lady of the Isle, made it over to her new Cistercian house at Buckland founded for the sake of the souls of the king and of her own family. It was owned by the Cistercians until the Dissolution.[64]

4.9 Detached territories: Bickleigh and Sheepstor.

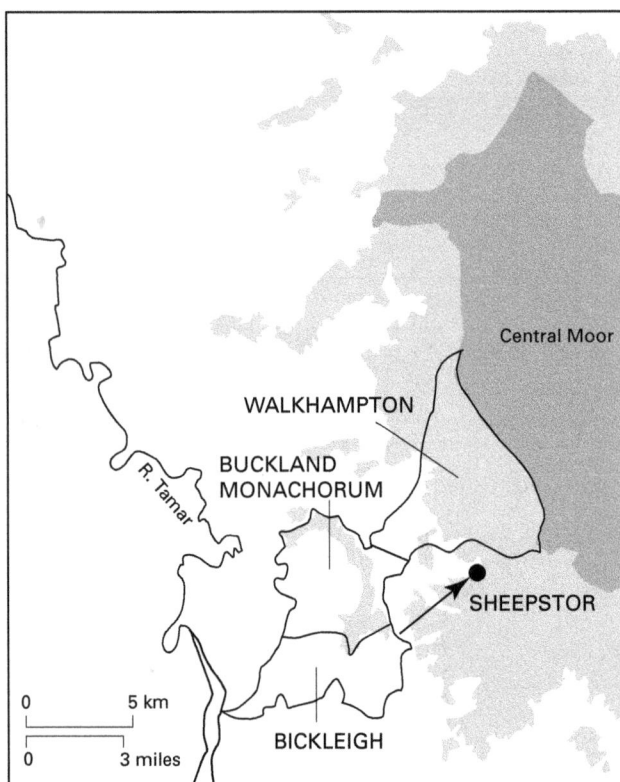

The most instructive document concerning this block of land is not Amice's foundation charter but its ratification in 1291 by Isabella, Countess of Devon, who clearly wished to leave absolutely no doubt about the territorial rights of the monks.[65] Her charter includes a record of a detailed perambulation of the block of land, of great interest because it includes some boundary points on the outer moors. But it is her enumeration of the constituent parts of the block of land which concerns us most here, because it mentions an interesting linkage: 'the manors of *Boclond*, *Bykelie* and Walkampton ... and the land and villeins of Torre at *Shitestorr* belonging to the manor of *Bykelie*'. The *Shitestorr* of the charter is Sheepstor today, a parish with much rough grazing and hard up against the central moor, the 'p' in the name being a recent substitution for 't' in order, as the editors of *Place-names of Devon* coyly put it, 'to prevent the unpleasant suggestions of the old form of the name'.[66] All later sources confirm that part of the moor-edge parish of Sheepstor belonged to the Tavy-side manor of Bickleigh. Sheepstor was a chapelry of Bickleigh, as recorded in the Taxation of Pope Nicholas (1291) and in later ecclesiastical sources.[67] The Taxation also records that Buckland Abbey had rents 'in *Dertemore*' and these were certainly the Sheepstor property. Manorial evidence, for example a lease of 1434, confirms that Bickleigh's share of Sheepstor was called Tor or the like (as in the charter of 1291), but it is not easy to locate it precisely.

Again we have a very strong and persistent link between a river valley territory and a smaller moor-edge block. Simple spatial convenience (Fig. 4.9) would suggest that the part of Sheepstor which became the property of Buckland Abbey, had it been a 'free-standing' block of land in terms of ownership, should have been attached to the abbey's manor of Walkhampton, which it adjoins. That it was regarded as part of more distant Bickleigh, both manorially and ecclesiastically, indicates a link of some strength and antiquity, going back at least as far as a time as the early eleventh century when the de Redvers family had acquired Bickleigh but had not yet been given Walkhampton.

Sheepstor is one of very few moor-edge parishes bearing a name which does not appear in Domesday Book. This omission is significant: its resources may, in part, have been included in the Domesday entry for Bickleigh and perhaps also in other entries for other manors which had land in what was later to become Sheepstor parish; there is a reference, for example, to 'the way of the men of Plympton going to Sheepstor'. Probably, the parish was colonised by permanently occupied farms relatively late in the day and, again significantly, its church is dedicated to St Leonard, who has been described as a 'wilderness saint'.[68]

The significance of the detachments

Some historical studies which have used the topographical evidence of boundaries, for whatever purpose, have not always been received kindly, partly because a certain type of historian finds it difficult to follow and to appreciate lines of argument which are essentially topographical (even though they may be grounded on documents, as in all of the thumb-nail sketches presented above), partly because those who use such methods have sometimes made claims which go wildly beyond what a pattern of boundaries might be telling us. We shall make no wild claims here but we shall discuss the possible significance of the detached parts on Dartmoor through use of logic and comparative evidence.

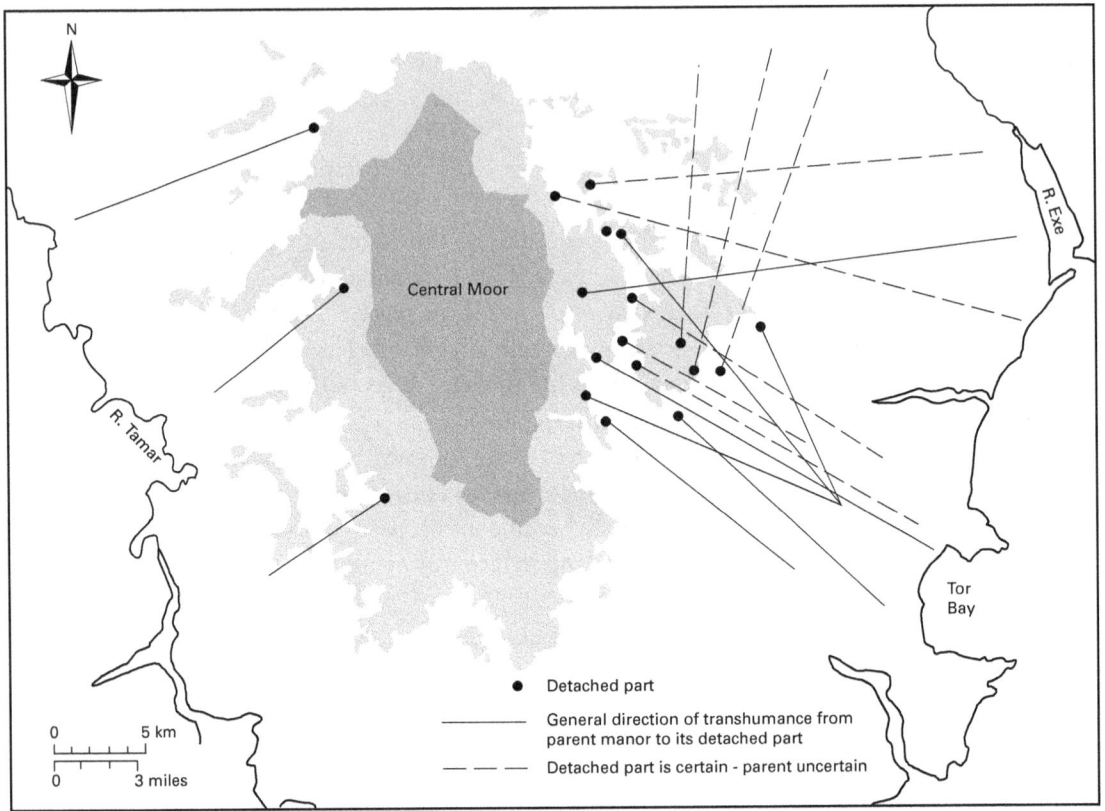

We shall be faithful to our sources and we hope that the reader, in return, will
not lack faith and imagination in following our interpretations.

Fig. 4.10 is a synthesis of the nine case-studies presented above and may be
thought of as problematic in the minds of some readers because it is a multi-
period map. The links shown—between manorial centres and detachments
on Dartmoor—are in some cases not documented until relatively late in the
day which, in the context of this book, may mean the thirteenth century
(although in no instance has use been made of late cartographic evidence
alone). For example, the first reference to Lifton's outlier is from 1275/6. On the
other hand, the evidence for some of the linkages is respectably early by any
standards. Documentary evidence for Ipplepen's detachment dates from 956, for
Paignton's from the eleventh century, for Tavistock's from the late Saxon period
and for Cockington's from 1066–1086—and, in the last case, the place-name
Cockingford suggests that the link to Dartmoor was earlier than Domesday
Book. Where the manorial documentation is good (and it is especially explicit
for the linkages between parent manor and outlier in the cases of Kenton and
Cockington) it usually shows that the links could be very strong and that the
lords of the parent manors maintained their jurisdictions over their outliers for
many centuries. The proven antiquity of the linkages in some of our examples

and their strength as indicated by the manorial documentation means that, even where we have only relatively late evidence for an outlier, it is very probable that the arrangement predates the Norman Conquest. That is to say, to return to the example of Lifton's detached outlier, we can state categorically only that the connection is as old as 1275/6; but we may reasonably surmise that it may be far older than that.

Manorial links originating in seigneurial estate administration

It will be argued later that the links between down-country manors and their detached parts on Dartmoor had an ecological and economic rationale—that they were forged in order to give the inhabitants of the former the benefits of access to moorland pastures in the latter for the livestock which formed part of their livelihoods. The links were at the level of the *manor* and were not in the nature of the linkages between manors existing at the level of a lord's *estate*, which were of a more administrative nature. From a methodological point of view it is very important to make this distinction. Failure to do so can easily lead the researcher into reaching invalid conclusions by muddling linkages of different kinds, which has been done elsewhere, for there are many traps into which the unwary may fall.

An estate (as the word is generally used by historians) at the time of the Norman Conquest, and later, was a collection of manors and sub-manorial properties all in the ownership of one lord and dispersed geographically to a smaller or greater degree. It was largely at the level of lordship and seigneurial administration that there were links between its constituent manors. The manors were linked together by visits of the lord's steward for the purpose of holding courts and other types of supervision, by movements of livestock, for the purpose of seeking out fresh pasture (largely a privilege of lords, with their extensive command over land), and by the sending of seed-corn from manor to manor in an attempt to offset 'in-breeding'—all of which movements were co-ordinated by lords, their stewards and their councils. Some lords perambulated their manors in a predatory fashion: 'plan your sojourn for the whole of the year and for how many weeks in each place [i.e. manor] ... and in no way burden the places where you stay' was the advice that Robert Grosseteste gave to the dowager Countess of Lincoln in the thirteenth century.[69] The manors of an estate were all linked to the estate centre by flows of rents, surplus produce and perhaps labour services to the lord's chief residence there. These flows were to the profit of the lord at the centre, but there were also movements of cash of a centrifugal kind, as for example when investment on one of the manors was financed from the coffers of the estate at large. For the inhabitants of the different manors on the same estate there were some links for some purposes— as where tenants in outlying manors were obliged to perform labour services at the centre—but they were by no means as strong as those forged by and for

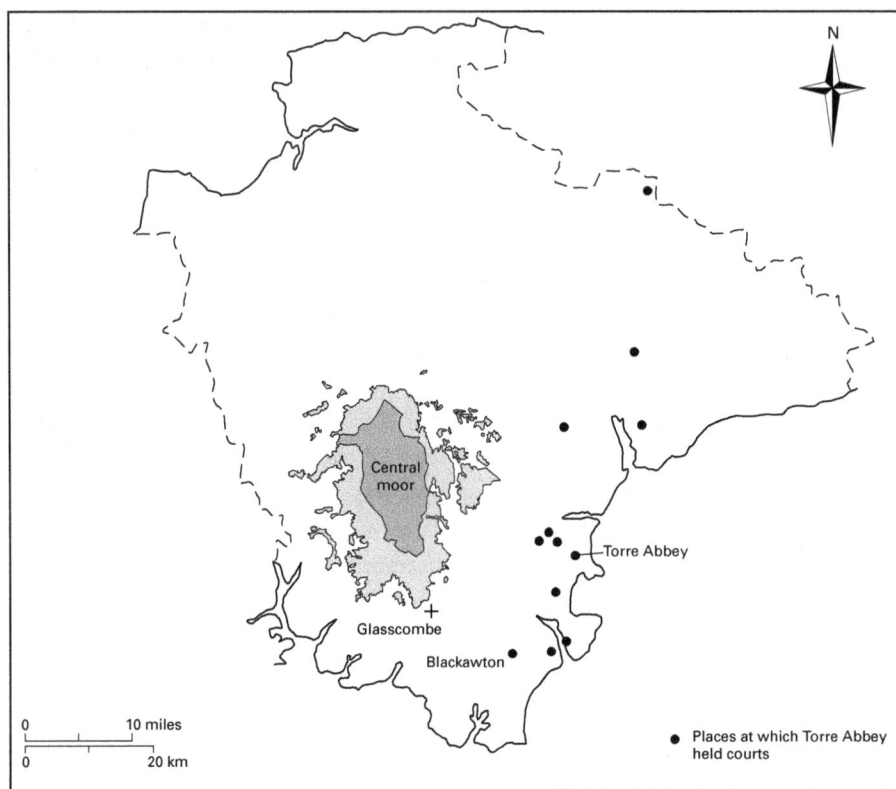

the lord and his administration. For example, when the manor of Braunton was added to the estate of Glastonbury Abbey in the late ninth century, specifically 'for the taking of fish', this act was not in any way to the benefit of the people of the abbey's other manors, for the fish were destined for the table of the abbot.[70]

What was simply an administrative link between two places within an estate, with little effect on the people of the two properties, may be illustrated by the connection which existed in the Middle Ages between Glasscombe and Blackawton. Around the middle of the thirteenth century, William de Lestre augmented the estate of Torre Abbey by giving a farm and wood in Glasscombe, in the valley of the Glaze Brook and close to open moorland in the moor-edge parish of Ugborough and manor of Langford Lester. The abbey used the farm for its rental income, so that we find, for example, Abbot John (around 1350) confirming its occupancy to William Atteffenne for 5s. yearly rent, a relief of 10s. and suit of court at the abbey's manor of Blackawton, 11 miles away in the deep South Hams.[71] The farm was a free tenement, so the tenant would do suit of court at Blackawton only twice a year, with an annual or biannual visit by the tenant to Torre Abbey in order to have his tenancy acknowledged. The benefits of the link between Glasscombe and Blackawton to the people of those places were *nil*, the link being purely an administrative convenience

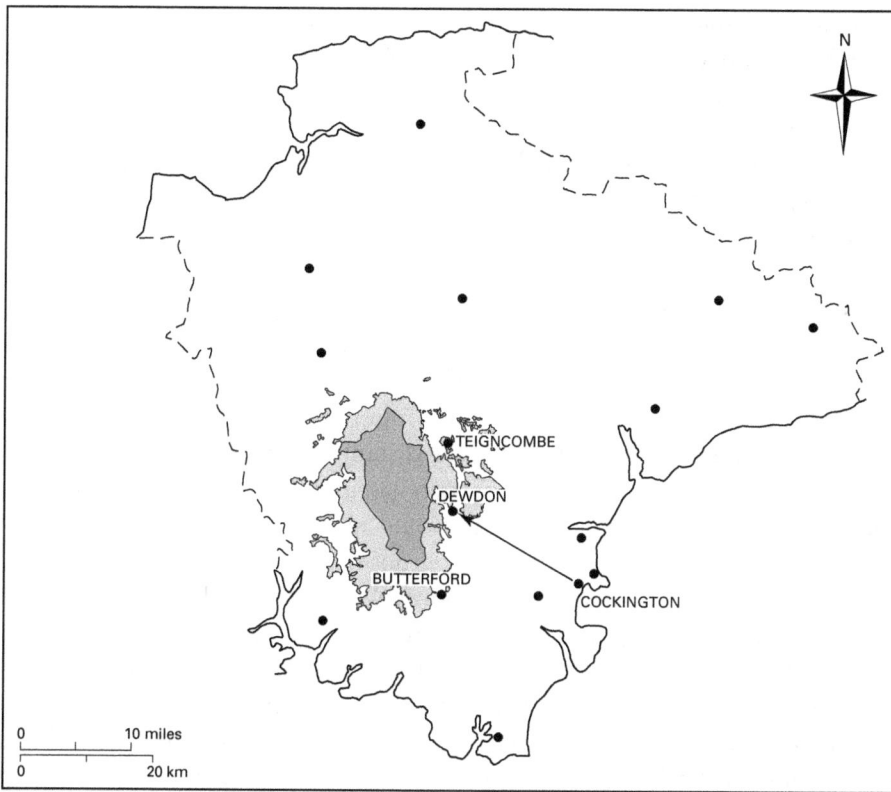

4.12 Alric's Domesday estate.

Source: Domesday Book.

within Torre Abbey's estate. That suit of court was done at Blackawton can be explained by the geography of the estate, for of all the places at which the abbey held manorial courts, according to the Valor Ecclesiasticus of 1535, that manor was closest to Glasscombe (Fig. 4.11).[72]

With the discussion of the foregoing paragraphs in mind it is worth returning as an example to the link between Cockington and *Dewdon*, subject of the first of the case studies made earlier in this chapter. Was this a linkage for administrative convenience on an estate or one with a deeper economic rationale which touched upon the lives of the people of Cockington? Coastal Cockington and upland *Dewdon* were held by Alric in 1066 and were part of an estate whose geographical extent at the time of the Norman Conquest may be reconstructed accurately through identification of that landowner's manors (and other properties) as they were listed under his name in Domesday Book (Fig. 4.12).[73] Alric's lands were widely distributed throughout Devon and this pattern brought three of them closer to *Dewdon* than that place was to Cockington. For the purpose of administration the small property at *Dewdon* could have been managed from Butterford or Teigncombe, for example, but this was not the case. It was managed from, and linked to, Cockington—indeed Domesday Book states that it was part of that manor—and the link was maintained despite distance, suggesting an economic not an administrative necessity, and one which touched the lives of the people of the coastal part of the manor. It must be added that what has been said here about Alric's lands applies only to 1066, the year for which we have evidence in Domesday Book, and not to any earlier period when the estate which included Cockington could have been very different in its size and the distribution of its manors from that shown on Fig. 4.12.

Manorial detachments originating in transhumance

After these long but necessary comments on methodology we may return to the rationale of the links to Dartmoor shown on Fig. 4.10. In almost all cases, it is possible to show that these links were not purely administrative connections within an estate, as described above; the distant detachments were not to the nearest down-country manor on an estate (as in the case of Glasscombe and Blackawton, above) but to places which would appear to have been eccentrically chosen had they been selected for the purpose of estate administration (as in the case of *Dewdon* and Cockington, above). We therefore suggest an ecological and economic rationale, not an administrative one. That this rationale was for transhumance is suggested by comparative evidence from other parts of England. In our discussion of this comparative evidence we shall begin with the example of Warwickshire where territories with detached parts have been studied in some detail and then move on to the Weald of south-eastern England where traces of transhumance and linked properties are strong and continuous from very early times; there then follows a briefer discussion of detached parts in a marshland environment, the Norfolk Broads.

The evidence for transhumance towards the wood-pastures of what later came to be called the 'Forest' of Arden in Warwickshire, as we have seen in chapter 1, was assembled by Ford.[74] He explored the link between Brailes, near the Stour (a tributary of the Avon), and Tanworth in Arden, 25 miles away, taking his cue from the seventeenth-century topographer Sir William Dugdale who had noted that the large amount of woodland listed in Domesday Book for Brailes was unlikely to have lain in that place, being 'for the most part champion' (i.e. open, not wooded) but was situated at Tanworth, a detached dependency of the main part of the manor.[75] Ford pointed out that Tanworth was regarded as a chapelry and hamlet belonging to Brailes in the twelfth and thirteenth centuries and was a detached part of the Hundred of Fexhole in which the parent settlement lay, pushing the link between the two places back before the Norman Conquest. Ford used Anglo-Saxon charters to demonstrate some of his linkages and also the evidence of linked place-names. He was convinced that the detached parts in Arden were being exploited on a seasonal basis and that the region was a 'striking area of transhumance' and, more recently, Della Hooke's detailed studies have led her to conclude that 'the linkage here may have been initially one of transhumance'.[76] It is all too easy to make an imaginary leap between territorial links and transhumance, but it is reasonable also to ask what the alternatives might have been. The lengths of the links between Arden and places in the lowlands of the Avon and its tributaries were relatively great in some cases and the use of the detached parts on a daily basis would not have been possible. The lowlands were ancient champion lands, almost certainly well cultivated and highly exploited before the Norman Conquest, as Hooke's studies of charter boundaries show. Pasture was scarce in these champion lands. By contrast, to judge from the evidence of place-names and Domesday Book, and also from the detailed studies of field systems in Arden (including the vicinity of Tanworth) made by Skipp and Roberts, the reverse applied in that region: colonisation had begun, but had not speeded up, in the late Saxon period and by about 1300 improved land still comprised only a multitude of small islands surrounded by seas of wood and heath.[77] This regional contrast was very marked and significant. It was of just that kind which, among a people highly skilled in observing, seeking out and making use of differences in resources, would have set in motion seasonal movements of their animals in search of pasture. Moreover, as Hooke has noted, there is a marked pattern of parallel lanes and tracks which all lead in a consistent direction towards Arden and which bear all the characteristics of droveways for animals, although they were no doubt also used for the carting of timber and faggots.

Detached, outlying territories in a wooded environment are best recorded for the Weald of Kent and Sussex and, of all English examples, these have been the most thoroughly studied and frequently noted. The earliest evidence is provided by place-names, as Stenton observed: for example, *Limenweara Wold*, *Weowera Weald* and *Tenetwaradenn* recall portions of the Weald belonging to Lyminge and Wye and the *denn* (woodland pasture for swine) of the people of Thanet. These Old-English names, all containing the element *wara*, must be of some antiquity because that element tends to occur in early names. Then, perhaps a little later than this first stratum in the evidence, there are pre-Conquest charters with their indisputable references to detached portions in the Weald. Thus in 814 Cenwulf, king of Mercia, gave Bexley to the See of Canterbury, his charter ending with a list of swine pastures, some of them in the Weald; in 804 St Augustine's Abbey at Canterbury received land at Lenham with thirteen swine pastures in the Weald 'belonging to that land by ancient right'—the links were already regarded as very old in the early ninth century. A further stratum in the evidence is added by Domesday Book's entries for Kent where some (but by no means all) of the detached Wealden swine pastures are enumerated under their parent manors, although the relevant information is unfortunately omitted from the other south-eastern counties with a share in the Weald. Post-Conquest manorial sources also refer to detached dens in the Weald and they also provide some evidence about how transhumance to that region was organised, about the movement of pigs and other animals together with their keepers.[78]

The Wealden evidence is important because it is continuous and comprehensive. It begins with early place-names, then continues with the evidence of pre-Conquest charters, Domesday Book and later sources; it is comprehensive because it speaks not only of detached parts, from which we may begin to infer transhumance, but also of the livestock movements themselves. In our final comparative example of detached manorial and parochial outliers, we turn to coastal matters and to the Norfolk Broads, the evidence for which is somewhat less complete than that from the Weald, but nevertheless seems satisfactory enough. The pattern shown in Fig. 4.13, based on the detailed work of Tom Williamson,[79] is one of inland parishes with detached parts, in many cases 5–6 miles away and adjoining the banks of the Rivers Bure, Yare and Waveney. Probably already in place by around 1100, at the very latest, these detached portions gave the people of the parent parishes access to a rich variety of resources which were not available inland and which were managed on a seasonal basis. Peat, clearly, was one and it was the exploitation of this commodity which has given the 'broads', rivers widened into placid pools by digging and which impart character to the region today and gave it its name. The detached parts also gave access to fisheries and salt pans. In this connection the evidence from the Broads has parallels on other coasts of England, in the South West for example, where there are coastal outliers or narrow tongue-like extensions of parishes reaching out to coast or estuary or river, the latter represented by Towednack (Cornwall), Stoke Fleming and Teigngrace (Devon) and Luccombe (Somerset), the former by several parishes or manors in Devon, of which one (Ottery St Mary) is recorded as early as 1061 and then again in 1086.[80] Finally, the detached portions in the Norfolk Broads gave inland manors access to sheep pastures on the marshes which supported large flocks according to the evidence of Domesday Book and all later sources. Here most of the distances between the detached parts and their respective parent manors are relatively short, although a few are of six miles or more, but nevertheless people from the inland parishes set up dependent buildings in the Broads, for example the 'cotes belonging to the ... marsh' recorded in a lease of 1494.[81] Place-names incorporating the element 'cot', used in A.H. Smith's sense of a 'shed for certain crafts or the manufacture or storage of materials' (salt, fish, barrels, boats, etc.),[82] and perhaps also serving as dwellings at certain times of the year, are frequently found along the coasts of England, Seacoats and Saltcoats being common names in coastal environments.

To sum up the comparative evidence, divided manors with 'home' cores and detached parts were to be found in many parts of England, giving the people who lived in the former access, at a remove, to a variety of resources which they did not have at home. In many cases they can be shown to have a respectable

4.13 Parishes with distant detachments in the marshes along the rivers Bure, Yare and Waveney, Norfolk and Suffolk. Based on T. Williamson, *The Norfolk Broads: A Landscape History* (Manchester, 1997), p. 45, Fig. 12.

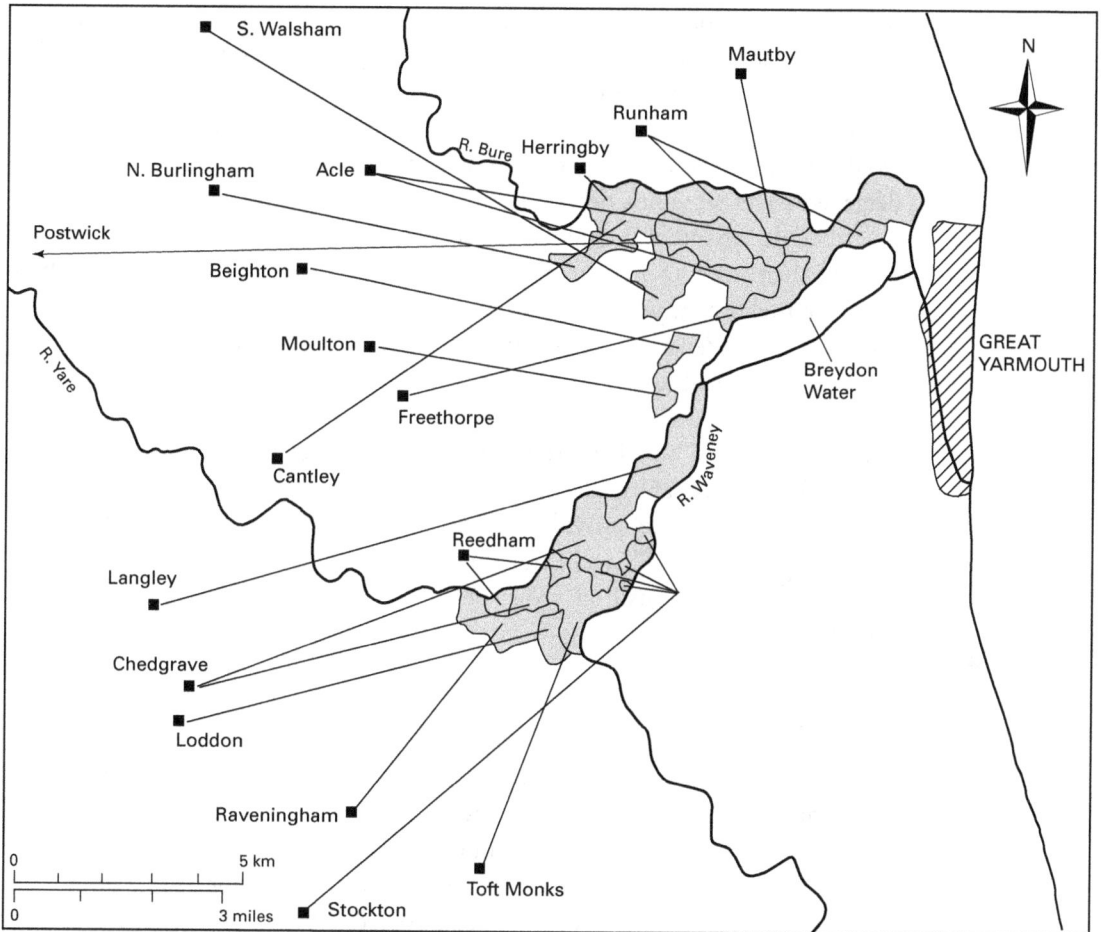

pedigree taking them back before the Norman Conquest, although it would be rash to claim a more remote, prehistoric ancestry for them. Where the detached parts lay at a distance too great for use on a daily basis and where the exploited resource was feed for livestock—pasture, wood-pasture, pannage—or coastal resources such as fish or salt, they set in motion seasonal movements of people, that is, transhumance.

Detached portions of land on Dartmoor belonging to manors many miles away were not necessary in order to give the people of down-country places common rights on the uplands. The status of the uplands as public pastures, common grazings for the whole shire, is very clear in all of the documentation: common rights on Dartmoor were strongly entrenched and never disputed (chapter 2). Moreover, the detached portions cannot have existed for the purpose of daily movements, the distances being too great; nor is it possible that they were toe-holds to give down-country places access to, say, rushes or bracken, for those commodities were too low in value to be brought very far. This being so, the only rationale for a detached part was to serve as a *pastoral base* for down-country people and their livestock living on the moors for the duration of the summer grazing season; the lowland manor was the home territory, the detached part was in the nature of a camp surrounded by its own pastures and from which further, daily, journeys might be made onto adjacent hills. The detached parts were not necessary in the system of impersonal transhumance described in chapters 2 and 3: under that system the owners of livestock handed them over to herdsmen-guardians and did not need a moorland base camp or toehold in which to live during the summer. This means that they represent an *older* type of arrangement, personal transhumance, involving seasonal settlement and tides of men (and/or women) as well as movements of livestock. They take us back to an ancient custom which, on Dartmoor, died out very long ago, but they are not the only evidence for it: information from archaeology, topography and place-names (and a single documentary reference to movement of people) provides additional glimpses of personal movements of people to the moors. This additional information is teased out in the following chapter, and the transition from personal to impersonal transhumance is discussed in chapter 6.

Conclusion

Important evidence for the earlier, impersonal phase of transhumance to Dartmoor can be found in a number of down-country manors which had detached territories on Dartmoor and its flanks. With a few exceptions these links cannot be documented for any earlier date than Domesday Book, and in some cases not until a century or two later, but they are likely to pre-date the Conquest considerably, and to have originated in a period when lowland communities exploited Dartmoor's pastures directly through seasonal satellite settlements (care must be taken to distinguish these connections, of an economic and agrarian nature, from merely tenurial links originating in seigneurial estate administration). Only a few such territorial detachments can be identified on Dartmoor (though parallels can be found in other parts of Britain, such as the Warwickshire Arden, the Weald of Kent and Sussex, and the Norfolk Broads), but those that survived into the late medieval period were doubtless only a fraction of a much larger number formerly in existence—once the seasonal settlements became permanent and the transition to impersonal transhumance had taken place many would have ceased to be subordinate to their down-country parent.

CHAPTER FIVE

Personal transhumance

Archaeology, topography, place-names and history

Transhumance in which people moved on to the upland to live with their livestock was still practised in parts of the British Isles in recent times, giving us detailed accounts of life on the hillsides.

> Talking about old customs, there is an old custom of which I heard as a lad and of which you hear no mention now, here or there, up or down. That is the practice which people had long ago of going to the mountain to pasture in the summer and returning home with their stock about November Day. At night the cattle were close around the shieling and when daybreak came the girls got up and herded them up on the hillside and they stayed there, quiet and peaceful all day until evening came. There was a nice stream coming down there from a lake which is on top of the hill, called Loch an Duine. In my mother's time the floors of the shielings were not made of flagstones or bricks. They cut a couple of loads of fresh green rushes and laid it thickly on the floor. Then they brought in the black sedge and piled it on top, to lift their beds high above the floor and the cold. The girls rose from these beds as fresh as trout. When they were going up from the homes to the shielings, the heavy things to be brought, such as the churns, tubs, cans and mugs, the men brought up all of those things on the backs of horses, except that each woman took her spinning wheel behind on her shoulders, and they were as airy as if they were going to a wedding. They had no earthenware crocks to hold the butter. It was all wooden vessels then and the vessels to store the butter were just like a cask or a stoup. The best of oak was in them. When the men were building the shielings they made other little houses too like caves and no matter what heat came in the summer the butter inside would be hard as an icicle as in winter. A girl who went to the pastures and was in the shieling usually took care of more cows than those of her own father. She might be in charge of the stock of three or four households. The grazing was very good up there. I heard the old people saying that in those days the grass was up to the animals' ears. When the

potatoes were dug [on the home farms] and the harvest gathered in, and all that done, then they brought down the cattle. [In the shielings] they had good salt fish from Tory Island in those days, and lots of sweet milk. That was their dinner. The girls had plenty of work to do. They began to card the wool and to spin and knit it, and worked away like that until the time for coming home. Occasionally the young men came up from their neighbourhood far away, and they had a nice merry night, with their own music and dancing and fun. My mother would tell us that long ago in the shieling she heard the song from this one or that, some from fine boys who went to America and were killed in the Civil War and never more returned. When they were on the hillside one girl could keep her eye on all of the cattle there.

The summer pasturing continued in this district until my mother was twenty years or more. That was about ninety years ago [i.e. *c*.1850]. I heard her say that the last summer was the most beautiful and pleasurable they ever had.

About that time a mine of silver was found up there and hundreds of miners were brought over from England to work the place. The fathers and mothers of the girls thought it was not good enough to have their young daughters on the same shoulder of the hills as these miners from England, for although some of those were good, dependable, respectable, there were others who were not.[1]

This evocative and very full account relates to County Donegal in the middle of the nineteenth century and is introduced here simply to guide our discussion of personal transhumance to Dartmoor in the centuries before the Norman Conquest—for which the topographical evidence has been discussed in the previous section.

Archaeology and topography

The seasonal dwellings at Hound Tor

The attention given by the narrator from Donegal to the making of dwellings at the shieling reminds us that personal transhumance involves seasonal habitation on uplands by the owners of the livestock and, for Dartmoor, we are lucky to have one site where some of the structures associated with that custom have been excavated, at Hound Tor in Manaton parish (Plates 10–12). The landscape of settlement at Hound Tor is a palimpsest, so we must first strip away the later phase of permanent occupation which has partially obscured the earlier one of seasonal use. The life of the permanent settlement came to an end by stages towards the end of the fourteenth century. At its prime of life the settlement was small: in Sandy Gerrard's words, it is 'often described as a village but . . .

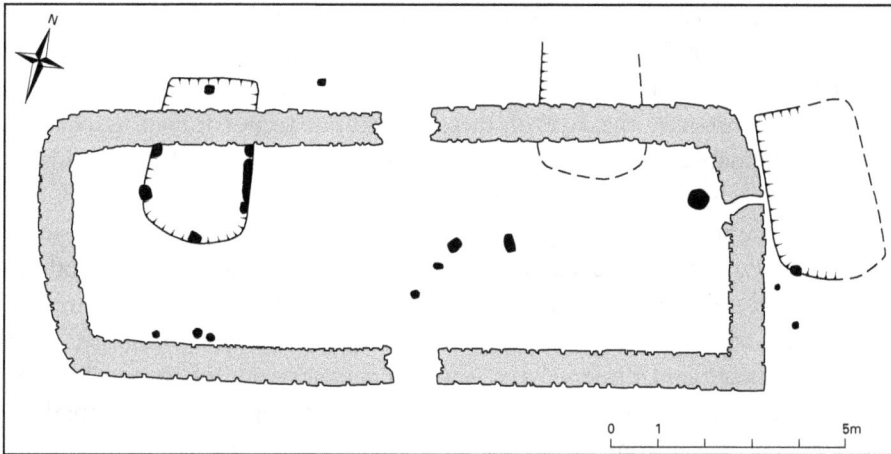

5.1 Three sunken-floored huts at Hound Tor underlying a thirteenth-century longhouse.

Based on G. Beresford, 'Three deserted medieval settlements on Dartmoor: a report on the late E. Marie Minter's excavations', *Medieval Archaeology* 23 (1979), pp. 98–159, Fig. 7.

[is really] a hamlet', containing four stone-built longhouses, four smaller dwellings and some associated agricultural buildings including three corn-drying kilns for removing moisture from grain harvested in damp conditions. About 300 yards away is a subsidiary settlement, a single farmstead with one longhouse and three associated agricultural buildings. Clear traces of an arable field system are associated with the main settlement, testifying, along with the kilns, to cultivation of cereals at this remote site in its final phase. Most would now agree that the permanent settlement and its field system were created in the thirteenth century and, remote, high (1200 feet) and on thin soils derived from granite, this island of cultivation in a sea of moor is therefore excellent testimony to pressure of population at that time.[2]

The thirteenth-century structures at Hound Tor were completely excavated by Mrs E. Marie Minter and her team in the 1960s. Central to the subject of this book, and sealed beneath one of the thirteenth-century building, the sealing so well illustrated in Fig. 5.1 (and see Plate 10), were three sunken-floored huts which Guy Beresford, the author of the excavation report, described as shielings, that is, as seasonally occupied pastoral huts. They were set into the growan (decomposed granite) by a few inches, never exceeding nine, they had rounded corners and were of uniform size. Two had hearths but the third did not. They were remarkably small, roughly 12 feet long and 7 feet wide. The excavators found that the fill of the sunken floors was of decomposed turf, possibly indicating that the walls had been made partially of that material, with some timber, suggested by slots and post-holes dug into the growan. Opposing post-holes in one hut show that the roof had a ridge piece but about the roofing material we can only speculate: hides, which could be removed for the winter when the huts were not in use, are a possibility; there is also a tradition on Dartmoor of roofing in rushes, heather and bracken.

In his report, Guy Beresford was convinced that the sunken-floored huts at Hound Tor were seasonally used herdsmen's dwellings, and that view has never been challenged. It seems all the more likely given the wealth of evidence for transhumance to Dartmoor which is now gathered together in this book. Moreover, the size of these structures argues for an association with transhumance, for the custom often involved a division of labour within the family, each unit sending up one member to the summer pastures, and Peter Herring has strongly argued the case for single occupancy of the small, stone-built huts which he has discovered on the open pastures of Bodmin Moor (Plate 13). Fig. 5.2 shows a plan of the best preserved of the sunken-floored huts at Hound Tor and, for comparison, plans of other buildings used in transhumance and designed for single occupancy: one of several huts on Brockabarrow Common on Bodmin Moor, an example from Cumberland and a booley house from Achill Island, off the west coast of Ireland. Further comparison is invited by plans of two permanently occupied medieval dwellings designed for whole families: a thirteenth-century longhouse from Hound Tor itself and a substantial fifteenth-century farmhouse from Chilverton, in the Culm Measures countryside to the north of Dartmoor. The difference between the spaces occupied by single people on the one hand and families on the other are strikingly demonstrated here.[3]

The sunken-floored nature of the huts at Hound Tor lends some support to the view that they were used by people engaged in transhumance because there are good parallels at sites which had similar economies. Three English examples are instructive. One is from the parish of North Marden, Sussex, where a single sunken-floored building was excavated, of early or middle Anglo-Saxon date, and having two opposing post-holes at each end to support a ridge-piece for the roof, as at Hound Tor. It was on hilly ground and distant from the present-day village. The dimensions were 8 feet by 8 feet and the excavators were surprised to discover no other similar huts nearby, because such structures are 'seldom found individually', that is, other excavated examples are usually parts of proto-villages. The context of the hut is interesting, because North Marden is on the South Downs, a region where transhumance was practised in the past. At Salmonby, Lincolnshire, a single sunken-floored hut was excavated in 1972, measuring about 13 feet long and a little less wide and at some distance from the present-day village. The location is again highly significant, for it is on the Lincolnshire Wolds, a region used for transhumance in the Anglo-Saxon period, as I have argued elsewhere. If we interpret the hut in the context of transhumance, then difficulties which place-name scholars have had with the name Salmonby, a Scandinavian name in -by belonging to a settlement where earlier Anglo-Saxon ceramics have been found, almost disappear: we can now say that the earlier English settlement was for seasonal use and its pastures were taken over in the ninth century for permanent settlement by Scandinavian immigrants who re-named it. One other excavated sunken-floored building is highly significant,

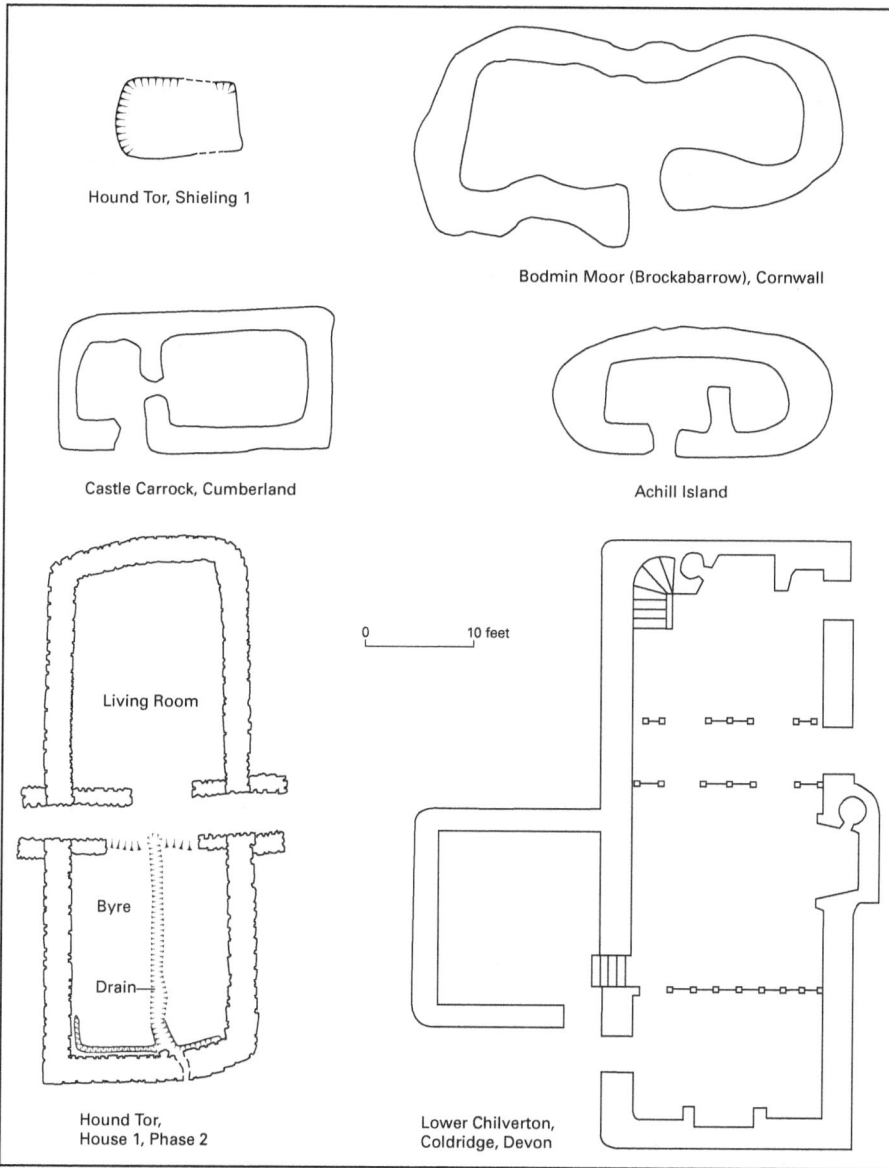

5.2 A transhumance hut from Hound Tor with comparisons.

All drawn to the same scale.

Sources: see text, n. 3.

because it comes from our adjacent county, Cornwall. It is near Stencoose (St Agnes) on the once extensive downlands of that parish. The hut's dimensions are 18 by 19 feet; a little larger than the Hound Tor and Bodmin Moor huts, but its radio-carbon dates were from the fifth to eleventh centuries, a period during which we know, from place-name evidence, that transhumance was practised in Cornwall. All of the parallels discussed above strongly support Guy Beresford's interpretation of the structures at Hound Tor as 'shielings', though that North Country word is rather a misfit in the South West. It is interesting to note the widespread use of sunken-floored huts by people involved with transhumance in Basse Alsace, the Auvergne and Switzerland, where some of these structures were seasonally occupied by livestock keepers and others served as cool stores for butter and cheese.[4]

The dating of the sunken-floored huts at Hound Tor is not really affected by the debate about the chronology of the permanent settlement of longhouses. We need not go over the debate in detail here, but simply say that the long sequence of successive rebuildings proposed by Guy Beresford on the basis of alignments of post-holes has now been discredited by work from three directions—re-excavation, palaeoenvironmental study of peat deposits from a site very close to the settlement, and new comparative research on ceramics found at the site and also at other deserted settlements on Dartmoor. All concur in giving the longhouses a thirteenth-century date, which fits in well with what we know of pressure of population at that time. The sunken-floored huts are sealed below the longhouses of the permanently occupied, if short-lived, settlement and must therefore be earlier than it. Sunken-floored huts have long been discussed in the literature and Hamerow's recent survey of England and north-west Europe more generally concluded that they were not much used after the tenth century, although there were no doubt pockets of survival later than that, among people who were used to traditional customs, and in out-of-the-way places. The same dating applies to the demise of round-cornered huts. For Hound Tor, where no ceramic evidence was found to date these structures, all that we can say is that it is likely that they belong to the Saxon period although they may have survived in seasonal use a little longer than that.[5]

It is a characteristic of research into this early phase of transhumance on Dartmoor that the evidence is patchy and sporadic. For Hound Tor the archaeological record for the three huts is excellent, as we have seen, but documentary evidence which might tell us about the parent manor of this seasonal settlement is non-existent. Moreover, the archaeological record begs some questions. For example, was the hamlet (and its nearby single farm) only one of a number of seasonally used sites belonging to its parent manor in the down-country? In other words, was it part of a local system of seasonally occupied settlements which may have co-operated to some degree in managing the pastures? To answer those questions we turn to another territory in the parish of Manaton (in which Hound Tor is situated), the territory of Heatree, reconstructed speculatively in the following paragraphs as it was in its early stages.

The seasonal phase of settlement at Heatree: a reconstruction
The territory known as Heatree, at least in later documents, lay in Manaton parish, as did Hound Tor, and was separated from the latter by the tor itself and the great hill of Hayne Down. It was a detached part of the manor of

Kenton on the shore of the Exe, and earlier we have argued that the rationale of these detached portions was for transhumance. We have detailed rentals of this territory from the sixteenth century onwards and we can therefore reconstruct the sites of the farms within it (Fig. 5.3). In bringing this map to bear upon the settlement landscape associated with the phase of personal transhumance, one speculative leap in method must be made: we must imagine that the later permanently occupied farms were on the sites of the earlier seasonally occupied settlements associated with that phase. This seems a very reasonable suggestion, given the sequence at Hound Tor and elsewhere in England. Moreover, common sense would suggest that a colonist creating a permanently occupied farm would place it on a previously seasonally used

5.3 Early modern farms in the territory of Heatree.

site because there the land was well manured, night and day, by livestock brought to it through transhumance.[6]

The spacing of the settlement sites is regular and is determined by the availability of low-lying land, some of it meadowland. The territory later called Heatree contains a great deal of hilly ground, 'very poor, cold and hungry ground, full of rocks and naturally heathy' according to a survey of around 1690, by which time the phase of seasonal use had long been replaced by permanent occupation; it contains 'some of the wildest scenery of Dartmoor' according to a nineteenth-century directory.[7] The survey adds that 'there are some meadows between the hills' and these may be identified in the field as follows: in the east an undulating patch served by several headwaters of the Hayne Brook, now

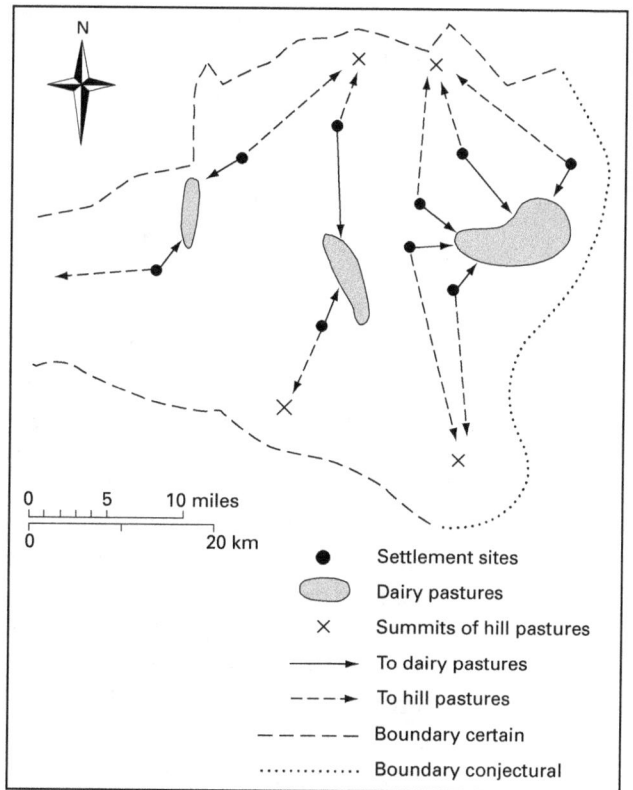

slightly diverted so as to follow field boundaries, and, in the west, three small, elongated patches along streams, both of which (today at least) have small pools suitable as watering places. On a recent visit, I was told by playwright Mark Beeson, the occupier of a farm here, that one of the wet patches is known as 'Frogs Parlour' and that he could recall seeing, as a boy, cows splashing about in its cool, lush pasture. The low-lying land and meadows have been reconstructed on Fig. 5.3 where they are called 'dairy pastures'. There is clearly a relationship between settlement sites and meadows, because five of the settlements cluster around the largest patch while all but one of the others relate to the two smaller ones. Here, on the best grassland, partly overflown in winter and receiving the first flush of new springing grass in springtime, dairy cattle would have grazed: evidence of dairying at seasonally used sites on Dartmoor is presented in the following section. In all probability the meadows were managed communally by the occupiers of the sites nearest to them: that is what the map seems to suggest.

Behind each of the settlement sites lie rounded hills, some over 1,300 feet, the 'heathy' land of the survey of around 1690, and here the grass is poorer than in the meadows and the growing season starts later. The survey makes it quite clear that each of the hills was regarded as the territory of particular farms, and this would probably have been the case in the phase of seasonal occupation. We may therefore reconstruct a little of the pastoral management of this detached territory, a sophisticated but common-sense allocation of time and space between common cores of meadowland, where dairy cattle were carefully supervised and where stocking density was highest, and hillslopes, where other livestock, probably sheep, grazed at lower density and with less supervision (Fig. 5.3): 'when daybreak came, the girls got up and herded . . . [the cattle] up on the hillside and they stayed there, quiet and peaceful all day until evening came' (from the Donegal account given above). It may well have been that, in this phase of transhumance, dairy cattle were led up from the parent manor of Kenton earlier in the season than other livestock, because of differing times in first grass growth, between the meadowlands and the hillslopes.

Settlement sites in this territory are remarkably similar in terms of their altitude, for all are at between 900 and 1,100 feet on the slopes of hills which rise to 1,300 to 1,400 feet. Need for shelter and need for access to water, for humans and animals alike and for dairying, were in part responsible for siting. In addition, and perhaps a paramount consideration, is the visibility of the pastures. Peter Herring has noted how panoramic views are essential for buildings associated with transhumance and this is no doubt another reason for the siting of the seasonally used settlements shown in Fig. 5.3.[8] They are low down on relatively gentle slopes, each having a good, close outlook on dairy cows in the meadows below them, now hedged but, in the phase of seasonal settlement, presumably unhedged and therefore all the more visible; and also panoramic, sweeping views of the hillslope above where, weather permitting, the figures in our reconstructed landscape could observe other livestock at their grazings.

Seasonal settlement at Cudlipp: a reconstruction

We follow our reconstruction of seasonally used sites in Heatree by another of the territory of Cudlipp, named from one of the settlement sites within it.[9] It was the moorland appendage of Tavistock (as discussed in chapter 4), and for it we have lists of permanently occupied farms and hamlets in documents from the fourteenth century to the eighteenth. Again, we have no documentary evidence of an antecedent phase of seasonal use, nor any archaeological record, for none of the sites has been excavated, but given the proven sequence from seasonal to permanent settlement at Hound Tor, that sequence is likely also in the territory called Cudlipp. Moreover, we have argued earlier that these moorland detachments were for seasonal use. Later we shall argue that dairying was important at seasonally used sites and in this connection it is significant that three places in the territory of Cudlipp have names incorporating Old-English words for dairy products.

As at Heatree, the territory of Cudlipp was a mixture of rough hillslope pasture and lusher lower-lying land fed by streams. Of the latter there were two main blocks and three outliers. Recently I visited both of the main ones. The northern, roughly oval, block is large, gently sloping and well watered, with many springs from which would once have issued winding rivulets, although these have now been straightened for improvement. It would have been ideal as a dairy pasture. The area is much esteemed today and has been greatly improved through re-seeding; field boundaries have been removed, to give it a rather stark appearance. It was bare of livestock when I saw it in very early April: they would come later. The elongated southern block is scenically much more attractive, a valley enlivened by much wood, good grass and more frequent field boundaries although there has also been some removal of these here. As at Heatree, the largest block attracted a ring of seasonally used settlements around it, all in positions to supervise animals grazing on it. The smaller blocks were also overlooked by settlements, though for each there were fewer of them.

On the most northerly of the hillslope pastures, also now improved, a large flock of sheep was being driven on that bright April day, making the point that different types of livestock have their different seasons: cattle were not yet out on the lusher pastures but hardier sheep were already on the hillslope. I gained the impression that they had just arrived. As at Heatree distinct areas of these hillslopes would have been regarded as the territory of a particular farm.

Following from this discussion of the siting of seasonally used settlements in the detached territories of Kenton and Cudlipp, we may recall the site of Hound Tor. Recently I revisited the site. 'I had been there before,' first with my mother 'on a cold, cloudless day in April', as an eager young research student, then on many other occasions—'and though I had been there so often, in so many moods, it was to that first visit that my heart returned on this, my latest.'[10] Coming over the flank of the tor itself, I noticed how the cold wind ceased, and we saw below us the settlement in its gentle green col, a perfect situation for a pastoral outpost. From the settlement itself may be viewed all the south-eastern flanks of Hound Tor itself and also the north-western ones of Greator Rocks, while a short walk uphill brings into view another good, flat grazing ground. Downhill from the settlement are two springs for water supply and these feed a patch of land which is now a marsh overgrown with scrub, but which would once have been meadow, supplying good pasture as well as rushes for floor-covering, as in the account from Donegal given above. It is noticeable that, once at the marsh, the panoramas are largely lost, so that is why the settlement was not sited there. All of the sites which we have been discussing (in the territories of Heatree and Cudlipp and at Hound Tor) were chosen with visual command over grazing animals in mind, as stressed in the account from Donegal given above.

Place-names and history: economy and society

Many aspects of transhumance to Dartmoor in its personal phase must remain obscure because the custom came to an end so long ago, in general by the eleventh century. We are on our surest ground with the structures and settlements discussed above and with their specialised pastoral economies, to which we now turn. We should not necessarily expect that the types of livestock kept at these settlements were the same as those which were taken to Dartmoor under the impersonal system, in which dairying was out of the question because the number of cattle was so great and the number of people employed to look after them was too small for the labour-intensive tasks of milking and of making dairy produce; under that system Dartmoor became a land of steers and herdsmen (chapter 2). In the earlier phase of personal transhumance, place-names quite clearly indicate that dairying was one object of the custom; the names thus take their place alongside our reconstruction above of the cores of meadowland in Heatree, the detached part of Kenton manor, and one of the sunken-floored huts at Hound Tor which had no hearth and may be interpreted as a store for dairy produce. There are no practical objections to the idea of dairying in this remote region: butter could be stored away in cool caches, as in the Irish account given above, expertly placed in wooden or earthenware containers like those which Risdon noted later, commenting that Devon butter potted better than any other. The butter could be sold to down-country farms not involved with transhumance, especially to those with few dairy cattle and especially for winter use; there were five urban settlements in late Saxon Devon, exerting a demand for this product.[11]

Butter-making: smeoru

When we consider the faint figures engaged in dairying on Dartmoor when transhumance was in its first, personal, phase, three place-name elements are relevant, *smeoru* and *butere*, both meaning 'butter', and *wic*, 'dairy farm'. I first encountered *smeoru* when researching the detached part of Hurdwick (Tavistock) manor, for in it is a place called Smeardon Down. Looking the name up in *The Place-names of Devon* I found that it 'was probably applied to the hill because it gave rich pasturage', *smeoru*, 'butter, implying good grazing', plus *dun*, 'hill or down' plus another tautological down.[12] It is always exciting for the researcher when two quite different types of evidence reinforce one another: in this case my mind raced towards the idea that the detached parts of down-country manors on Dartmoor were used for dairying, and that idea will be followed up below. Subsequently, researching droveways to the north of Dartmoor, I came across Smerdon Down in Inwardleigh parish. It is not in *The Place-names of Devon*, probably because the researchers for that work could find no early forms for it. This repetition of a name in *smeoru*, on the west and north flanks of Dartmoor, made me interested in the element and, thanks to a data-base which is being compiled for *The Vocabulary of English Place-names*, I was able to compile and publish a list of English names which incorporate the word.[13]

The national list of place-names containing the element *smeoru* is not complete because in general it is based on the county volumes of the English Place-name Society, whose survey is still ongoing. In all it contains twenty-one names, ranging from Smerrill Grange in Derbyshire (plus *hyll*, 'hill') to Smarden in Kent (plus *denn*, 'wood pasture'). Three points may be made about this corpus. First, names in *smeoru* are rarely combined with words meaning 'valley', for example *cumb* or *denu*. Second, they are rarely combined with words which have pastoral connotations, for example *feld*, 'open pasture', *haeth*, 'heath', or *moed*, 'meadow' which might be expected if 'good pasturage' was the meaning; Smarden in Kent is the only exception. Third, when inspected on the map and in the field, places with names containing this element have the appearance of being on inferior, not 'good', land. This certainly applies to one of our Dartmoor places in *smeoru*, Smeardon Down in Peter Tavy parish: Tom Greeves writes to say that the hill 'is exceedingly rocky, so highly doubtful as good pasture (it may be a Dartmoor joke, of course)'. Inspection in the field confirms that it is full of rocks, with some scrub, its slopes unlike the smooth and verdant ones of adjacent hills.

The word *smeoru* clearly means something which is smeared or spread. *OED* under 'smear' gives 'fat, grease, lard; ointment', citing sources from the eighth century onwards. A.H. Smith also gives 'fat, grease, lard' but adds 'butter' from the evidence of the word *smeoru-mangestre*, one *que mangonant in caseo et butiro*. E. Ekwall, from a country where *smør* means butter today, gives that for OE *smeoru*.[14] Where the word occurs in place-names (except habitative ones) it is usually translated as 'rich pasturage' (Smith) or 'good grazing' (Ekwall).[15] Meanings of this type are given in the county volumes of the English Place-name Society and in most national dictionaries of place-names, and there are also some rather strange interpretations, for example 'land so productive that the farmer can expect to live on butter'.[16] Margaret Gelling gives 'butter hill' for Smerrill (Derbyshire), coming closer to the literal interpretation which will be proposed in this paper, but only A.D. Mills makes a thoroughly literal translation, 'woodland pasture where butter is produced' for Smarden (Kent).[17]

If a name like Smeardon means 'hill on the flanks of which butter is produced', what then was the historical context of this practice? We shall suggest here that the context was that of transhumance in which the making of dairy products could not have been carried out in the diminutive hutlets associated with the custom but was done in the open air. The excavated sunken-floored huts at Hound Tor on Dartmoor were far too small for both sleeping and dairying, and this would have applied also to still visible huts on Bodmin Moor which were used by people engaged in transhumance, and to similar structures which have been excavated or observed elsewhere in England. The hutlets at Hound Tor (Fig. 5.2) are about 12 feet long and 7 feet wide, approximately the same dimensions as a structure noticed by Estyn Evans in the Mourne Mountains (Northern Ireland); likewise, in Cumberland and Northumberland the simplest huts at shieling sites were no more than 10 feet long and smaller in width; on Bodmin Moor some huts probably used for transhumance are roughly square in shape, 12–13 feet by 12–13.[18] Other examples have been mentioned above (Fig. 5.2). Dairying would have been difficult in these structures, which were barely large enough to house some bedding for a single person and a few personal possessions. Dairying required several pails and pots and also a churn, which was a reasonably large piece of equipment; there is good evidence for it from Saxon Devon, namely from the vessel of one of the Exeter riddles, into which the strapping churl 'thrust something stiff'.[19] Because of the small size of the huts associated with transhumance, these implements were used and stored in the open air.

The idea that names in *smeoru* are associated with transhumance is supported by Cornish and Welsh evidence. In Cornwall, *amanen*, 'butter', especially when combined with words for hills, 'is connected with the custom of making butter on the summer pastures when transhumance was a common form of husbandry'. In Wales, Nant Manyn (Carmarthenshire, from Welsh *nant* plus *ymenyn*, 'butter valley') has been described as a place of 'butter production' associated with 'transhumant dairying activity'.[20] Turning to England, almost all of the places in the corpus of names in *smeoru* were in regions in which transhumance was practised in the past. A Westmorland example comes from a county where transhumance is well documented and was first described in print in a short but graphic description in William Camden's *Britannia*. It has also been much studied by historians and geographers.[21] Others come from the Weald and North Downs of Kent and Sussex where transhumance has been studied by Witney and Everitt respectively, and from Yorkshire and Gloucestershire where there is also evidence for the custom. We can now understand why a great proportion of names in *smeoru* have a second element which means 'hill'. Seasonally occupied settlements were on the hills, permanent ones down below.

Butter-making: butere

Butere occurs in twelve Devon place-names, six of which are near or on Dartmoor or Exmoor, the latter also being a region where transhumance was practised.[22] Of the five Dartmoor names, four are of hills, the same preponderance of hill names which we found nationally with *smeoru*.[23] The authors of *The Place-names of Devon* conclude that, where it is compounded with a topographical term, *butere* 'may refer to land which provided good pasturage'.[24] Similar interpretations are given by those who have considered the element nationally: for example, 'rich pasture which produced good butter', 'apparently complimentary, referring to rich pasture'.[25] In other words, we have the same type of interpretation which is encountered with *smeoru*. So confident are these writers about the non-literal meaning of *butere* in place-names that when they encounter it combined with a word for water, they come up with some bizarre interpretations. Thus in the name Butterford (North Huish and Inwardleigh parishes, south and north of Dartmoor respectively) the element 'may have had some reference to the appearance or colour of the water'.[26] I have been to the former place and the water is not yellow, nor is it of greasy appearance. Moreover, the ford is very close to a droveway, leading off Dartmoor, down which butter could have been carried.[27] *Smeoru* when combined with water words is usually treated in the same way as *butere*: thus Smorel (Warwickshire), *smeoru* plus *wiell* ('well'), 'must have had reference to the colour or appearance of the water'. In a few cases, of course, this may possibly have been the meaning: Paul Cullen writes to me, of Smersole (Kent, *smeoru* plus *sol*, 'soil'), where a pond nearby is 'the most mucky, slimy, bubbling and vile example of a *sol*' that he has ever visited.[28]

If we are right about *smeoru* nationally (see above), some names in *butere* combined with a topographical term should also refer to places where butter was made. It should be added that personal observation and local opinion do not suggest that the Dartmoor hills with names in *butere* support better pasture than adjacent summits and slopes; they form a ring around the border of Dartmoor and are markedly poorer than the lower lands which surrounded the Moor, as evidenced, for example, by medieval land values. These names cannot have been coined in connection with butter-making at the later permanently settled farms which eventually developed at the feet of the hills, for that activity would have been carried out indoors, for example in the kitchen end of a longhouse.[29]

Dairying: wic

Wic is a common place-name element in Devon. Nationally, *wic* is very often compounded with elements relating to dairying, for example Butterwick (many counties) and Cheswick, Chiswick or Keswick (cheese, many counties). A Cowick (Devon and other counties) was clearly a dairy farm while Gatwick (goats, Surrey) and Shapwick or Shopwick (sheep, several counties) were also places specialising in dairying, for milk was an important produce from goats and sheep.[30] There are numerous names in *wic* along the Essex coast, some of them in detached parts of manors, and these produced the large Essex cheeses the nastiness of which was sung by Piers Plowman and John Skelton.[31] On the marshland manors of Glastonbury Abbey were tenants known as *wicarii* who rented land and cows from the lord and, presumably, paid him back with dairy produce.[32] Writing on *wic*, Ekwall concluded that 'probably the most common meaning is "dairy farm"' and this is echoed by A.H. Smith. *Wic* in place-names has many other meanings and 'dairy farm' is simply one of a sub-set which imply a settlement with a particular specialisation. In a recent discussion of the element, Richard Coates concluded that one of its meanings was '"farm specialising in some product" or "in animals yielding produce", in other words, not a subsistence farm, which requires ... minimal diversification'. Another meaning, he writes, is 'camp, temporary encampment', a place of 'discontinuous occupation'. This is fascinating, for if we put the two meanings together we have a dairy settlement seasonally used by people engaged in the custom of transhumance.[33]

In Devon there are two names in *wic* very close to Exeter, Exwick and Cowick, whose people must have supplied the Anglo-Saxon inhabitants of Exeter with milk (we find the same near other early towns).[34] Some Devon names containing this element are pastoral farms or hamlets way out in their parishes near the boundary, such as Week in Burrington which retained its pastoral specialisation quite late, as shown by a poem coined by the people of the parish's other settlements to describe their rude and remote neighbours:

Out to Week beneath the trees,
Barley bread and vinid cheese,
Risty bacon as thick as a thong,
That's how Week boys git along.[35]

Dartmoor and its surroundings have a greater concentration of names in *wic* than any other region in Devon.[36] Altogether there are twenty of them, including, for example, Runnage (Lydford, Renewych in 1317) and Weeks-in-the-Moor (Beaworthy); Cholwich and nearby Bromage (Bromwic in 1249, both in Cornwood), the former, 'the coldest *wic*', being higher and more exposed than the latter. Spitchwick (Widecombe in the Moor) is, as we have seen, 'the settlement of the fat-bacon people', the first element, *spic*, being very rare in English place-names,[37] Fuidge (Spreyton, La Fowych in 1289) is the 'cattle *wic*'. Stickwick (Bovey Tracy) bemused the editors of *The Place-names of Devon*, but the first element, probably Old English *sticca*, may refer to the flimsy nature of the walls of huts occupied only in the summer, perhaps akin to those observed near Newry (Ireland) in 1690, made of hurdles and removed in winter.[38]

For two of Dartmoor's names in *wic* we have some evidence of date. One, Spitchwick, named in the Domesday Book, was discussed in the previous chapter because it was a detached part of a down-country manor, its pastoral place-name reinforcing our conclusion that these detachments were for the purpose of personal transhumance, as with Smeardon in Peter Tavy (above, p. 148), also a detached part. Its name is evidence for the driving of pigs to distant woodlands for the mast season and, presumably, for other forage before that time; the practice is well known from other parts of Anglo-Saxon England.

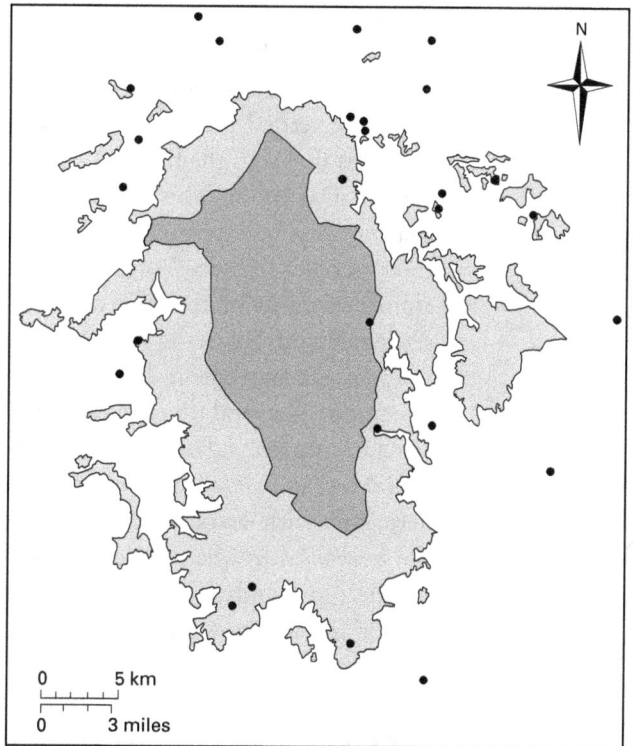

5.4 Distribution of placenames relating to dairying.

The area of the manor is still well wooded today, especially the steep slopes down to the River Webburn where, in the Saxon period, when the name was coined, we must envisage structures similar to the 'respectable house' in a wood which the pig-keeper of Christow was expected to build and inhabit in 1521. We can push this seasonally occupied, specialised pastoral settlement well back before the Norman Conquest because by the date of Domesday Book it had had time to develop into a normal small manor with a demesne, slaves on the demesne, ploughlands, villains and smallholders, the last no doubt attacking the woodland edge; perhaps significantly no pig-men are recorded here, as they are for a number of Devon manors.[39] The other name in *wic* for which dating is possible is Runnage (spelled Renewych in 1317) because it is compounded with an Old English personal name, Raegna, of a type which was becoming exceedingly rare by, say, 1130 and is probably much older than that.[40]

Distribution of dairying place-names

The distribution of place-names relating to dairying is shown on Fig. 5.4. The dating evidence discussed above pushes at least some of these settlements back in time into at least the late Saxon period, when personal transhumance was still the custom. The names are another important strand in the evidence for that custom. Many of these names are within the parishes which, with their outer moors, touch on the central hub. The map also shows a ring of pastoral names which are today some way away from the moorland edge, in the next rung of parishes, such as Fuidge in Spreyton parish and Smerdon Down in Inwardleigh, discussed above. Could it be that these represent the moorland edge at some distant time in the past? It is not possible to answer this question, which must remain a speculation.

Droveways

We can see society on the move towards the seasonally used settlements, on one occasion directly and very clearly, in other cases more obliquely. Figures on the move, the seasonal ebb and flow of transhumance, are directly referred to in a Saxon charter of 1031 which mentions, somewhere in one of the manors of Meavy, 'the highway of the dwellers of Buckland', using the word *saete* for those settled people seasonally on the move. Buckland is a manor which stretches down to the bank of the River Tavy and is about four miles from the edge of Dartmoor. This is too far for daily movements with livestock, so the charter must be interpreted as referring to seasonal movement among some of these people; the 'way' of Buckland's people into the heart of Dartmoor was almost certainly on the same course as the present-day road linking the modern settlements of Yelverton and Princetown.[41]

Frequent movement by the people of a down-country manor towards Dartmoor—several times in early summer with livestock of different types, the same in autumn and other contacts in between—must have led to certain tracks becoming associated with certain people; we are not dealing with ownership here, but with association by frequent use. Cockingford (above p. 111) was the ford used by the people of Cocca who also gave his name to Cockington on the coast and lies directly on a determined droveway linking the coastal manor and its known detached part on Dartmoor, analysed later in this book. Colesworthy, formerly *Chauelesweye* in Ilsington parish, is now the name of a settlement but means 'the way of Cafel', an individual who occurs again in Keyberry near the River Teign. *Chauelesweye* is on a straight line leading from Keyberry to the edge of Dartmoor and on a track which comes to be called Green Lane as it nears the moorland. Pinchaford, 'the ford of Puneca', also in Ilsington, must be on a droveway between lost place-names south of Ashburton, named as *Puneces worthi* in an eleventh-century document, and Dartmoor.[42] The two are about four miles apart, and above Pinchaford there are swelling moorland slopes which lead on to Haytor and Hound Tor. The tracks we have been discussing relate directly to the phase of personal transhumance. Cocca, our first figure, must go back to before the Norman Conquest, perhaps well before, because by 1066 Cockington had come to be owned by a person called Alric; Cafel and Puneca are names not likely to have been in use after the eleventh century. The tracks or droveways we return to in chapter 7, where their impact on the landscape is discussed. There were many of them—they form a multiplex pattern made up of many parallel strands—and more may once have been named after particular people. Many of these names became lost when personal transhumance was replaced by the later, impersonal, type—a development to be discussed soon in the following chapter.

Social composition of transhumant groups

The names discussed above show figures on the move, but the social composition of the groups who undertook personal transhumance is difficult to establish. In our reconstruction above of seasonally occupied settlements in Heatree, a detached part of the coastal manor of Kenton, nine sites were identified. In Domesday Book forty tenants are recorded on Kenton manor,[43] so we should envisage a degree of co-operation at home in the choice of which members from the community should make the summer journey, a single individual taking to Dartmoor the cows of more than one farm in the down-country: a girl 'might be in charge of the cows of three or four households' (from the Donegal account). Kenton manor had many scattered hamlets, a type of settlement which was the basis of small-scale, intensely local co-operation, so we might expect that the choice was made at the level of the hamlet. Once on Dartmoor the chosen delegates would have needed to co-operate, for example in managing livestock on the best pasture which many of the sites overlooked; co-operation between shieling settlements was a feature of the custom where it survived in Britain relatively late in the day. We have used the word 'delegates' for these figures for lack of more precise knowledge. One thing which is certain is that it was not the custom for whole families to move to Dartmoor for the duration of the transhumance season, for the size of the sunken-floored huts at Hound Tor is against that interpretation: they were for single occupancy, as Peter Herring has always argued for similar buildings on Bodmin Moor, each having space enough only for a 'bed, open fire and some storage'.[44]

Maidens

Of the gender of the occupants we can only speculate, noting that transhumance was in the female domain where it lingered to recent times in Scotland and Ireland (as in the Donegal account given above); and that the management of steers and oxen was traditionally in the male domain (especially management of immature stock such as those described as 'wild' in a fourteenth-century inquisition from a Devon manor)[45] while dairying, on the other hand, was a female occupation as far back as we can trace it in medieval and Anglo-Saxon documents. Some English place-names incorporating Old English *maegden*, 'a maiden', have locations where we might strongly suspect an association with transhumance. A.H. Smith gives examples of place-names in which the word is compounded with *leah* (wood), *dun* (hill), and *cot* (humble dwelling), all of these words making good sense in the context of transhumance. He was writing at a time when the custom was not much studied in England and he did not consider seasonal occupation by maidens as a possible explanation. One of his suggested meanings, 'something that has never been taken', could well apply to fortresses such as Maiden Castle in Dorset and in Edinburgh, but his 'secluded place where maidens could indulge their fancies unobserved' is a little strange.[46] Some English place-names in *maegden* are in locations where transhumance was practised, and in both Cumberland and Cornwall, where it was the custom, we have Celtic names meaning 'the high ground of the maidens'. On Dartmoor we have only Maiden Tor in Sheepstor parish, certainly an area to which transhumance was practised in the past, as described above in the section on distant detachments, and Maiden Hill in the central moor, east of Peter Tavy, but because there are no early recordings of either name, further speculation is not possible.[47] It is rather unlikely that in the Victorian period maidens walked here in these remote and wild spots, but how much earlier than that age the names are, we cannot say. Maiden Tor on Bodmin Moor, on the other hand, was recorded as early as the seventeenth century, but may derive from a Cornish word, as its earliest form is *Meadna*.[48]

The findings from Hound Tor, the reconstruction of Heatree and Cudlipp, the place-names associated with dairying—all of these point to a world less rough and rugged than that which prevailed under the system of impersonal transhumance. That was a male world of herdsmen and their male assistants, of many male, frisky steers, of sudden death (animals crushed in stampedes, murder of a herdsman) and of loud noise, when at the drifts animals had their movement directed by men blowing horns from the top of tors.

We do not wish to compose a pastoral idyll about the earlier world, as did the Donegal maidens about their months on the mountains in the nineteenth century, but it could well have been less harsh than the later one, perhaps a female world, with sleek lumbering cows in calf and the soft sounds of the churn and of milk plashing into pails on the summer hillslopes so long ago.

Conclusion

Hints gleaned from archaeological excavation reports, topographical analysis, place-names, Anglo-Saxon charters and late medieval historical records can be combined and interpreted in the light of modern accounts of transhumance practised more recently in other regions to produce a glimpse of the personal phase of transhumance to Dartmoor in the centuries before the Norman Conquest. Unlike the impersonal transhumance practised later, it is likely to have been as much focused on dairying as ranching, and to have involved young women as well as men. Place-names incorporating Smear- and Butter-, and also those with Maiden-, may identify locations where butter was made, and places named -wick would have originated as seasonally occupied sites. The tiny one-roomed shelters found at Hound Tor, some with hearths, others without and probably used for storage of dairy products, are likely to have been typical. Their small size suggests occupation by single individuals, perhaps each looking after the livestock of several lowland families, or of a single hamlet. No doubt also typical was these shelters' situation, close to low-lying marshy meadows but with panoramic views of the adjacent hillside pastures. Hound Tor's shielings lay beneath much larger longhouses, designed for family occupation and dating from the thirteenth century, which suggests that seasonal occupation was converted to permanent settlement and personal transhumance became impersonal transhumance before the thirteenth century.

CHAPTER SIX

Domesday Book and beyond

The transition from personal to impersonal transhumance

In this chapter we first discuss the role of colonists in the transition from impersonal to personal transhumance and in that context we have to confront the difficult question of the dating of the colonisation of Dartmoor which gave the region the farms and hamlets we can still see in the landscape today. Was it a thirteenth-century 'journey to the margins', as described by William Hoskins and Maurice Beresford, or did the journey take place earlier? And when was the origin of the system by which middlemen on the moor-edge manors earned income by taking in the livestock of down-country farmers? We next turn from the role of colonists to the role of lords in appropriating and slicing up the moorland edge to produce that remarkable spoked boundary pattern noticed in chapter 1. How old are the spokes? The question is a simple one but the arguments and evidence which are needed to answer it are complex indeed. Finally, we turn from the spokes of the wheel to the hub, for which there is strong evidence of royal ownership since the beginnings of recorded time. What role did the Crown have in dividing up Dartmoor? Was there contest between lords and state in this process?[1]

The role of colonists

The theme of this section is that colonists began to settle permanently at the seasonally used sites and to transform their economies and cultures. They made them into permanent homes with cultivated fields, where only pastures had existed earlier. In the phase of personal transhumance explored in the previous two chapters, men, and perhaps women, many of them young, made frequent visits to the summer pastures. They became well acquainted with the better grassland and with the more bare hillslopes, both well manured through years of seasonal use. No doubt in the summer these appeared alluring enough and, in the mind of a young man, their permanent colonisation would have had two advantages. First, he would be able to marry without having to wait for a vacancy on his home farm after his father's death; or, if he was a younger son, he would gain land to which, normally, he would not have had access. Second, he would be able to escape from immediate lordship, at least for a time. The disadvantages would be separation from kin and the hard work of transforming a once seasonally used settlement site into a permanent farm.

What would be the advantages of this transition to the down-country farm which once sent dairy cattle to a seasonal site as described in the previous chapter? The new colonist and his wife would have their own dairy cattle to look after, and could not take in more because of the labour-intensive nature of dairying. So the down-country farm would keep its dairy cattle at home, where the feed was certainly better than that on Dartmoor: good, fresh grass leys (temporary grass awaiting ploughing), shooting earlier in the spring than on the moors, and lush meadows between the June mowing and late October. The dairy cows, formerly sent to Dartmoor, would remain on the down-country farm and displace other livestock, which would now be sent to the moors, probably immature males, hardier than females, but with some females. The new colonist would act as a middleman. And so developed that tradition of grazing young bovines on Dartmoor, which is so apparent in all later records. The transition was accompanied by a flip-over in the gender of the livestock pastured on Dartmoor, now that young males as well as females came to the moors (also perhaps a flip-over of gender for their keepers, if in the earlier phase of personal transhumance females were the keepers of dairy cattle, as in the account from Donegal given in chapter 5).

At the formerly seasonally used site, its transformation into a permanent farm would take time. New fields had to be created, their walls, often still to be seen today, made from stones gathered from the land as clearing proceeded. A new house fit for a family would have to be built and there was experimenting to be done with new crops such as rye, which would have played a minor role on the colonist's farm in the down-country (if he came from the south) but was to play a major one on the newly colonised moor-edge farm. Creating fields and buildings, experimenting and in general learning to live in a new environment with soils, weather and wildlife very different from those at home: all of these took time. At first, therefore, the new colonist would have to find a means of making some extra income, but not a labour-intensive one, such as tin-working (if tin was being exploited in the late Saxon period), because the new farm absorbed so much time. A simple strategy adopted by the new colonist was to become a middleman, taking in young cattle displaced from the down-country farm by the returning dairy cows, perhaps his father's or from other farms in his home neighbourhood. They would need little attention, for they could be given a lair on a hillslope, visible from the new farm which, being heir to a seasonally used settlement, was sited with visibility in mind, as described earlier; they would need no new buildings, and at first the colonist would not have had to pay fees for use of the public pastures, for only later did these become appropriated by lords, as discussed in the following section. And so developed that system of middlemen, acting for down-country farmers, which is so apparent in all of the later documentation.

Dating the transition: archaeological and historical evidence

When did the transition from seasonally used settlement to permanent occupation, described above, take place? In an attempt to answer this question, there are two obstacles to be cleared away, first, the evidence from excavation by archaeologists and, second, the writings of historians. Excavation has taken place at a number of moor-edge farms and hamlets now deserted. Single farms are represented by Dinna Clerks, hamlets by Hound Tor, where there is much good evidence for antecedent seasonal use, the nameless settlement on Sourton Down, and the buildings which were destroyed when Okehampton Park was created in the thirteenth century. John Allan's recent re-evaluation of all of Dartmoor's excavated medieval dwellings concluded with authority that 'none of the ... settlements ... yielded pottery firmly dating before *c.*1200'; in other words, they are of thirteenth-century date, because we should not expect new farms in the fourteenth and fifteenth centuries, when there was a lessening of pressure of population on the land. We shall show later that many moor-edge farms were colonised far earlier than the thirteenth century and can only conclude that the excavated sample of deserted sites is a misleading one, and cannot be used to generalise about sequence of settlement on Dartmoor generally. It is in any case a small sample, given the total number of moorland farms. Many of the excavated sites are high and relatively exposed: one of the excavators at Sourton Down told me that his team virtually perished of cold there. All of the sites are deserted and may conform to the model of 'last to come, first to go', although that concept cannot be applied universally in England at large. The excavators found that the seasonally occupied hutlets at Hound Tor are aceramic, as to be expected of dwellings which were cleared out at the end of the summer grazing season and were occupied by dairying pastoralists who probably used wooden vessels in any case. Other archaeologists have found the same thing, Barker and his team concluding that in the Cicolano Mountains of Central Italy, evidence of transhumance 'would be difficult ... to detect' while Chang, writing of northern Greece, states that 'mobility strategies employed by pastoralists cannot be easily discovered in the archaeological record'.[2]

In order to make the case for transition from seasonal occupation to colonisation and permanent settlement in the late Saxon period we have to clear away not only the evidence of excavation but also the writings of historians, based on place-names and documents. W.G. Hoskins made the extraordinary claim that 'most of Dartmoor remained unknown until the twelfth century'.

Then came the "tin rush" after about 1250 and prospectors and settlers flocked in. 'Many new farms,' he continued, 'were created in these years (between about 1150 and 1250) on the edge of the Moor, of which Brisworthy in the upper Plym valley is a good example, surrounded by its tiny irregular fields, fields dotted with granite boulders and bounded by granite also.' Clearly, Hoskins had been on one of his day-trips, to the Plym valley, but in view of the place-name, Brisworthy, which we shall discuss later, his choice of example was not a happy one. He went on to say that 'we hear of many farmsteads well into the Moor by the closing years of the thirteenth century and the early years of the fourteenth'. His views have been followed by others. For example, M.W. Beresford and J.K. St Joseph wrote of 'the last great burst of medieval colonisation' in the early thirteenth century, and D. Brunsden described Dartmoor as 'the goal of colonisation in the twelfth to fourteenth centuries'. M.M. Postan, in an influential chapter in the *Cambridge Economic History of Europe*, wrote that 'most of Devonshire's combes and valleys ... were not fully occupied until the thirteenth century', and he too must have been relying upon the writings of Hoskins. These views of Hoskins on chronology coincide with the results of excavation, but they were coined long before deserted sites on Dartmoor were excavated. The evidence which he used was largely that of first references to the names of Dartmoor farms in the pages of *The Place-names of Devon*, for example the first to Brisworthy, mentioned above, being from a royal charter confirming lands to Plympton Priory, from the reign of Henry II (1155–88). This is a dangerous method, because a place can exist for many centuries before being first documented. For example, only a very small number of place-names in England generally are recorded in documents from before 730—in the writings of Bede, in a few early charters and in the Anglo-Saxon Chronicle—and have been analysed by Barry Cox, but thousands of places already existed before that date.[3]

The Place-names of Devon, under the name of the farm called Cholwich in Cornwood, gives its source as 'B.M.' and that reference probably led Hoskins to the British Museum and to his only sustained work on the documents of a Dartmoor settlement, an isolated farm perched on the edge of the moorland, 'the coldest, i.e. colder, dairy farm', as opposed to nearby Bromwich, 'broom dairy farm', which is lower. This led him to write a brilliant paper on the family of Cholwich of Cholwich. A crucial document in his work was a charter of the early thirteenth century by which Guy de Bryttavilla, Norman lord of Cornwood, granted 'all of his land of *Cholleswyt*' to a free tenant for a modest rent. The land is bounded in detail in the charter and the tenant was allowed common rights 'in dry and wet' for the grazing of livestock and the taking of hay, turf, peat (called 'coal' in the document) and 'other necessary things'. Elsewhere Hoskins describes documents of this kind as the 'foundation charters' of new thirteenth-century free holdings, probably having in mind the formal charters by which new urban settlements were created at the same time. Was the recipient of the thirteenth-century charter really the first person to reside at Cholwich? This seems unlikely, for two reasons. First, and perhaps not so secure as the second, the property already had boundaries by the date of the charter, although these could just possibly have been the bounds of an empty piece of land. Second, and indisputably, the second element in the name, *wic*, often meaning 'dairy farm', is of the type which place-name experts describe as 'habitative', that is, a spot where somebody lives, even if only seasonally. In chapter 5 we concluded that names in –*wic* were given to seasonally occupied dairy farms.[4]

Hoskins' vignette on Cholwich of Cholwich is therefore incorrect in one important respect. The place-name indicates very clearly that the thirteenth-century document is not a 'foundation charter' and that people had been there before, if only seasonally. The document could be a record of transition from seasonal to permanent use, in which case it is a very late example of that, but it need not be so. In all likelihood it is simply a confirmation of the rights of the family living there, later taking their name from the name of the farm. (Cholwich of Cholwich eventually moved to Oldstone in the warm South Hams, a place, when seen by Hoskins, being a ruined house 'among the chestnuts, the nettles and the elder').[5]

Dating the transition: place-names incorporating Anglo-Saxon personal names

In sum, neither excavation, nor place-names as treated by Hoskins nor the Cholwich charter are evidence of colonisation in the thirteenth century. What other method may we use to date the transition? Here we first turn again to place-names, not to the date at which they were first recorded but to the elements of which they are made up. Some of these elements contain no clues as to the dating of the names, such as the interesting name Summerhill in Ashburton parish or the many Dartmoor farms called Longstone, all taking their names from proudly upright prehistoric standing stones. One is mentioned as early as the first years of the eleventh century, while another is disguised today as Launceston Moor in Peter Tavy parish, *Langeston More* in a rental of 1488. Others contain only vague clues, so that, for example, Bowdley, also in Ashburton, contains a first element *boga*, 'curve', and a second *leah*, 'woodland clearing', and the latter is seldom found in Cox's corpus of elements earlier than 730 mentioned earlier in this chapter. There is, however, a method by which a group of names may be shown to be for the most part Anglo-Saxon and that is by using those where the first element is a Saxon personal name.[6]

The first question to ask in this investigation is: when did Saxon personal names such as Beorhtwine in Brisworthy (*Brutereswurdam* in the eleventh century) cease to be given as personal names, to be replaced by continental names such as Thomas and Richard (though not Harry)? The pace of change in name-giving habits differed between one part of England another and between different classes. It would have been all the more rapid among a fashion-conscious free peasantry who were often, but not always, the colonists of Dartmoor. It seems to have been early in Devon, probably because of frequent contacts with a close continent, contacts which would not have been made by farmers but by merchants and lords whose new names would then have been imitated by others. To answer the question about pace which was posed at the beginning of this paragraph we took three documentary sources, the early *acta* or written acts, mostly deeds with some writs, of bishops of Exeter, the cartulary of Canonsleigh Abbey and the small, early cartulary of Tavistock Abbey, a religious house close to Dartmoor, both of which contain charters from before 1150.[7]

In the *acta* no bishop had a Saxon personal name after Leofric's reign. Of other individuals, elevated archdeacons and lesser mortals such as clerks of works and canons, 46 per cent had Anglo-Saxon names in the period between 1075 and 1100, as we should expect because many of these people were born before the Norman Conquest. By the period 1126–1150 the proportion was 17 per cent. Thereafter it plummeted: the period between 1100 and 1150, and almost certainly the earlier part of that period, say before 1130, was the great turning point—the triumph of continental Thomas, Richard, Walter, Robert and William—and percentages of Anglo-Saxon names were never above 4 per cent after 1130. The second source, Canonsleigh's cartulary, produced similar figures from 1150 onwards, as did Tavistock's cartulary.

Now to return to place-names on Dartmoor. The method employed was as follows. For all of the moor-side parishes and the central parish of Lydford the entries in *The Place-names of Devon* were examined. Those which contained Saxon personal names were extracted through use of the long list of such names near the end of that reference work. So we find Bicca at Beckaford in Manaton, Pulla who gave his name to Pullabrook in Bovey Tracey, Raegna who gave his name to one of the 'ancient tenements', Runnage, of the central moor, and so on. These names are indisputably Anglo-Saxon: some of them crop up in Germanic sources from the continent, they are never found in Norman contexts and they have name-forming patterns which are thoroughly Germanic.[8]

The next step was to plot the names on a map (Fig. 6.1) which also shows the present-day moorland boundary, already presented in our first chapter. As was explained earlier in this book, we show only the outer boundaries of the great central block of moor and of the smaller surrounding blocks, not the islands of cultivation within them. This explains why some of the places plotted appear to lie within moorland, for example the 'ancient tenements' of Runnage (Raegna) and Babeny (Babba) in the east. Other dots within moorland on Fig. 6.1 represent landscape features not settlements, for example Bagga Tor (Bacca) in

Peter Tavy and Eylesbarrow (Elli), first mentioned, as a boundary marker, in the great perambulation of the central moor made in 1240. Presumably Bacca was an individual who lived on the slopes of Bagga Tor. There is no settlement there now so one may argue for a seasonally used site somewhere on the slopes of the hill which has a south-west facing slope above a minute stream, very typical of the sites of such settlements.[9]

6.1 Place-names containing Anglo-Saxon personal names.

All we can say is that the people who named the farms shown on Fig. 6.1 were of Saxon stock. It is highly unlikely, if not impossible, that all of the farms were colonised in the period between 1066 and, say, 1130 when Old-English personal names were still common: that would not have been demographically possible, especially if we consider the certainty that we must add to the symbols on Fig. 6.1 a good number of other Saxon place-names which do not incorporate diagnostic Old-English personal names. A few of the farms shown on Fig. 6.1 may have originated between 1066 and 1130, and a very few in the period after 1130, when the proportion of Saxon personal names in Devon was minute. But a good number must belong to the Saxon period, which came to an end in 1066. Dartmoor cannot have been 'unknown' until the twelfth century as Hoskins stated. How early in the Saxon period these names are we cannot say, although Dr Mike Thompson, who kindly carried out for me some of the analysis of personal names in documents, discussed earlier, acutely observed that names on Dartmoor,

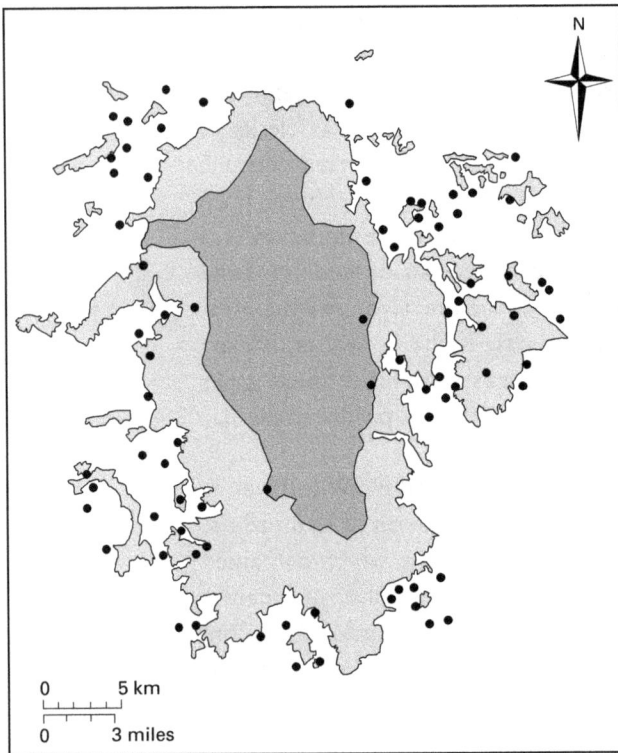

and elsewhere in Devon, are of types which do not appear in those documents: possibly they were archaic by the time of the Norman Conquest and, if so, that pushes them well back from 1066.

Dartmoor was well-peopled at least in the later Saxon period. People farmed at their *worthig* farms, a word meaning 'enclosure', as at Brisworthy (Beorhtwine), Godsworthy (Gode), Wapsworthy (Waebeorht) and Willsworthy (Wifel), all on the western side of Dartmoor. Whether the word means enclosure of the farmstead or fields is uncertain, although a clause in the late seventh-century law-code of King Ine of Wessex suggests the latter, which means that enclosed fields already existed around the moor's edge in the late Saxon period at least. These people pushed back the limits of the moorland, as is very clear from Fig. 6.1, which shows many sites with place-names incorporating Saxon personal names virtually perched on the modern limits of the moorlands. Others are half a mile or a mile from those limits and it is possible, if we connect these with a line in the mind's eye, to reconstruct the edge of moorland in the Saxon period. As explained earlier, the map does not show these diagnostic names if they are more than 1 mile from the edge of present-day moorland. If, say, we were to include those which were two miles away from it, we might reconstruct an even earlier Dartmoor.[10]

They cleared the woodlands of the edge of Dartmoor, as did Cifa at Chuley and Gydda at Gidleigh, the second element in both cases being *leah*, 'a woodland clearing'; some of them lived in remote coombes, Podda in Puddicombe, Pulla along a stream called Pullabrook.[11]

As we have said, we do not know when in the Saxon period these colonists arrived, nor do we know how many of them permanently settled at sites more seasonally occupied, as described in the imagined development drawn at the beginning of this section. But that this transition did take place, and by the date of the Norman Conquest, if not earlier, is clear from documents relating to three places. First, and the earliest, is *Bittelworth*, Bittleford in Widecombe in the Moor parish. It was a detached part of Ipplepen in the down-country of the South Hams and was therefore once a seasonally used site, as we have argued earlier in this book for all of the detached portions. It is mentioned as such in a Saxon charter of 956, but it was by then already named as a *worthig*, meaning a farm with enclosed fields. In this case we know for certain that Bitela was the young man who colonised it permanently at some time before 956, confirming our dating inference from place-names given above. Second, perhaps slightly later, we know the name of another of these strong youths who went to farm on Dartmoor and to transform seasonally used sites, Hyfa, who did this at Heatree, a detached part of Kenton. His name occurs in a boundary perambulation of the early eleventh century discussed earlier in this book (*on hyfan treow*) and also in the next section of the present chapter.[12]

Third, Domesday Book allows us to see, and count, but not to name, the people who farmed in 1086 at some of the once seasonally occupied sites around Dartmoor, perhaps the successors of the first colonists. Bagtor was a detached part of Holbeam (in Ogwell parish), Spitchwick of Littlehempston and Ashburton of Paignton. Each, by the time of Domesday Book, had become a manor in its own right, a development which must have taken some time, confirming our dating of the transition to the (late?) Saxon period. At Spitchwick, King William had a demesne (the lord's own land) on which four slaves worked. There were eight villeins and four bordars. The latter comprised one-third of the population of the manor (excluding slaves), a high proportion, perhaps confirming the view that bordars were literally 'at the edge' (French *borde*), a relatively new colonist: they would have been at farms like Cator, at the edge of the manor, which has a Saxon personal name, Cada, as its first element, or Corndon, at the end of its lane, with a name, 'corn down or hill', in which we can virtually see its first occupier clearing the land, enclosing and sowing it. Between them the eight villeins had four ploughs, so we must envisage some sort of sharing, which perhaps also produced the miniature strip-field system at Uppacott, remains of which are shown on an eighteenth-century map of the manor. Domesday Book also mentions, in Spitchwick manor, a relatively large acreage of pasture, which always means rough pasture in Devon, the remnants of which may still be seen today in areas such as Cator Common, savannah-like now that the gorse has been allowed to grow into small trees through lack of browsing. In addition there was woodland twice as long as it was wide, no doubt in the valley of the Webburn where woods may still be seen today. Possibly the woodland may once have had a larger area than at the time of Domesday Book, having been destroyed by the pigs which gave Spitchwick its name (p. 152) Spitchwick began as a pastoral place, its inhabitants perhaps living in the woods, as was the custom at Christow much later, and rendering a food-rent of bacon to its lord, hence the name; but by 1086 it was more arable, and its pig-men, recorded in Domesday Book for some other manors, had gone.[13]

In summary, the transition from occupation on a seasonal basis to permanent settlement had taken place at at least some of the sites with Anglo-Saxon personal names in their place-names, although we have no means of knowing what proportion of these sites had antecedent seasonal use. It had certainly taken place at *Bittelworth* by 956, at Heatree by the early eleventh century and at Ashburton and at the detached, moorland, portions of hundreds, such as Spitchwick, by 1066. More we cannot say: the difficulty in this chapter and in the two previous ones is that we are dealing with customs and events which took place in a misty, ancient period from which the evidence is almost lost and from which archaeology so far has not dispelled the mist, except at Hound Tor. Luckily, in chapter 7, where we explore, first, the landscape of droveways, the evidence is ever-present and robust. In that chapter where, second, we explore how medieval farm economies were affected by transhumance, the documentary evidence is satisfactory, though not excellent.

The role of lords

The newly colonised farms which we have discussed in the previous section were set in what were still public pastures, as described in chapter 2. The distinction between a single inner central moor and plural outer moors, as we call them in this book, had not yet developed. Each new farm was close to private land, the land of one of the moor-side lords and here, as in the previous section, we present a scheme, in this case of the activities of lords not colonists, of how these great men—abbots and kings as well as lesser owners—reacted to the presence of the new colonists. Those lords knew well the public pastures adjoining their improved land, because they used them for grazing their own livestock, which they sent to them at sunrise, taking them back at dusk, as described in documents from the fourteenth century onwards.

There were several reasons why these lords would wish to appropriate part of the public pastures closest to them, to slice up the public grazings, to draw them to themselves, now for the first time creating the 'outer moors' as we describe them in this book. First, no doubt they perceived the new colonists beginning to make profits as middlemen, taking in the animals of down-countrymen, as described in the previous section. How could a lord himself profit from this new development? The simple answer was to charge a guardianship fee per head of cattle. We have seen in chapter 3 that lords of moor-side manors charged such fees, made large profits from them and employed their own herdsmen to look after the livestock of outsiders. This system of fee-paying could well have come into being on Dartmoor before the Norman Conquest, because there is good and clear evidence for it on Exmoor in Domesday Book.[14] If a lord of a moor-side manor began to introduce the system on moorland adjacent to his manor, at the same time as his neighbouring lords were doing the same, how could he police it and ensure that only the livestock for which he received a fee pastured on his land? The simple answer was to bound the moorland, if only in the mind's eye. And so developed that distinctive spoke-like pattern of boundaries, with manors appropriating slivers of moorland, mapped as Fig. 1.5, and complex jurisdictions and systems of pastoral management discussed earlier in this book: drifts to count animals and collect fees, systems for the apprehension and claiming of strays. The outer moors were now distinct from the central moor.

A second reason for lords to appropriate slices of moorland next to their manors was to make profits by charging small rents from the new colonists who were clearing the moors on their doorsteps. Lords perceived these new families on land close to them and looked upon them with avarice: here was rent to be had. So lords acquired new rents as well as new guardianship fees, to their obvious advantage. The new tenants attached themselves to adjacent lords; formerly each had been free with no lord but the monarch, and in the words of Domesday Book, largely in its East Anglian entries, he 'could go with his land with whatever lord he would' and 'become his man'. Such entries are rare in the Devonshire folios of Domesday but one which has been noticed relates to the border of Dartmoor, significantly for us. Under the heading of the manor of Bridestowe, Domesday states that Saewin Tuft, Doda (two holdings), Godwin (two) and Sihtric held farms which did not belong to the manor at the time of the Norman Conquest 'and could go with their land to whichever lord they would', but by 1086 had become attached to Bridestowe's lord. The farms are named as Kersford, Battishill, Combebowe, Ebsworth, Fernworthy and Way and most of them are very close to moorland. The advantage to the tenant, now attached to a lord, was that he had protection, he had a putative court where he could seek justice, he had a church to go to without feeling an outsider and he now felt part of the community of a manor and parish, however weakly developed that community was. In the case of the Bridestowe men, there was the added advantage of being protected by very powerful lords, because the manor was held by Ralph de Pomeroy under Baldwin the Sheriff. One might add that there could well have been some compulsion here from these highly influential men.[15]

There were, thirdly, miscellaneous reasons for lords to appropriate slices of waste. They may have seen themselves not only as taking profits from grazing fees, but also as providing good lordship and order, for example in apprehending and fining rustlers, as we have seen them doing at a later date in chapter 3.

In appropriating the outer moors to themselves, lords saw off the commoners of Devon and henceforth only their own tenants had rights of common, as described in an earlier chapter. This seems harsh, but the huge central moor was still common to the whole shire and all that probably happened was that livestock were displaced to it from the outer moors. There is evidence from the late medieval period onwards to show that the outer moors were collectively called 'The Commons of Devon',[16] yet, as shown earlier in this book, they patently were not common to the whole shire when detailed documentation about them begins, in the thirteenth century. They were the private moors of lords, commoned only by those lords' tenants. It is probable, therefore, that the term harks back to the period before the lordly appropriations described here.

The moorlands now in Manaton parish may have been the last remaining commons not appropriated by a lord, because the name means 'common territory', from (ge)maene, 'common' and *tun* which here, as often, means area not settlement. In a period when all of Dartmoor was common, this name would not have made sense, so it is reasonable to suggest that it was so called because its moors were the very last to which the commoners of all Devon had access (although there are other explanations). They would have had access to the central moor at this time, and this perhaps explains the extraordinary elongated corridor of Manaton towards the centre, noted by Angus Winchester in his book about boundaries in England generally, where he calls it a 'pan-handle', the pan being the main block of Manaton parish, the handle being the corridor.[17]

From the imagined, undated developments proposed above we turn, as in the section on colonists, to the evidence, which comes not largely from place-names as in that section but from five documents: Domesday Book; two lost Saxon charters of which we have only a description; another document which is often called a charter but which is certainly not; a surviving charter; and the wording on a single cross standing lonely on the moors. These documents and the wording on the cross help us to confirm and date the developments imagined above.

Dartmoor's pastures in Domesday Book

For the title of this chapter I borrow from an enduring work in early social history, F.W. Maitland's *Domesday Book and Beyond: three Essays in the Early History of England* published in 1897. In part, I admit, it is the sonority of his words which attracts me, but the method used here is his, to begin with Domesday Book and then to try to discern the dim 'beyond' of late Anglo-Saxon arrangements. 'The Beyond is still very dark,' boomed Maitland, 'but the way to it lies through the Norman record' (Domesday Book), with help from whatever other scraps of evidence that are available. In the pages that follow the few Saxon writings which have any bearing on the borders of Dartmoor will be brought into play, including those written on stone. The beyond is still very dark but shadowy shapes are discernable in the darkness and we must trace them as best we can.[18]

There is a certain irony in the title of this section, for the name of Dartmoor does not appear anywhere in the Devon folios of Great Domesday or in its local predecessor, the *Liber Exoniensis*. The outer moors, divided into elongated segments and slithers by the distinctive and remarkable spoke-like pattern of boundaries which was introduced early in this book and discussed earlier in this section, may however be inferred from references to pasture in the Domesday entries for moor-edge manors.

Domesday Book, in its surviving version, is deficient in its record of pasture for England at large. For some counties, such as Lincolnshire, there are no references to it at all, which must simply reflect the way in which information was collected or summarised, for we should expect much rough grazing on the Heath and the Wolds at the end of the eleventh century and also in the Marsh and the Fens; and, indeed, sources from the last region, not too distant in time from 1086, reveal abundance of rough pasture there. For other counties, those who compiled the information to be included in the final Domesday folios made a systematic effort to mention pasture where it existed. With a few minor exceptions, the 'pasture' of Domesday was always rough grazing, what documents of a later age would call 'waste', though without the implications of 'wasted' or 'useless'; it was not mown meadowland which, because of its great value, has separate entries in the record, nor was it fallow pasture resting after an arable crop, for this was subsumed within the data on ploughlands. The record of Domesday pasture is a record of the grazing potential of moors, heaths, downs and marshes: in Oxfordshire it was a notable feature of manors in the Cotswolds and of those with land stretching up onto the Chiltern Hills, while in Essex, where the Domesday entries specify pasture for sheep, it was present almost exclusively on manors with coastal marshland or with access to the coast through detached parts. Dues were already being collected from peasants grazing their livestock on rough pastures at the time of Domesday.

Devon is one of those counties where pasture is recorded systematically, for it occurs in almost 80 per cent of Domesday entries. In this county the pasture was not the ley grass which was nurtured and mown in fields when they were not under the plough, but the rough pastures of hills and moors and, occasionally, marshes, as is clear from its distribution, with concentrations, for example, on the long hill ranges of east Devon, around the Haldon Hills and around Exmoor and Dartmoor; in all of these regions later sources from the thirteenth century onwards reveal abundant rough hill grazings. The 50 acres recorded for Powderham, on the low-lying shore of the Exe, was marsh, for the name (*Poldreham* in 1086) means 'land reclaimed from the sea' and there is very good evidence of marshland reclamation here in later centuries. Some of the Domesday pastures of Devon are described as 'common' although inclusion or omission of the adjective is probably random. There are two references in the Domesday folios for Devon, in the entries for Woodbury church and Molland manor near Exmoor, to fees collected from tenants who used a rough pasture, but these are unusual entries, although the practice may have been usual enough.[19]

The many statements about pasture in the Domesday folios for Devonshire usually refer to it in measurements either of length and breadth or of area. Thus, if we take examples from Dartmoor, the pasture of Sourton was 1 league in length and half a league in breadth and that of Shapley in North Bovey was given as 10 acres, while a variation of the former type of entry occurs when only one linear measurement is mentioned, for example 'pasture 1 league' for Peek in Ugborough. It must be said at once that there is no consensus about the equivalent of these measures in modern miles and acres. A Domesday league is thought to have equalled 12 furlongs, and thus 1½ miles, but that is based on twelfth-century evidence from Sussex, and there may well have been local variations. The acres of Domesday are likely to have been far larger than today's acres: for example, Walkhampton manor had 100 acres of pasture according to the Norman record but the parish, in which there were no other Domesday manors, reported 6,500 acres of commons to the Royal Commission on Common Lands in 1958.[20]

Given these problems it is best to approach the topic of the Domesday entries for the moor-edge manors through analysis of *types* of entry rather than through any attempt at conversion to modern acres. In Table 6.1 we have abstracted data on pasture from Domesday entries for about two thirds of

Table 6.1 Domesday pasture entries for moor-edge manors (a., acre; fl, furlong; lg, league)

Manor		Pasture	Manor		Pasture
Harford	L	1 lg long, ½ lg wide	Okehampton	L	1 lg long, ½ lg wide
Cornwood	L	1 lg long, ½ lg wide	Belstone	L	1 lg
Blachford (Cornwood)	L	1½ lgs	Sampford Courtenay	L	2 lgs long, 1 lg wide
Fardel (Cornwood)	a	300 a.	South Tawton	L	4 lgs long, 4 lgs wide
Dinnaton (Cornwood)	L	½ lg	Throwleigh	L	½ lg long, 4 a. wide [sic]
Plympton	a	20 a.			
Baccamor (Plympton)	L	½ lg long, 2 fls wide	Gidleigh	–	none mentioned
Hemerdon (Plympton)	a	60 a.	Drewsteignton	a	60 a.
Shaugh Prior 1	L	½ lg long, 4 fls wide	Teigncombe	L	3 lgs long, 1 lg wide
Shaugh Prior 2	L	½ lg long, 4 fls wide	Chagford 1	a	60 a.
Coldstone (Shaugh P)	L	½ lg long, 2 fls wide	Chagford 2	a	40 a.
Pethill (Shaugh P)	L	½ lg long, 2 fls wide	North Bovey	L	1 lg
Fernhill (Shaugh P)	L	½ lg long, 2 fls wide	Moretonhampstead	a	60 a.
Meavy 1	L	½ lg long, 2 fls wide	Manaton	a	12 a.
Meavy 2	L	5 fls	Houndtor (Manaton)	L	1 lg
Meavy 3	L	½ lg	Bovey Tracey	a	50 a.
Meavy 4	a	100 a.	Ilsington	L	2 lgs, 8 fls long, the same wide
Bickleigh	L	1 lg long, 4 fls wide			
Walkhampton	a	100 a.	Bagtor (Ilsington)	L	1 lg long, ½ lg wide
Buckland Monachorum	L	1 lg long, 1 lg wide	Ashburton	L	1 lg
Sampford Spiney	L	½ lg long, 1 fl wide	Buckland in the Moor	L	4 lgs
Whitchurch	L	1 lg long, 4 fls wide	Spitchwick (Widecombe)	a	100 a.
Peter Tavy	L	16 fls long, 9 fls wide	Stoke (Holne)	L	½ lg
			Holne	L	1 lg
Willsworthy	L	2 lgs long, 1 lg wide	Buckfast	-	none mentioned
Tavistock	L	10 fls long, 10 fls wide	Skerraton (Dean Prior)	a	60 a.
			Dean Prior	L	1 lg
Mary Tavy 1	L	½ lg long, 6 fls wide	South Brent 1	L	1 lg long, ½ lg wide
Mary Tavy 2	L	1 lg long, ½ lg wide	South Brent 2	a	30 a.
Lydford	–	none mentioned	Ugborough	a	50 a.
Bridestowe	a	30 a.	Langford (Ugborough)	a	200 a.
Sourton	L	1 lg long, ½ lg wide	Peek (Ugborough)	L	1 lg

Source: C. Thorn and F. Thorn, *Domesday Book: Devon* (Chichester, 1985). Compiled by the editors.
Note: *DB* records at least 100 manors which might have contained parts of the outer moors. Many of them, particularly minor sub-infeudated manors, recorded very little pasture (40 a. or less, always measured in acres) and some none at all—most of these have been excluded from this table. They may perhaps have shared in the common pasture of a nearby dominant manor, though in some cases where it seems impossible that the manor could not have included large areas of moorland, and certainly did so at later dates (notable examples are Lydford and Buckfast) the entries are unusually terse and may simply have omitted some of the information usually recorded, including perhaps substantial moorland pastures.

the hundred-odd moor-edge manors which could have had slices of the outer moors, beginning with Harford in the south, then arranging them clockwise around Dartmoor (manors with only small areas of pasture—under 40 acres—or none at all have mostly been excluded). In the second column of the table the entries are classified according to whether they are given in linear measures or in acres and the details appear in the third column.[21] It is clear that linear measures dominate, being used for about two-thirds of the manors recording more than 40 acres and a larger proportion of those with substantial areas of pasture. This dominance is brought home if we compare the moor-edge manors with places in other parts of Devon. In east Devon, where there was a good deal of rough pasture, on the hill ranges between the lush valleys of the Rivers Exe, Otter, Yarty and Axe, and on the Blackdowns, less than one fifth of references to pasture are in linear measures and in the southern part of the South Hams, where rough pasture was generally scarce according to Domesday Book and all later types of record, the figure falls to 1 per cent.[22] Dominance of linear measures is one interesting feature of Table 6.1. Another feature, especially intriguing in light of the elongated shapes of many of the outer moors, is that 90 per cent of the entries in linear measures specify pastures which were longer than they were broad. In this calculation I have included entries in which only one dimension is given (for example, 'pasture 1 league') on the grounds that this is shorthand for 'pasture 1 league in length but far less in breadth', an interpretation which seems to fit in with the shapes of the moors belonging to some manors with entries of this kind.[23]

In many cases there is a good correlation between the Domesday measurements and the configurations of the outer moors as shown on maps of a much later age, although it is a very general coincidence of shapes rather than any strictly mathematical relationship—as we should expect, because the Domesday figures are clearly rounded generalisations. Thus at Ilsington, on the south-eastern side of Dartmoor where the normal spoke-like pattern of boundaries is interrupted for some reason, the pasture was 2 leagues and 8 furlongs in length and also in breadth, allowing us dimly to discern a rough square, and that is certainly the shape of the moorland of the parish in later times. Both Peter Tavy and Harford are attributed in Domesday Book with pasture about twice as long as it was wide and both have elongated moorlands today, the latter's being less than half a mile wide at its narrowest point and over five miles long.[24]

Domesday Book does not give us a highly focused picture of the outer moors at the time of the Norman Conquest, nor does it tell of their management, although we may conclude that, being systematically listed and measured, if only roughly, they were regarded as valuable assets. But two things seem reasonably clear from the record, first that the outer moorland was already appropriated by the lords of moor-edge manors in the manner envisaged above and, second, that the private manorial moors so formed in many cases had elongated shapes. Private ownership implies the existence of boundaries, if drawn only in the mind's eye, and elongated moors imply elongated boundaries, so we can say that the remarkable spoke-like pattern (Fig. 1.5) already existed in whole or in part in 1086. Beyond that we would not venture to go with the evidence of Domesday: some of the boundaries of Fig. 1.5 may still have been imperfectly formed in 1086, some may have been in dispute, recalling the disputes of later ages, and a few, perhaps, awaited strict definition. But a mould had been set, the basic elements of a pattern established.

Brent Moor's Anglo-Saxon bounds

Something of this pattern of boundaries existed earlier than 1086: that we know from four pre-Conquest documents and a mysterious cross standing on the moorland. Three of the documents have their problems, two being ghosts of charters seen long ago, faint marks on a shroud, while the purpose for which the third was drawn up is nowhere stated, although we shall make a reasonable conjecture about its context. We shall begin with the two ghosts, which deal with the boundaries of Brent Moor. They occur in a document already discussed earlier in this book (p. 98), 'The instructions of & for the titell of the monastery of Our Lady of Buckfast ... to their three mores ...' made in 1446/7. At dispute were the bounds of Buckfast Abbey's moors of Buckfastleigh Moor, South Holne Moor and Brent Moor, although it is only the last which concerns us here. A lawyer, John Fitz, was employed to search the abbey's evidences and found a 'black register book' containing a copy of a record of the boundaries of Brent and, among the abbey's loose documents, some fourteenth-century and later account rolls giving details of the fees paid by people whose animals grazed that moor and collected by the abbot's servants. Portions of the 'black' cartulary, including the perambulation, have survived, as have account rolls of the manor of Brent, and a check shows that, so far, the lawyer's transcriptions are accurate. He next turned to the 'whit register book': Buckfast Abbey possessed two cartularies, a large one which was black and a smaller one which was white and now lost which, like Tavistock's small cartulary, contained the earliest evidences. In the white cartulary he saw two royal charters 'yn danys spech' (i.e. Old English) granting Brent to laymen and the charters very importantly included descriptions of the boundaries of Brent Moor. Herbert Finberg admitted that the lawyer's 'palaeographical and linguistic attainments were not of the highest order'—for example, the description as 'Danish' for language which must really have been Old English—and a mis-copying of the dates—but he was 'reasonably certain' that what the lawyer saw was a transcript of two Saxon charters, probably from the reign of Edwy or Edgar (third quarter of the tenth century).[25]

Four points may be made in support of Finberg's conclusion about the authenticity of these transcripts. First, the lawyer can be shown, as is done above, to have been honest in his transcription of other documents. Second, had he invented the Anglo-Saxon charters that would have been a foolish move because in any case in law he could have been challenged to produce the cartulary itself. Third, it is, of course, entirely usual for royal charters granting lands in favour of laymen to have been copied into the cartulary of the monastery which eventually came to own those lands. Finally, there is the question of *two* grants. Finberg was slightly bemused by this but the reason is quite clear, for there were *two* adjacent manors of Brent, possibly the result of division at some time before the third quarter of the tenth century; they were separately listed as the property of Buckfast Abbey in Domesday Book and there is some hint of a bipartite organisation still in the thirteenth century, though after that the two came to be managed as one manor. The *two* grants are not bemusing but are another reason for believing the authenticity of the lost charters, because it would have taken a mind most ingenious to have gone that far in an invention.

The lost 'white' cartulary of Buckfast Abbey, then, contained copies of charters in Old English relating to Brent Moor, seen by our lawyer in the fifteenth century. Might the originals or the copies have been forged by the monks of Buckfast before the compilation of the cartulary, perhaps in the thirteenth century? This seems very unlikely, because another charter in the cartulary, one also noted by the lawyer, has all the signs of authenticity. It is the foundation charter of Buckfast Abbey which seems correct in date, in the name of the founding king, Canute, in the name of the founding lay landowner, Æthelweard, and in general diplomatic; moreover, there is corroborative evidence, although possibly not entirely independent of the monks, for the existence of this charter. The charter apparently named the places given in the foundation endowment, including, presumably, the two manors called Brent. In a way it rendered the two earlier charters for the two manors superfluous as evidence for title, which makes it all the more likely that they are authentic.

To conclude, the two charters seen by Fitz were neither a fabrication by him in the 1440s, nor were they falsified by Buckfast Abbey. Brent Moor had already been appropriated to the two manors of Brent in the third quarter of the tenth century, and its boundaries were perambulated when the two charters were drawn up, unless they were inserted from oral testimony or copied from an existing document—the beginnings perhaps of a tradition which was to persist for centuries. The spokes were already approaching towards the hub by the third quarter of the tenth century. But how far would they get?

The eleventh-century bounds of Ashburton's moors
If only the fifteenth-century lawyer had not been, as we say of some students, undistinguished in palaeography; if only he had transcribed the boundary

Table 6.2 Eleventh-century bounds of the manor of Ashburton

1 where the Ashburn (*æscburne*) shoots out to Dart stream (*dertan*)	22 by the way (*þone weg*) as far as the great dyke (*þa greatan dic*)
2 as far as Webburn and up the Webburn	23 as far as the dyke
3 as far as withy marsh (*widi mor*)	24 to the spring (*þone wille*)
4 to the middle of calf's hill (*cealfadune*)	25 to the head of the marsh (*þæs mores heafod*)
5 as far as seven stones (*sufonstanas*)	26 by the stream to the swallowing (?whirlpool)
6 to Hyfa's tree (*hyfan treow*)	
7 to treasure fort	27 to *Yederes* barrow or hill (*yederes beorh*)
8 to deer ford	
9 to long stone	28 as far as the great lime tree
10 to *Eofede* tor	29 to the middle of *Dyra* detached piece of land (*dyra snæd*)
11 to the front of high hill	
12 to the hidden spring	30 to white ford (*hwita ford*)
13 to *writelan* (?babbling) stone	31 to dirty ford (*fulanford*)
14 to rough hill or barrow	32 to Hild's ford (*hildes ford*)
15 to the furze (gorse) enclosure or hill	33 to Hild's wood (*hildes lege*)
16 to the head of herb coomb	34 northwards to *sole* gate (*sole get*)
17 to ramshorn (*rammes horn*)	35 to *Brynes* knoll (*brynes cnolle*)
18 to *Lulca* stile	36 southwards to *Puneces worthig* (enclosure)
19 to the head of wick (dairy farm) coomb (*wice cumes heafod*)	37 to the head of ravens (?) coomb (*hremnes cumes heafod*)
20 to Lemon stream (*lymen stream*) as far as where Ogwell stream shoots out	38 to the streamlet (*þa ride*) as far as the Ashburn (*æscburne*)
21 by the stream as far as the head of the Ogwell (*wocgawilles heafod*)	39 thence by the stream to Dart (*dertan*)

Source: D. Hooke, *Pre-Conquest Charter-Bounds of Devon and Cornwall* (Woodbridge, 1994), pp. 217–22.

description which he was struggling to read—then we would have been able to journey across the purple moors of Brent as they were in the tenth century. Luckily, there is one document in Old English which allows us to make a similar journey, across the moorlands northwards of the present parish of Ashburton, and which confirms the inference which may be drawn from the Brent charters, namely that boundaries across the outer moors were of some concern even before the Norman Conquest. The document is discussed twice in this book, first, in an earlier chapter on detached parts of manors, and second here, where we explore the probable reason for its compilation. It dates from a little later than the Brent charters, from the first half of the eleventh century.

It is not a charter but a simple recitation of the course of a boundary, but there is nothing unusual in that, for other such documents exist, although not in large numbers. The core of the territory which it describes is what was later to become the manor of Ashburton, belonging to the See of Exeter.[26]

In discussing the possible course of this boundary we may usefully classify the thirty-nine phrases or clauses which the document mentions into three stretches (Table 6.2 and Fig. 6.2). The first group of points, 1 to 2, is a river stretch offering relatively few problems. The two phrases are 'where Ashburn shoots out on Dart stream', 'to the Webburn and up the Webburn'. The junction of the Ashburn and the Dart, the Dart itself and its junction with the Webburn may all be indisputably located on modern maps. The Webburn divides into two, presenting us with our first problem: which Webburn? A second problem is how far up the stream the boundary went. Most of the many commentators on the document have assumed, with only slight justification, that the East Webburn is the correct solution and if we further assume that the boundary went to the head of the stream, again without much justification, this first stretch is a long one, of about eight miles, but that is not remarkable because these streams are secure boundaries and those who made the perambulation in the early eleventh century had no reason to add any refinement to their description here.

The second stretch, clauses 3 to 17, is of more interest topographically and of much relevance to the subject of this book, because it is a 'moorland stretch'—it traverses the outer moors and, if only we could be certain of the precise route taken by the boundary makers of the eleventh century, we would be able to traverse those moors along with them. Of the fifteen points on this stretch, eleven may be said to be typical of, but not all exclusive to, a moorland landscape: in order, these are a marsh with willows, a calf's down, seven stones (i.e. a prehistoric circle or row), a barrow with treasure, a longstone, a tor, a high down, a rough hill or barrow, a gorse-covered enclosure or hill, a tree, and a hill shaped like a ram's horn. There are no people in this landscape except that the tree is said to belong to Hyfa (*on hyfan treow*), presumably a prominent tree marking the boundary of the farm called Heatree today, perhaps still in seasonal occupation in the early eleventh century when the document was drawn up. We encounter instead the lonely moorland landscape with its pastoral associations, a landscape strewn with prehistoric features, including a circle of seven stones and one of those magnificent single, tall, Dartmoor longstones, and the abiding hills, tors and streams. We are lost, as often I have been, on the moors, for of the fifteen boundary points eleven might be anywhere in that landscape. With the remaining four points we are on more certain or slightly more certain ground. First, the farm called Soussons today (*Soueston* in the fifteenth century), usually taken to mean seven stones, stands close to a stone circle (though one of 22 stones) and both are near the

Neadon

Langstone
Langstone
Cross

hyfan
treow?
Hayre Brooke
Heatree
Cross
Manaton

Lustleigh

Heatree
Down

Challacombe Down
Natsworthy

Houndtor

Soussons
Down
Challacombe

Soussons
Farm

cealfadune

sufonstanas?

West Webburn R.

East Webburn R.

? widi mor

Haytor
eofede tor?

Widecombe
in the Moor

Ilsington

Dunstone
Blackslade

Scobitor

Bagtor

Penn
Wood

Sigford

Combe

rammes horn

Ramshorn
Down

lulca stile?

Lurcombe

Buckland in
the Moor

R. Webburn

wice cumes heafod

Bickington

lymen stream

wede
burne

R. Lemon

þa greatan
dic

þone
wille
þaes mores
hæford?

wocgawilles heafod

W. Ogwith

Torbryan

Burrow
Cottage

yederes
beorh

þone
weg

Ashburton

dyra snæd
hwita ford

Denbury

þa ride

Woodland

R. Ashburn

R. Dart

R. Yealan

hremnes
cumes heafod

sole
get?

hildes
lege

fulanford?

Knowle
Hill

hildes ford?

R. Hems

R. Asheburn

- - - - - Parish boundary

◆ Settlement

0   1   2 km

0   1   2 miles

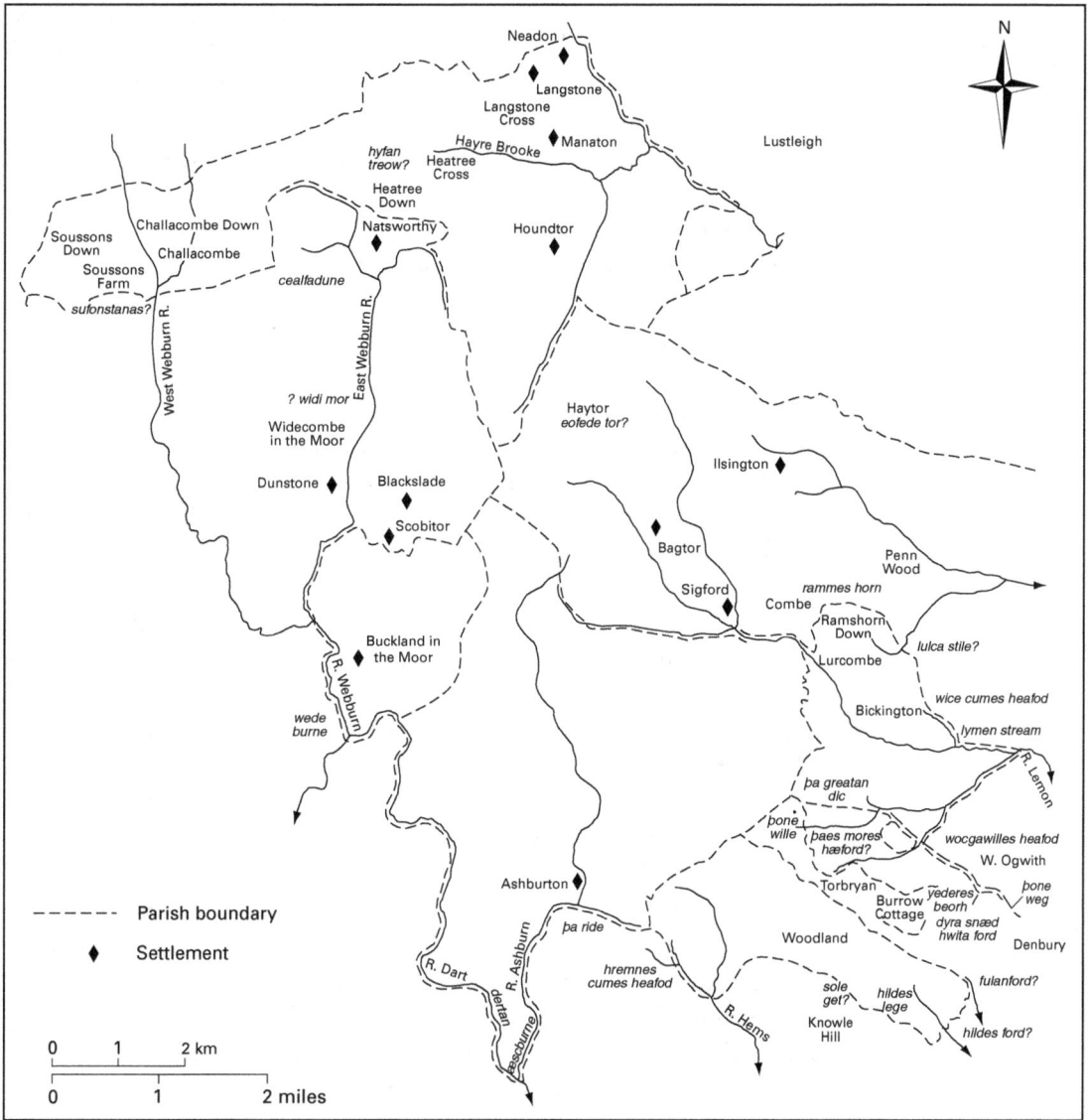

West Webburn of the first stretch of the perambulation: these considerations accurately fix its location.[27] Second, about three miles from Soussons as the crow flies is the farm called Heatree, for which we now have medieval spellings not available to the compilers of *The Place-names of Devon* (e.g. *Hevittre* in 1300); the farm must lie close to the Hyfa's tree of the perambulation. Third, the hill shaped like a ram's horn is Ramshorn Down today: it comes at the very end of the second stretch being considered here and the feature lies close to points on the third stretch, to be discussed shortly. It is aptly named, for I have seen it from the east and the dark shape of the hill appears to be down-turned and tapering, just like a ram's horn. Fourth, the modern Haytor, *Idetor* in 1566 and *Ittor* in 1687, may possibly be the *eofede tor* of the perambulation, although the etymology is uncertain. These four fixed points on the perambulation are shown in Fig. 6.2. If joined by straight lines they give a boundary of over nine miles, but the actual perambulation would have covered much more ground than that, because it would have had deviations which we cannot reconstruct now. We can conclude that those who made the perambulation in the early eleventh century covered many miles of moorland yet noted relatively few boundary points, and this is understandable given the open nature of the landscape and therefore a good deal of inter-visibility between the features which they noted.

In marked contrast is the third stretch of the boundary. It covers only about five miles, again a rough approximation, for deviations cannot be accounted for, yet the record includes no less than twenty-two points (18 to 39 in the table), suggesting that it was drawn through a more complicated, probably partly enclosed, landscape. Some of the clauses along this stretch refer to natural features, but others are man-made and part of a cultural landscape—a *wic*, that is a dairy farm, in a valley, a *weg* or road, a great dike, a land division, several fords and an enclosed farm. Moreover, there are humans in this landscape, several features being associated with, probably occupied by, named individuals. As in the case of the second stretch, some features, for example the way and the knoll, were and are so common in the landscape that there is no point in attempting to identify them now; but the personal name Lullca, which is attached to one of the boundary points, takes us to the settlement called Lurcombe today (*Lulcacumba* in the twelfth century); the River Lemon; and the stream which runs into the Ashburn (where the perambulation began) may both be placed with certainty, giving us a general idea of where the boundary lay (Fig. 6.2). Those who made the perambulation were confident as they rode this last stretch of the boundary, picking their way around properties, noting ownership and making their way to fords for an easy crossing.

Fig. 6.2 shows that the territory perambulated in the eleventh century included, in the south, all of the later parish of Ashburton, all of Buckland in the Moor (a parish once dependent on Ashburton), much of Bickington and perhaps part of Woodland; these were, or had been, episcopal property according to Domesday Book and later sources. In other words, here the perambulation was made around existing episcopal lands. The map also shows that the perambulation extended into Widecombe in the Moor and Manaton parishes, taking in large tracts of open moorland and not respecting the boundaries of those parishes as they are today. Here no episcopal holdings were recorded in Domesday or in later centuries and here those who made the perambulation appear at their least certain. Several commentators on the document have noted the fact that the northern part of the boundary appears to be a mis-fit, the editors of *The Place-names of Devon* noting that the record 'does not follow, so far as can be determined, the present boundaries of those parishes, while Sue Pearce states that, to the north, the bounds 'do not relate to the parish boundaries'.[28] She further suggests, most interestingly, that the territory which was perambulated in the north was 'rather ephemeral' and 'soon broke up' and I think that we can extend that suggestion, with a slight change of emphasis, by making the following proposal about the nature of and reason for this eleventh-century document: to the south it recorded the known and established boundaries of episcopal lands, but to the north it simply recorded a *claim* to a segment of the outer moors—but one which was never allowed. Had the claim been allowed it would have given Ashburton a tongue of moorland similar to those of Holne, Buckfastleigh, and North Bovey (Fig. 1.5). But this never happened and the spoke-like pattern of boundaries around Dartmoor is broken here. The suggestion that the document we have been considering is a *claim* not a grant is confirmed by the fact that it is not a charter, as has been claimed. It is not dispositive, that is, it does not dispose of anything. Probably it arose from a dispute, with the bishop claiming part of the last (of what were to become the outer moors) to remain common to all the people of Devon. The dispute would have been taken to the shire court, and in England and other parts of Europe at this time, resolution of disputes over land were often accompanied by perambulation. That is the correct context of this non-dispositive document.

This section has shown that lords of the moor-edge manors were already, by the time of Domesday Book, claiming elongated slices of the rough pastures of the outer moors and that, by implication, the spoke-like pattern of parish boundaries was in place by then. It has also shown that perambulations were being made even earlier, for Brent's moor in the tenth century and for Ashburton, an optimistic and unsuccessful claim to moorland, in the early eleventh.

A manorial moor in Meavy in 1031

One other Saxon document concerns the outer moors and offers less than the others, although previous scholarship has been rather confused. It is a charter of 1031, by which King Canute granted half a hide (*mansa*) at *Maewi* (Meavy) to Aetheric, minister (*thegn*).[29] The very first point to make about this grant is that it is of a tiny property, 60 acres if a hide equalled 120 acres, and this point has not been emphasised enough by previous commentators. In addition, they do not seem to have looked up Meavy in Domesday Book, where they would have found five manors with that name, four of them held by Iudhoe 'of Totnes', with lesser lords holding under him, each probably providing the services of a knight when needed for fighting. Meavy itself, Goodameavy and Hoo Meavy are still named on present-day maps. The existence of a small half-hide unit at Meavy in 1031 shows that the division, probably into six, had occurred by then. There may have been areas which were disputed at the time of the division, because Callisham Down in Meavy parish contains the element *calenge*, 'challenge' or 'claim'. All of this is important, because it has been claimed by Sue Pearce and others that boundaries around Dartmoor were ephemeral because the limits of the *Maewi* of the charter patently do not follow the present-day parish boundaries. There is absolutely no reason why they should have done so, because the charter granted only one-sixth of the area of the parish. My contention in this section of the book is that boundary patterns around the central moor were set in the late Saxon period and that, *mutatis mutandis* perhaps, they remained so set until recent times, perpetuated by perambulations of the people and by documents.[30]

What remains to be done in this section, the purpose of which is to show that the outer moors were for the most part created by the late Saxon period, is to see whether or not the boundaries of this tiny manor of Meavy had a 'moorland stretch'. I do not propose to reconstruct the boundaries of 1031 in detail, because my fieldwork is still incomplete as I write this, and such an exercise is made difficult by clauses in the document, which could be virtually anywhere in Meavy parish, for example a 'boundary mark stone', perhaps set up when Meavy was divided into six, which has not left a trace in field-names, as recorded in the tithe apportionment, nor in place-names. The boundary clauses include an 'eel brook', which commentators have linked with Elford in Meavy parish, but that is not necessarily correct, because the editors of *The Place-names of Devon* give the derivation of the name as 'the ford of Ella', one of our Anglo-Saxon personal names. Perhaps the most interesting boundary clause reads *to boc saetena hig weg*, 'to the highway of the settlers of Buckland' (later Monachorum) and is a clear reference to transhumance towards the moorland (the text is a little corrupt here and in other places, but there is no way in which one can get to the 'hay wagon way' of some commentators, because the people of Buckland would not have transported hay over long distances.[31]

We must return to our main investigation, the discovery of a moorland feature in the boundary, and that is initially quite easy, because towards the very end of the perambulation we find *to edswythe torre*, 'to Eadswith's tor'. A tor is an abiding feature of moorland landscapes, seldom found outside them, and it is significant that this clause comes at the end of the perambulation, which would have begun 'at home' and ended with a moorland stretch. Previous commentators have been well off the mark here, taking the boundary into another parish, which is unlikely because of the small size of this fragment of Meavy. Moreover, Tom Greeves has discovered a document of around 1550 which mentions common of pasture in Meavy, on Eaddystorre and Ringmoor Down while a brook (now Legislake) was called *Yaddabrok* in 1291, 'Eadda's stream'. Given the licence of a little miscopying, the forms here are sufficiently close for us to say with confidence that the tor of the Anglo-Saxon perambulation is what is now called Legis Tor, next to Ringmoor Down, in Meavy parish.[32]

So we can say that this small manor of Meavy had its share of the outer moors by 1031. The larger moor of the original, undivided, manor of Meavy had been divided into smaller slices when the manorial sub-division took place. To conclude in general: the spoke-like pattern of boundaries around the edges of Dartmoor was already in place by the eleventh century, in large part at least. But what of the hub at the centre, to which we now turn?

The role of the Crown

In the previous section we have seen how the lords of manors on the borders of Dartmoor began, in the tenth century, to slice up the lower moorlands for their own profit, creating the boundary pattern which still exists today. Now, in this section, we look at the role of the Crown, which takes us to the central hub, which is still today in royal ownership.

Anglo-Saxon origins of tithings and hundreds

We begin by examining a growing concern about theft of cattle evident in royal law codes in the tenth century, because this concern, we shall argue, lay behind the definition of the boundary of the central hub. Few Anglo-Saxon laws contain no reference to cattle, which is unsurprising, because an ox or cow was a person's most valuable moveable possession. The laws of Ine of Wessex, from the very end of the seventh century, mention cattle theft, but it is not until the tenth century that we find detailed instructions about the apprehension of men who had stolen livestock and driven them away. The laws of Edward the Elder, issued at Exeter in the first quarter of the tenth century, ordered that 'everyone shall have always ready on his estate men who will guide others wishing to follow up their own [cattle]' presumably stolen or straying. This looks like a system of self-help which could be brought into being in the case of theft: a man's cattle are stolen or stray, he calls on the help of neighbours ('others'), who themselves enlist the help of experts in tracking cattle ('men who will guide'). This law may merely have codified existing practice. Certainly it was not a pious expression of how things should be, because a document exists from Edward's reign recounting, among other things, a theft of cattle from land at Fonthill (in Wiltshire); they were driven to Chicklade but were discovered there because a man knowledgeable in the tracking of livestock followed the trail.[33]

Later laws, from the end of the tenth century, add territorial details. When a theft was reported, as many as possible of the men of the locality were to ride out following the trail. When the trail was lost, one man delegated by every ten, presumably from the locality where the theft took place, was to continue the search; the search was to be taken up by neighbours should it be necessary to cross boundaries.[34]

Groupings into ten were called tithings. They began, in the words of Henry Loyn, as groups for 'voluntary self-help' in order to 'ensure protection against cattle-rustling and other forms of theft'. There was one further development in the concept of the tithing, either organic or imposed by Cnut in his great law code of the early 1020s: if one man in a group of ten committed an offence the whole tithing would be fined; in other words, people were discouraged from offending because they knew that they were being closely watched by neighbours. The body which fined the tithing was the court of the hundred, a territorial unit so-called because it supposedly contained one hundred hides of land. We first hear of these courts early in the tenth century, in the code of Edward the Elder made at Exeter, although they are not specifically called hundred courts there. The court was held at the meeting place of the hundred and here too taxes (the geld) were rendered and the army (*fyrd*) assembled, for hundreds were financial and military units as well as legal ones.[35]

It will be clear that the tithing and hundred system abhorred a vacuum. If a place or district was outside the tithing—that is, belonging to no tithing—it was likely to become a den of thieves; in the context of cattle rustling it would become an obvious place to which to drive stolen beasts. This is a concept which we can apply to the centre of Dartmoor in the tenth century. The centre was both royal land and public pasture. It was open land and huge, around 50,000 acres, and a man who had stolen livestock could, say, enter the moorland in the west, traverse it, then leave it in the east where the crime would be unknown and where he could pretend that the animals were his own. This kind of problem did not apply to the moorlands surrounding the centre because, as we have seen, the lords of the moorside manors were carving these into slices and expropriating them in the tenth century; in Devon most, but not all, tithings were based on manors, so these moorlands automatically came to be part of the tithing system as it developed in the tenth century and came to be policed, subject to neighbourhood watch and to cooperation between communities in the tracking of livestock. As for the central moor, we might envisage a royal ealdorman supervising the creation of hundreds and tithings and, perceiving a vacuum at the centre of Dartmoor to which livestock could escape, making that area into a tithing in its own right, attached to the royal fortress of Lydford, probably a relatively large town in the tenth century, the king's reeve at Lydford having supervision of this tithing. This scheme of development is supported by the fact that the whole pattern of hundreds and tithings surrounding Dartmoor was determined by a need to control livestock on the move, as described later in this section.

Desire for good order, which lay behind the tithing system and the hundred court, may not have been the only motive behind central Dartmoor's constitution as a separate tithing, and the definition of its boundaries: there may have been economic reasons, too, namely a desire to introduce and profit from the guardianship fees which played such a large part in the profits from the central moor in later times. It is not possible to assert firmly that the Crown took profits of this kind on Dartmoor in the late Saxon period, but it is likely that this was the case, because of parallels elsewhere. Domesday Book records in Cambridgeshire and Essex fees paid by tenants for grazing, either in shillings and pence or in ploughshares; this would not have been grazing on the fallows after cropping, which tenants would have enjoyed freely as an adjunct to their rented holdings, but on permanent pasture, probably rough. A crucial reference comes from Devon, where 'every third grazing animal' on the moors of Molland was taken by the Crown, according to Domesday Book, a reference, probably, to Exmoor, which Molland adjoins. An ox was of great value, but we do not know why payments for grazing were so high on Exmoor at the time of Domesday Book and very much lower on Dartmoor.[36]

'Spokes and hub' boundary patterns

We have concluded that the boundary of what we call the central moor was drawn as part of the construction of the tithing system. That seems very likely, but two topographical problems remain. They will not be so easily resolved. The first concerns the relative chronology of what we have called the 'spokes and hub' pattern of boundaries on Dartmoor. The comparative evidence is suggestive, because it indicates that spoke-like patterns of parish boundaries, which are not uncommon in England at large in localities where formerly common resources have been divided up, are not usually accompanied by a large central hub. Dartmoor is not unique, but it is out of line. Fig. 6.3 shows several examples: from the Leicestershire Wolds where the hub was a very small extra-parochial place occupied only by a pub, much used for cock-fighting and other illegal games; from Brown Clee Hill in Shropshire, where the boundaries of eight parishes converge on three points along the summit ridge of a large hill pasture; from Goonhilly in Cornwall, where six parish boundaries converge at a place called Dry Tree; and from Rymer in Suffolk, where no less than ten parish boundaries converge on a cluster of small meres. These may be compared with the pattern of boundaries on Dartmoor in Fig. 1.5 (p. 23).[37] These four cases are examples of what Angus Winchester has called 'converging boundary patterns',[38] but Dartmoor stands out because convergence is incomplete there. Because a converging pattern seems to be the norm, we can suggest that its absence on Dartmoor is because the hub was already there when the boundaries which make up the spokes were drawn; the hub is older than the spokes and prevented their convergence. In other words, the initiative in the making of this boundary pattern was taken by the Crown, which created the central tithing of Dartmoor for the judicial and financial reasons already discussed, and the

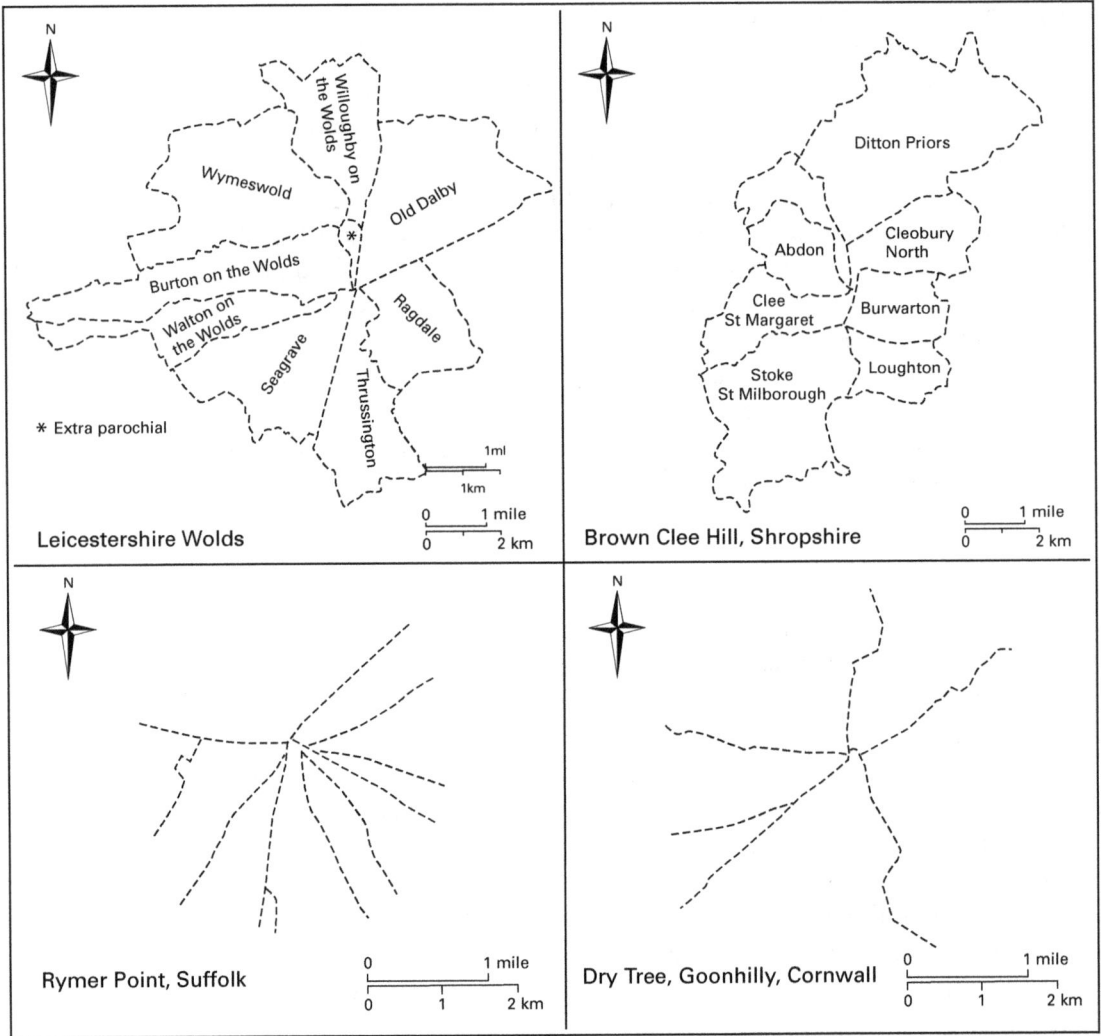

N

Willoughby on the Wolds

Wymeswold

Old Dalby

Burton on the Wolds

Walton on the Wolds

Seagrave

Ragdale

Thrussington

* Extra parochial

1ml

1km

0   1 mile
0   2 km

Leicestershire Wolds

N

Ditton Priors

Abdon

Cleobury North

Clee St Margaret

Burwarton

Stoke St Milborough

Loughton

0   1 mile
0   2 km

Brown Clee Hill, Shropshire

N

0   1 mile
0   1   2 km

Rymer Point, Suffolk

N

0   1 mile
0   1   2 km

Dry Tree, Goonhilly, Cornwall

6.3 'Hub-and-spoke' patterns in parish boundaries around England.

Sources: see text, n. 37

lords of moor-side manors were then encouraged to complete the tithing system by extending the boundaries of their manors, and therefore their tithings, to meet the outer limits of the hub. If this were the case, we have discovered a very early, tenth-century, example of a planned pattern of boundaries. There is, however, a second possibility, namely that the spokes are earlier than the hub and formerly converged in their respective localities, as seems to have been the norm. In this second possibility we must envisage that the Crown, in creating the central moor, slightly truncated the rights of some of the moor-edge tithings, manors and grazings.

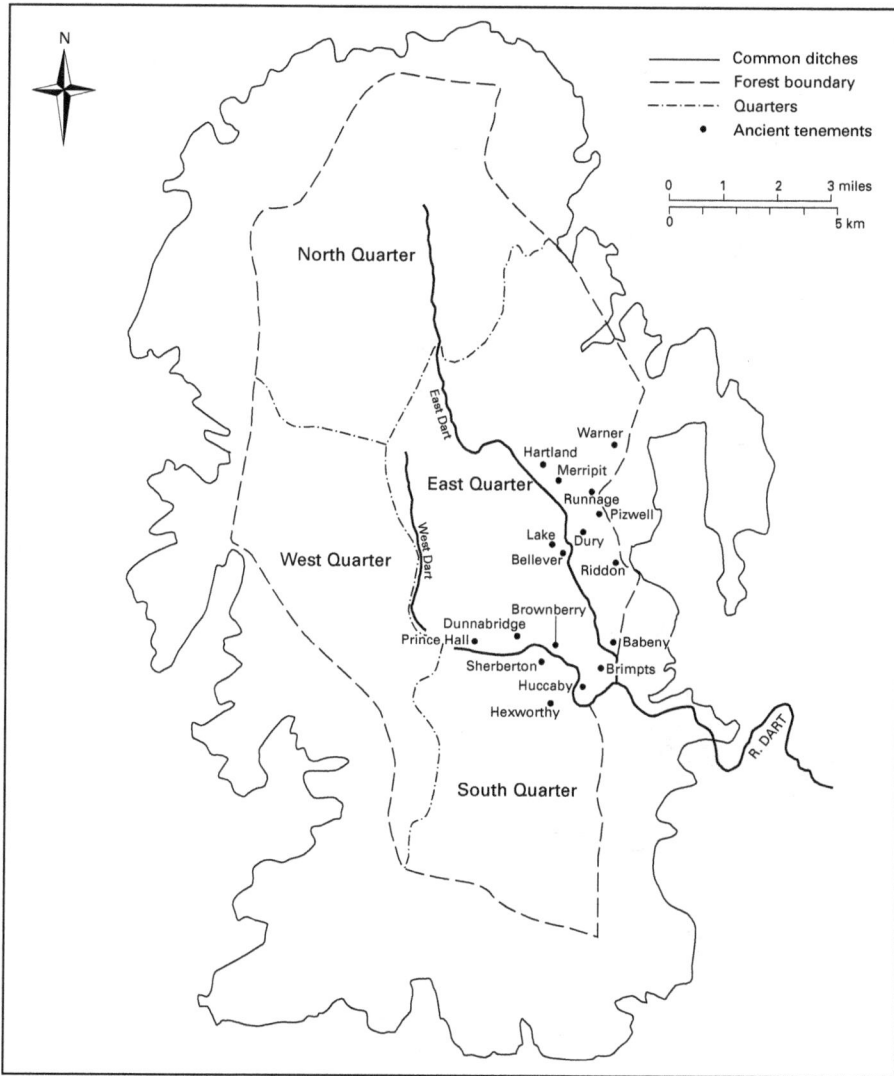

6.4 Dartmoor's 'ancient tenements'.

Based on J. Somers Cocks, 'Saxon and early medieval times', in C. Gill (ed.), *Dartmoor: A New Study* (Newton Abbot, 1970), Fig. 12, and M. Havinden and F. Wilkinson, 'Farming' in *ibid.*, Fig. 15.

The ancient tenements

A second topographical problem concerns the farms known as the 'ancient tenements', the only permanently occupied places in the central hub of the moorland. They are shown on Fig. 6.4, which is reconstructed from post-medieval sources, but reflects the medieval situation relatively accurately. The Crown had no arable demesne on Dartmoor, so the occupiers of the 'ancient tenements' were not expected to plough and reap for their lord as those of other Devon manors did, if rather lightly burdened. Instead, as has been discussed above (chapter 3), each had to assist, with one man in attendance, at the drifts when livestock were rounded up and counted. Their labour services thereby perfectly reflected the pastoral nature of Dartmoor.

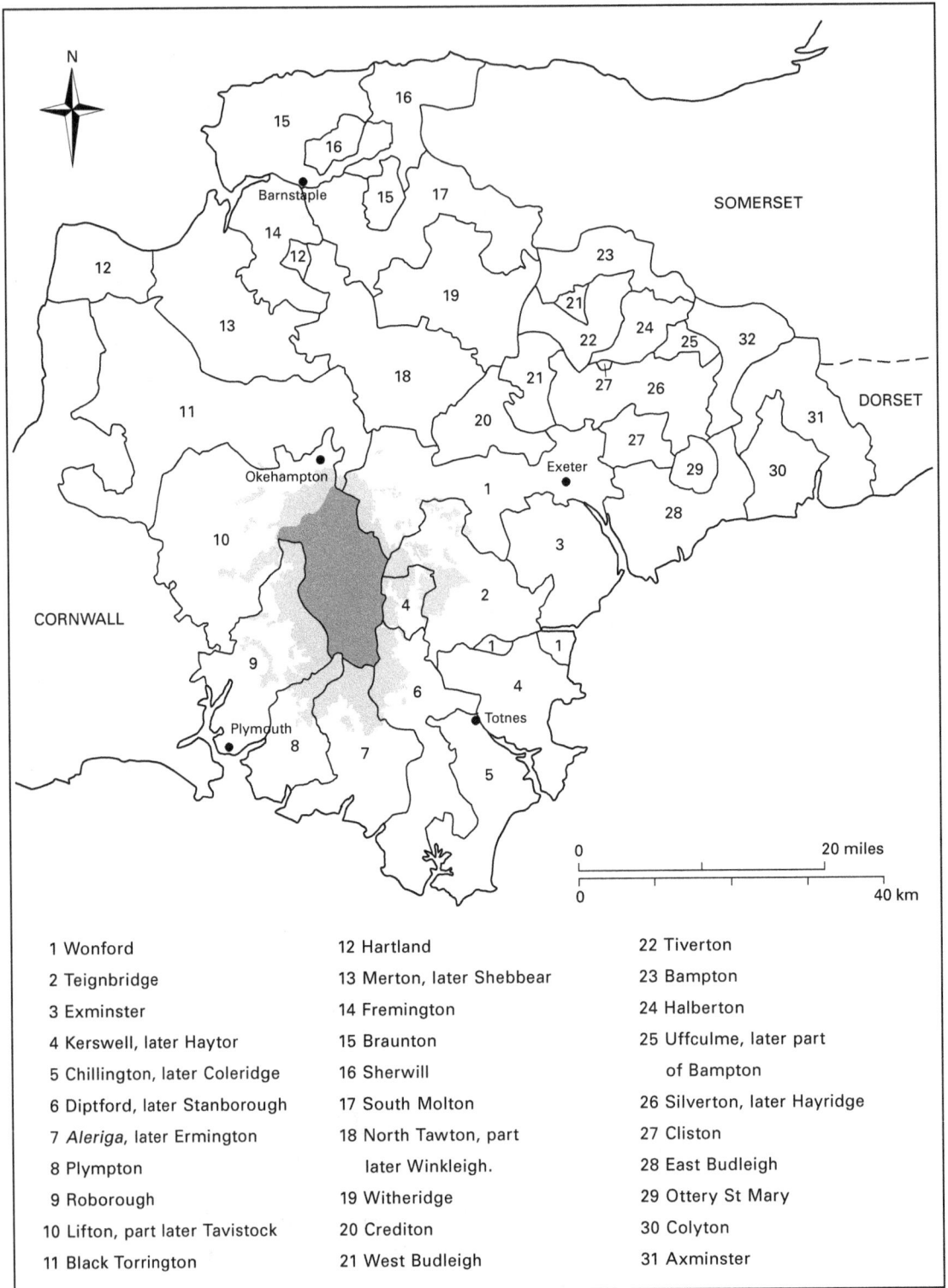

N

SOMERSET

Barnstaple

DORSET

Okehampton

CORNWALL

Exeter

Plymouth

Totnes

0   20 miles

0   40 km

1 Wonford	12 Hartland	22 Tiverton
2 Teignbridge	13 Merton, later Shebbear	23 Bampton
3 Exminster	14 Fremington	24 Halberton
4 Kerswell, later Haytor	15 Braunton	25 Uffculme, later part
5 Chillington, later Coleridge	16 Sherwill	of Bampton
6 Diptford, later Stanborough	17 South Molton	26 Silverton, later Hayridge
7 *Aleriga*, later Ermington	18 North Tawton, part	27 Cliston
8 Plympton	later Winkleigh.	28 East Budleigh
9 Roborough	19 Witheridge	29 Ottery St Mary
10 Lifton, part later Tavistock	20 Crediton	30 Colyton
11 Black Torrington	21 West Budleigh	31 Axminster

Current scholarship dates the 'ancient tenements' to the thirteenth and fourteenth centuries, and this undoubtedly applies to some of them, for example Dunnabridge, presumably named after a bridge on the Dart, for which we have a document recording its establishment by a syndicate of named new tenants in the first decade of the fourteenth century—a rare piece of evidence in the annals of settlement in England at large.[39]

However there is reason to think others may be older still. Two of the 'ancient tenements' bear Saxon personal names as their first elements, Babeny being 'the watery land of Babba' and Runnage (*Renewych* in 1317) 'the dairy farm (*wic*) of Raegna'. It is highly unlikely that Saxon personal names such as these would have persisted later than the first years of the twelfth century, as we have shown above, and there is therefore a very high probability that the settlements to which they belong were established in the Saxon period. Were they already present in the landscape when the Crown 'organised' the central moor in the late Saxon period? This suggestion might be supported by the fact that some of the 'ancient tenements' lie along a stream known as the Wallabrook, 'the brook of the Welsh', possibly indicating that there was some settlement along it in the Celtic period, before the eighth century.[40] However, this is not a strong argument, because there is no proof of continuity between then and the twelfth century. An intriguing discovery concerns numbers. If we subtract, first, tenements known to have been established late, such as those at Dunnabridge, second, those which are not mentioned in the early documents, such as Prince Hall, and third, 'far out' places likely to be late, then the total number of settlement sites is ten. Given the view, expressed above, about the origins of the central moor as a tithing, this is intriguing and suggestive, though no more than that. As for the origins of those ten places, some, such as Babeny and Runnage, were probably already in existence when central Dartmoor was constituted as a tithing in the tenth century. Others may have been deliberately planted by the Crown at that time: there are other examples, although later, of settlements being established by the Crown in areas where livestock needed supervision, such as the northern upland vaccaries, some of which began as royal or seigneurial demesne outposts but developed into peasant farms and hamlets.[41]

6.5   The Devon hundreds in Domesday Book.

Based on W.G. Hoskins, *Devon* (London, 1954), p. 51, and *DB*.

Hundredal boundary patterns

These two topographical problems—first, the relative chronology of spokes and hub, and second, the origins of the ancient tenements—are not easily solved. But what is clearer is that the creation of Dartmoor tithing was part of an act of territorial organisation which also involved the creation of a pattern of hundreds which locked into the central hub. What is most striking about the pattern of the hundreds of Devon is that so many of them converge on the central moor, no less than eleven in all out of a total of around thirty (Fig. 6.5).

One, Black Torrington Hundred, was engineered in such a way that it deviates from its 'natural' shape and makes a turn to arrive at Dartmoor in the vicinity of Belstone, and to a lesser degree Plympton Hundred does the same.[42]

Around Dartmoor the pattern of hundreds seems to have been greatly influenced by the needs of a pastoral society, and one which was on the move. What were these movements? First, there were many movements to and from Dartmoor by people practising the ancient custom of transhumance, as we have seen. It was relatively easy to steal livestock on the move in large numbers; the possibility that an animal might stray down one of the many side-lanes which met the droveways was ever present; gates into fields along the droves might be left open or broken and the stock might cause damage to crops or grass. For those people who followed the trails of lost or stolen livestock, and who hurried to a neighbouring tithing in order to report theft, loss or damage, a pattern of tithings forming an elongated strip with Dartmoor as one of its destinations was a logical and useful one. Second, there were, potentially, many trails of stolen livestock being led to Dartmoor by thieves who hoped to use the moorlands as an escape route, entering them at one point and leaving at another, distant one where neither man nor beast would be recognised. In the apprehension of such men, and the passing on by the tithings of word about their crimes, what would have been more useful and natural than a pattern of tithings forming a strip extending towards Dartmoor?

The boundaries of the hundreds around Dartmoor marched with the droves, and in places the former followed the latter. On the map and the from the air this is a landscape of parallel lines, occasionally to be seen in the field, lines strikingly formed by the needs of movements of animals and their owners, especially the tides of transhumance.

It is possible that the siting of the meeting places of the hundreds surrounding Dartmoor was also influenced by transhumance. A first clue comes from an entry in Domesday Book relating to Moretonhampstead, close to the moorland border. The entry reads: Moretonhampstead receives the third penny of the hundred, that is, one-third of the income from fines at the hundred court. But this is curious, because Moretonhampstead is in the Hundred of Teignbridge, which stretched from a bridging point on the River Teign, four miles from its mouth, northwards to Shapley, which touched the central moor (Fig. 6.5). It is quite clear, then, that Teignbridge Hundred had two foci, one, after which it is named, at a bridge across which livestock from the east would have come on their way to Dartmoor, from manors such as Kenton, the other at the end of their upward trail, at Moretonhampstead, near Dartmoor. That the two foci were at the two ends of the transhumance trail is intriguing, although the precise connection between the custom and the institution is not clear at this distant remove; could it have been that at one time flocks and herds on the move were collected together at the down-country hundredal focus,

Teignbridge, then passed from the supervision of one tithing to another until they finally collected together at Moretonhampstead, before being sent to the open moorland? Teignbridge-Moretonhampstead Hundred was called simply *Moreton* in a list of landowners compiled in the fourteenth century.[43]

All of this helps explain the curious name Moretonhampstead. The three last elements are all habitative, that is they denote a place where people live. Why they are strung together in this way, here and in places in other counties, is not known and the question has vexed place-name scholars for some time. However, it is the first element, which simply means 'moor', which needs explaining in the present context. Every settlement near Dartmoor could be a 'moorton' or a 'moorworthy' or a 'moorwich', so why has this particular one been singled out? The answer is that it was named in relation to the hundred: it was the 'moor settlement' of Teignbridge Hundred, possibly having the specialised function proposed above.

Other hundreds south of Dartmoor may have had two foci in the past. Diptford Hundred, so named in a late eleventh-century geld roll (a list of hundreds compiled for the purpose of taxation), is called Stanborough Hundred later on; a hundred called *Aleriga* in the same source becomes Ermington later on; Kerswell Hundred became *Heithornhundredum* (Haytor) at some date after 1086. Frank Thorn believed that these apparently new foci may in fact represent revivals of old ones; if this was the case then each of these hundreds, too, may once had two foci. Diptford is a parish at one remove from Dartmoor, approximately as close to the moorlands as Moretonhampstead is; Stanborough is in the deep South Hams (south Devon), very close to Halwell, a minute, failed Saxon *burh* or fortress where the hundred court may have met. So here again we have twin foci, one towards Dartmoor and one at a distance from it. It is not surprising to find that at Stanborough a number of droveways from the deep South Hams converge, from Strete, Slapton, South Allington and Soar, for example. The locations of *Aleriga* and *Heithorn* are uncertain, but their twins, Ermington and Kerswell respectively, are in the south and therefore, if the southern-moorland location of the foci is repeated in these hundreds, one would expect to find these 'lost' places towards Dartmoor in the north.[44]

Conclusion

The transition from personal to impersonal transhumance, and from seasonal settlement to permanent occupation, is likely to have occurred in a much earlier period than the late twelfth and early thirteenth centuries proposed by Hoskins and others. This is not reflected in the archaeological evidence, but seasonal transhumance may be nearly invisible archaeologically. An early appearance of permanent settlement can instead be discerned in the names of many of the farms and settlements around the moorland edge, places likely to have originated as seasonal settlements; many of these place-names incorporate Anglo-Saxon personal names and so must have been named before about 1130, when such names went largely out of use. Some at least must have become permanent settlements well before the Conquest, since they appear in Domesday Book as arable-farming communities, and for a handful there are pre-Conquest documentary references.

The initial impetus for the permanent occupation of these sites is likely to have been the enterprise of individual peasant families, but lords soon followed, extending their manors up onto the moors to incorporate the new permanent settlements and large slices of the still-unenclosed moorland around and above them. That this process had already occurred by the Conquest can be seen in the shapes and large sizes of the manorial pastures recorded in Domesday Book, and in late Anglo-Saxon charter bounds which included slices of moor — though the eleventh-century Ashburton bounds appear to be an attempt, ultimately unsuccessful, to claim a then still undivided part of the moor.

Just how the Crown came to appropriate the central hub is uncertain; do the private manorial moors represent encroachments onto a formerly more extensive royal moor, or was the royal centre carved out of the innermost stretches of pre-existing private moors? Its origins may be connected to the creation of the hundreds and tithings in the tenth century; certainly the shapes of the hundreds, radiating out from Dartmoor and carefully adjusted to give even quite distant regions access to it, must reflect a society heavily dependant on transhumance.

CHAPTER SEVEN

Dartmoor and beyond[1]

To regional historians the chosen region is always a seductive temptress; there is a tendency to claim uniqueness, to plead an especial importance. So we shall not claim here that Dartmoor was in history the most distinctive of all the regions of southern England, rather and simply that the region takes its place among others in the South as a district with special reserves and systems of management and utilisation which are unlikely not to have exerted an influence on its surroundings, in the same way that, for example, the New Forest did, or the Weald of the South East. In the past some histories of Devon have been written around the theme of her naval and maritime history, mistakenly, perhaps;[2] and while it would be equally mistaken to write the history of the county from the viewpoint of Dartmoor, it is nevertheless true that these granite hills, set central in the shire, and especially the systems of transhumance which they have always generated, cannot but have influenced the landscapes in which the county's people lived and their ways of living, far beyond any boundaries drawn on geological lines.

This chapter has two very simple aims. The first is to ask how transhumance to and from Dartmoor influenced landscapes beyond the region itself. Here we shall concentrate on droveways, with some general comments on the landscapes of roads and tracks and on the characteristics of droves in particular, before looking at those of Dartmoor, with the use of two new methodologies. The second aim is to ask how transhumance affected the economies of the farms of the down-country. Pastoral farming is discussed first, with a speculative treatment of tenanted holdings, and then data from two demesne farms. Transhumance also affected arable farming in several ways, not least by influencing the pace of enclosure, so here we return to the landscape and ask about the connection between the custom and the small enclosed fields which are so characteristic of Devon's landscapes.

Droveways

The historian would expect that transhumance towards Dartmoor over so many centuries would have left marks in the landscape, etched by constant movements of animals to and from the hills, by many communities as they sent cattle to the summer grazings and saw them return again, perhaps by many different movements as stock of differing types and ages were made to pass and re-pass the lanes along which beckoned, in one direction, the blue grazings in the distance, and in the other, the home comforts of permanent homesteads and relationships. Yet when the historian comes to attempt to study these droveways, it is found that there are very few guideposts and markers to help in the investigation.

The study of routes, tracks, ways, paths and rights of way has been a late-comer in the discipline of landscape history, especially the medieval landscape, of which they are perhaps the least studied feature. However, there are some exceptions to that generalisation. Roman roads have been thoroughly analysed, for example by Ivan Margary, and there is some work on the saltways along which an indispensable commodity was carried.[3] A large literature exists on the routes by which drovers took their livestock to market, as well as on the drovers themselves, because of the undoubted economic importance of that trade and its romantic associations, though many such books focus more on the romantic than the economic.[4] Finally, there are two general books on roads, a few regional studies and comments on roads in general works on landscape history. The two general books are both excellent: Christopher Taylor's *Roads and Tracks of Britain* (1979) and Brian Hindle's *Roads, Tracks and their Interpretation* (1993). Regional studies include Sheldon's *From Trackway to Turnpike* (1928), an analysis of routeways in east Devon, and Raistrick's *Green Tracks on the Pennines* (1962). For the Kingdom of the Hwicce in the west Midlands, Della Hooke has made an innovative study of routeways as recorded in the descriptions of boundaries found in Anglo-Saxon charters. David Hey's work on carriers and their routes in the Pennines, *Packmen, Carriers and Packhorse Roads* (1980), is equally novel. There are comments on roads and tracks in general works on landscape history, for example *The Making of the English Landscape* (1955), in which W.G. Hoskins discusses those shown on a single 1-inch Ordnance Survey map covering parts of Oxfordshire and Northamptonshire. Richard Muir's *The New Reading the Landscape* (2000) refers to 'droveways ... associated with short-distance movement of stock to commons' (this is, strictly, not transhumance and such tracks are properly called 'drifts' not droveways) but he then veers off to a discussion of droving to markets. Oliver Rackham, in *The History of the Countryside* (1986), has many perceptive ideas on roads, but when he reproduces a map of tracks on elevated land between the Nene and the Ouse, Huntingdonshire, almost certainly droveways in origin, his only comment is: 'for what purpose?'[5]

Transhumance is dependent on routeways, and it is natural therefore that some studies of the custom contain information about the ways along which livestock were taken to the new pastures. For continental Europe we have,

7.1 Droveways in the Forest of Arden, the North Downs in Kent and High Leicestershire.

Source: see text n. 7.

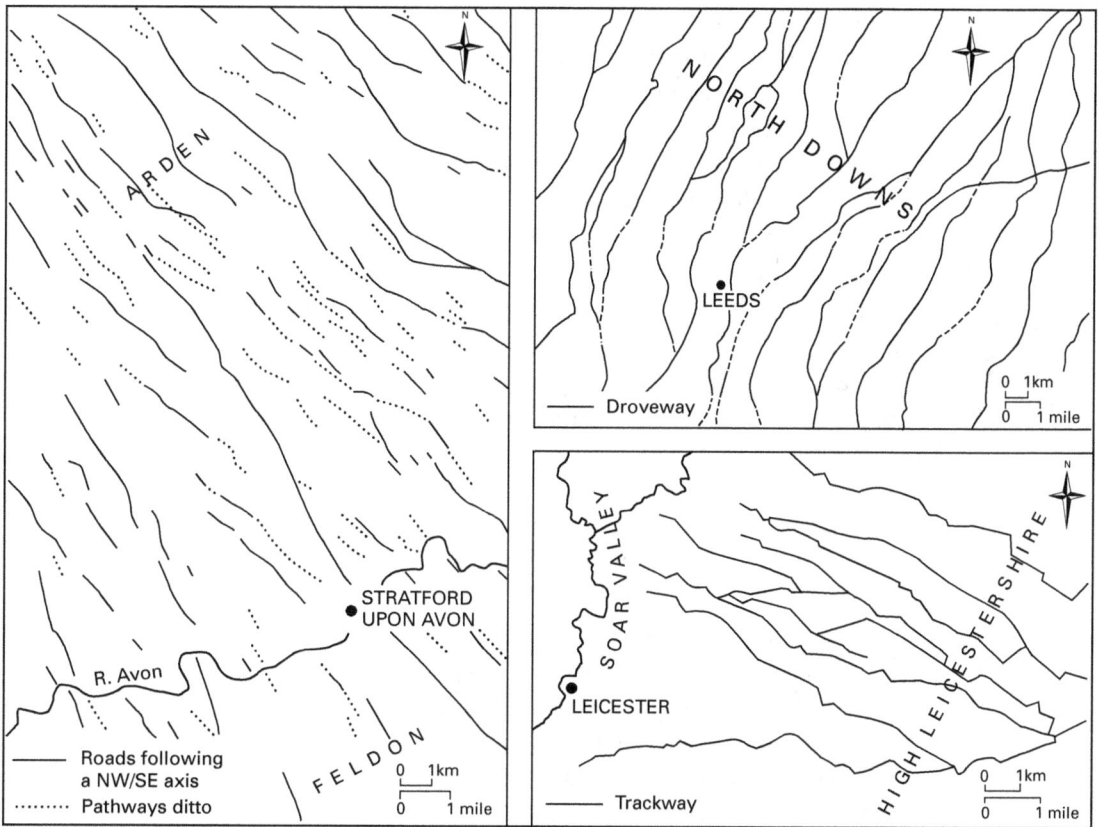

for example, discussion of the wide Spanish *canadas* along which ebbed and flowed the woollen wealth of the nation, and of the Italian *tratturi* which linked mountain and plain.[6] For England only four works touching on transhumance have discussed droveways specifically. They are, in chronological order of publication, K.P. Witney's *Jutish Forest* (1976), a study of the Weald of Kent, and Alan Everitt's *Continuity and Colonisation* (1986), which has a map of droveways to the Weald of Kent, as well as very detailed case-studies of those in other parts of the county. He makes the astute point that many of the droveways to the Weald contain stretches too steep to have been used by wheeled vehicles; they were created for livestock only. My own paper on 'The people of the wolds' (1989) has an experimental map of tracks leading from the Soar Valley eastwards to the wolds of High Leicestershire, and Della Hooke's 'Pre-Conquest woodland' (also 1989) has a map of tracks between the Avon Valley and the 'Forest' of Arden. Discussion of the tracks mapped in these last two brief works is limited in the extreme.[7]

Finally, in this brief review of the literature, some of the general works on the history of the roads and tracks, mentioned in the previous paragraph, briefly discuss droveways, for example the 'transhumance tracks' at Knoydart,

7.2 Two droveways, from Cockington to Dewdon and from Paignton, Stoke Gabriel and Marldon to Dartmoor.

Prepared by the editors, based on a draft found in Professor Fox's papers.

Scotland. One of them confuses transhumance with droving, so it is necessary to make some distinctions here.[8] Transhumance has already been defined in this book: it is 'the seasonal transfer of grazing animals to different pastures', the livestock returning to their point of origin after a season at a distance. Droving is the driving of animals to markets, usually urban ones, from which they did not return. However, the literature on droving is significant to the scholar of transhumance, because both involve movements of livestock and both generate tracks or roads and need for facilities *en route*.

The English publications mentioned above, dealing with transhumance and droving to markets, were focused on localities and written independently from one another, and therefore do not make many general points. But thanks to them we can now make four simple generalisations about droveways used for transhumance. Droveways have a striking directness; patterns of droveways are multi-flex, having many strands; the tracks have facilities along the way; finally, they are of some antiquity. These characteristics will be dealt with, first in relation to the existing literature then in relation to the tracks which converge on Dartmoor.

In Fig. 7.1 maps taken from some of the English studies mentioned above have been re-drawn to the same scale. The multi-flex pattern of these droveways will be discussed a little later, but as equally striking is their *directness*. They do not wander much or deviate from their purposeful routes: they are determined and there is a certain urgency, an impatience about them. Oddly enough, most of the authors of these studies do not comment on this characteristic. Certainly I did not do so in 'The people of the wolds', and the same applies to the work of Everitt and Hooke. Only Witney's comments on the Wealden droveways have any bearing on this subject: he describes them as 'always penetrating [directly] towards the heart of the forest'.[9] Perhaps this characteristic of directness has not been commented upon because its reasons are self-evident and very simple, but they will nevertheless be introduced here because they take us to the very heart of what it meant to be in charge of animals on the move. At the beginning of the summer grazing season, livestock were weaker than at the end of it; they therefore needed to be driven or led to their fresh pastures with as much economy as possible. Watering places, discussed below, might be infrequent and this was another reason for making the journeys, in both directions, as short as possible. Finally, some of the animals taken to summer pastures were young and weak—for example, the calves which were sent to Dartmoor in the Middle Ages—and they especially needed economically planned droveways. These, I think, are the main reasons, very simple, for the directness of the droves.

Patterns of droveways are *multi-flex*, as Fig. 7.1 shows. Individual droveways head for their destination while the patterns which they form together are many-stranded. For Kent, Fig. 7.1 shows a stretch of downland studied by

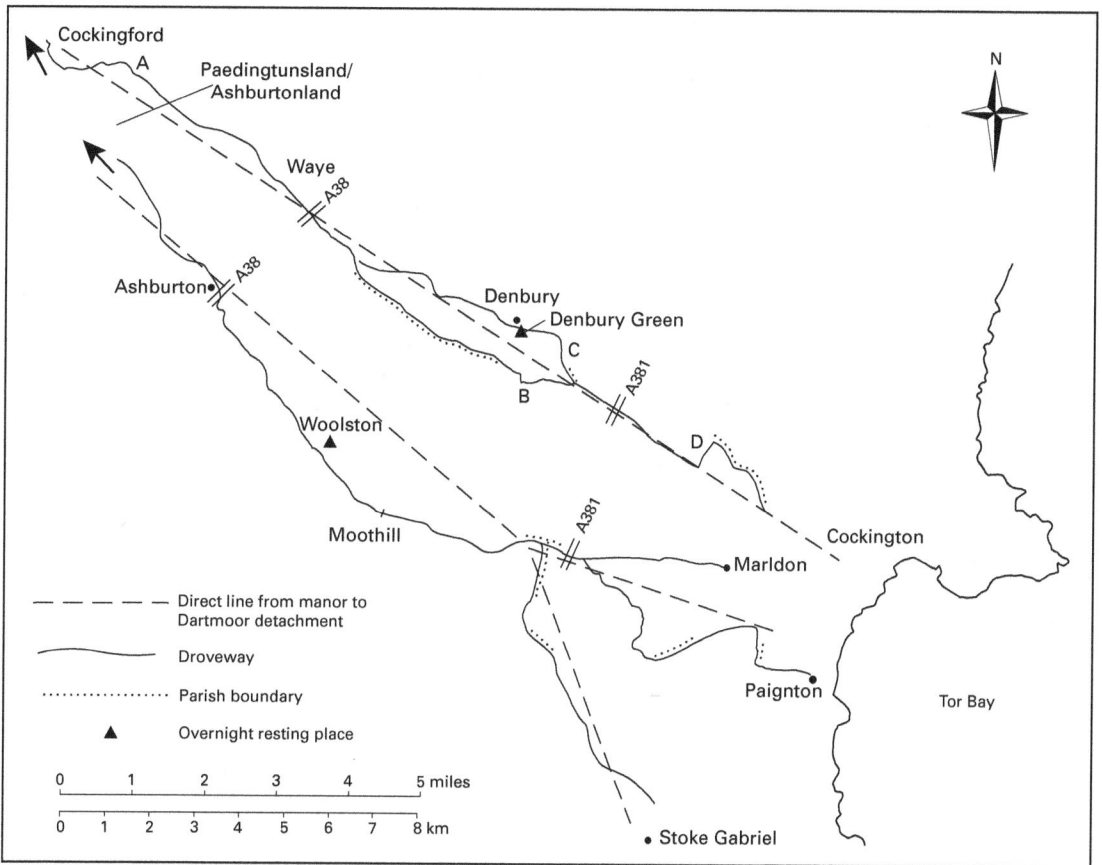

Cockingford
A
Paedingtunsland/
Ashburtonland
Waye
A38
Ashburton• A38
Denbury
Denbury Green
C
B
Woolston
D
Moothill
A381
Cockington
Marldon
A381
Paignton
Tor Bay
Stoke Gabriel

- - - - Direct line from manor to Dartmoor detachment
——— Droveway
.... Parish boundary
▲ Overnight resting place

0 1 2 3 4 5 miles
0 1 2 3 4 5 6 7 8 km

Alan Everitt, only about 12 miles from west to east, but containing no less than thirteen parallel droveways at intervals of between one and two miles, heading for the Weald. Della Hooke, in her work on the ecological links between the Avon valley, Warwickshire, and the woodlands of the 'Forest' of Arden, presents a map of droveways, some continuous, some slightly broken in places, some still in use as roads or lanes, some marked only by field tracks. In the sample stretch of country which she maps, 16 miles wide, there are about eighteen droveways, many of them less than 1 mile apart. In my own work on the tracks leading up to the wolds-country of High Leicestershire I counted seven droveways, some of them followed by parish boundaries, in the space of about four miles.

None of the authors referred to above made an effort to explain the multi-flex patterns which they map. I was as guilty as the rest. Why do we have this myriad of individual droveways? The answer would appear to be fairly simple: if the livestock of many farms and communities used a single droveway there would be a danger of congestion, of tail-backs so to speak, the more so since some of the comings and goings had fixed dates, as in the north of

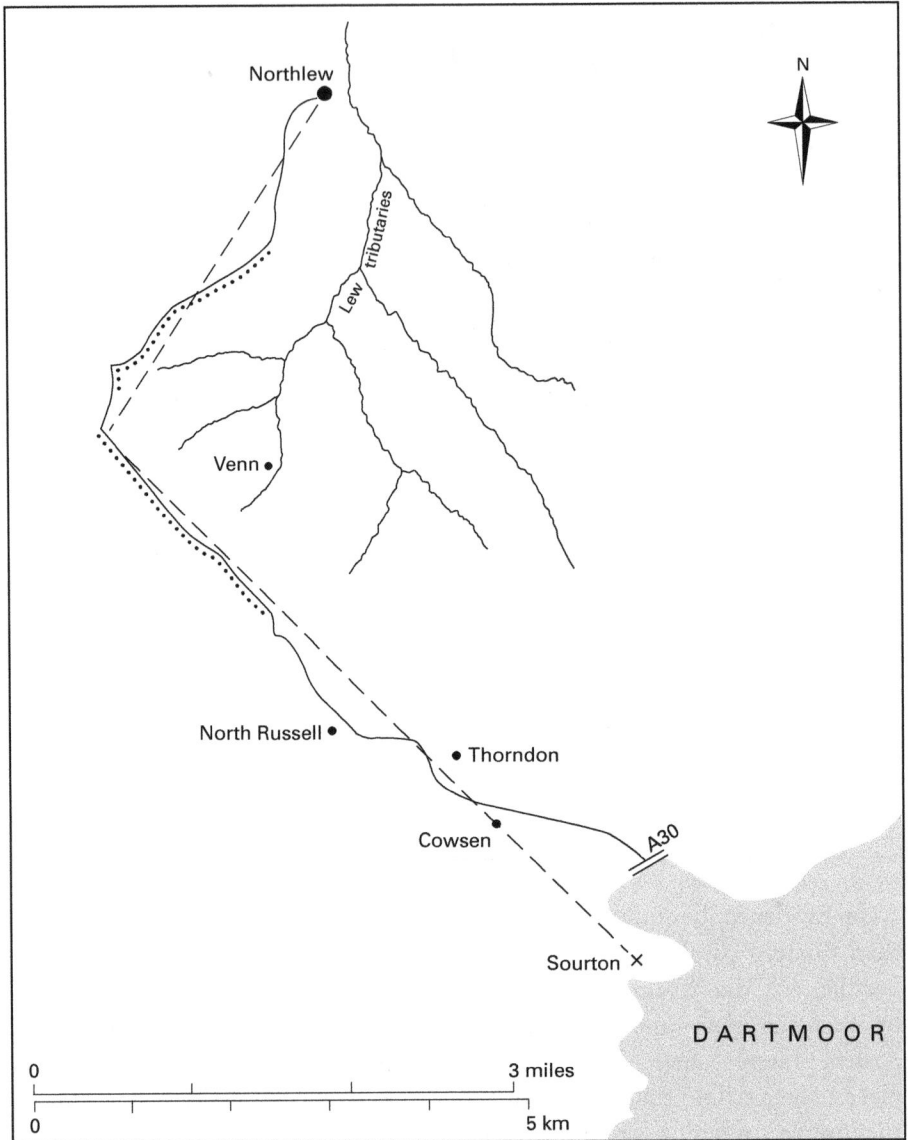

7.3 The droveway from Northlew to Dartmoor.

Prepared by the editors, based on an annotated map found in Professor Fox's papers.

England and on Dartmoor (for the spring movement). Droveways are narrow in many stretches, narrowness being a result of encroaching farmland, so the inconvenience of congestion would have been all the greater. Livestock needed water and pasture at stopping places along droveways, and large numbers on a single route might exhaust supplies. Finally, the need for directness in droveways, discussed above, dictated that there should be many parallel tracks; had there been a single one it could not have been direct from all of the lowland settlements to the pastures which were the object of transhumance.

Facilities en route have been discussed more in the literature on the routes which drovers took than in works on transhumance. However, Alan Everitt noted that the High Street of Sevenoaks in Kent was part of the droveway between Otford and the Weald, so the origins of the town was partly connected to servicing the needs of people and animals on the move; he also noted that it was the droveway, not the London road, which here became the High Street and market of the town.[10] The literature on droving roads mentions four types of facilities: watering, grazing, accommodation for the drover, and places where cattle could be shod. As for watering, Stephen Rippon has pointed out to me the board which still exists at a drinking pond at Hawkesbury Upton, Gloucestershire, which reads 'Ancient drovers' pool'—this was for the cattle drovers from Wales who gave numerous names in 'Welsh' along their ways through the Midlands, for example Welsh Road West, near Offchurch, and Welshman's County, near Milcote, south of Stratford-on-Avon. Grazing for the livestock of the drovers was provided largely by their practice of renting fields *en route*, which often thereby acquired names such as Wales field, or Smithfield, Holborn or London field (after the drovers' destination), or Halfpenny field (for the fee paid for an overnight stay). Drovers' inns provided evening rest and refreshment and can be recognised by names such as The Drovers' Arms (Glossop, Derbyshire; Erwood, Powys; Ruthin, Clwyd).[11]

Only one commentator on droveways used for transhumance has speculated on their *antiquity*. Alan Everitt, in presenting his map of droveways crossing the North Downs, also showed the Pilgrims' Way (not depicted on our reproduction of the map, above Fig. 7.1). This runs more or less at right angles to the droveways and is probably of pre-Anglo-Saxon date. Everitt perceptively noticed that in general where younger tracks meet an older road they 'tend either to terminate at that point or to continue ahead by a zig-zag or "dog-leg" alignment'. The droveways which intersect at many points with the Pilgrims' Way do not do that: they appear to sail across it without deviation. This characteristic, continues Everitt, 'does not definitely prove that they antedate it ... but it is one of many little details in the Kentish landscape that probably point, in the last resort, to those Celtic peoples who gave *Cantion* its name'. He was rightly too cautious to go further, but if the Pilgrims' Way is of pre-medieval origin, then the droveways which pay it so little respect must be older. They, and transhumance, are of great antiquity.[12]

Droveways to Dartmoor: directness

From these general considerations we turn, with a sigh of relief perhaps, to the droveways which converge on Dartmoor. The first general characteristic of droveways is their directness, and we need a simple methodology to explore this feature for the ways leading up to Dartmoor. As an example we shall take the first of the distant detachments discussed in chapter 4: we know that the people of the manor of Cockington, on the final leg of their journey to the summer pastures, crossed the East Webburn at Cockingford on their way to Dewdon and our method first simply involves superimposing, on the first edition of the Ordnance map, a straight line which is a supposed most economical route between the manor and the ford, a hypothetical droveway. Then, as a second step, the lanes which run parallel to that line and are closest

7.4   Roads running (a) south from Hatherleigh towards Dartmoor, (b) from the South Hams towards South Brent and (c) from Tor Bay towards Dartmoor.

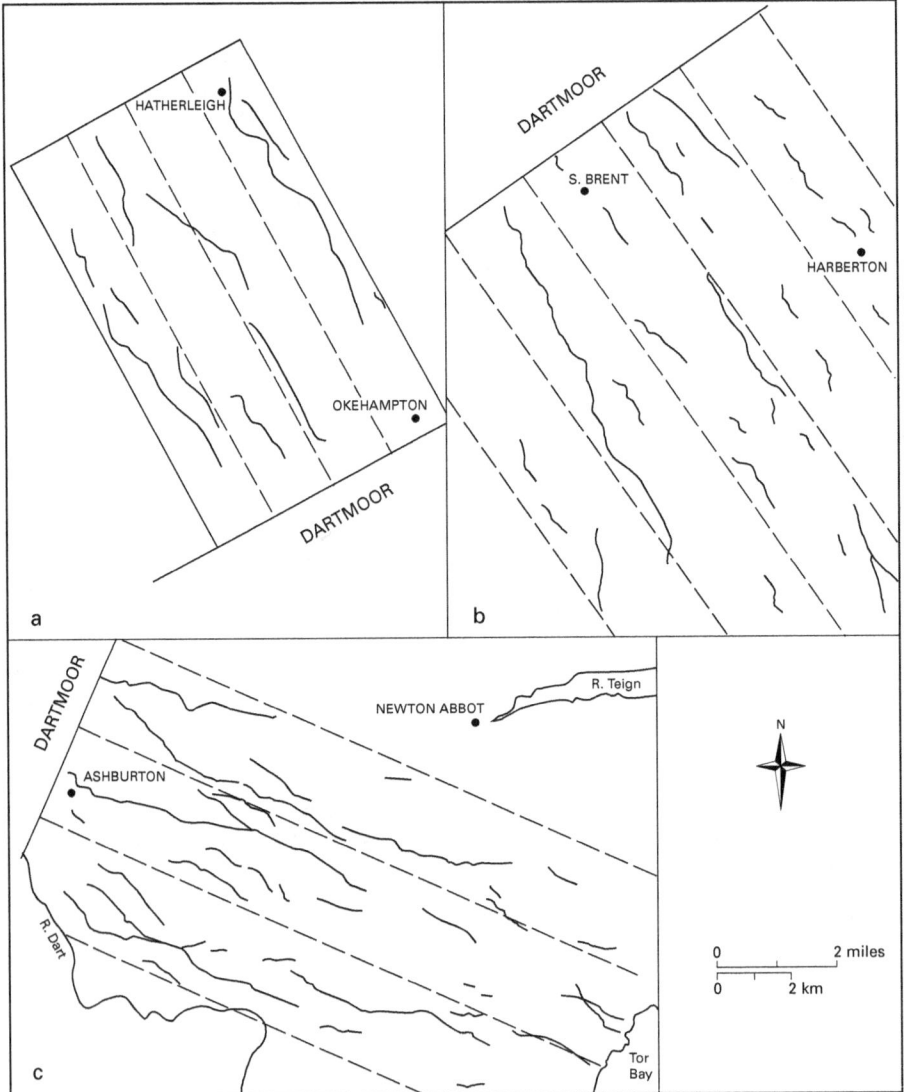

to it are identified (Fig. 7.2). The results are instructive, for along almost all of the length of the straight line there are lanes which roughly run alongside it and are rarely more than half a mile away. Along one stretch of the line it is not easy to select which of two ways might have been used by the people of Cockington, and alternatives are therefore shown on the map. The droveway reconstructed here crosses only one stream large enough to be picked out in blue on modern 1-inch maps, a very small tributary of the Webburn, and here there is a slight deviation (A on the map). The deviations at B, C and D, especially the last, mark the avoidance, by the people who used this droveway, of ascending hills at right angles to their slopes; in these vicinities the hypothetical droveway, the most economical route in terms of distance, does just that and use of this route, had it existed, would not have been economical in terms of time. For those who walk this droveway, a notable feature is the lack of farmsteads along the route. Farms appear to avoid the drove, raising the possibility that the route is the older feature.

It is difficult to decide upon which of the two alternative ways shown on the map was used. The most northerly one runs through the settlement of Denbury, but that is not a factor against it because the built-up street here is a borough established in the thirteenth century,[13] and would not therefore have been present in the landscape when the way was first used for transhumance, although when that was we do not know. In support of this alternative is the existence of a large green, Denbury Green, with excellent watering facilities, for later we shall argue that these are diagnostic of droveways. (Plates 16 and 18) The more southerly one is marked by parish boundaries for a significant proportion of its length, which makes it a good candidate. Perhaps both were used.

More briefly we shall introduce two other studies of the directness of droves, first for that belonging to Paignton on the coast of south Devon, which, as we have discovered, had a detached Dartmoor portion in the vicinity of Ashburton. A first problem in this exercise is to ascertain the initial stretch of this drove. Unlike Cockington, which was a small and simple manor, Paignton was sprawling and complex, comprising the place of that name and also Stoke Gabriel, now a separate parish, and Marldon, likewise now a separate unit. The three medieval churches of these places are about 2–3 miles apart. If we project the most economical route for each of them towards the border of Dartmoor, the three lines converge at the first obstacle to be surmounted, the River Hems (Fig. 7.2 — only the two outer routes are shown) at a spot called Hemsford near the Tallyho Inn. The droves reach that spot through the tangle of lanes behind the urban sprawl of Paignton, the routes being marked by parish boundaries along part of their courses. This fact gives the researcher some hint of their antiquity: there is no reason for a route to follow a parish boundary, but there is a rationale, among those who drew the bounds of parishes, and of the manors which they mirrored, to bring them up to a droveway etched into the landscape through constant use and therefore an indisputable legal limit. The droveways are therefore probably older than the parish boundaries. These early miles in the upward journey to Dartmoor are not easy to reconstruct but beyond and north of Hemsford exciting discoveries may be made. A straight line from the ford to the boundary of Dartmoor near Ashburton is closely followed by a droveway. It passes Moothill Cross, a name which must mean 'hill of assembly' (Old-English *mot*) and later we shall argue that meeting places were connected with droveways. Then it goes on to Woolston Green, the half-way overnight resting place (Plate 17), as was Denbury Green on Cockington's droveway. Finally, the drove reaches the edge of Dartmoor in the vicinity of Buckland in the Moor (Plate 20). This was the earliest droveway which I explored on foot and I can still recall my excitement, first of my armchair exploration with the 1-inch map, in my upstairs study in my mother's Exeter house, then dashing down by an early morning train to Totnes on a cold December day after Christmas and walking upwards along the drove, small notebook in hand. There are no or very few early houses or settlements along this route, the church at Landscove, with its atypical spire in a land of towers, being a nineteenth-century building donated to serve the families of a slate quarry here. In places the droveway is wide, with grass verges (Plate 19), while elsewhere the verges have been encroached; in other places the way is narrow, constricted and sunken, as when it plunges down Chuley Hill (Plate 21), opposite Yolland Hill near Ashburton, my lunchtime destination. It is improbable that wheeled vehicles could have used the way here; as Alan Everitt noted for his Kentish droveways, it is a track for livestock.[14]

A third example of a droveway is that from Northlew towards Dartmoor. What lanes south of Northlew towards Dartmoor have the characteristics of droveways which we have already identified? Using the characteristics of directness, of lanes followed by parish boundaries and of few farmsteads along the route, we arrive at a droveway in two stages (Fig. 7.3), the reason for this dog leg being to avoid the channel of a tributary of the River Lew. The tributary runs through a formation known as the Culm Measures which are muddy and difficult to cross, especially in wet springs and autumns, the seasons of most traffic on the droveways. There are very few old settlements on this route, North Russell, Thorndon and Cowsen, for example, being deliberately situated at a short distance from it. The route, in both of its legs, is followed by parish boundaries.[15]

Dartmoor's droveways: multi-flex routes

A second general characteristic of droveways is that they form multi-flex patterns. Another very simple methodology has been devised to ascertain if such patterns may be found around Dartmoor. Bearing in mind the directness which is necessary in droveways, it is to be expected that they will head directly to the moorland; therefore, if we imagine the moor's edge to be a straight line, droveways should lead towards it at right angles. The simple methodology which has been devised is to imagine the moor's edge as a straight line and to isolate on a map those roads and lanes which run at right angles to it, allowing for a limited amount of deviation. The sources which were used in this experiment were the first edition 1-inch Ordnance Survey map from the early nineteenth century, checked against more modern Ordnance maps. The three tracts of country are the land between Tor Bay and Dartmoor to the west; south of Hatherleigh in countryside where the bold silhouettes of Dartmoor can clearly be seen to the south; and rolling deep South Hams country with droveways leading up to points west and east of the moor-edge manor of South Brent.

The methodology produces maps in which the droveways appear to be broken in places (Fig. 7.4); the missing stretches are deviations from the hypothetical straight lines at right-angles to the edge of Dartmoor. This is sometimes because they wander a little in order to ascend hills in an economical fashion, not too steeply, or to avoid river crossings. Time has prevented an examination of all of these cases of deviation and I hope that a reader of this book will carry out the analysis for me, to confirm or refute the reason I have given.

The similarity between these multi-flex patterns and those, for example, in Kent heading for the Weald (Fig. 7.1), is very striking, and in Kent, of course, the lanes are known from documentary sources to have been used for leading livestock to and from the Weald, and some of them are in fact called 'The Drove'. That the rationale of multi-flex patterns of this type, as explained above, was to 'spread out' transhumance, each track being used by a number of particular down-country farms, is supported by the evidence of names and documents. The track used to reach Dartmoor by the people of Cockington crosses the River Webburn at Cockingford, and it is reasonable to speculate that it was once called Cockingway, just as *Chauelesweye*, once the name of a lane in Ilsington parish, a few miles south of Dartmoor, is 'the way of Cafel', who was probably the owner of Keyberry, near the River Teign (Cawbiry in early documents, from *Cafa*). The people of Buckland had their own way to Dartmoor, explicitly mentioned in a Saxon document of 1031 (p. 154).[16]

Greens

Of facilities on droveways the greens are undoubtedly the most fascinating. In the Saxon period and later Devon was not in general a 'land of villages', to use Maitland's term, and therefore not a land of village greens. However, a few villages did exist and some had greens. The spacious and unusual piazza-like squares at the centres of some of these villages, such as Chittlehampton and Ugborough, were once greens, though now covered with tarmac. Chittlehampton in north Devon is not on a droveway, so there must be some other reason for its green; probably the houses set on four sides of the square formed a defensive grouping, as W.G. Hoskins argued, the back walls or banks of their crofts serving as a first line of defence, with the green a place of refuge. At Thorverton, another village once with a green at its centre, the open space is in fact called The Bury, that is, 'defended place' (*burh*) and there is some other circumstantial evidence for the interpretation given by Hoskins. Ugborough's green *is* on a droveway, a straight track leading from the River Erme towards Dartmoor, but its role as a resting place for livestock and people engaged in transhumance was probably a secondary one. Many of the other greens of Devon, those not associated with nucleated villages, were common space for the three or four farmhouses which made up a hamlet. They were used for grazing geese, for the placing of gorse-ricks and as cultural space, for gossiping and games; the green of the hamlet of Langham (Dolton, north Devon) was used 'for a wake or revel on Whitsun Wednesday'. Finally, another category of greens are those which served the droveways.[17]

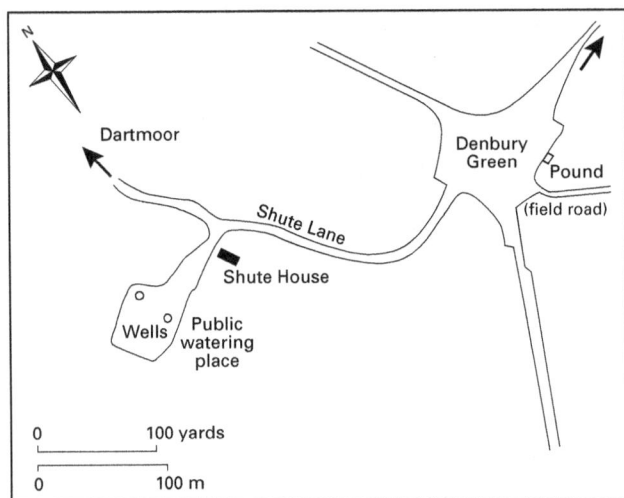

7.5 Denbury Green.

Transhumance facilities shown on the 1839 Tithe Map and 1886 O.S. Six Inch sheet CXV NW.

We can begin with Denbury Green, as an example (Plate 16). It lies on Cockington's droveway and, significantly, is roughly half way between the coast and Dartmoor, used as an overnight resting place on a droveway too long for a single day's journey. How many miles might be covered in a day by livestock and their keepers engaged in transhumance? The only information on the pace of driven cattle comes from relatively modern times and from the literature on droving to markets. Early in the eighteenth century, cattle from Devon being driven for sale in London, *via* Salisbury, Winchester, Basingstoke and Hounslow, took nine days for the journey; cattle from Hereford and Gloucester took eight days to reach London. These figures, and others, give a rate of roughly 15 miles per day for relatively fit, agile and predominantly male animals, fattened for the market and therefore strong; 9, 11 and 15–20 miles per day are also figures which have been quoted. In the phase of personal transhumance to Dartmoor, the livestock were female milkers, more ponderous and, at the beginning of the summering season, weaker and slower, having been kept indoors during the winter. Moreover, the journey was ever upwards towards the high moorlands. Cockington's droveway is 15 miles long, so the upward journey to Dartmoor would not have been covered during a single day. Denbury Green was therefore a necessary resting place along the way.[18]

The morphology and facilities of Denbury Green are instructive (Fig. 7.5). It is triangular in shape, with three narrowing entrances across which some kind of barrier could be put, like the 'bar' which was thrown over the entrances to medieval market places; this would have prevented livestock from escaping overnight. The green was not of the hamlet type, having no farmhouses clustered around it: it must have had some other purpose. Especially significant is the presence of watering facilities close to Denbury Green, all the more

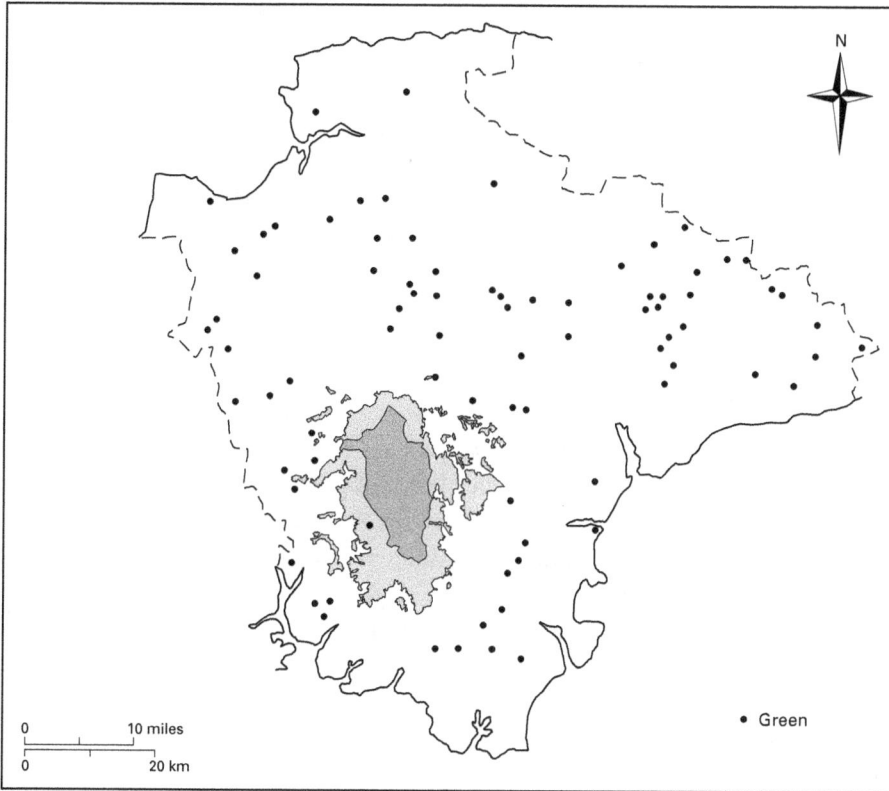

7.6 Distribution of greens in Devon.

necessary because droveways tended to avoid streams if at all possible. The tithe map shows a 'public watering place' near the green and eighteenth-century court rolls mention a rate levied 'for cleaning out the Shute Lake'. Inspection on the ground brings us to Shute Lane, Shute House, just off the green and a spout gushing apparently perpetually and fed by an aquifer in the rocks below. The editors of *The Place-names of Devon* almost invariably choose Old-English *sciete*, 'a corner of land', for the relatively numerous Shute names of Devon, though they have to admit that Watershoot, in Parkham parish, must mean 'place where the stream shoots out', both because of the first element in the name and also because of the presence of the source of a stream here. Shute Lane and House near Denbury Green must surely be named after the water-source at this spot, used among other things by people and animals engaged in transhumance.[19]

A few other examples of other greens on droveways are Woolston Green on Paignton's drove (Fig. 7.2); Taw Green, on one of the northern droveways and bounded by the River Taw at which the livestock watered; and Churchland Green, on a determined droveway running northwards between the Rivers Erme and Avon, a place-name which probably has a Celtic word, *cruc*, 'hill or barrow' as its first element. The distribution of greens in Devon is of considerable interest (Fig. 7.6). Most of those shown on the map are associated with hamlets, but there is a notable string of greens to the south of Dartmoor, approximately halfway between the moorlands and the coast and others north-east and west of the region. All of these need to be researched in more detail in order to discover if they were similar to Denbury Green—that is, on droveways and lacking settlement around them—and therefore likely to have been part of a system of facilities which made transhumance to and from Dartmoor more easy.

Agistment pastures

The greens which we have been studying were half-way stopping places and were not for long stays. But there is evidence, albeit late, that some Devon farmers rented pasture, perhaps for a week or so, on their way to Dartmoor. The stock rested and they grazed on grass different from that on their home farms, relishing the change as animals always do. They were waiting, perhaps, for the grassland of Dartmoor to become suitable for grazing, waiting for the formal 'opening of the moorlands', described earlier in the chapter on the central moor. The evidence for this comes from place-names containing the Old French word *agistement*, 'rented pasture land'. A.H. Smith, in his *English Place-name Elements*, lists one place under this word, a farm called Justment in the parish of South Tawton, north of Dartmoor, spelled *Agismont* in 1713 (it disappeared at some point in the twentieth century, though its name survives, attached to a copse and a crossroads east of Itton, near the parish boundary with Spreyton). The farm stood just a few yards away from a determined droveway from the north leading towards Dartmoor, being one of the pattern of multi-flex droves identified in the map exercise described above. It is five miles from the edge of moorland as it exists today. While I was carrying out fieldwork on droveways and greens in the vicinity I noticed a board at a farm gate reading Jussament, which must be the same word, if not the same place. In both cases 'an agistment' has become 'a gistment' or 'a jistment' among people not familiar with Old French who understandably thought that the initial 'a' was the indefinite article. 'Justment', a dialect word denoting rented pasture, was still in use in north Devon as late as 1900. Not far away is a farm in Sampford Courtenay parish called Agistment.[20]

Since this exciting discovery, *The Vocabulary of English Place-names* covering the letter 'a' has been published. The editors still list Justment in South

Tawton as the only English settlement with a name taken from *agistement*. So the discovery of Jussament and Agistment has doubled, perhaps trebled the corpus of English place-names containing this element. The *Vocabulary* additionally gives two field-names containing the element, from Gloucestershire and Westmorland, both counties in which transhumance was practised.[21]

That these three, or perhaps two, Devon farms—Justment, Jussament and Agistment—were used by farmers taking livestock to Dartmoor, on the northern droves, is suggested by a rental of 1608 made for Andrew Cholwich of Cholwich in the parish of Cornwood, on which several drove–roads converge. The farm of Cholwich adjoins open moorland and the family had properties elsewhere in the parish. Andrew was drawing £27 6s. 8d. a year from seven 'justment rents' of varying values. Probably we lack the data with which to turn these sums into the acreage of pasture which was agisted but precision is not the important point. The point is that here, just to the south of Dartmoor, the same agricultural practices took place as they did to the north, and that fact associates them with transhumance. For richer farmers transhumance was not urgent and hurried but was carried out in two stages.[22]

Inns and smithies

The literature on droving to markets stresses the importance of inns for drovers to rest at along the way. On the edge of Denbury Green is a public house (the Union Inn—see Plate 16). Just north of Churchland Green is an isolated inn called California Cross, while on Cockington's droveway is Tallyho Inn, at a river crossing and also isolated. Ordnance Survey maps name an isolated Half Way House Inn on a road west of Newton Abbot, and one is bound to ask the question: half way between where? Recent owners have now provided the answer, for they have re-named the inn Halfway Dartmoor. A simple exercise in measurement on the map tells us that it is half-way between the edge of Dartmoor and manors such as Highweek and East Ogwell, so it was the people of those places who gave the inn its name, on their way to and from the moors. All of these inns are at places which people engaged in transhumance would have passed and it is likely that those people would have used their facilities. No claim is being made here as to their antiquity (although the inn sign at California Cross claims that it is of medieval origin; such claims can often be exaggerations). There is probably little doubt that these inns were used by men taking livestock to and from Dartmoor in relatively recent times and a possibility that this was so in the Middle Ages too.

Another facility for animals on the move, noted in the literature on droving to markets, is the blacksmith's shop for shoeing. These were clearly necessary on the routes taken by the drovers, in order to provide a facility for repairing cattle shoes which had become damaged on the journey. There is plenty of evidence, most of it quite late, for the shoeing of cattle before they were driven to market, for example from Wales. In some counties oxen working on farms were also shod, as in Yorkshire and Sussex. This was not the case in medieval Devon, however, because no manorial accounts contain expenses for shoeing. Nor was it necessary to shoe cattle undertaking transhumance to and from Dartmoor, for the distances were too short, unlike the drovers' routes.[23] However, there were blacksmiths' shops in places which were clearly on droveways. One is at North Bovey, where a deed of 1426 mentions a house called *la Smytth*. It probably stood on the green there and we have seen that greens were associated with transhumance. The green is on a droveway linking places west of Exeter to the moorlands of Dartmoor just to the west of North Bovey. One other example of a blacksmith's shop on a droveway is instructive because it was completely isolated, not in a settlement or near a parish church. The evidence is from a relatively late map of Owlacombe Common, in Ashburton parish, on the Cockington droveway. It is possible that these smithies were employed partly to shoe horses being taken to and from Dartmoor.[24]

Droveways and other routes

We turn, finally, to the *antiquity* of droveways. Two aspects will be examined: the relationships between droveways and other roads and the names of the droves. Alan Everitt noted how droveways never deviated in the vicinity of the Pilgrims' Way which runs from west to east towards Canterbury. If they had been younger than the Way, he thought, some would have come up to it from the north then followed its course for a while, then would have struck out again to the south and their destination in the Weald. We can adopt his methodology for two roads in Devon, those which skirted Dartmoor to the north and south, in order to avoid the rugged centre of the moorland. Both were important in the eleventh, twelfth and thirteenth centuries because medieval boroughs were established on them, South Zeal and Okehampton (already there, though rather feeble, in 1086) on the northern route, Chudleigh, Ashburton and Plympton on the southern one. In three of these towns the main street carries the ancient route. At South Zeal the route was diverted when this pocket-sized borough was planted: here the slopes along which the old route ran were too steep for town foundation so the way was diverted into what became the town's main street (it is fascinating to find the former course fossilised in field patterns as shown on the tithe map). A similar diversion may have been engineered at Plympton. Clearly, medieval town-planners were trying to catch passing trade, merchants on their way to Cornwall's tin-producing areas and to the important medieval towns of Plymouth, Tavistock, Launceston and Bodmin, pilgrims to Landulph and other ports, where they embarked for Compostella and elsewhere, and many others, including those who visited Dartmoor in order to get tin or administer the industry, to hunt or to fetch millstones. The locations of medieval towns are our best evidence for tracing medieval long-distance routeways, in the absence of other means of doing so, although the Gough map of the fifteenth century shows the northern route to Cornwall *via* Okehampton.[25]

These two medieval routeways were, then, important in the eleventh, twelfth and thirteenth centuries, when the towns mentioned above were founded. How much older than the eleventh century were they? Luckily, we have evidence to show that they are at least as old as the eighth century. The northern routeway passes through the present-day parish of Drewsteignton and very close to it is a farm called Harepath, named after no hare, but from Old English *herepaeth*, 'route taken by the army': when trouble occurred westwards, the Anglo-Saxon army based at Exeter would set forth along this route. By chance the name was mentioned in the charter of 739 by which King Aethelheard of Wessex gave 20 hides based on Crediton to the Bishop of Sherborne. The charter has a record of the boundary of the estate including reference to the *herepaeth*. The southern routeway passes through the present-day parish of Harford, *Hereford* in Domesday Book, a name which shares the same derivation as *herepaeth*.[26]

After this necessary digression on the antiquity of these two routeways skirting Dartmoor, we turn to the question of their relationship with droveways. Clearly, all that we can do is to rely on relatively modern maps. Let us begin with the printed map of Devon compiled by Benjamin Donn, published in 1765. On it the two routeways are shown very clearly and there are many examples of droveways intersecting with them in a way which we shall call 'perfect': in other words, the intersecting lane sails across the routeway, usually at right angles and certainly without even a small deviation along it. On the southern route there are excellent examples of perfect intersections between South Brent and Bittaford and south of Dean Prior. Inspection of modern maps shows that some of the intersecting lanes have all the characteristics of a droveway, for example the drove which starts near Oldaway (of which more later) quite close to the coast, goes northwards to the vicinity of Churchland Green, then further north towards Dartmoor. Some of the perfect intersections here belong to the tracks which were identified in the map exercise carried out to demonstrate the multi-flex character of patterns of droveways (p. 200): different strands in the evidence are fitting nicely into place. The droves which link Cockington to Cockingford and Paignton to Ashburton, mapped in Figs. 7.2 and 7.3, are also shown by Donn to have 'perfect' intersections with the southern routeway. Turning to the northern one, we find more perfect intersections on Donn's map, for example of the track which comes from the north in the vicinity of Winkleigh, then avoids the village of Sampford Courtenay, then crosses Chapple Moor (where it is only a footpath today) and heads for Dartmoor in the vicinity of Belstone.[27]

An earlier printed map is that published in 1675 by John Ogilby, 'His Majesty's Cosmographer and Master ... of Revels', covering some of the principal main roads of England and Wales, which are shown in strip form, as was once done for motorways in handbooks produced by the Automobile Association. The routeway north of Dartmoor is not included, but that to the south is, considered by Ogilby to be the principal 'road from London to the Land's End'. Traversing this route, Ogilby would have been very much aware of Dartmoor's hills to his north and at several places on his map he writes 'to ye Moor', and in one place 'to Dartmore *vulgo* to the Moor', for lanes which head northwards. If we try to locate on Ogilby's map the same perfect intersections found on Donn's, many of them are repeated on the former map. Unpublished plans also portray some perfect intersections between droveways and the two ancient routeways north and south of Dartmoor. For example, the tithe map for Ashburton shows the southern routeway's intersection with the droveway from Cockington on the coast to Cockingford near Dartmoor: it is a perfect intersection, with no deviation. In short, there is abundant evidence around Dartmoor for droveways which, when meeting an ancient routeway, do not, in Alan Everitt's words, 'continue ahead by a zig-zag or "dog-leg" alignment'. We should conclude, as he did, that our droveways are more ancient than the ancient routeways. We are lost in antiquity here.[28]

Droveway names

There is good evidence to show that, locally, droves were known as 'old ways'. As recounted above, the first droveway which I walked was Paignton's, from the Tallyho public house, to Moothill Cross in Staverton parish, then *via* Woolston Green to Dartmoor. Afterwards, researching this way in documents, I found that it had in the past a very strong influence on field-names: 'Westaway', 'Westways', 'Easterways', 'Boveway', 'Tweenways', 'Between the Ways' are all fields listed in Staverton's tithe apportionment dating from 1842. There is also a field called 'Yellow Way', which interested me immediately because I recalled that 'yellow' in Devon place-names is a corruption of 'ye old'; thus Yellowland in Holsworthy parish was spelled *Yeoldelonde* in 1390. The editors of *The Place-names of Devon* note that names containing the element *eald*, 'old'—the West Saxon form of *ald*—are frequent in the county, perhaps, when referring to land, valleys, hills and so on, having an archaeological significance, namely 'land . . . worn out by cultivation . . . [or] passed out of cultivation altogether'.[29]

The name in the tithe apportionment, 'ye old way', referring to Paignton's drove, is intriguing. It is possible to check the reference in an independent source, namely a survey of the manor of Staverton made in 1805 which names fields called 'Lower Yellaway' and 'Higher Yellaway'. There is plenty of other evidence to show that this name was attached to droveways in Devon, the earliest coming from the Saxon charter for Crediton dated 739. Oldaway is a south Devon farm in West Alvington parish, a few yards from a determined route which goes northwards to Dartmoor, *via* Moreleigh (a failed medieval borough far younger than the road) then to the border of the moorland in the vicinity of Zempson. In the manor of Doccombe (Moretonhampstead) is a 'Yoleway', probably the sinuous road which comes in from the vicinity of Exeter in the east, winding to avoid steep slopes in very difficult country above the steep valley of the Teign. The manor was given to Canterbury Cathedral Prior by William de Tracy in order to atone for the murder of Thomas à Becket. Its court rolls still survive at Canterbury, the earliest reference in them to 'Yoleway' being from 1492. 'Oldway' is a name in Brixham parish, recorded in a survey from the very early sixteenth century, and could name the beginning of a way which runs from this coastal place to Hemsford (on Paignton's droveway); parish boundaries meet it at three places along its course.[30] The sense of the word is not too clear. Local people in the past would have been aware of the sunken nature of the droves, at least in some of their stretches, but we cannot be sure that they would have equated deepness with age. At a time when boundaries were of crucial importance they would have been aware of the fact that droveways were often farm boundaries, so they may have imagined them to be older than the outer parts of farms. They would have been aware of the fact that parish boundaries follow droves but it is not very probable that they had a sense of the date and nature of parochial formation, except that it occurred beyond the memory of men and women. Finally, one may speculate that there were local folk memories which passed down, from generation to generation, the idea that transhumance to Dartmoor along the old ways was ancient custom, undertaken as a time-honoured and predictable part of the farming year, as the days lengthened and another pastoral season began to reach its zenith.

So much more work could be done on the droveways which we have been exploring. For example, a sustained examination is necessary of the relationships between parish boundaries and droveways, mentioned in passing several times above. The determined route between Kingston in south Devon and Churchland Green is followed by the boundaries of several parishes for almost all of its route and the eastern boundary of Okehampton parish follows a way which heads straight for Dartmoor. There are many problems in the interpretation of evidence of this kind. If parish formation belonged to the late Saxon period we could possibly say that droves were as old as that. We know that in many cases parish boundaries simply followed the limits of existing estates, but of the antiquity of those estates we know nothing. Again we find ourselves lost in the past. Finally, much work needs to be done on droveways and the boundaries of farms. This line of enquiry began with inspection of farm holdings in the parish of Staverton through which Paignton's droveway runs: few of their boundaries seem to cross the drove, but further expert research is necessary on this topic.

Pastoral husbandry

It is hardly necessary to emphasise the fact that the practice of transhumance is designed, in part, to benefit the pastoral husbandry of the farms whose owners remove their livestock to the rough grazings. Stress must be laid on the words 'in part' because, as the following section will show, systems of transhumance in many parts of the British Isles were set in motion in order to benefit the arable. Here, however, we concentrate on pastoral farming and attempt some degree of quantification of the benefits, drawing where possible from the period between the beginning of the fourteenth century and the early sixteenth century, but introducing some figures from more modern times when the medieval data fail us.[31]

Model 60-acre farm

In trying to explore the benefits of transhumance to a down-country farm holding in medieval Devon, we shall consider a model tenant holding of 60 acres, a size which would have been relatively rare in the twelfth and thirteenth centuries but was not uncommon by the end of the fifteenth century and beginning of the sixteenth, as Table 7.1 shows. Some of these large holdings of 60 acres or more were a result of the accumulation by a single tenant of two or more farms which had previously been occupied by separate tenants; where the standard size of farms was around 30 acres (a Devonshire ferling) and where, as was usual in the county, tenants who were able to accumulate land did so by adding holding to holding rather than by picking up parts of holdings, our threshold of 60 acres would be reached quite frequently, despite the strains on investment which this may have caused. An example is provided by the south Devon manor of Stokenham, where in 1548 the average holding size was 54 acres, and over 60 per cent of the eighty-seven tenants held more than 35 acres. Other holdings of 60 acres or over might be formed by the addition of leased demesne to the customary holding, like the 33 acres of demesne which John Chudley had added to his 37-acre holding on the manor of Woodbury (1525) or the 20 acres of demesne closes which brought the holding of Richard Dun in Uplyme (1516) up to a total of 80 acres.[32]

Proportions of meadow, ley and permanent pasture

On a model Devon holding of 60 acres, how much might be available as pasture for non-working cattle? The first step to make when we attempt a calculation of this kind is to deduct stream-side meadow land, the hay and grazing of which, we may reasonably assume, would be reserved for the oxen which pulled the plough; these acres can be deducted, for their produce should probably be considered as part of the 'arable' budget of the farm—as early as the date of Domesday Book, meadow was associated with that most important

Table 7.1 Mean farm sizes in Devon, early sixteenth century

Manor	No. of tenants	Mean holding size (acres)	No. of holdings of 50a. or more	Two largest holdings (acres)
Brendon, 1525	18	67	9	69, 400
Bishops Tawton, Landkey and Swimbridge, 1525	126	31	10	89, 109
Hartland, 1566	19	46		
Ashwater, 1523	25	42	6	70, 73
Coldridge, 1525	17	31	3	75, 153
Morchard Bishop, 1525	29	55	14	142, 150
Knowstone, 1525	10	66	4	133, 240
Woodbury, 1525	58	38	13	89, 99
Uplyme, 1517	32	37	6	115, 127
Stoke Fleming, 1523	41	55	19	150, 150
Stokenham, 1548	87	54	36	150, 180

Compiled by the editors from data contained in Professor Fox's research notes.
These figures may under-estimate holding sizes, as the surveys occasionally fail to state the size of free holdings (which had to be excluded from the data, though some of them were clearly very large) and, less frequently, of closes (which have been included in the calculations at a conservative 1 acre).
Sources: (Hartland) DRO, Z17/3/19, printed in R.P. Chope, *The Book of Hartland* (Torquay, 1940), App. I; (Ashwater, Stoke Fleming) DRO, Cary Mss, 1523 surveys of Lord Dinhams' lands; (Uplyme) BM, Eg. Ms 3034; (Stokenham) TNA:PRO, SC 11/168; (all others) TNA:PRO, E 315/385.

of animals, the plough ox, without which there would be no ploughing, and therefore no grain production. Manorial surveys do not normally give details of the land-use on tenants' holdings, being content to measure them in terms of customary units, in Devon the ferling, usually of about 30 acres, and its multiples and divisions. There are occasional exceptions to this generalisation, for example a detailed survey of the properties of Cecily, Marchioness of Dorset made in 1525, which is exceptional in giving the acreage of all types of land-use, arable, meadow and pasture, and occasionally woodland and moor. From these sources we can say that it was relatively rare for a tenant holding to contain more than 10 per cent of meadow in itself, although, by the fifteenth century, some tenant farmers were competing eagerly to add demesne meadowland to their farms, paying high rents and fines for them. Of the land-use of our model 60-acre farm we have allocated 10 per cent to meadow, that is 6 acres. Keeping

7.7 South Brent livestock market tolls.

Livestock pastured on Dartmoor might be sold at one of the market towns which ringed the moor. South Brent's market may be of post medieval origin, but the town certainly had an annual three-day fair from at least 1353, held at the end of September.

to our assumption that the produce of these 6 acres would have been largely reserved for plough oxen, it is possible that they could have maintained a team of four, which would have been fed meadow hay during the winter (say five months), being the produce of the meadows during the spring growing season, and would have grazed the after-math of the meadows after the hay had been lifted. Four oxen would have made a rather feeble plough-team (extra animals could, of course, be hired or borrowed) but, on the other hand, this number was rather extravagant for the acreage which would have been ploughed in a 60-acre farm (for which, see below): the evidence of the demesne accounts shows that eight oxen (one team) were considered sufficient for the ploughing needs of about 50 acres of cropped land, and far less would have been under crops on our hypothetical 60-acre tenant's holding.[33]

We turn now to the acres not occupied by stream-side meadow. Of these, how many were 'arable'—a term which in medieval Devon universally meant what it literally means, 'capable of being ploughed'? Some of the same sources which were used to calculate the percentage of holdings under meadow can be employed here, and these suggest that it was usual in the fifteenth and early sixteenth century for between 50 and 60 per cent of holdings to be arable—with some significant regional variation, the percentage being highest in south Devon south of Dartmoor and lowest in north Devon and mid-Devon (between the northern flanks of Dartmoor and the coast), where meadow and permanent pasture was of much importance. Taking the figure of 60 per cent, this would mean that 36 acres of the model holding would be under the plough at some time. Throughout Devon, though in varying degrees over time and from region to region, convertible husbandry held sway, a system which avoided bare fallows and under which every arable close or piece of land was cropped for a few years and was then allowed to revert to ley grass for a long period. Writers who commented on the agriculture of Devon in the eighteenth and nineteenth centuries wrote of the practice as strongly traditional and deeply rooted in time—it is certainly much in evidence in the Middle Ages, from the thirteenth century, when the documentation becomes full enough for us to witness it, and in all probability was more ancient still, not an innovation of the Middle Ages, but a common-sense adaptation to a climatic regime in which, farmers knew full well by observation, mild springs and generally high rainfall give herbage so good and valuable for livestock that bare fallows were truly wasted land.[34] For the purposes of our calculation we need to know how much of the arable might have been under crops in any one year. We have set this figure at 20 per cent, a figure based on a sample of demesne accounts and probably quite realistic (perhaps a little high) for a tenant farm in the fifteenth century, when the trend in most parts of Devon was towards pasture. This would give 7 acres under crops which, if we calculate for 3 acres under oats, 2 acres under wheat and 2 acres under rye (a good, typical Devon mixture) and use sowing rates and yields derived from demesne accounts, gives a total output of about 70 bushels of grain after tithe had been deducted –enough to provide a family and a servant with bread and ale (though ale made from oats), with a little to spare as fodder for a horse. The remainder of the 'arable' would be under ley grass awaiting its turn for conversion to cropland.[35]

We have considered meadow, arable (and its two components, cropland and ley grass) and it remains therefore to consider permanent pasture. This differs from grass ley in that it was never ploughed for crops, perhaps because it was on inferior ground or steep slopes. The evidence suggests that about 30 per cent of a holding might be under permanent grass, a figure which translates to 18 acres on our model farm of 60 acres.[36]

Number of animals on a breeding and rearing farm

How many animals could the pasture of such a farm support (bearing in mind that we have already consigned away the hay of the stream-side meadows to the arable sector, for the feed of the plough oxen, and that, unrealistically, we have considered the farm to have bovines only and no sheep)? In order to simplify the calculations (posted in Table 7.2) we shall have to make more assumptions here, though they are easy ones to understand. First, we assume that the prime purpose of the farm is to rear bovines until they become adult oxen or cows (at four years old, according to medieval reckoning) and are sold (Fig. 7.7). Second, the calculations allow for no animals to be bought in at any stage: the farm is entirely self-sufficient, its cows producing calves which, each year, graduate to the next stage towards maturity, according to the theoretical rules followed by reeves and accountants in charge of enumerating demesne livestock, to be read in practice in many a medieval manorial account roll. Third, we assume an 85 per cent fertility rate for the cows (not too unrealistic)

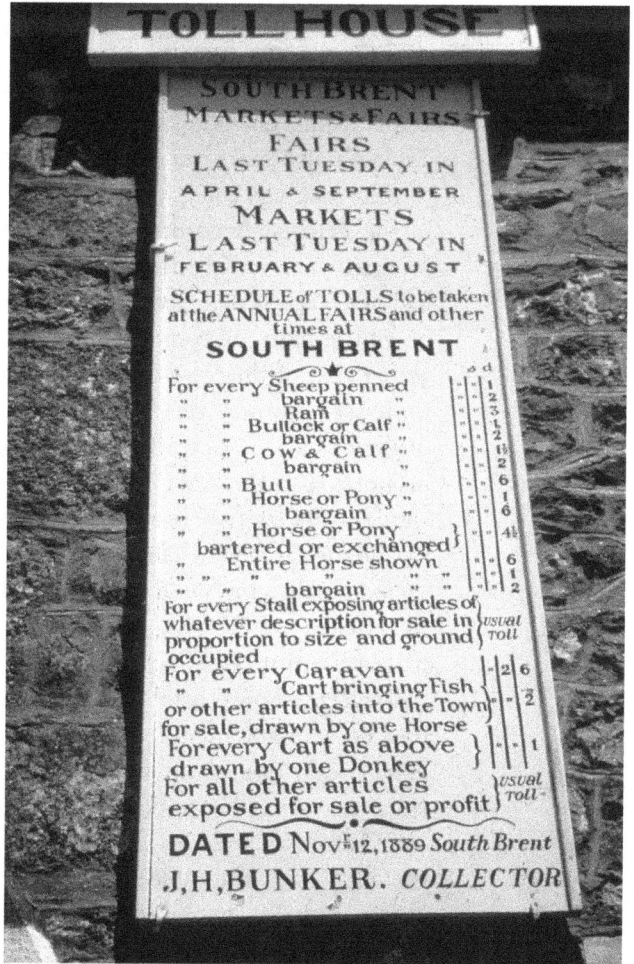

and a mortality rate of nil for bovines of all ages. The next assumptions concern the feed of the herd. Figures from the late eighteenth century and the nineteenth suggest that, during the summer months, a full-grown animal could feed from 2 acres of grassland and that another 1½ acres would have to be set aside to be mown for the hay which sustained it during the winter (and medieval data from the South West indicate that it was very rare indeed for bovines to be fed on any other fodder than hay—they were fed partly on oats in some parts of England, but south-western practice, influenced by entrenched pastoral traditions and a long growing season for grass, separated arable from pastoral husbandry in a more rigorous way).[37] The calculations in Table 7.2 also make various assumptions about the acreage of pasture required to feed each age category of cattle, based upon the prices which they fetched in the market. According to demesne accounts, almost always drawn up at Michaelmas, yearling cattle (those which had passed their first Michaelmas but had not reached their second, and which might therefore be twelve months old, or a little older or younger, depending on their month of birth) fetched only 30 per cent of the price of mature cattle, and similar figures may be calculated for beasts of other ages.[38] Medieval cattle prices were determined by the weight of the carcass in meat, hide and other by-products which should be in rough proportion to the amount of feed consumed (in terms of acres of grass)—and similar calculations are made today by those who determine the prices which should be fetched when farmers sell cattle at market or rent grassland for them. Finally, the table makes no allowance for a bull: on this model farm its services were hired, as on many Devon demesnes in the fourteenth and fifteenth centuries.

Table 7.2 shows that a total of twenty-six cattle might have been maintained on a 60-acre holding (of which 18 acres were permanent grassland), although a good proportion of the beasts were immature. Each year, five bovines would reach maturity, of which, say, two might be needed to replace the breeding stock of cows and the oxen (the latter, it will be remembered, having been excluded from the table because of their reliance on meadow hay, which is also excluded). The remaining three could be sold, giving a cash yield of 33s., a figure derived from a mean price of 11s. per beast (a mean for cows and oxen, based on a national price series, but adjusted slightly to take account of contemporary Devonshire prices).[39]

Number of animals on a rearing-only farm

Figures for another type of 60-acre model farm are given in Table 7.3. We have called this a 'rearing farm', because no breeding was carried on: instead, calves were bought at an early age (from farmers who wished to concentrate on dairying, and who sold weaned calves early on in order to conserve their mother's milk) and bred up until they became adults, at which point they were

Table 7.2 Livestock capacity of a 60a. Devon breeding and rearing farm

Assuming: 6a. meadow (reserved for plough oxen)
  7a. sown with crops
  29a. ley grassland } 47a. of grassland to feed non-working
  18a. permanent grassland } livestock.
  60a. total.

Without Dartmoor pasture

	Feed ratio (a)	Acres of pasture per beast (b)	Number of beasts	Total acres required
Cows	0.86	3.01	6	18.1
3 year-olds	0.68	2.38	5	11.9
2 year-olds	0.56	1.96	5	9.8
Yearlings	0.30	1.05	5	5.3
Calves	0.11	0.39	5	2.0
Totals			26	47.1 a.

With Dartmoor pasture

	Feed ratio	Acres of pasture per beast (c)	Number of beasts	Total acres required
Cows	0.86	3.01	8	24.1
3 year-olds	0.68	1.36	7	9.5
2 year-olds	0.56	1.12	7	7.8
Yearlings	0.30	0.60	7	4.2
Calves	0.11	0.22	7	1.5
Totals			36	47.1 a.

Profit from cattle sales

Without Dartmoor pasture

  3 beasts sold @ 11s.   33s.

With Dartmoor pasture

  5 beasts sold @ 11s.   55s.
  Deduct guardianship costs (28 beasts @ 6d.)   14s.
  Profit   41s.

  extra profit = 8s.
  % increase in profit = 25%

(a) derived from B.M.S. Campbell, *English Seigniorial Agriculture, 1250–1450* (Cambridge, 2000), p. 106.
(b) Assuming 2a. for summer grazing and 1½a. for hay for winter feed (adjusted by the feed ratio).
(c) Only the cows now need 2a. (adjusted by the feed ratio) for summer grazing plus another 1½a. for winter hay; the immature beasts spend the summer on Dartmoor and need only 1½a. (adjusted) for winter hay.

Table 7.3 Livestock capacity of a 60a. Devon rearing-only farm

Assuming: 6a. meadow (reserved for plough oxen)
7a. sown with crops
29a. ley grassland   ⎫ 47a. of grassland to feed non-working
18a. permanent grassland ⎬ livestock.
6oa. total.   ⎭

Without Dartmoor pasture

	Feed ratio (a)	Acres of pasture per beast (b)	Number of beasts	Total acres required
3 year-olds	0.68	2.38	8	19.0
2 year-olds	0.56	1.96	8	15.7
Yearlings	0.30	1.05	8	8.4
Calves	0.11	0.39	8	3.1
Totals			32	46.2 a.

With Dartmoor pasture

	Feed ratio	Acres of pasture per beast (c)	Number of beasts	Total acres required
3 year-olds	0.68	1.02	19	19.4
2 year-olds	0.56	0.84	19	16.0
Yearlings	0.30	0.45	19	8.6
Calves	0.11	0.17	19	3.2
Totals			76	47.2 a.

Profit from cattle sales: rearing-only farm

Without Dartmoor pasture

7 beasts sold @ 11s.	77s.
Deduct purchase of 8 calves (@ 14d.), 9s. 4d., say 9s.	9s.
	68s.

With Dartmoor pasture

17 beasts sold @ 11s.		187s.
Deduct purchase of 19 calves (@ 14d.),	say 22s.	
Deduct guardianship costs (76 beasts @ 6d.)	38s.*	60s.
		127s.

extra profit = 59s.
% increase in profit = 87%

(a) derived from Campbell, *English Seigniorial Agriculture*, p. 106.
(b) Assuming 2a. for summer grazing and 1½a. for hay for winter feed (adjusted by the feed ratio).
(c) All the livestock spend the summer on Dartmoor and need only 1½a. (adjusted) for winter hay.

sold. The carrying capacity in terms of total numbers of beasts is increased to fifty-six, simply because the farm does not have to bear the burden of breeding stock. The number of beasts reaching maturity each year is therefore greater than in the first example—seven, of which perhaps only one would need to be kept to maintain the necessary number of plough oxen—the gross profit (11s. each from six beasts) being 77s., from which about 9s. should be deducted to take into account purchase of calves.[40] Clearly, there were greater profits to be had from the practice of buying, rearing and selling cattle than from breeding and selling them. None of the farm's grassland was consumed by breeding stock, all of it instead going to animals with a potential sale value; profits were derived from the farm's herbage, and, with a little luck provided by optimum weather conditions for growth of grass—a mild spring, a wet summer in which grass did not parch, and a late autumn—and with the input of considerable expertise from the farmer, who must needs know the optimum use for each field and the optimum timing for its use, profits would accrue as a matter of course.

Effect of transhumance to Dartmoor

The model farms for which profiles are given in Tables 7.2 and 7.3 are self-contained, meaning their occupiers have no access to grassland beyond the bounds of their 60 acres. We now introduce transhumance into the picture. To put the matter in the simplest possible of terms, farmers who sent some of their livestock to Dartmoor for the summer grazing season were able to conserve some of their summer grazing fields, which could then be mown for hay, which could be used to sustain more cattle in the winter months. We assume that breeding cows (in the first model) would have been excluded from transhumance because, if they were carrying calves, the journey would have been too great and because, under the system of guardianship prevailing in the fifteenth century, they and their new-born calves would not have received the necessary care on the moors; but that all other stock, the immature animals included, were sent away from the farm during the summer months. Greater numbers of animals retained over the winter translate into greater numbers reaching maturity and thus greater numbers able to be sold: the figure is seven on the breeding and rearing farm (Table 7.2) and about nineteen on the rearing-only farm (Table 7.3) at a total sale value of 77s. on the former and 187s. on the latter (from both should be deducted the costs of transhumance, namely the guardianship fees discussed in chapter 2, perhaps amounting to 14s. and 38s. respectively,[41] and 22s. should be deducted from the rearing-only farm's profit for purchase of calves). In short, the practice of transhumance might have increased sale values by 25 per cent in one case and 87 per cent in the other. The financial benefits of transhumance to the farmers who practised it were considerable; the ancient customs of the hills, dating back no doubt to ages when commercial considerations were less important, could be turned to considerable advantage by farmers in the fifteenth century.

Our models of the stocking densities on two types of farm, and of the benefits which would accrue to them through transhumance, are highly simplistic, of course, because many farmers would have mixed their strategies, both breeding stock and buying in young store cattle for fattening, sending some animals to Dartmoor and not others, differing from one another in the attention they gave to arable husbandry. Nevertheless, examples may be found of real pastoral regimes which permitted impressive numbers of livestock to be maintained and which bear some of the characteristics of those outlined in our crude models above. Both of the examples given below come from the demesne sector, simply because our knowledge of the composition and demography of the herds and flocks of tenant farmers will always be very limited indeed; nor can it be proven, in one of these examples, that transhumance to Dartmoor played a part in its management strategy, although it is likely to have done so, given the large total numbers of animals sent to the moor in the late fourteenth century and the fifteenth.

Sir John Cary's demesne farm at Northlew, 1388

Our first example comes, not from a demesne account, but from an inventory of livestock, made in 1388 on the demesne of Sir John Cary at Holloway, in Northlew parish, with associated land in the adjacent parish of Highampton; the two properties were clearly worked as one unit, as will be shown below.[42] These were not large demesne properties, but the type of livestock husbandry practised was nevertheless highly specialised and on a grand scale. Arable husbandry was of small importance. The inventory, taken in April, includes spring-sown crops as well as those which had been sown the previous autumn: a total of about 28 acres were under crops, principally oats and rye, as is typical of the region. Animals to work the arable included oxen in teams of eight (as we know from the valuation of their 'gear', said to be for eight beasts) and a few horses, which might also have been for domestic or personal use. Totally outnumbering working animals, largely consigned to the small arable sector, were non-working animals kept specifically for their pastoral products. At Holloway itself were no less than sixty-five cows with a bull. This was clearly a breeding and dairying herd: if we use a reproduction rate of 66 per cent (taking into account sterile cows and those whose calves were weakly and died young), we would expect forty-three calves, yet Sir John had only thirty-two, which indicates that some (around eleven) had been weaned and sold; the rest were also weaned and sent to Highampton, allowing their mothers to be used in a dairy enterprise at Holloway, where a dairymaid called Alice was rewarded by being allowed to keep one cow among the lord's herd (and presumably taking a due proportion of the dairy produce as part of her wages).[43] Because we do not have manorial accounts for this manor, we do not know what profits Sir John drew from it, although they could have been as high as a theoretical £13 from sales of cheese and butter, from which we should deduct the consumption of the lord's household at Holloway. After weaning the calves were sent the two or three miles to Highampton, where they were kept over the winter months for three years; the inventory mentions 32 calves, 20 yearlings, 24 two-year-olds and 29 three-year-olds, the roughly equal numbers of each immediately suggesting to us that the estate policy was to maintain a mean of around twenty-six cattle of each age-group (the slight variations from this mean in each age-group probably being a result of the occasional death or sale or slaughter of a beast for the lord's larder). Eight of the mature oxen were also kept at Highampton, giving a total of 94 beasts, an impressive number for such a small demesne. Given the stocking densities which we have discussed in previous paragraphs, and given that a proportion of the land there would have had to be reserved for hay for winter feed, it is unlikely that the demesne would have carried all of these beasts throughout the year. We know that Sir John's steward sent some animals to Dartmoor because, as previously mentioned (chapter 4), the commissioners who made the inventory had to recover four mares with their foals 'out of *Dertmore*'—these would have been horses which had over-wintered on the moor. The young cattle would have been sent to Dartmoor too, but since the inventory was made in April, they had not yet been removed there (twelve of them were sold by the commissioners for a low price 'because the beasts were wild', which perhaps points to an upbringing on the moor).

In short, Sir John Cary maintained a specialised vaccary. The very large herd of cows was the economic base of this enterprise and gave him dairy produce for sale way beyond the needs of his household. The cows also produced calves, many of which were carefully reared until they reached maturity, when some of them were sold, their number being too great for maintenance of the breeding herd and the plough oxen. A specialist enterprise of this size, as has been argued above, must have relied on the summer pastures of Dartmoor in order not to over-burden the limited acres of the demesne, but even with this help there was no space for a flock of sheep. The inventory mentions no sheep of any kind (only eleven goats, a rare animal on demesnes at this time) and, because it is so detailed, and extends to Sir John's properties in other parts of Devon, we can take this lack of mention at face value, indicating a dedication to cattle rearing in part abetted by the summer pastures of Dartmoor, close to hand.

Sir John Daumarle's manors in the South Hams, 1365–93

Another demesne which had a specialised economy, yet one which differed from Holloway, was Sir John Daumarle's property at North Huish, to the south of Dartmoor. This was not a moor-edge manor but lay at one remove from the moor—in the Middle Ages the edge of the moor would have been between three and four miles away. Sources for the Daumarle estate are rather fragmentary, but those which do survive are good. There are inventories (though not, unfortunately, for North Huish itself), made upon the death in 1393 of Sir John Daumarle, sheriff of Devon three times between 1353 and 1377; for North Huish manor itself there is a single financial account for the year 1365–66.[44] Of the manors which he kept in hand, three lay in the South Hams of Devon—North Huish, in the north of the region, towards Dartmoor as has been stated, billowing, hilly land with relatively little meadow; Flete Daumarle, close to the coast, with lush meadows along the bank of the estuary of the River Erme; and Aveton Giffard, a few miles away and also estuarine, on the lower Avon, with its meadows and marshes. In the management of cattle these three manors were closely integrated. The breeding herd was kept on the manors near the coast, where there were twelve cows in 1393. A few young cattle were kept there, the ratio of mature to young beasts being 44:20, a little over the number needed to replace the breeding herd and the plough oxen. The regime at North Huish, towards Dartmoor, was quite different: a team and a half of oxen worked the arable there, but of non-working beasts there was only a solitary cow, together with the impressive number of forty young cattle of various ages. The account of 1365–66 tells us how this demographically very imbalanced situation was arrived at, for it states that the calves there had been received from Sir John's reeve and bailiff at his coastal manors of Flete and Aveton Giffard. Clearly, calves on these coastal manors were quickly weaned in order to preserve their mother's milk for the dairy. They were then sent to North Huish where they were reared through all of their formative years (including possibly their first year as calves), during which the nearby moorland pastures of Dartmoor provided their summer keep. The manor of North Huish was thus used as a kind of highly specialised staging-post in the rearing cycle, receiving the off-spring of the smiling meadows of the coastlands and sending them to the sombre moors for the summer grazing season. A long, distinctive droveway links Flete and North Huish, while from the latter a number of lanes lead towards Dartmoor.[45]

The implications of transhumance for lowland farming

So far the main concern has been to indicate the methods of transhumance which enabled thousands of animals and particularly cattle to be driven to summer pasture on Dartmoor. We have speculated on the profit that lowland farmers gained from the practice. The availability of this great pasture resource also influenced the ways in which the lowland farmers managed their arable lands. Devon agriculture had various special features, and one of these was the very early enclosure of open fields, by agreement, so that by 1600 Devon land was mainly held in hedged fields, well in advance of much of England. Villages in the Midlands, for example, experienced some early piecemeal enclosure or enclosure by agreement, but many of them had to wait until parliamentary enclosure in the eighteenth or early nineteenth centuries.

In Devon, farmers who sent some of their livestock to Dartmoor for the summer season would clearly have recognised its benefits in separating animals from crops during the months when trampling of the stalks was to be minimised at all costs, as a safeguard to farm incomes and living standards. It can be argued that the motivation which is being discussed here—desire to protect crops as one reason behind the practice of transhumance to Dartmoor—would have been all the stronger when the down-country Devon landscape had a far more 'open' appearance than it does today; when many villages and. especially, hamlets were surrounded by fields divided into unenclosed strips. Enclosure of strips to produce an intricate network of enclosed fields was a long drawn-out process in Devon, beginning in places during the latter half of the thirteenth century, gathering momentum during the late fourteenth century and fifteenth, yet not quite complete at the end of the sixteenth.[46] It is notable, however, that there is no correlation between this trend and the number of livestock pastured upon central Dartmoor: large numbers of bovines were sent to the summer pastures despite the progress of enclosure of the down-country fields. This suggests that in Devon the prime motive behind transhumance to Dartmoor was not, as might be imagined, to facilitate the conversion of arable to pasture, but instead was to allow already existing grassland on the down-country farms to be converted from summer grazing to hay meadow, as discussed earlier.

Another contribution of transhumance to arable husbandry in medieval Devon concerns its role in *facilitating* enclosure of arable strips: the argument to be developed here is that the practice of sending livestock to Dartmoor allowed the development of related systems of pasturing on the arable fields and that these facilitated enclosure, when circumstances were appropriate for it. In the early thirteenth century, in many parts of Devon, the face of the countryside was marked by patches of strip cultivation, some around the relatively few large medieval villages which then existed, many more—strip-field systems in miniature—associated with small hamlet settlements. Their origins—in many ways obscure, although a concept of sharing among the people of the close-knit community of a hamlet may in part account for them—need not concern us here. Better documented and understood, and a highly important process for the agrarian history and agrarian landscape of Devon, was enclosure of strip-field systems, a development which stretched in time from the late thirteenth century until the seventeenth but reached its height in the period between 1350 and 1500, when population levels were low and when, therefore, exchange and enclosure of strips were more easily achieved.

All the evidence indicates that practices of pasturing animals on the strip fields of Devon were relatively relaxed. It was natural that patches of unenclosed strips in intermixed occupation should have been grazed in common by the animals belonging to their occupiers. The practice had many benefits: the stubble of grain crops, and the grass and weeds growing among it, provided sustenance for the livestock; cattle which were moved from grassland to stubble on a daily basis—like those at Halstock in the sixteenth century, which were driven to the arable 'every forenoon and not the afternoon'—were essentially transferring nutrients from pasture to the cropland which they dunged.[47] We thus find references to common pasture on the strip-field systems of Devon: for example, a thirteenth-century grant of land in the hamlet of Ogbear in Tavistock gave the grantee common of pasture 'throughout the whole of my land of Ogbear ... except meadows and standing corn.[48]

Theoretically the greatest obstacle to enclosure should have been the existence of rights of common grazing over the arable strips. This was the case in the highly developed common field systems of the Midlands of England—where widely exercised and valued rights of common could delay enclosure—but was not the case in Devon, where we find clear examples of lords and tenants who willingly relinquished their rights. For example, in 1394 lord William Bonville extinguished pasture rights over the whole of Borcombe's arable, granting in return to some of his tenants part of 'a certain field called Estfield' which he had newly hedged, and the quitclaims of pasture rights over part of the arable at Uplyme, exacted from the tenants by its lord in *c.*1337, may likewise have been a preliminary to enclosure.[49]

Two distinctive features of common rights over the arable in midland field systems were absent from Devon. First, all of the animals of a midland tenant used the common pasture of the fallow field (except in those townships where a separate area of grass was set aside for milking beasts, the cow common, which was a post-medieval innovation). Second, and related, in the Midlands the animals were on the fallow field through absolute necessity, because arable field systems in many areas pressed hard on the township's boundary and, beyond the boundary began the fields of the neighbouring village. In Devon, by contrast, most farmers with a stake in strip-field systems also occupied closes of their own and on the horizon of many parishes were rough pastures which could accommodate livestock. Moreover, on far horizons were the blue hills of Dartmoor where all had common rights, which were never under threat in the Middle Ages. The droveways which led livestock towards Dartmoor were safety valves which allowed more relaxed systems of grazing on the strip-fields and more relaxed attitudes to their extinction. We shall never be able to put a quantity on these facts but there can be little doubt that the existence of rights on Dartmoor prepared the people of Devon, both mentally and in terms of the convenience of their pastures, for enclosure in the down-country.

Conclusion[50]

A history of Dartmoor might appear to be a localised story of a specialised, exceptional landscape. In fact we learn from a study of the moor a great deal about the region in which it lay, and by comparison it teaches us about the countryside across England and in continental Europe.

The moor, far from being cut off, was closely connected with the down country by a series of roads and droveways, every mile or so, radiating from the moor like the spokes of a bicycle wheel, each connecting upland and lowland. There were many more roads in the later Middle Ages than exist now, and they were provided with resting places and sources of water for the animals, and inns for those who accompanied them.

The study of the moor and the farms that used it allows us to appreciate the skilful management of the great pasture, and the profits that could be gained by the farms, large and small, in the down country. So much of our attention is traditionally fixed on arable farming that we forget that breeding, feeding and rearing animals required special techniques and could yield high returns. Pasture and arable worked together in complementary systems, and a by product of feeding animals by a transhumance system was the early enclosure of the arable strip fields in the districts around the moor. In the Midlands of England, where no large pastures were available, the pasture on the stubbles and fallows of the corn fields were a vital resources, and enclosure was resisted because it threatened the balance of the farming system.

Conclusion

When Harold Fox wrote the conclusion to his book on fishing villages, he in effect added another detailed chapter, about parallels for the Devon fishing villages in other parts of the country, and he also took the story of the settlements onwards into modern times. He probably did not intend to write a similar conclusion for this book, as he included parallels for Devon transhumance in the text of the rest of the book, and also dealt with its continuation after the Middle Ages. We do not know what he planned, and the best that we can do is to refer back to the general questions posed in the introduction, and identify the main points of this book, and its novelties of interpretation. We will also indicate, as he would have done, the potential for further research.

The significance of pastoral farming is the first important general historical question to which this book contributes. As explained in the introduction, arable cultivation has been given much attention by historians, partly because it is more fully documented, yet this book shows that evidence can be discovered for pastoral farming if there is a careful search. Harold Fox showed that agricultural resources were not as inadequate as is often assumed, because large areas of good grazing could be found on the moor, and even unpromising plants like gorse could be treated to make them edible. The air was healthier for the animals on the high ground, and contemporaries commented on the high quality of the meat. These advantages could only be exploited through good management of the grazing, and this was provided by the herdsmen on the inner moor, the middlemen who took in the animals, and the lords of the adjacent manors and their officials. The technology of pastoral farming lay in the care taken of the animals, and the facilities for moving them about, on drove roads with stopping places and water supplies. Pastoral husbandry required less labour than ploughing, sowing, weeding and harvesting, but the organisation, training and deployment of labour were still crucial. In the days of personal transhumance the herders lived next to the animals and probably practised dairying, but impersonal transhumance meant that the animals (in that period mostly beef cattle) were not attended so closely, though they were still in the care of specialist herdsmen.

Harold Fox's pioneering achievement, based on well-informed speculation, was to indicate the costs and benefits of pastoral farms in the fifteenth century by comparing one calculation based on breeding and dairying with another based on rearing of young animals for sale, many of which were to be used for beef. Not only do these figures suggest the substantial profits of pastoral farming, but they also prove the great benefit that lowland farmers derived from their access to moorland pasture. Perhaps it was intended by Harold Fox that a conclusion would have had more to say about the sale of the animals and their ultimate destination. We know that the fairs held on the fringes of the moor, at places like Ashburton and Moretonhampstead, were held in late autumn, after the grazing season had ended, and these were perhaps one of the main points of sale of cattle that had spent their last summer on the moor.[1] Harold Fox believed that the Dynham family in the fifteenth century were acquiring more animals from the Hartland district than they needed for their household in order to fatten them in the east Devon lowlands for sale to butchers, so perhaps a similar trade operated in the south of the county.[2] Some cattle dealers from south-west Devon were trading in Exeter in the late fourteenth century, and Exeter consumed much meat, as a result of which the city had a large surplus of hides.[3] No doubt some local beef was salted for provisioning the many ships which operated from Devon ports such as Plymouth and Dartmouth. But even this extra source of local demand cannot account for the hundreds of surplus animals available for sale each year, and one suspects that Devon cattle were driven much further to the east to satisfy the demand in the larger towns of the South and even London. Not all young animals were destined for the table, as in their third year they were categorised as oxen, and the arable farmers to the south and east of Dartmoor bought them to haul their ploughs. It is also important to emphasise the changes over time, as the demand for beef was rising in the fifteenth century. The records of the Tavistock estate show that oxen were bought and sold before the Black Death of 1348–49 for prices which ranged from 8s. to 11s. each, but in the second half of the fifteenth century animals generally were traded at between 10s and 22s., with a median around 15s.[4]

The second question that we posed on Harold Fox's behalf in the introduction concerned the approach to regions and their character. Dartmoor, along with other moors and stretches of upland, can be caricatured as remote and empty wastes, cut off from the civilised world and supporting a backward society. The 'otherness' of Dartmoor was well expressed by Conan Doyle in the *Hound of the Baskervilles*, in which a landscape of bogs and rocks threatened visitors from the urban world with superstitions and unknown terrors. Dartmoor had its Hound in fiction, but nearby Bodmin Moor in recent times supposedly had a real 'Beast'. Moors, in the perception of modern outsiders, were and are dangerous places, in which visitors unused to the terrain and its sudden changes of weather occasionally have to be rescued.

Harold Fox's Dartmoor was a very different place; 'alluring' for the cattle and their owners, but also for many other users of the moor. Its land was profitable, with many valuable assets, such as turf, heather, furze and stone, as well as the abundant grazing for livestock. Far from being remote and closed off, access to the moor was provided by dozens of roads. Not only was the moor linked with the many lowland settlements which sent their animals for grazing, it also had connections, both direct and indirect, over a much larger area, including Exeter, as we have already seen. Like other pastoral areas, its inhabitants had limited opportunities for self sufficiency since their ability to grow cereals was constrained by soils and climate, and they had to live by selling their livestock, dairy produce and wool. The tinners were obviously producing for distant markets, and they were even less likely to be able to grow their own grain. The people of Dartmoor and its fringes were more connected to the commercial economy than those practising a more mixed husbandry in south Devon and other arable landscapes. They bought goods from afar, such as the pottery, including good quality glazed jugs, found on Dartmoor settlements, and some of the iron, salt, linen, and preserved fish known to have been imported by traders based in the south Devon ports would have found its way on to the moor.[5] The middlemen who managed cattle grazing, and no doubt the graziers and butchers who appear in the Exeter documents, were caught up in complex dealings and exchanges. It was a commercial and industrial region, and was not trapped in timeless poverty.

The moor, like other uplands, was inhabited permanently in villages, hamlets and farmsteads which have survived into our own time, and for at least a century (from *c.*1200 until after 1300) in the case of some of the settlements that have been abandoned. The central moor contained fewer permanent settlements, but in the summer its upland pastures, like those of the outer moors, were full not only of animals but also of a good number of people looking after them, in the early Middle Ages including herdsmen and dairymaids living in shielings. The people of Dartmoor had special characteristics, including a hardy independence and a distrust of strangers, but for them the moor was not a wilderness, but a known environment, with its routes and waymarkers, and boundaries invisible to outsiders.

In short, Dartmoor can be recognised as a specialised *pays* with its distinctive topography, economy, society and mentality, which was integrated into the wider society of the South West, and which should be regarded as an unusual but by no means backward, primitive or remote place.

The third question which this book has illuminated is the emergence of private property. The moor seems to present an obvious example of the universal transition from common rights to private property, at least on the slopes of the moors where many manors developed and took over areas of rough pasture for the use of the lords and their tenants. The story, however, is a complicated one, as even the inner moor had its 'ancient tenements'. The manors on the edge of the moor, and the detachments belonging to more distant manors, suggest that rights of property had been established over much of the area before the Norman Conquest, and changes after that date were limited in scope. The tenth and eleventh centuries, as in so many aspects of settlement, economy and government, emerge as the formative period when property relations on the moor and its surroundings were defined. Transhumance, which we normally associate with very traditional societies, has the reputation of having been a communal activity, but certainly in its 'impersonal' form it was based on clear definitions of individual ownership, with each animal marked and its owner responsible for paying the fee to the royal herdsmen.

The moor is a good example of the way in which a number of layers of ownership and use rights extended over the same piece of land: the ultimate lordship of the king; the royal right to hunt and to prevent others from hunting, under forest law; the common rights of the people of Devon; the more specific rights of the ancient tenements and the venville farms; the privileged rights of the tinners to prospect, extract and smelt the tin ore; in the outer moors the seigniorial rights of the manorial lords; the rights of pasture, turbary and to exploit other resources enjoyed by their tenants; and even the contractual rights, to pasture or peat or granite, sold by the lords to outsiders from further afield.

This book has provided information and ideas which contribute to the discussion of the three questions discussed above. In addition Harold Fox coined new terminology, based on new thinking. The idea of English transhumance itself is one which has been accepted rather slowly and reluctantly by English agrarian and local historians, but this book is one more proof that the practice really was a feature of English farming. It has been suggested here that 'personal transhumance' should be distinguished from an 'impersonal' variety (what Peter Herring has termed 'transhumance by proxy'), which did not require the presence of the owners of the animals. Harold Fox was also anxious to affirm a distinction, made by others, between lesser transhumance, when the animals were moved off the arable land to a pasture only a short journey away, usually within the parent settlement's own territory, and greater transhumance, when the animals were moved from one type of pasture to another and over much greater distances (and to distinguish both from mere daily moves from farm to hillside and back). Perhaps the greatest achievement of this book, though inevitably based on some speculation, has been the reconstruction of pre-Conquest practices from later evidence, and the suggestion that on Dartmoor personal transhumance was abandoned in the tenth and eleventh centuries.

If Harold Fox was writing this conclusion, he would have regretted that he devoted so little attention to tin mining and other moorland activities such as turf-cutting and the production of peat charcoal, millstone making and the exploitation of other natural resources such as gorse, heather, bracken and rushes, or deer, rabbits, wildcats, plovers and honey. In fact he had begun writing chapters concerning them, but sadly they could not be incorporated in this book. No doubt others will research and write about these subjects in the future, one hopes with the same imagination and sympathetic explanations of human behaviour, which Harold showed in this, his last book. We know that he had gathered so much knowledge and had gained numerous insights into the history of his native Devon, and had he lived he would have written at least one more book, perhaps a survey of the landscape and society of the whole county.

Harold Fox would certainly also have commented on other areas where further work remains to be done. Identification and mapping of the network of droveways leading to Dartmoor from the surrounding down-country, and their associated greens, watering places and other facilities, might well have been top of the list, especially as much of his work on this subject was done too recently to have been written up and will have to be repeated by someone else. He would no doubt also note that although he integrated a wide variety of evidence into his thesis, it remained heavily dependent on documentary sources, and much remains to be done to investigate and assemble other forms of evidence for transhumance, especially in its earlier, personal phase, for which few written records exist. The archaeological evidence for transhumance is still very patchy, and many of the physical remains on Dartmoor are still imperfectly understood—for example, it is uncertain whether the drift pound at Dunnabridge is a Bronze Age, Anglo-Saxon or later medieval structure, and different dates and purposes have been proposed for the many small stone huts on the moor. More paleo-environmental work needs to be done, similar to that of the Shaugh Moor project and Ralph Fyfe's work on Exmoor.[6] The folklore of Dartmoor and its region has never been studied academically, and a phenomenological approach to the region's history, especially to the droveways, could be rewarding. In landscapes of severely dispersed settlement the numerous minor place-names become significant historical sources, usually pre-dating the written record, and this book makes great use of them. However the principal source available for their interpretation, *The Place-names of Devon*, was produced in 1931–32 and is now out of date, especially as regards Celtic names, and a re-examination of many of Devon's place-names would probably cast new light on aspects of Dartmoor's Anglo-Saxon and Celtic past.

Lastly, although the two other great south-western uplands, Exmoor and Bodmin Moor, have been the subject of some recent archaeological investigation, no detailed historical research into their medieval pasts similar to this book exists, yet it is likely that each similarly attracted a seasonal tide of pasturing livestock from a large region.[7] Comparable research into either of them would likely illuminate conditions on Dartmoor.

Notes

Notes to Introduction

1 H.S.A. Fox., 'A Geographical Study of the Field Systems of Devon and Cornwall', unpublished Ph.D. thesis, University of Cambridge (1971).

2 H.S.A. Fox, 'Approaches to the adoption of the midland system', in T. Rowley (ed.), *The Origins of Open-Field Agriculture* (London, 1981), pp. 64–111; *idem*, 'The alleged transformation from two-field to three-field systems in medieval England', *Economic History Review*, 2nd ser., 39, no. 4 (1986), pp. 526–48; *idem*, 'The people of the Wolds in English settlement history', in M. Aston, D. Austin and C. Dyer (eds), *The Rural Settlements of Medieval England* (Oxford, 1989), pp. 77–101.

3 H.S.A. Fox, 'Subdivided fields in south and east Devon', *Trans. Torquay Nat. Hist. Soc.* 16, pt 1 (1970–71), pp. 12–17; *idem*, 'Field systems of East and South Devon, pt I: East Devon', *The Devon Historian*, 4 (April, 1972), pp. 81–135; *idem*, 'The study of field systems', *Trans. Devonshire Association*, 104 (1972), pp. 3–11; *idem*, 'Outfield cultivation in Devon and Cornwall: a reinterpretation', M. Havinden (ed.), *Husbandry and Marketing in the South-West, 1500–1800* (Exeter, 1973), pp. 19–38; *idem*, 'The chronology of enclosure and economic development in medieval Devon', *Economic History Review*, 28 (1975), pp. 181–202; *idem*, 'The boundary of Uplyme', *Trans. Devonshire Association*, 102 (1970), pp. 35–47; *idem*, 'The functioning of bocage landscapes in Devon and Cornwall between 1500 and 1800', Proceedings of *Écosystèmes Bocagers* conference at Rennes (1976), pp. 55–61, 97–101'; *idem*, 'Contraction: desertion and dwindling of dispersed settlement in a Devon parish', *Medieval Village Research Group Annual Report* 31 (1983), pp. 40–42; *idem*, 'Peasant farmers, patterns of settlement and *pays*: Transformations of the landscapes of Devon and Cornwall during the later Middle Ages', in R. Higham (ed.), *Landscape and Townscape in the South West*, Exeter Studies in History 22 (Exeter, 1989), pp. 41–74; H.S.A. Fox, 'Occupation of the land: Devon and Cornwall', 'Farming practices and techniques: Devon and Cornwall' and 'Tenant farming and tenant farmers: Devon and Cornwall', in E. Miller (ed.), *Agrarian History of England and Wales*; *III 1348–1500* (Cambridge, 1991), pp. 152–74, 303–23 and 722–43.

4 H.S.A Fox, 'Exploitation of the landless by lords and tenants in early medieval England', in Z. Razi and R. Smith (eds), *Medieval Society and the Manor Court* (Oxford, 1996), pp. 518–68; H.S.A. Fox, 'Servants, cottagers and tied cottages during the later Middle Ages: towards a regional dimension', *Rural History* 6, no. 2 (1995), pp. 125–54.

5 H.S.A. Fox, *The Evolution of the Fishing Village: Landscape and Society along the South Devon Coast, 1086–1550* (Oxford, 2001).

6 H.S.A. Fox, 'The people of Woodbury in the fifteenth century', *Devon Historian* 56 (1998), pp. 3–8; *idem*, 'Medieval urban development', 'Medieval rural industry' and 'Medieval farming and rural settlement', in R. Kain and W. Ravenhill (eds),

Historical Atlas of South-West England (Exeter, 1999), pp. 273–80, 322–29 and 400–7; *idem*, 'Farmworkers' accommodation in later medieval England: Three case studies from Devon', in D. Hooke and D. Postles (eds), *Names, Time and Place: Essays in Memory of Richard McKinley* (Oxford, 2003), pp. 129–64; *idem*, 'Taxation and settlement in medieval Devon', in M. Prestwich, R. Britnell and R. Frame (eds), *Thirteenth Century England X : Proceedings of the Durham Conference 2003* (Woodbridge, 2005), pp. 168–85; *idem*, 'Two Devon estuaries in the Middle Ages: fisheries, ports, fortifications and places of worship', *Landscapes* 8, 1 (2007), pp. 39–68.

7   H.S.A. Fox, 'Medieval Dartmoor as seen through the account rolls', *Proceedings of the Devon Archaeological Society* 52 (1994), pp. 149–72; *idem*, 'Introduction: Transhumance and seasonal settlement', in *idem* (ed.), *Seasonal Settlement* (Leicester, 1996), Vaughan Paper No. 39, pp. 1–23; *idem*, 'From seasonal to permanent settlement: fishing sites along the South Devon coast from the fourteenth century to the sixteenth', in P. Holm, O.U. Janzen (eds), *Northern Seas Yearbook* (1997), pp. 7–19; *idem*, *The Evolution of the Fishing Village*; *idem*, 'Fragmented manors and the customs of the Anglo-Saxons', in S. Keynes and A. Smyth (eds), *Anglo-Saxons: Studies presented to Cyril Roy Hart* (Dublin, 2005), pp. 78–97; *idem*, 'Butter place-names and transhumance', in O.J. Padel and N. Parsons (eds), *A Commodity of Good Names: Essays in Honour of Margaret Gelling* (Donnington, 2008), pp. 252–64.

8   M.M. Postan, *The Medieval Economy and Society. An Economic History of Britain 1100–1500* (London, 1972) typifies the approach; F. M. Page, '*Bidentes Hoylandie*: A medieval sheep farm', *Economic History* 1 (1927), pp. 603–13.

9   M.M. Postan, 'Village livestock in the thirteenth century', in *idem*, *Essays on Medieval Agriculture and General Problems of the Medieval Economy* (Cambridge, 1973), pp. 214–48.

10 K. Biddick, *The Other Economy: Pastoral Agriculture on a Medieval Estate* (Berkeley, CA, 1989); M. Stephenson, 'Wool yields in the medieval economy', *Economic History Review*, 2nd ser. 41, no. 3 (1988), pp. 368–91.

11 M. Page, 'The technology of medieval sheep farming: some evidence from Crawley, Hampshire, 1208–1349', *Agricultural History Review* 51, pt 2 (2003), pp. 137–54; D. Stone, 'The productivity and management of sheep in late medieval England', *AHR* 51, pt 1 (2003), pp. 1–22; A.J.L. Winchester, *The Harvest of the Hills: Rural Life in Northern England and the Scottish Borders, 1400–1700* (Edinburgh, 2000).

12 U. Albarella and S.J.M. Davis, 'Mammals and birds from Launceston Castle, Cornwall: decline in status and the rise of agriculture', *Circaea: The Journal of the Association of Environmental Archaeology* 12 (1996 for 1994); C. Dyer, 'Sheepcotes: Evidence for medieval sheep-farming', *Medieval Archaeology* 39 (1995), pp. 136–64.

13 D. Stone, *Decision Making in Medieval Agriculture* (Oxford, 2005), pp. 263–67; C. Dyer, *An Age of Transition? Economy and Society in England in the Later Middle Ages* (Oxford, 2005), pp. 203–6.

14 R. Britnell, *The Commercialisation of English Society 1000–1500* (Cambridge, 1993); *idem* and B.M.S. Campbell (eds), *A Commercialising Economy: England 1086–c.1300* (Manchester, 1995).

15 Personal comment by S. Broadberry at the Economic History Congress, Utrecht, 2009.

16 A. Everitt, 'River and wold: Reflections on the historical origins of region and pays', *Journal of Historical Geography*, 3 (1977), pp. 1–19.

17 S. Epstein, *Freedom and Growth: The Rise of States and Markets in Europe, 1300–1750* (London, 2000), pp. 7–10.

18 Bruce Campbell tells the story of a convivial dinner at Darwin College in 1973 which Harold left, shortly after coffee but with the evening far from over, saying: 'I am sorry, I have to go now, I have a footnote to write.'

Notes to Chapter One

1 S. Moore and P. Birkett, *A Short History of the Rights of Common upon the Forest of Dartmoor and the Commons of Devon* (Plymouth, 1890), pp. 65–66; F.C. Hingeston-Randolph (ed.), *The Registers of Walter Bromescombe and Peter Quivil* (London, 1889), p. 204; DRO, 1508M/Devon/Surveys vol. 7 (a 1787 survey of Kenton).

2 W. Marshall, *The Rural Economy of the West of England including Devonshire . . .; ii*, (1796, reprinted Newton Abbot, 1970), p. 24–25; (Simpson) DRO, Z17/3/8; H. Tanner, *Essay on the Cultivation of Dartmoor* (London, 1854), pp. 35, 39.

3 *Gentleman's Magazine*, May 1836, p. 519; A. Mee, *Devon* (London, 1938), p. 412.

4 M. Havinden and F. Wilkinson, 'Farming', in C. Gill (ed.), *Dartmoor: A New Study* (Newton Abbot, 1970), pp. 139–82, at p. 142; S. Baring-Gould, *A Book of the West, I: Devon* (London, 1899), p. 178. See also C. Vancouver, *General View of the Agriculture of the County of Devon* (London, 1808), p. 347, where Dartmoor is said to be 'in a dry summer . . . one of the best sheepwalks in the kingdom'.

5 *DB* 10,1, 20,13, 32,4; (charters) DRO, 123M/TB/7–9, 12, 15; (early mowing) *Short History*, p. 95.

6 Jehan de Brie, *Le Bon Berger ou le Vray Régime et Gouvernement de Bergers et Bergères*, ed. P. Lacroix (Paris, 1879); (John French) Personal communication from Tom Greeves, quoting the reminiscences of a Dartmoor-born farmworker; (blossom'd furze) Oliver Goldsmith, 'The deserted village' in *Essays and Poems* (London, 1807), p. 256; (Okehampton 1292 survey) TNA:PRO, C 133/62/7.

7 (Lutton) BM, Add. Ch. 26137 (printed in W.G. Hoskins, 'Cholwich', in W.G. Hoskins and H.P.R. Finberg (eds), *Devonshire Studies* (London, 1952), pp. 78–94, at p. 79); (1382) TNA:PRO, C 145/224/3 (printed in *Cal Inq Misc IV: 1377–88*, p. 94); (Brixham) DRO, 1392M/T/Brixham; (Tavistock) Marshall, *Rural Economy*, ii, p. 9.

8 R. Evans, *Home Scenes; or Tavistock and its Vicinity* (Tavistock, 1846), p. 76; (partridges) Exeter Cathedral Archives, D&C Exeter VC/22279.

9 R.H. Worth, 'Presidential Address', *Trans. Devon. Assoc.* 62 (1930), pp. 49–115, at p. 51.

10 (South Teign) TNA:PRO, SC 2/168/29, courts of 12 Henry IV; (Lustleigh) DRO, 410Z/F/1, printed in H.M. Peskett, 'The probate inventory of Sire John Daumarle, 1393', *DCNQ* 32 (1971), pp. 79–82; (Tavistock) H. Finberg, *Tavistock Abbey: A Study in the Social and Economic History of Devon* (Cambridge, 1951), p. 98; (ale) A. Borde, *The First Boke of the Introduction of Knowledge*, ed. F.J. Furnivall, EETS extra ser. 10 (London, 1870), p. 122; M.J. Blake, 'Hooker's Synopsis Chorographical of Devonshire', *Trans. Devon. Assoc.* 47 (1915), pp. 334–48, at p. 345, fn. 90; F.E. Halliday (ed.), *Richard Carew of Anthony: The Survey of Cornwall etc.* new edn. (London, 1953), p. 103; (Chagford, 1220) *Curia Regis Rolls, 3–4 Hen. III* (London, 1938), pp. 267–68; (rye a staple food) Fox, 'Peasant

farmers, patterns of settlement and *pays*', pp. 41–74, at p. 62; and *idem*, 'Farming practices and techniques: Devon and Cornwall', in *AHE&W III*, pp. 303–23.

11 A. Pollard (ed), *Works of Robert Herrick*, i (London, 1891), pp. 125–26.

12 C.G. Henderson and P.J. Weddell, 'Medieval settlements on Dartmoor and in west Devon: the evidence from excavations' *PDAS* 52 (1994), pp. 119–40; D. Austin, 'Excavations in Okehampton Deer Park, Devon 1976–1978', *PDAS* 36 (1978), pp. 191–239; P.J. Weddell and S.J. Reed, 'Excavations at Sourton Down, Okehampton, 1986–1991', *PDAS* 55 (1997), pp. 35–147; G. Beresford, 'Three deserted medieval settlements on Dartmoor: A report on the late E. Marie Minter's excavations', *Medieval Archaeology* 23 (1979), pp. 98–158; D. Austin and J. Thomas, 'The "proper study" of medieval archaeology: A case study', in D. Austin and L. Alcock (eds), *From the Baltic to the Black Sea: Studies in Medieval Archaeology* (London, 1997), pp. 43–78.

13 (Ashburton) A. Hanham (ed.), *Churchwardens' Accounts of Ashburton, 1479–1580*, DCRS, new ser., 15 (1970), pp. xiii–xiv; (Moorman) T.L. Stoate (ed.), *Devon Lay Subsidy Rolls, 1524–27* (Bristol, 1979). P.H. Reaney offered 'marsh-dweller' as the name's meaning in his *Dictionary of English Surnames* (Oxford, 1958).

14 (1699) *Short History*, p. 81; (1382) TNA:PRO, C 145/224/3 (printed in *Cal Inq Misc IV: 1377–88*, p. 94); (1331) DRO, 1508M/ Moger/241.

15 A.M. Everitt, 'Country, county and town: Patterns of regional evolution in England', *Journal of Historical Geography* 3 (1977), pp. 1–19, at p. 2 (reprinted in *idem*, *Landscape and Community in England* (London, 1985), p. 12); (yearly drifts) *Short History*, p. 146, and see p. 89; (poaching) *CPR 1317–21*, pp. 18–19.

16 (Buckland, 1332) A.M. Erskine (ed.), *The Devonshire Lay Subsidy of 1332*, DCRS new ser. 14 (1969), p. 6; (Buckland, 1378) *Cal InqPM, vol. 15, Ric. II, 1377–84*, p. 430; (Widecombe) *PnD*, p. 526.

17 (Lettaford) TNA:PRO, SC 6/826/21–3, *Cal Inq Misc V: 1387–93*, p. 151; (1219) *Short History*, p. 3; ('more remote') *Short History*, pp. 80, 85.

18 (1345 survey) TNA:PRO, SC 11/802, printed in *Short History*, p. 152–6; (late enclosures) J. Somers Cocks, 'Exploitation', in C. Gill (ed.), *Dartmoor: A New Study* (Newton Abbot, 1970), pp. 245–75; (Nuns Cross, Snaily House) E. Stanbrook, *Dartmoor Forest Farms: A Social History from Enclosure to Abandonment* (Tiverton, 1994), ch. 7; (detested depradations) William Simpson's Survey of the Forest of Dartmoor, DRO, Z17/3/8; (Dartmoor Pres. Assoc.) J. Somers Cocks and T. Greeves, *A Dartmoor Century 1883–1983: One Hundred Years of the Dartmoor Preservation Association* (Postbridge, 1983).

19 S. Turner, *Ancient Country: The Historic Character of Rural Devon*, Devon Archaeological Society Occasional Paper 20 (2007), pp. 96–112, 146–53.

20 (Hound Tor) D. Austin and M.J.C. Walker, 'A new landscape context for Hound Tor', *Medieval Archaeology* 29 (1985), pp. 132–52; A. Fleming and N. Ralph, 'Medieval settlement and land use on Holne Moor, Dartmoor: The landscape evidence', *Medieval Archaeology* 26 (1982), pp. 101–37, at p. 132.

21 (Peter Tavy) DRO, T1258M/E15; (Harford) DRO, Harford tithe map, 1841.

22 (Four quarters) Fox, 'Medieval Dartmoor as seen through the account rolls', pp. 149–72, at pp. 150, 159; and see Fig. 16 in Havinden and Wilkinson, 'Farming', pp. 139–82; J. Somers Cocks, 'The Stannary bounds of Plympton and Tavistock', *DCNQ* 32, pt 3(1971), pp. 76–79; (glebe terriers) Exeter Cathedral Archives.

23 E. Gawne, 'Field patterns in Widecombe Parish and the Forest of Dartmoor', *Trans. Devon. Assoc.* 102 (1970), pp. 49–69, Fig. 1; D. Brewer, *Dartmoor Boundary*

Markers (Tiverton, 2002); (Haytor) DRO, Z17/3/19, fol. ciii d; R.H. Worth, 'Dartmoor 1788–1808', *Trans. Devon. Assoc.* 73 (1941), pp. 203–25; (1291) *Short History*, pp. 105–6.

24 (Spitchwick) DRO, 48/14/142/1a; (Halstock) DRO, 1508M/Devon/Surveys/vol. 4, plan XXV.

25 R.H. Worth, 'The tenants and commoners of Dartmoor', *Trans. Devon. Assoc.* 76 (1944), pp. 187–214, at p. 205.

26 M. Dobson, '"Marsh fever": The geography of malaria in England', *Journal of Archaeological Historical Geography* 6 (1980), pp. 357–89; P. Herring and J. Nowakowski, 'Beehive huts', in N. Johnson and P. Rose, *Bodmin Moor: An Archaeological Survey*, vol. 1 (London, 1994), pp. 98–100, at p. 100; F. Aalen, 'Clochans as transhumance dwellings in the Dingle Peninsula', *Journal of the Royal Society of Antiquaries of Ireland* 94 (1964), pp. 39–45; F.W.L. Thomas, 'Beehive houses in Harris and Lewis', *Proceedings of the Society of Antiquaries of Scotland* 3 (1857–60), pp. 127–29; K.P. Witney, *The Jutish Forest: A Study of the Weald of Kent from 450 to 1380 AD* (London, 1978), p. 175; *OED*, s.v. shieling, citing the register of Paisley Abbey; W. Nall, 'Alston', *Transactions of the Cumberland and Westmorland Antiquarian and Archaeological Society* 7 (1886), p. 14; Fox, *The Evolution of the Fishing Village*, pp. 12, 129–38; Hasted's *History and Topograpical Survey of the County of Kent*, cited in A.M. Everitt, *Continuity and Colonisation: The Evolution of the Kentish Settlement* (Leicester, 1986), p. 64; M. Gardiner, 'A seasonal fishermen's settlement at Dungeness, Kent', *Medieval Settlement Research Group Annual Report* 11 (1996), pp. 18–20.

27 BL, Harleian 6380, quoted in J. Whetter, *Cornwall in the 17th Century* (Padstow, 1974); T. Greeves, 'The Devon Tin Industry 1450–1750: An archaeological and historical survey', unpub. PhD thesis, University of Exeter (1981), p. 169 and J.A. Buckley (ed.) *Thomas Beare's The Bailiff of Blackmore 1586* (Camborne, 1994), p. 57; D. Austin, G.A.M. Gerrard and T.A.P. Greeves, 'Tin and agriculture in the Middle Ages and beyond: Landscape archaeology in St Neot parish, Cornwall', *Cornish Archaeology* 28 (1989), pp. 5–251, at p. 132; D. Knoop and G.P. Jones, *The Medieval Mason* (Manchester, 1949), pp. 52, 68. For seasonality in the building and mining industries respectively, see Knoop and Jones, *Medieval Mason*, pp. 129–33, and I. Blanchard, 'Labour productivity and work psychology in the English mining industry', *EHR*, 2nd ser. 31 (1978), pp. 1–24, at pp. 2–3.

28 Thoresby's *Excursions in Leicestershire* (1790), cited in W.G. Hoskins, 'Croft Hill', in his *Provincial England* (London, 1963), p. 178.

29 *OED*, s.v.; M.I. Newbiggin, *Modern Geography* (London, 1911), p. 179; M. Beresford, *The Lost Villages of England* (London, 1954), p. 204. For discussion of the term, see P. Vidal de la Blache, *Principles of Human Geography* (1926 trans. of French edn of 1922), p. 131; E.H. Carrier, *Water and Grass: A Study of the Pastoral Economy of Southern Europe* (London, 1932), pp. 6–7; J. McDonnell, 'The role of transhumance in northern England', *Northern History* 24 (1988), pp. 1–17; H.G. Ramm, R.W. McDowall and E. Mercer, *Shielings and Bastles* (London, 1970), pp. 1, 4; and other works cited in Fox, 'Introduction', esp. fns 2, 5–10.

30 F. Braudel, *The Mediterranean and the Mediterranean World in the Age of Philip II*, vol. 1 (London, 1972), p. 87.

31 E. Davies, 'The patterns of transhumance in Europe', *Geography* 25 (1940), pp. 155–68, at p. 155.

32 (1604 survey) cited in Ramm, McDowall, Mercer, *Shielings and Bastles*, pp. 1, 4;

(Middleton, 1588) W. Camden, *Britannia*, ed. P. Holland (London, 1610), I, p. 806, cited in Ramm, McDowall, Mercer, *Shielings and Bastles*, pp. 1, 4; Halliday (ed.), *Richard Carew of Anthony*, p. 86; verse cited in M. Johnson and P. Rose, *Bodmin Moor: An Archaeological Survey*, I, *The Human Landscape to c.1800* (Truro and London, 1994), p. 80; 'Remarks' by J.T., in T. Risdon, *The Chorographical Description; or, Survey of the County of Devon* (1714, edition of 1811), p. ix.

33 A.J.L. Winchester, 'Shielings in upper Eskdale', *Transactions of the Cumberland and Westmorland Antiquarian and Archaeological Society* 84 (1984), pp. 267–68; G. Elliott, 'Field systems of northwest England', in A.R.H. Baker and R.A. Butlin (eds), *Studies of Field Systems in the British Isles* (Cambridge, 1973), pp. 41–92, at p. 74.

34 *VCH Cumberland*, ii, p. 334; and see A.J.L. Winchester, *Landscape and Society in Medieval Cumbria* (Edinburgh, 1987), pp. 92–96; (Tynedale) Winchester, *The Harvest of the Hills*, p. 87; B. Colgrave (ed.), *Two Lives of St Cuthbert* (Cambridge, 1940), pp. 71, 171; For *scela, skali, saetr, erg* place-names, see A.H. Smith, *English Place-name Elements* (London, 1956), i, p. 157, ii, pp. 95–96, 123; G. Fellows-Jensen, 'A Gaelic-Scandinavian loan-word in English place-names', *Journal of the English Place-name Society* 10 (1977–78), pp. 18–25; and M.C. Higham, '*Aergi* place-names as indicators of transhumance: Problems of the evidence', in H.S.A. Fox (ed.), *Seasonal Settlement* (Leicester, 1996), Vaughan Paper No. 39 pp. 55–60.

35 Albert Bil, *The Sheiling, 1600–1840: The Case of the Central Scottish Highlands* (Edinburgh, 1990); P. Herring, 'Transhumance in medieval Cornwall', in Fox (ed.), *Seasonal Settlement*, pp. 35–44.

36 J. Klein, *The Mesta: A Study in Spanish Economic History, 1273–1836* (Harvard, 1920).

37 R. Lopez, 'The origin of the Merino sheep', *The Joshua Starr Memorial Volume: Studies in History and Philology*, Jewish Social Studies 5 (New York, 1953), pp. 151–68 (quoted in Braudel, *Mediterranean*, I, p. 93).

38 D. Oschinsky, *Walter of Henley and other Treatises on Estate Management and Accounting* (1971), p. 424. For examples of *pays* used by English landscape historians, see Everitt, *Landscape and Community*, pp. 11–40, or J. Thirsk (ed.), *Rural England: An Illustrated History of the Landscape* (Oxford, 2000).

39 E. Power, 'Peasant life and rural conditions', in J.R. Tanner, C.W. Previte-Orton and Z.N. Brooke (eds), *The Cambridge Medieval History*, vol. 7 (Cambridge, 1932), pp. 716–50, at p. 747; the statute is printed (with different attribution and date) in F.M. Powicke and C.R. Cheney (eds), *Councils and Synods, with other documents relating to the English Church, II: AD 1205–1313* (Oxford, 1964), 2, pp. 794–5; (Statutes of Winchester) C. Deedes (ed.), *Registrum Johannis de Pontissara, Episcopi Wyntoniensis AD MCCLXXXII–MCCCIV*, vol. i, Canterbury and York Society 19 (1915), pp. 213, 231; (arbitration) Staffordshire Record Office, D593/A/1/14/4.

40 G. Bray (ed.), *Tudor Church Reform: The Henrician Canons of 1535 and the Reformatio legum ecclesiasticarum*, Church of England Record Society 8 (2000), pp. 108–9; and see R. Swanson, 'Economic change and spiritual profits: Receipts from the peculiar jurisdiction of the Peak District in the fourteenth century', in N. Rogers (ed.), *Harlaxton Medieval Studies, III: England in the Fifteenth Century, Proceedings of the 1991 Colloqium* (Stamford, 1993).

41 C. Dyer, 'Seasonal settlement in medieval Gloucestershire: Sheepcotes', in Fox (ed.), *Seasonal Settlement*, pp. 25–34.

42 Biddick, *The Other Economy*, chs 4 and 5, esp. pp. 84–85 and 102–6.

43 F. Page, '*Bidentes Hoylandiae*: A medieval sheep farm', *EHR* 1 (1926–9), pp. 603–13; R.A. Donkin, *The Cistercians: Studies in the Geography of Medieval England and Wales* (Toronto, 1978), pp. 96–98; D. Postles, 'The Oseney Abbey flock', *Oxoniensia* 49 (1984), pp. 141–52, at p. 143; M.A. Atkin, 'Land use and management of the upland demesne of the de Lacy family of Blackburnshire *c*.1300', *AHR* 42 (1994), pp. 1–19, at p. 18.

44 (Cheshire) R. Trow-Smith, *A History of British Livestock Husbandry to 1700* (London, 1957), pp. 210–11, and see also A.M. Everitt. 'The marketing of agricultural produce', in J. Thirsk (ed.), *Agrarian History of England and Wales; IV 1500–1640* (Cambridge, 1997), pp. 539–42, at pp. 540–41; (Romney etc.) S. Hipkin, 'The structure of landownership and land occupation in the Romney Marsh region, 1646–1834, *AHR* 51, pt 1 (2003), pp. 69–94, at pp. 72–73; N. Neilson, *A Terrier of Fleet, Lincolnshire*, British Academy Records of the Social Economic History of England and Wales 4 (1920), pp. xii, lii; M. Williams, *The Draining of the Somerset Levels* (1970), pp. 89–91.

45 Dyer, 'Sheepcotes: Evidence for medieval sheep farming', pp. 136–64; J. Goodacre, *The Transformation of a Peasant Economy: Townspeople and Villagers in the Lutterworth Area, 1500–1700* (Aldershot, 1994), pp. 101–2; W.O. Ault, *Open-field Farming in Medieval England* (London, 1972), pp. 143, 167, 169; (Goosehill) P. Christie and P. Rose, 'Davidstow Moor, Cornwall: The medieval and later sites. Wartime excavations by C.K. Croft Andrew 1941–2', *Cornish Archaeology* 26 (1987), pp. 163–94, at p. 180 and P. Herring, 'An Exercise in Landscape History: Pre-Norman and Medieval Brown Willy and Bodmin Moor', unpublished M.Phil. thesis, University of Sheffield (1986), Appendix 1, p. 115.

46 F.R.H. du Boulay, 'Denns, droving and danger', *Archaeologia Cantiana* 76 (1961), pp. 75–87. For Lincolnshire and Somerset, see above.

47 Fox, 'The people of the Wolds', pp. 77–101; K. Cameron, *English Place-names* (1961; 3rd edn, London, 1977), p. 79; Everitt, *Continuity and Colonisation*, pp. 32–39, 52–57.

48 M. Bloch, *Les Caractères Originaux de l'Histoire Rurale Française* (Oslo, 1931), p. 7; W.J. Ford, 'Some settlement patterns in the central region of the Warwickshire Avon', in P.H. Sawyer (ed.), *Medieval Settlement: Continuity and Change* (1976), pp. 280–81, and *idem*, 'Pattern of Settlement in the Central Region of the Warwickshire Avon', unpubl. M.A. thesis, University of Leicester (1973), pp. 50–56; D. Hooke, 'Pre-Conquest woodland: its distribution and usage', *AHR* 37 (1989), pp. 115–16.

49 Bil, *The Sheiling*, pp. 51–57; Biddick, *The Other Economy*, pp. 84–85, 102–6.

50 Blake, 'Hooker's Synopsis', pp. 344–45; C. Pearse, 'Sheep creeps and holes', *Dartmoor Magazine* 61 (2000), pp. 34–35; Ault, *Open-field Farming*, p. 167.

51 J. Coker, *A Survey of Dorsetshire* (London, 1732), p. 5 (the survey was actually compiled *c*.1630–40, by Thomas Gerard), cited in Trow-Smith, *History of British Livestock Husbandry*, p. 179, and generally see chapter 7, especially n. 4.

52 Herring, 'Transhumance in medieval Cornwall'.

53 Emmanuel Le Roy Ladurie, *Montaillou: Cathars and Catholics in a French Village 1294–1324* (1978; English trans. London, 1980), ch. 5; Dyer, 'Seasonal settlement in medieval Gloucestershire'; (wilderness for sheep) R. Powell, *Depopulation Arraigned* (London, 1636; reprinted Amsterdam, 1976), p. 54.

54 Beresford, *Lost Villages*, pp. 99–101.

55 O. Greig and W. Rankine, 'A stone-age settlement system near East Week,

Dartmoor: Mesolithic and Post-Mesolithic Industries', *PDAS* 5 (1953), pp. 8–26; *PnD*, pp. 482, 287; Beresford, 'Three deserted medieval settlements on Dartmoor', pp. 104–5, 110, 134; A. Fleming, *The Dartmoor Reaves: Investigating Prehistoric Land Divisions* (London, 1988; 2nd edn, Bollington, 2007), and *idem*, 'The reaves reviewed', *PDAS* 52 (1994), pp. 63–74.

56 *PnD*, pp. xviii–xxiv; O. Padel, *Cornish Place-name Elements* (Nottingham, 1985), pp. 147 (*lether*), 104 (*glynn*) and 66 (*corn, cors*); T. Greeves, 'Was Brentor a Dark Age Centre', *Dartmoor Magazine* 71 (2003), pp. 8–10; (Was Tor) *PnD*, p. 214.

57 Herring, 'Transhumance in medieval Cornwall'; Padel, *Cornish Place-name Elements*, p. 129; E. Okasha, *Corpus of Early Christian Inscribed Stones of Southwest Britain* (London, 1993); S. Pearce, *South-western Britain in the Early Middle Ages* (London, 2004), pp. 57–58; T. Greeves, 'The start of history—two inscribed stones from western Dartmoor', *Dartmoor Magazine* 91 (2008), pp. 8–10.

58 H.L. Gray, *English Field Systems* (Cambridge, 1915).

Notes to Chapter Two

1 P. Herring 'Cornish uplands: medieval, post-medieval and modern extents', in I.D. Whyte and A.J.L. Winchester (eds), *Society, Landscape and Environment in Upland Britain*, Society for Landscape Studies 2 (2004), pp. 37–51; Halliday (ed.), *Richard Carew of Anthony*, p. 86; Johnson and Rose, *Bodmin Moor*, p. 80.

2 'Down-country', an expression used by Dartmoor people, means the areas beyond and below the moor-side parishes, and is used in this sense throughout this book (see above, p. 27).

3 'come to the kynges forrest by sonne, and goo home by sonne', *Short History*, p. 47.

4 (Red tides) Havinden and Wilkinson, 'Farming', pp. 139–82, at p. 169; (Ashprington) ECRO C.R. 20,103, m. 1 (Pie Powder court held in the eve of St Peter, 18 Hen.VI); (Werrington) DRO, W1258M/D/70, court held Sat. after Ascension, 40 Edw.III; (Holsworthy) TNA:PRO, SC 2/167/34.

5 *Short History*, pp. 2–14.

6 C. Wickham, *Land and Power: Studies in Italian and European Social History, 400–1200* (London, 1994), pp. 158–59; *Rotuli Chartarum in Turri Londoniensis Asservati*, i, pt 1, Record Commission (London, 1837), p. 132; *Short History*, p. 2.

7 *Short History*, pp. 76, 83; (Barnstaple) a recent authority considers that *Pilletune* in the version of the burghal hidage probably written in the tenth century could have been Barnstaple; another version, made before 1066, has *Piltone that is Bearstaple*: D. Hill and A.R. Rumble, *The Defence of Wessex: The Burghal Hidage and Anglo-Saxon Fortifications* (Manchester, 1996), pp. 26–27 (texts), 38, 47 (dating), 213–14 (interpretation). The two places are adjacent. For further discussion, see J. Haslam, 'The towns of Devon', in J. Haslam (ed.), *Anglo-Saxon Towns in Southern England* (Chichester, 1984), pp. 251–56; H. Miles and T. Miles, 'Pilton, North Devon: Excavations within a medieval village', *PDAS* 33 (1975), pp. 268–70.

8 *Short History*, pp. 43–91.

9 (1388 inquisition) TNA:PRO, C 145/242/10; printed in *Cal Inq Misc IV: 1387–93*, p. 120 and *Short History*, pp. 28–29; (1275 Hundred Rolls) *Rotuli Hundredorum*, i (London, Record Commission, 1812) p. 77; (1204 charter) *Rotuli Chartarum in Turri Londoniensis*, p. 132; *Short History*, p. 2.

10 (Witnesses) *Short History*, pp. 56–91; (Gorddwr) A.J. Kettle, 'Agriculture, 1300–1540', in *V.C.H. Shropshire*, 4 (Oxford, 1989), p. 113; (Balsham) A. Rumble (ed.),

Domesday Book: Cambridgeshire (Chichester, 1981), 5,6; (Molland) *DB*, 1,41; (Woodbury) *Exon DB*, fol. 96b.

11 TNA:PRO, C 145/242/10; printed in *Cal Inq Misc IV: 1387–93*, p. 120 and *Short History*, pp. 28–29.

12 *Rotuli Hundredorum*, i, p. 77.

13 (Sixteenth century) *Short History*, p. 47; (1382, 1388) TNA:PRO, C 145/224/3 and /242/10; printed in *Cal Misc Inq, iv: 1377–88*, p. 94 and *v, 1387–93*, p. 120 and *Short History*, pp. 27–29; (1345) TNA:PRO, SC 11/80, abstracted in *Short History*, pp. 18–19, 156–60; (1297) TNA:PRO, SC 6/827/38, printed in L.M. Midgley, *Ministers' Accounts of the Earldom of Cornwall 1296–97*, ii, Camden Society 3rd ser. 68 (1945), pp. 219–20 and abstracted in *Short History*, pp. 9–10.

14 *Short History*, pp. 18, 19, 55, 66, 156–60.

15 *Short History*, pp. 39–40, 60; (1525 subsidy) Stoat, *Devon Lay Subsidy Rolls*.

16 A.E. Bray, *A Description of the Part of Devonshire bordering on the Tamar and the Tavy . . .*, vol. 1 (London 1836), pp. 35; G. Spooner and F. Russell (eds), *Worth's Dartmoor* (Newton Abbot, 1953; 1967 edn), p. 345; *OED*, s. v.; (venville, Buckfastleigh) *Short History*, pp. 39–40, 45–46.

17 (eighteenth, nineteenth century) William Simpson's Survey of the Forest of Dartmoor, DRO, Z17/3/8, and J. Somers Cocks, 'Saxon and early medieval times' and Havinden and Wilkinson, 'Farming', pp. 96–98, 148–65; (1345) TNA:PRO, SC 11/802; (both periods) *Short History*, pp. 18, 89–90.

18 Marshall, *The Rural Economy of the West of England*, ii, p. 26; *Short History*, pp. 80, 85.

19 (Tavistock) DRO, W1258M/D/52/2, 3, quoted in Finberg, *Tavistock Abbey*, p. 131; (Halsford) Exeter Cathedral Archives, D&C Exeter 5120; (Trematon) TNA:PRO, SC 6/823/24.

20 TNA:PRO, SC 6/826/21–3, *Cal Inq Misc IV: 1387–1393* (London, 1962), p. 45; (Bickleigh) West Devon RO, Acc. 70/51; (Monkleigh) DRO, C.R. 1132; (Parswell) DRO, W1258M/D43/6.

21 (1296–97) TNA:PRO, SC 6/827/38, printed in Midgley, *Ministers' Accounts*, and abstracted in *Short History*, p. 9; (1366–77) TNA:PRO, SC 2/166/37.

22 (Agistment lists) TNA:PRO, SC 6/828/18 (1347), /828/20 (1351), SC 2/166/45 (1410s, several), /166/46 (1420s–60s, several), SC 6/Hen.VII/88 (1493), /Hen. VII/89–91 (1496), SC 12/6/57–58 and SC 2/166/52, /167/1–13 (temp. Eliz., many), /167/14–24 (temp. Jas I); (Subsidies) Stoat, *Devon Lay Subsidy Rolls*.

23 (Torre, Clement) *Short History*, pp. 66, 91; (Palmer v. Sladd) TNA:PRO, SC 2/166/37, m. 3; (1331) DRO, 1508M/ Moger/241; (average farm size) No doubt based on an analysis of the holding sizes recorded in a large number of manorial extents, surveys and rentals, too many to list here, in which Professor Fox was engaged at the time of his death. See also H.S.A. Fox, 'Tenant farming and farmers: Devon and Cornwall', in *AHE&W III*, pp. 723–25.

24 (1347) TNA:PRO, SC 6/828/18; (1345) SC 11/80, abstracted in *Short History*, pp. 156–60; and (1496) SC 6/Hen VII/89–91.

25 TNA:PRO, SC 6/828/18.

26 Vita Sackville-West, *The Land* (London, 1929), p. 107.

27 (Staunton) *CPR, Henry VI, vol. 2 (1429–36)*, p. 272; E. Acheson, *A Gentry Community: Leicestershire in the Fifteenth Century, c.1422–c.1485* (Cambridge, 1992), pp. 100, 251; (Dinham) *CPR, Edw. IV, Edw. V, Ric. III, 1477–1485* (London, 1901), p. 386, abstracted in *Short History*, p. 38, and see *DNB, s.n.*

For the foresters and herdsmen generally, see Fox, 'Medieval Dartmoor as seen through the account rolls', pp. 149–72, at p. 159.

28 (£4 wages) C. Dyer, *Standards of Living in the Middle Ages: Social Change in England c.1200–1520* (Cambridge, 1989; revised edition, 1998), pp. 222–33; (Radbourne) *idem*, *Warwickshire Farming 1349–c1520: Preparations for Agricultural Revolution*, Dugdale Society Occasional Paper (1981), pp. 19–21; (tempests and floods) Hingeston-Randolph (ed.), *The Registers of Walter Bromescombe and Peter Quivil*, p. 204.

29 Fox, 'Medieval Dartmoor as seen through the account rolls', p. 159.

30 TNA:PRO, SC 6/827/38, printed in Midgley, *Ministers' Accounts*, ii, pp. 219–20; Fox, 'Medieval Dartmoor as seen through the account rolls', p. 159.

31 TNA:PRO, SC 6/828/18.

32 C.L. Kingsford, *The Stonor Letters and Papers, 1290–1483*, i, Camden Society 3rd ser. 29 (1919), p. 64; Erskine (ed.), *The Devonshire Lay Subsidy*, pp. 8, 94.

33 W. Crossing, *Crossing's Dartmoor Worker*, ed. B. Le Mesurier (Newton Abbot, 1966), p. 21; *OED s.v.*.

34 J. Birrell, 'Deer and deer farming in medieval England', *AHR* 40, pt 2 (1992), pp. 112–26, at p. 116; M.C.B. Dawes (ed.), *The Black Prince's Register*, ii (London, 1931), p. 72; abstracted in *Short History*, pp. 21–22.

35 (*Bovettus*) TNA:PRO, SC 2/166/47, court held before feast of St Luke evangelist, 18 Edw. IV. The marks may have been not brands but earmarks, patterns of nicks in an ear, which have been used since at least the sixteenth century on both Dartmoor and Exmoor: Havinden and Wilkinson, 'Farming', p. 148, and M. Siraut, *Exmoor: The Making of an English Upland* (Chichester, 2009), p. 76, or horn-marks, also used on Dartmoor in recent times (information given to Tom Greeves by an elderly moorman).

36 (Taxation) Fox, 'Taxation and settlement in medieval Devon', pp. 168–85.

37 Dawes (ed.), *The Black Prince's Register*, ii, p. 175, abstracted in *Short History*, p. 24.

38 (1702) *Short History*, p. 84; (amercement) TNA:PRO, SC 2/166/48, mentioned in *Short History*, p. 97. In 1583 John Ellett and Robert French were each amerced 6d. for the same offence, Worth, 'The tenants and commoners of Dartmoor', pp. 187–214, at p. 193.

39 Baring-Gould, *A Book of the West, I: Devon*, p. 180; (1367) TNA:PRO, SC 2/166/37, court held Monday after Invention of the Holy Cross, 41 Edw. III.

40 (Population) C. Dyer, *Making a Living in the Middle Ages: The People of Britain 850–1520* (London, 2003), pp. 233–35, 322–23; (Werrington) DRO, W1258M/D/70, court held Friday after Assumption, 43 Edw. III, and two following; (N Devon pasture) Fox, 'Occupation of the land: Devon and Cornwall', pp. 154–58.

41 Fox, 'Medieval Dartmoor as seen through the account rolls', at p. 155.

42 (Halstock) DRO, 1508M/manor/Halstock/2.

43 (Ashburton) A.S. Napier and W.H. Stevenson (eds), *The Crawford Collection of Early Charters and Documents now in the Bodleian Library* (Oxford, 1895), pp. 23–24; D. Hooke, *Pre-Conquest Charter-Bounds of Devon and Cornwall* (Woodbridge, 1994), p. 186; (Cornwood, Brendon) *Exon DB*, fol. 218b, 337; (1468–81 court rolls) TNA:PRO, SC 2/166/47, 48; (1496 account), SC 6/Hen. VII/89–91; (Bishop's Clyst) DRO, W1258M/G/3.

44 (Place-names) *PnD*, pp. 221, 226, 239, 476; (Harwood, Cornwood) *Exon DB*, fol. 218b; (Highampton) TNA:PRO, SC 6/826/21–23, *Cal Inq Misc V: 1387–1393*,

p. 45; (Nymet Tracy) DRO, DD20/1471, quoted in A. Adams, *Zeal Monachorum: A Devon Rural Parish 1086–1801* (Zeal Monachorum, 2002), pp. 21, 145; (Shapley Hellion) DRO, 1508M/ Moger/241; (Spitchwick) North Devon RO, 50/11/12/1 and *PnD*, p. 528; (bans on goats) for example, in 1250 William de Albemarle excluded pigs and goats from a grant of common of pasture in his demesne lands at North Huish, DRO, 158M/T496; and in 1256 the Abbot of Buckfastleigh granted rights in his wood of Holne for 'all animals . . . except goats', F.C. Hingeston-Randolph (ed.), *Bishop Grandisson's Registers* 3 (London, 1899), Appendix, p. 1585; (1608) *Short History*, p. 55. For a comprehensive survey of medieval goat-keeping, see C. Dyer, 'Alternative agriculture: goats in medieval England', in *People, Landscape and Alternative Agriculture. Essays for Joan Thirsk*, ed. R. Hoyle (*AHR* supplement ser. 3, 2004), pp. 20–38.

45 Risdon, *The Chorographical Description*, p. ix; W. Burt (ed.), *Dartmoor: A Descriptive Poem*, by N.T. Carrington (London, 1826); A. Young, *Annals of Agriculture and other Useful Arts*, 45 vols (1784–1809); Vancouver, *General View of the Agriculture of the County of Devon*, p. 228; William Camden, *Britannia, or, a Chorographical Description of Great Britain and Ireland, together with the Ancient Islands / written in Latin by William Camden and translated into English with additions and improvements by Edmund Gibson* (4th edn, London, 1772), p. 161; Risdon, *The Chorographical Description*, p. 6; (pasture as good) TNA:PRO, E134 17 Chas. I, Mich. 21, quoted in J. Thirsk, 'Farming techniques: Grassland and stock', *AHE&W IV*, pp. 179–95, at p. 183.

46 (1376) TNA:PRO SC 2/166/37, mm. 4 *et seq.*, courts held Monday after the Invention of the Holy Cross, 51 Edw. III and following; (1479) SC 2/166/48.

47 (Vancouver) Vancouver, *General View of Agriculture of the County of Devon*, p. 345; (Black Prince) Dawes, *Black Prince's Register*, ii, p. 71; (Simpson) D120, Z17/3/8.

48 B. Le Messurier, 'The Post-prehistoric structures of central north Dartmoor: A field survey', *Trans. Devon. Assoc.* 111 (1979), pp. 59–73; P. Newman, *The Dartmoor Tin Industry: a Field Guide* (Newton Abbot, 1998), p. 51; J. Butler, *Dartmoor Atlas of Antiquities*, Vols I–V (Exeter, 1991–1997); W. Crossing, *A Hundred Years on Dartmoor* (Plymouth, 1901), p. 73.

49 (Throwleigh) TNA:PRO, E 179/95/14; (Tavistock) TNA:PRO E 179/95/12, in the Inquisition as to Tinworkers, 10 and 11 Edw. III, and the Tinworkers' return to the Fifteenth and Tenth, 13 Edw III, in both cases under Tavistock Borough; (Chagford) DRO, 314M/M/11.

50 (Alston, Norden, Beare) see chapter 1. S. Rowe, *A Perambulation of the Antient & Royal Forest of Dartmoor & the Venville Precincts* (Plymouth, 1848); Le Messurier, 'Post-prehistoric structures', p. 65.

51 W. Crossing, *Guide to Dartmoor* (Plymouth, 1912), pp. 217, 407; *idem, Hundred Years*, p. 105; Newman, *The Dartmoor Tin Industry*, p. 51; Butler, *Dartmoor Atlas*, ii, pp. 134, 158; Herring and Nowakowski, 'Beehive huts', pp. 98–100, at p. 100; A. Fox, 'A monastic homestead on Dean Moor, S. Devon', *Medieval Archaeology* 2 (1958), pp. 141–57, at pp. 142–44; (Holwell quarry hut) Butler, *Dartmoor Atlas*, i, pp. 25, 66.

52 H. Finberg, 'Childe's Tomb', in W. Hoskins and *idem* (eds), *Devonshire Studies* (London, 1952), pp. 40–58; Finberg, *Tavistock Abbey*, p. 4.; N.T. Carrington, *Dartmoor: A Descriptive Poem, with a Preface and Notes by W. Burt, esq.* (London, 1826).

Notes to Chapter Three

1   The 'central moor' was defined in chapter 1 (p. 27) as the area in Crown ownership, coterminous with the parish and manor of Lydford; the 'outer moors' are the privately owned areas surrounding the central moor, including the fragmented detached moors. Exmoor was similarly divided into a central royal forest and an outer ring of manorial commons; Siraut, *Exmoor: the Making of an English Upland*, Fig. 54 and pp. 37, 74–75.

2   (Brent) DRO, 123M/E/1024; (Plympton) DRO, CR 496; (Joel) West Devon RO, 70/53, and see H.S.A. Fox, 'The Millstone Makers of Medieval Dartmoor', *DCNQ* 37, pt 5 (1994), pp. 153–57, at p. 154; (Gidleigh) TNA:PRO, C134/46/23 (IpM of William le Prouz, 9 Edw II), printed in *Cal InqPM, 5, Edw. II, 1307–16*, p. 368; (Cornwood) TNA:PRO, C 135/88/2, printed in *Cal InqPM, 9, Edw. III, 1347–52*, p. 67; (Bovey Tracey) TNA:PRO, C 134/99; (South Tawton) TNA:PRO, C 139/194. Another survey of Bovey Tracey, from 1353, also refers to *pastura montana*: C 145/169/4, m. 8.

3   (Walkhampton) West Devon RO, 70/73; (South Brent) DRO, 123M/M1; (Brent Moor) DRO, 123M/E31; (Ilsington) DRO, Z17/3/19, fol. ciii.

4   (Writs) *Short History*, pp. xviii–xix, 3–4; (1359 council) Dawes (ed.), *The Black Prince's Register*, ii, p. 153, abstracted in *Short History*, pp. 23–24; (Privy Council report) TNA:PRO, SC 12/25/31, abstracted in *Short History*, p. 43; (Augmentation Office grant) *Short History*, pp. 43, 118.

5   (no lorde nor gentylman) *Short History*, pp. 164–66; (violent consequences) Baring-Gould, *A Book of the West, I: Devon*, p. 180.

6   The grants in Table 3.1 are: (Cornwood) Hoskins, 'Cholwich', pp. 78–94, at p. 79; (Spitchwick) North Devon RO, 50/11/12/1; (Holne) Hingeston-Randolph (ed.), *Bishop Grandisson's Registers* 3, Appendix, p. 1585; (S Brent) DRO, 123M/TB/7, 9, 12; (Okehampton) DRO, TD/51/Courtenay Cartulary, fol. 60–62; (Shapley Hellion, 1331, 1339) DRO, 1508M/ Moger/241, 158M/T71; (Willsworthy) DRO, 410Z/T10; (Ugborough) TNA:PRO, E164/19, fols 4/5; printed in D. Seymour, *Torre Abbey* (Exeter, 1977), p. 82; (Shapley Hellion, 1432) DRO, 1508M/ Moger/218.

7   (Brent) DRO, 123M/E31, 49/26/4/8–9; (Ilsington) DRO, Z17/3/19; (Meavy) DRO, Z13/1/10; (Halstock) DRO, 1508M/manor/Halstock/2.

8   (Shapley Hellion) DRO, 1508M/ Moger/218.

9   DRO, 1508M/Devon/special subjects/Okehampton Park/1–5.

10 (1262/3) TNA:PRO, C 132/29/4, printed in *Cal InqPM, 1, Hen. III*, p. 564; (1422) TNA:PRO, SC 6/1118/6; (fifteenth century) BL Add. Ch. 64683.

11 (1424/5) BL Add. Ch. 64663; (Park Books) DRO, 1508M/Devon/special subjects/ Okehampton Park/1–5; (1534/5) DRO, C.R. 532. A more detailed description of the Courtenays' management of Okehampton Park can be found in H.S.A. Fox, 'Lords and wastes', in R. Goddard, J. Langdon, M. Muller, *Survival and Discord in Medieval Society: Essays in Honour of Chris Dyer* (Turnhout, 2010), pp. 29–48, at pp. 42–48.

12 (Natsworthy) Cornwall RO, AR2/1289; (Brent) Sir Harris Nicolas (ed.), *Privy Council of England, Proceedings and Ordinances, 10 Richard II–33 Henry VII, (1386–1542)*, 7, Record Commission (London, 1837), p. 123, extracted in *Short History*, p. 46; (Harnatethy) P. Herring, 'Cornish uplands: Medieval, post-medieval and modern extents', p. 48; (1588) *Short History*, p. 146.

13 BL Add. Ch. 64663. The profits in 1534/5 were even larger—£24 8s., less the drift expenses; DRO, C.R. 532.

14 (Christow) probably DRO, W1258 M/G/1/60–70.

15 Fox, 'A monastic homestead on Dean Moor, S. Devon', pp. 141–57.

16 The cartulary appears in Hingeston-Randolph (ed.), *Bishop Grandisson's Registers* 3, Appendix. The memorandum, and the bounds to which they are appended, are at p. 1608, and also in Fox, 'A monastic homestead on Dean Moor, S. Devon', at p. 150.

17 (Ugborough/Wrangaton) *'Pole's Charters' (Extracts from deeds etc made circa 1616 by Sir William Pole of Shute)*, MS transcript (anon., 1915–16) held by DCRS, no. 204.

18 (Buckfast) *Short History*, p. 119; (Buckland) *Short History*, pp. 105–6; (Cornwood) Hoskins, 'Cholwich', p. 79; (Widecombe) DRO, 48/14/1/7; (Natsworthy, Ilsington) DRO, Z17/3/19, fol. ciii, dorse.

19 (divers writings) *Short History*, p. 119.

20 BL 37,640, fol. 25v–26v, quoted in *Short History*, pp. 49–50.

21 (1531 complaint) *Short History*, pp. 43, 119–20, and see also Hingeston-Randolph, *Bishop Grandisson's Registers*, 3, pp. 1563–65.

22 (Buckfast cartulary) Hingeston-Randolph, *Bishop Grandisson's Registers*, 3, p. 1608 (fol. 143).

23 (1541) *Short History*, pp. 45–46; (1446) DRO, 123M/E/1018–19.

24 DRO, 123M/E/1019; H.P.R. Finberg, 'Supplement to the Early Charters of Devon and Cornwall', in W.G. Hoskins, *The Westward Expansion of Wessex*, Department of English Local History Occasional Papers 13 (Leicester, 1960), pp. 23–25.

25 (Glastonbury survey) BL Eg. MS 3034, 3134; (Underdown) D. Underdown, *Revel, Riot and Rebellion: Popular Politics and Culture in England, 1603–1660* (Oxford, 1985), pp. 14, 81, 91.

26 *CPR 1317–21*, pp. 18–19. In 1371 the abbots of Buckfast and Tavistock, their monks and other priests, knights and inhabitants of the region were accused of similar behaviour, *CPR 1370–74*, p. 172.

27 (1315) *CCR, Edw. III 1313–18*, p. 238; (Birrell) J. Birrell, 'Who poached the king's deer?', *Midland History* 7 (1982), pp. 9–25, *eadem*, 'A great thirteenth-century hunter: John Giffard of Brimpsfield', *Medieval Prosopography* 3 (1994), pp. 37–66, and *eadem*, 'Peasant deer poachers in the medieval forest', in R. Britnell and J. Hatcher (eds), *Progress and Problems in Medieval England* (Cambridge, 1996), pp. 68–88.

28 (1361) Dawes, *Black Prince's Register*, ii, p. 178; (1314) H. Finberg, 'The Stannary of Tavistock', *Trans. Devon. Assoc.* 81 (1949), pp. 155–84, at p. 161; (tinworking) T. Greeves, 'The beamworks of Dartmoor—a remarkable heritage of the tinners', *Dartmoor Magazine* 75 (2004), pp. 9–11, S. Gerrard, *The Early British Tin Industry* (Stroud, 2000); P. Newman, 'Tinworking and the landscape of medieval Devon, c.1150–1700', in S. Turner (ed.) *Medieval Devon and Cornwall: Shaping an Ancient Countryside* (Macclesfield, 2006), pp. 123–43.

29 (Woolmer) D. Woolner, 'Peat charcoal', *DCNQ* 30 (1965–67), pp. 118–20.

30 (1347) TNA:PRO, SC 6/828/18; (1446) J. Hatcher, *Rural Economy and Society in the Duchy of Cornwall 1300–1500* (Cambridge, 1970), p. 188; (environmental impact) Discussed in T. Greeves, 'The Devon tin industry 1450–1750', where it is estimated that 10,500 tons of wet peat would need to have been dug annually to produce the 500 tons of charcoal required to smelt the annual output of tin metal in Devon in the first half of the sixteenth century.

31 (Dean Moor) Fox, 'A monastic homestead on Dean Moor, S. Devon'.
32 (Collishul) TNA:PRO, SC 2/166/37, m. 2; (Wonston) TNA:PRO, SC 2/166/37, 44–50; (Botreaux) TNA:PRO, SC 2/166/37, m. 1d; (over-wintering horses) TNA:PRO, SC 2/166/37, m. 1d; (1478) TNA:PRO, SC 2/166/47, court held before feast of St Luke evangelist, 18 Edw. IV.
33 (1444) TNA:PRO, SC 2/166/46; (1562) DRO, 123M/M1; (1566) DRO, 123M/E31; (Baring-Gould) Baring-Gould, *Book of the West, I: Devon*, p. 180.
34 (1354) Dawes, *Black Prince's Register*, ii, p. 72, and *Short History*, p. 22; (1276) *CPR 1271–1281*, p. 153; (1479) TNA:PRO, SC 2/166/48.
35 (1479) TNA:PRO, SC 2/166/48.
36 (Gidleigh) B. Cherry and N. Pevsner, *The Buildings of England—Devon* (London, 2nd edn, 1989), p. 456; (Gomerock) M.A. Watts, *Archaeological and Historical Survey at Gomerock, Kingswear, Devon* (Exeter, 1997); (Widecombe) S. Woods, *Uncle Tom Cobley and All—Widecombe-in-the-Moor* (Tiverton, 2000), pp. 90, 93; (Penhallan) G. Beresford, 'The medieval manor of Penhallam, Jacobstow, Cornwall', *Medieval Archaeology* 18 (1974), pp. 90–145; (Binhamy, Carminow, St Columb) A. Preston-Jones and P. Rose, 'Medieval Cornwall', *Cornish Archaeology* 25 (1986), pp. 135–85, esp. 169–73; (Blegberry) E.M. Jope, 'Cornish houses', in *idem* (ed.), *Studies in Building History* (London, 1961), pp. 214–22, at p. 214–15; (Roscarrock) Jope, *supra*, and Fox, *The Evolution of the Fishing Village*, p. 39, n. 16; (Cholwich) See the photographs in Hoskins, 'Cholwich'.
37 (1367) TNA:PRO, SC 2/166/37, m.7d, court held Thursday in the feast of St Peter in chains, 1 Ric. II; m. 6d, Friday before the feast of St Thomas apostle, 1 Ric. II; (1519) TNA:PRO, STAC 2/2/74 and 2/2/223, reported in Greeves, 'The Devon tin industry 1450–1750', pp. 113–14; (fled the stannary) for example TNA:PRO, E 179/95/14, where the subsidy was not collected from certain taxpayers *'qui fugit de stannaria'*.

Notes to Chapter Four

1 *DB*, 20,10; *PnD*, p. 527. Italics are here used to indicate old forms of place-names, where different from the usual modern spelling.
2 For example, Parkham and nearby Sedborough; Oakford and nearby Mildon: *DB* 16,33 and 19,37.
3 C.D. Linehan, 'A forgotten manor in Widecombe-in-the-Moor', *Trans. Devon Assoc.* 94 (1962), pp. 463–92; Cockington court rolls DRO, 48/13/2/1/1 (1434), /11 (1488), /14 (1490–1).
4 DRO, 48/13/2/2/1 for lists of both tenants and landless males; TNA:PRO, E179/95/15.
5 Moreover, early volumes of the English Place-names Society tended not to give names for which no early form could be found.
6 If loss of *ton* (for advice on which Professor Fox thanked Margaret Gelling) is postulated, this does not diminish the importance of the name, but its direct link to Cocca cannot be upheld.
7 W. de G. Birch, *Cartularium Saxonicum: A Collection of Charters relating to Anglo-Saxon History* (London, 1885–93), no. 952; P.H. Sawyer, *Anglo-Saxon Charters: An Annotated List and Bibliography*, Royal History Society Guides and Handbooks, 8 (London, 1968), no. 601; H.P.R. Finberg, *The Early Charters of Devon and Cornwall* (Leicester, 1953), no. 35; M.A. O'Donovan (ed.), *Charters*

of Sherborne (Oxford, 1988), no. 18; Hooke, *Pre-Conquest Charter-Bounds*, pp. 152–55.

8 O'Donovan, *Charters of Sherborne*, pp. lxviii–lxii.

9 *DB*, 7,2; O'Donovan, *Charters of Sherborne*, pp. lxi–lxii.

10 S. Keynes, *The Diplomas of King Æthelred 'the Unready' 978–1016: a Study in their use as Historical Evidence* (Cambridge, 1980), pp. 54–56, 64; O'Donovan, *Charters of Sherborne*, p. 63.

11 O'Donovan, *Charters of Sherborne*, p. 64 speculates that the line naming these two places may have been added when the charter was copied into the Sherborne cartulary. There is in fact no evidence to show that this happened. On the other hand, there is no evidence to show that the passage was in the original charter, although the existence of other old links between the lowlands and Dartmoor argues in favour of this one.

12 TNA:PRO, C 134/21/6.

13 Erskine (ed.), *The Devonshire Lay Subsidy*, p. 3.

14 For the medieval forms of Bittleford, see *PnD*, pp. 526, 682.

15 The 1332 Lay Subsidy records Geoffrey de Langeworthi in Ipplepen tithing: Erskine, *The Devonshire Lay Subsidy*, p. 3.

16 Linehan, 'A forgotten manor in Widecombe-in-the-Moor', pp. 475–76, places Bittleworthy in the sub-manor of Dewdon, but there seems to be little evidence for a connection before the eighteenth century.

17 N.J.G. Pounds (ed.), *The Parliamentary Survey of the Duchy of Cornwall*, DCRS, new ser. 25 and 27 (1982, 1984), p. 240.

18 O'Donovan, *Charters of Sherborne*, p. 64; Hooke, *Pre-Conquest Charter Bounds*, p. 155.

19 *PnD*, p. 467.

20 O.J. Reichel published copiously on the subject of the Devon hundreds in Domesday: see 'The Devonshire Domesday. V. The Hundreds of Devon', *Trans. Devon. Assoc.* 33 (1901), pp. 554–639, and a series of articles, each devoted to an individual hundred, in *Trans. Devon. Assoc*, scattered between vols 26 (1894) and 54 (1922) and its *Supplements* 1–10 (1928–38) (for a full list, see *DB*, i, 'Bibliography and Abbreviations'). Caroline and Frank Thorn, *DB*, ii, Note 1, and see F.R. Thorn, 'Hundreds and wapentakes', in F. Barlow and *idem*, *The Devonshire Domesday*, Alecto edition (London, 1991), pp. 26–42. See also P.H. Sawyer, 'The "Original Returns" and Domesday Book', *EHR* 70 (1955), pp. 177–97; and R. Welldon Finn, 'The making of the Devonshire Domesdays', *Trans. Devon. Assoc.* 87 (1957), pp. 93–123.

21 W. Dugdale, *Antiquities of Warwickshire* (London, 1656), p. 556.

22 Thorn, 'Hundreds and wapentakes', pp. 36–37.

23 Shapley (in Chagford) and Beetor (in N. Bovey) lay in Exminster Hundred (Thorn, 'Hundreds and Wapentakes', p. 31, n. 10; *DB*, 16,61–62, 45,1, 16,60); Bagtor, Sigford and Staplehill (all in Ilsington) lay in Wonford Hundred (Thorn, 'Hundreds and wapentakes', p. 29, n. 3; *DB*, 48,7, 35,23, 48,9); and Natsworthy, *Dewdon*, Dunstone, Blackslade and Spitchwick (all in Widecombe in the Moor) lay in Kerswell Hundred (Thorn, 'Hundreds and wapentakes', p. 34, n. 4; *DB*, 30,2, 20,10, 34,46, 1,48).

24 *PnD*, p. 528; *DB*, 1,48.

25 *DB*, 48,7.

26 Fox, *The Evolution of the Fishing Village*, p. 49.

27 Midgley (ed.), *Ministers' Accounts*, pp. 219–20; TNA:PRO, SC 6/828/5; C 133/95/2; E 142/71/7; DRO, 1508M/Lon/manorial/Kenton/6; 1508M/Devon/surveys/Kenton/6; R. Polwhele, *The History of Devon*, vol. 2 (London, 1793), p. 161 n.

28 DRO, 1508M/Lon./manorial/Kenton/3.

29 Erskine (ed.), *The Devonshire Lay Subsidy*, p. 123; TNA:PRO, E 179/95/6.

30 *Taxatio Ecclesiastica Angliae et Walliae Auctoritate P. Nicholas IV* (London: Record Commission, 1802), p. 150, does not mention the matter but it is recorded in a copy of part of the papal taxation made at Exeter by a local priest and inserted in one of the bishops' registers: Hingeston-Randolph (ed.), *Registers of Walter Bronescombe*, p. 459.

31 F.M. Powicke and C.R. Cheney, *Councils and Synods, with other Documents relating to the English Church, II: AD 1205–1313* (Oxford, 1964), p. 795.

32 Powderham Archive, 1787 Estate Atlas, map XXIV.

33 C.R. Stratton (ed.), *Survey of the Lands of William, First Earl of Pembroke*, Roxburghe Club, vol. 2 (Oxford, 1909), pp. 318–401, at pp. 345–49.

34 Inverted commas indicate 'lost' places or territories not appearing on modern maps.

35 Birch, *Cartularium Saxonicum*, no. 1323; Sawyer (ed.), *Anglo-Saxon Charters*, no. 1547; Finberg, *Early Charters of Devon and Cornwall*, no. 67; Hooke, *Pre-Conquest Charter-Bounds*, pp. 217–24. Dr Charles Insley kindly helped with the dating.

36 J.B. Davidson, 'Some Anglo-Saxon boundaries now deposited at the Albert Museum, Exeter', *Trans. Devon. Assoc.*, 8 (1876), pp. 396–419, at p. 404; *PnD*, pp. 462, 517; M. Swanton and S. Pearce, 'Lustleigh, south Devon: Its inscribed stone, its churchyard and its parish', in S. Pearce (ed.), *The Early Church in Western Britain and Ireland: Studies Presented to C.A. Ralegh Radford*, British Archaeological Reports (Oxford, 1982), p. 142; F. Rose-Troup, 'Anglo-Saxon charters of Devon', *DCNQ* 17 (1932–33), pp. 125–26; Finberg, *Early Charters of Devon and Cornwall*, no. 67; Sawyer (ed.), *Anglo-Saxon Charters*, no. 1547.

37 *PnD*, p. 517; F. Barlow, *English Episcopal Acta XI: Exeter 1046–1184* (Oxford, 1996–9), pp. 55, 132, 191, 247, 290.

38 *PnD*, p. 513; A.H. Smith, *The Place-names of Gloucestershire*, vol. 3 (Cambridge, 1965), pp. 3, 77.

39 Napier and Stevenson (eds), *The Crawford Collection*, pp. 23–24; Hooke, *Pre-Conquest Charter-Bounds*, p. 186.

40 M. Gelling, *Place-names in the Landscape* (London, 1984), p. 246, and *eadem*, *The Landscape of Place-names* (Stamford, 2000), p. 279.

41 P. Herring, 'Transhumance in medieval Cornwall', pp. 35–44; Padel, *Cornish Place-name Elements*, p. 129.

42 Population density was around 100 acres per person in Ashburton, around 140 in Paignton. In area the Domesday manor of Paignton included the present parishes of Paignton, Marldon and Stoke Gabriel and part of Bickington, and this has been taken into account in the calculation. None of these three last places is in Domesday, whereas almost all Devon parishes have a manorial equivalent in that record; their absence there points to subsumption within the entry for Paignton, and dependency of these places on Paignton is clear from many later manorial and ecclesiastical sources.

43 (Creation) M.W. Beresford and H.P.R. Finberg, *English Medieval Boroughs: A Hand-list* (Newton Abbot, 1973), p. 18; (spelling) *PnD*, p. 517.

44 J.J. Alexander, 'The beginnings of Lifton', *Trans. Devon. Assoc.* 63 (1931), pp. 349–58. One of Athelstan's charters is dated from Lifton, 12 November 1931: Sawyer (ed.), *Anglo-Saxon Charters*, no. 416.

45 D. Whitelock (ed.), *English Historical Documents, vol. I, c.500–1042* (London, 1955), p. 494; Sawyer (ed.), *Anglo-Saxon Charters*, no. 1507.

46 *DB*, 1,25; *Exon DB*, fols 93a, 496a.

47 *Exon DB*, fol 93a.

48 *DB*, 1,25, *Exon DB*, fol. 495b. Alfred's will and Lifton's Cornish dependencies are discussed in H.P.R. Finberg, 'The early history of Werrington', *EHR* 59, no. 234 (May, 1944), pp. 237–51, at p. 244, and Thorn, 'Hundreds and wapentakes', p. 27.

49 William of Malmesbury, *De Gestis Regum Anglorum*, ed. W. Stubbs, i (London, Rolls Series, 1887), pp. 148–49; H.P.R. Finberg, 'The making of a boundary', in Hoskins and Finberg (eds), *Devonshire Studies*, p. 19.

50 (Oratory) G.R. Dunstan (ed.), *Register of Edmund Lacy, Bishop of Exeter, 1420–1455*, vol. ii, DCRS new ser. 10 (1966), pp. 483, 723; (tithe map) DRO, Lifton tithe map.

51 R. Morris, *Churches in the Landscape* (1989; London, 1997), p. 227; J. Blair (ed.), *Minsters and Parish Churches: the Local Church in Transition 950–1250* (Oxford, 1988), p. 7.

52 (1330 survey) C 133/23/1, 24/1, mentioned in *Cal InqPM, 7, 1–9 Edw. III 1327–36* (London, 1909), p. 225; (account) TNA:PRO, SC 6/828/7.

53 Weddell and Reed, 'Excavations at Sourton Down, Okehampton', pp. 35–147, at pp. 46–50.

54 At the time of his death Professor Fox had not identified Lettaford as Northlew's outlier on Dartmoor—the identification has been made by the editors (using the material collected by Professor Fox—granted more time he would surely have made the identification himself), who have re-written this section accordingly.

55 TNA:PRO SC 6/826/21–23, printed in *Cal Inq Misc V: 1387–1393*, pp. 44–45.

56 *Cal Inq Misc V: 1387–1393*, p. 151.

57 C. Torr (ed.), *Wreyland Documents* (Cambridge, 1910), pp. 105–7.

58 *DB*, 1,57; *Exon DB*, fol. 108a; Thorn, 'Hundreds and wapentakes', p. 36, fn. 8

59 (c.1460) DRO, 4088M/16/325; (late fifteenth century) TNA:PRO, SC 12/6/59. The later rental also mentions the holding at Lettaford. A survey of 1561 (DRO, 4088M/16/34) does not mention either Lettaford or Venn, however. The association of *le Fenne* with Melbury in the 1388 inquisition might suggest that it was the Venn farm in Melbury parish, far away in north west Devon, but there is also a Melbury farm in Beaworthy parish (*PnD*, p. 130).

60 *DB*, 5,1.

61 Finberg, *Tavistock Abbey*, pp. 40–54.

62 Finberg, *Tavistock Abbey*, pp. 11–12, 44.

63 DRO W1258M/D/84/22.

64 *DB*, 21,19 and 20; J.H. Round (ed.) *Calendar of Documents preserved in France illustrative of the History of Great Britain and Ireland* (London, 1899), p. 235, no. 661; R. Bearman (ed.), *Charters of the Redvers Family and the Earldom of Devon 1090–1217*, DCRS new ser. 37 (1994), pp. 18–20, 36, 167–69, 174.

65 *Short History*, pp. 105–6.

66 *PnD*, p. 239.

67 *Taxatio Ecclesiastica Angliae et Walliae Auctoritate P. Nicholas IV* (London: Record Commission, 1802).

68 G. Jones, *Saints in the Landscape* (Stroud, 2007), p. 191.

69 Oschinsky (ed.), *Walter of Henley*, p. 397.

70 Finberg, *Early Charters of Devon and Cornwall*, no. 13.

71 TNA:PRO, E164/19, fols 97–80; printed in Seymour, *Torre Abbey*, p. 235.

72 J. Caley and J. Hunter (eds), *Valor Ecclesiasticus*, 6 vols, Record Commission (London, 1810–41), ii, pp. 361–62.

73 *DB*, Pt 2, Index of Persons. It was necessary to assume that there was only one person called Alric in the Devonshire folios of Domesday Book.

74 Ford, 'Pattern of settlement in the central region of the Warwickshire Avon', pp. 50–56 and Fig. 13, and *idem*, 'Some settlement patterns in the central region of the Warwickshire Avon', pp. 280–81.

75 Dugdale, *Antiquities of Warwickshire*, pp. 426, 556.

76 Ford, 'Pattern of Settlement in the Central Region of the Warwickshire Avon', pp. 42–43, 54; Hooke, 'Pre-Conquest woodland: Its distribution and usage', pp. 115–16.

77 V.H.T. Skipp, *Discovering Sheldon* (Birmingham, 1963), pp. 15–18; *idem*, *Discovering Bickenhill* (Birmingham, 1963), pp. 15–33; *idem*, *Medieval Yardley: The Origins and Growth of a West Midlands Community* (London, 1970), pp. 21–35; B.K. Roberts, 'A study of medieval colonisation in the forest of Arden, Warwickshire', *AHR* 16 (1968), pp. 101–13; *idem*, 'Field systems of the west midlands', in A.R.H. Baker and R.A. Butlin (eds), *Studies of Field Systems in the British Isles* (Cambridge, 1973), pp. 188–231.

78 F.M. Stenton, *Anglo-Saxon England* (Oxford, 1943), p. 280; Witney, *The Jutish Forest*, pp. 56–103, 154–86; E.M.J. Campbell, 'Kent', in H.C. Darby and E.M.J. Campbell (eds), *The Domesday Geography of South-East England* (Cambridge, 1962), pp. 527–32; du Boulay, 'Denns, droving and danger', pp. 75–87; H.P.R. Finberg, 'Anglo-Saxon England to 1042', in *idem* (ed.), *The Agrarian History of England & Wales, I, ii, AD 43–1042* (Cambridge, 1972), p. 410; Everitt, *Continuity and Colonisation*, p. 15; F.R.H. du Boulay, *The Lordship of Canterbury: An Essay on Medieval Society* (London, 1966), p. 50.

79 T. Williamson, *The Norfolk Broads: A Landscape History* (Manchester, 1997), p. 45, Fig. 12.

80 (1061) Canterbury Cathedral Archives, CCA-DCc-ChAnt/R/51, mentioned in *PnD*, p. 603; (1086) *DB*, 10,1.

81 Williamson, *Norfolk Broads*, pp. 43, 46, 49.

82 Smith, *English Place-name Elements*, i, p. 109.

Notes to Chapter Five

1 N. O'Dubhthaigh, 'Summer pasture in Donegal', *Folk Life* 22 (1983–84), pp. 42–54.

2 Beresford, 'Three deserted medieval settlements on Dartmoor', pp. 98–158; S. Gerrard, *Book of Dartmoor Landscapes Through Time* (London, 1997), p. 72.

3 Herring and Nowakowski, 'Beehive huts', pp. 98–100, at p.100; and also J. Nowakowski and P. Herring, 'The beehive huts on Bodmin Moor', *Cornish Archaeology* 24 (1985), pp. 185–96. However Peter Herring has also suggested that 'their small size makes it unlikely that the huts were anything other than refuges in inclement weather': P. Herring, 'Medieval fields at Brown Willy, Bodmin Moor', in S. Turner (ed.), *Medieval Devon and Cornwall: Shaping an Ancient Countryside* (Macclesfield, 2006), pp. 78–103 — at Fig. 45 there is a photograph of

one of the huts, Fig. 5.2, Beresford, 'Three deserted medieval settlements' pp. 110–12, Fig. 6, Shieling 1; N. Johnson and P. Rose, *Bodmin Moor: An Archaeological Survey*, I, *The Human Landscape to c.1800* (London, 1994), p. 82, Fig. 53, hut 9; Ramm, McDowall and Mercer, *Shielings and Bastles*, p. 37, hut 137; E.E. Evans, *Irish Folk Ways* (London, 1957), p. 37, Fig. 7, house 4; Beresford, 'Three deserted medieval settlements', p. 130, Fig. 13, Phase 2 house; P. Beacham, 'Rural building: 1400–1800', in N. Pevsner and B. Cherry, *The Buildings of England: Devon* (London, 1989), pp. 62–77, at p. 68, Fig. 4, house e.

4 P. Drewett *et al.*, 'The excavation of a Saxon sunken building at North Marden, West Sussex, 1982', *Sussex Archaeological Collections* 124 (1986), pp. 109–18; P. Everson, 'An excavated Anglo-Saxon sunken-featured building and settlement site at Salmonby, Lincolnshire', *Lincolnshire Hist. Archaeol.* 8 (1973), pp. 61–72; H.S.A. Fox, 'The Wolds before c1500', in J. Thirsk (ed.), *Rural England: An Illustrated History of the Landscape* (Oxford, 2000), pp. 50–61; A.M. Jones, 'The excavation of a multi-period site at Stencoose, Cornwall', *Cornish Archaeology* 39–40 (2000–1), pp. 45–94; (Alsace, Auvergne, Switzerland) H. Hamerow, *Early Medieval Settlements: The Archaeology of Rural Communities in Northwest Europe, 400–900* (Oxford, 2002), p. 34.

5 (excavation) Henderson and Weddell, 'Medieval settlements on Dartmoor and in west Devon', pp. 119–40; (peat deposits) D. Austin, 'Dartmoor and the upland village of the southwest of England', in D. Hooke, *The Medieval Village* (Oxford, 1985), pp. 71–80 and D. Austin and M.J.C. Walker, 'A new landscape context for Hound Tor', *Medieval Archaeology* 29 (1985), pp. 147–52; (ceramics) J. Allan, 'Medieval pottery and the dating of deserted medieval settlements on Dartmoor', *PDAS* 52 (1994), pp. 141–48; (Hamerow) Hamerow, *Early Medieval Settlements*, pp. 31–38.

6 The earliest, from 1578, is DRO, 1508M/Lon/manorial/Kenton/6.

7 DRO, 1508M/Devon/surveys/Kenton/6; *White's History, Gazetteer and Directory of Devonshire 1850*, p. 476.

8 Herring and Nowakowski, 'Beehive huts', p. 100.

9 Professor Fox had intended to illustrate this section with a map, similar to that at Fig. 5.3, but no draft of it could be found among his papers.

10 E. Waugh, *Brideshead Revisited* (1949), the opening sentence of ch. 1, slightly altered.

11 Risdon, *The Chorographical Description*. The five late Saxon towns were Exeter, Barnstaple, Lydford, Tavistock, and Totnes: Beresford and Finberg, *English Medieval Boroughs*, pp. 87–99; also Haslam, 'The towns of Devon', pp. 249–83.

12 *PnD*, p. 232.

13 H.S.A. Fox, 'Butter place-names and transhumance', in O.J. Padel and N. Parsons (eds), *A Commodity of Good Names: Essays in Honour of Margaret Gelling* (Donnington, 2008), pp. 252–64, Table 1 at p. 355. Paul Cullen kindly provided me with the information from the database.

14 Smith, *English Place-name Elements*, ii, p. 130; E. Ekwall, *The Concise Oxford Dictionary of English Place-names* (3rd edn, Oxford, 1947), *s.v. smeoru*.

15 Smith, *English Place-name Elements*, pt 2, p. 130; Ekwall, *Dictionary*, p. 407.

16 For example, the volumes for Derbyshire, Devon, Gloucestershire, Surrey, Westmorland and Yorkshire WR (see references in Table 1); J. Field, *English Field-names: a Dictionary* (Newton Abbot, 1972), p. 208.

17 M. Gelling, *Place-names in the Landscape* (London, 1984), glossarial index, 312,

    although the first element is classified as 'vegetation' on pp. 96, 171; A. D. Mills, *A Dictionary of English Place Names* (Oxford, 1991), p. 300.

18 Beresford, 'Three deserted medieval settlements', p. 111; Evans, *Irish Folk Ways*, p. 37; Ramm, McDowall and Mercer, *Shielings and Bastles*, p. 11; Johnson and Rose, *Bodmin Moor*, p. 82 (huts 3 and 4).

19 Crossley-Holland , K. (ed. and trans.), *The Exeter Riddle Book* (London, 1978), p. 77. For illustrations of traditional churns see E.E. Evans, *Irish Heritage* (Dundalk, 1942), p. 122.

20 Padel, *Cornish Place-name Elements*, p. 5; A. Ward, 'Transhumance and place-names: An aspect of early Ordnance Survey mapping on the Black Mountain commons, Carmarthenshire', *Studia Celtica*, 33 (1999), pp. 335–48, at p. 345.

21 Camden, *Britannia*, ed. Holland, vol. 1, p. 806. The earliest work appears to be T. H. Bainbridge, 'A note on transhumance in Cumbria', *Geography* 25 (1940), pp. 35–36. The latest is Winchester, *The Harvest of the Hills*, pp. 84–93. For work published between these dates, see Fox, 'Introduction', pp. 18–19.

22 E.T. MacDermot, *The History of the Forest of Exmoor* (Newton Abbot, 1973 edn), pp. 210–15.

23 The names on or near Dartmoor are as follows, with page numbers from *PnD*: Butterberry, formerly Boterworthi, in Peter Tavy (232), Butterdon Hill in Moretonhampstead (485), Butterdon Hill in Ugborough (287), Butterford in Inwardleigh (150), Butterford in N. Huish (303). Buttern Hill in Gidleigh and Butteridge Hill on the boundary of Tavistock and Peter Tavy parishes (neither in *PnD*) are possibilities. The two farms in Peter Tavy called Butterberry are deserted and are not on modern maps; their sites are shown in C.D. Linehan, 'Deserted sites and rabbit-warrens on Dartmoor, Devon', *Medieval Archaeology* 10 (1966), pp. 113–44, at p. 138.

24 *PnD*, p. 40.

25 Smith, *English Place-name Elements*, pt 1, p. 65; D.N. Parsons and T. Styles, *The Vocabulary of English Place-names, Brace-Caester* (Nottingham, 2000), p. 99.

26 *PnD*, p. 40.

27 Droveways around Dartmoor are discussed in detail in chapter 7.

28 J.E.B. Gover, *The Place-names of Warwickshire* (Cambridge, 1936), p. 277; Paul Cullen, personal communication.

29 Tom Greeves helped Professor Fox with these observations, commenting that Smeardon Down in Peter Tavy 'is exceedingly rocky' and that the other Dartmoor names are for slopes with pasture which is not 'significantly better for grazing than surrounding hills'.

30 Smith, *English Place-name Elements*, pt 2, p. 262.

31 J. H. Round, 'Domesday survey', in *VCH Essex*, vol. 1 (Westminster, 1903), pp. 368–74; B. Cracknell, *Canvey Island: The History of a Marshland Community* (Leicester, 1959), pp. 10–14.

32 *Rentalia et Custumaria Michaelis de Ambresbury, 1235–1252, et Rogeri de Ford, 1252–1261* (Taunton, 1891), pp. 39, 51.

33 Ekwall, *Dictionary of English Place-names*, p. 491; Smith, *English Place-name Elements*, pt 2, pp. 257, 259; R. Coates, 'New light from old wicks: the progeny of Latin *vicus*', *Nomina* 22 (1999), pp. 97, 105–6.

34 For example, Weeke outside the walls of Winchester and Bathwick outside those of Bath.

35 R. Stanes, *The Old Farm: A History of Farming Life in the West Country* (Exeter, 1990), p. 53.

36 They are listed here with the element with which *wic* is combined, if any, and the page numbers of their entries in *PnD*. Broomage in Cornwood (plus *brom*, 'broom', 269); Cobham Week in Bridestow (178); Cholwich in Cornwood (plus *cealdost*, 'coldest', 269); Cossick in Moretonhampstead (485); East Week in S. Tawton (450); Fuidge in Spreyton (plus *feoh*, 'cattle', 316); Great Weeke in Chagford (426); Middle Week in S. Tawton (450); North Wyke in S. Tawton (450); Runnage in Lydford (plus possibly the personal name Raegna, 197); Spitchwick in Widecombe in the Moor (plus *spic*, '(fat) bacon', 528–9); Stickwick in Bovey Tracy (probably plus *sticca*, 'stick', 468); Warwicks in Bovy Tracy (plus *wall*, 'wall', 469); Week in Sourton (207); Week in Spreyton (447); a lost Week in Chagford surviving in Week Cross (not in *PnD*) unlikely to be named from Great Weeke (see above) because the crossroads is not near that place; a lost Week near Hexworthy, either in Lydford parish or Widecombe in the Moor, surviving in Week Ford (not in *PnD*); Weeks-in-the-Moor in Beaworthy (131); West Wyke in S. Tawton (450); Wickeridge in Woodland (525). The spelling of West Wyke in S. Tawton is from modern O.S. maps, which differ from *PnD*. The name Avon Wick in N. Huish (303) is said to have been coined in 1878; it is on the River Avon, so the first element is easy to understand, but it seems strange that nineteenth-century locals should have invented a 'wick' here.

37 Smith, *English Place-name Elements*, pt 2, p. 137 gives only Spitchwick. 'Fat bacon' is his translation of *spic*; *PnD*, p. 528 gives simply 'bacon'.

38 Evans, *Irish Folk Ways*, p. 37.

39 (Christow) DRO, W1258M/G1/G8; (Domesday) *DB*, 17,61–2.

40 See Chapter 6, p. 163.

41 Hooke, *Pre-Conquest Charter-Bounds*, p. 199.

42 *PnD*, pp. 475, 477.

43 *DB*, 1,26.

44 Herring, 'Transhumance in medieval Cornwall', pp. 35–44, at p. 39.

45 *Cal Inq Misc V: 1387–1393*, p. 45.

46 Smith, *English Place-name Elements*, pt ii, pp. 31–32.

47 For physical descriptions of Maiden Tor and Maiden Hill, see E. Hemery, *High Dartmoor: Land and People* (London, 1983), pp. 160, 1019.

48 A 1639 deed relating to 'one Messuage 20 acres of land, five acres of meadow, and forty acres of pasture with the appurtenances in Slade Meadna-torr and St. Brewer . . . held of the Lord of the Manner of Brounwellie in free socage'; Royal Institution of Cornwall, HF/8/27, quoted in Herring, 'An Exercise in Landscape History', Appendix 1.

Notes to Chapter Six

1 W.G. Hoskins, 'The making of the agrarian landscape', in Hoskins and Finberg (eds), *Devonshire Studies*, pp. 315–24; *idem*, *Devon* (London, 1954), pp. 69–73; M.W. Beresford and J.K.S. St Joseph, *Medieval England: An Aerial Survey* (Cambridge, 1979), p. 91.

2 (Dinna Clerks) Beresford, 'Three deserted medieval settlements on Dartmoor', pp. 98–158; (Sourton) Weddell and Reed, 'Excavations at Sourton Down, Okehampton', pp. 39–147; (Okehampton) D. Austin, 'Excavations in Okehampton Deer Park, Devon 1976–1978', *PDAS* 36 (1978), pp. 191–239; J. Allan, 'Medieval

pottery and the dating of deserted settlements on Dartmoor', *PDAS* 52 (1994/1996), pp. 141–47, at p. 145; (Italy) G. Barker and A. Grant (eds), 'Ancient and modern pastoralism in Central Italy: an interdisciplinary study in the Cicolano mountains', *Papers of the British School at Rome* 59 (1991), pp. 15–88, at p. 84; (Greece) C. Chang, 'Archaeological landscapes: The ethnoarchaeology of pastoral land use in the Grevena province of Greece', in J. Rossignol and L. Wandsnider (eds), *Space, Time and Archaeological Landscapes* (New York, 1992), pp. 65–89, at p. 87.

3   W.G. Hoskins, *Dartmoor*, National Park Guide no. 1 (London, 1957), pp. 27–38; Beresford and St Joseph, *Medieval England*, p. 93; D. Brunsden, *Dartmoor*, British Landscapes Through Maps 12 (Sheffield, 1968), p. 32; M.M. Postan, 'Medieval agrarian society in its prime: England', in M.M. Postan (ed.), *The Cambridge Economic History of Europe, I: The Agrarian Life of the Middle Ages* (Cambridge, 1966), pp. 548–632, at p. 550; (Brisworthy) *PnD*, p. 229; B. Cox, 'Place-names of the earliest English records', *English Place-name Society* 8 (1975–76), pp. 12–66.

4   *PnD*, p. 269; W.G. Hoskins, 'Cholwich', in Hoskins and Finberg (eds), *Devonshire Studies*, pp. 78–94.

5   Hoskins, 'Cholwich', p. 94.

6   *PnD*, p. 465 (Summerhill); pp. 61, 232, 240 (Longstone); pp. 37, 463 (Bowdley).

7   (Brisworthy) *PnD*, p. 229; (adoption of continental names) D. Postles, *The Surnames of Devon* (Oxford, 1995), pp. 162–63, and *idem, Naming the People of England, c.1100–1350* (Cambridge, 2006), chs 2, 3; (*acta*) F. Barlow (ed.). *English Episcopal Acta; 11 &12: Exeter, 1046–1184 & 1168–1257* (Oxford, 1996); (Canonsleigh) V.C.M. London, (ed.). *The Cartulary of Canonsleigh Abbey (Harleian Ms. No.3660): A Calendar*, DCRS, new ser. 8 (Exeter, 1965); (Tavistock) W. Dugdale, *Monasticon Anglicanum*, ii (1819), pp. 493–503.

8   *PnD*, pp. 191, 194, 197.

9   *PnD*, pp. 232, 468, 483.

10 *PnD*, pp. 229, 232; (Law-code of Ine) Whitelock, *English Historical Documents*, p. 403, where *worthig* is translated as 'homestead': Smith, *English Place-name Elements, ii*, p. 275.

11 *PnD*, pp. 434, 438, 464, 468.

12 (Bittelworth) see Chapter 4, pp. 113–14; (Heatree) *PnD*, p. 482.

13 (Spitchwick) *DB*, 1,48; (Cator, Corndon) *PnD*, pp. 526, 529; (Uppacott) DRO, 48/14/142/1a.

14 *DB*, 1,41; *Exon DB*, fols 95a, 499b.

15 *DB*, 16,7; *Exon DB*, fols 288b, 495a.

16 *Short History, passim*, the very title of which refers to the Commons of Devon.

17 *PnD*, p. 481; A.J.L. Winchester, *Discovering Parish Boundaries* (Princes Risborough, 2000), p. 66, Fig. 19.

18 F. W. Maitland, *Domesday Book and Beyond: Three Essays in the Early History of England* (Cambridge, 1897), p. 19.

19 H.C. Darby, *Domesday Geography of South West England* (Cambridge, 1967), pp. 264–69, 382–87; *idem, Domesday England* (Cambridge, 1977), pp. 154–57; (Powderham) *DB*, 22,1; (Woodbury) *DB*, 1,33, note in *Exon DB*, 1; (Molland) *DB*, 1,41.

20 (Pasture) *DB*, 3,86, 52,44, 15,71; (league) Darby, *Domesday Geography*, pp. 264–68, 382–85; *Domesday England*, pp. 154–55; (Walkhampton) *DB*, 1,19–22; (Royal

Comm.) W.G. Hoskins and L. Dudley, *The Common Lands of England and Wales* (London, 1963), p. 266. It used to be said that Dartmoor was not recorded in Domesday, but Hoskins pointed out that it was implied by the unusually large areas of pasture recorded by the moor-edge manors; *Common Lands*, pp. 17–18.

21 A similar exercise was carried out by Somers Cox, though he arrived at slightly different conclusions; J. Somers Cocks, 'Dartmoor and Domesday Book', *DCNQ*, 30 (1965–67), pp. 290–93.

22 The comparison is brought out visually in Darby, *Domesday Geography of South West England*, Fig. 60.

23 It has been argued that such entries mean, for example, 'one league in length and breadth'; Somers Cox, 'Dartmoor and Domesday Book', p. 290, but *cf.* Darby, *Domesday Geography of South West England*, p. 266.

24 *DB*, 32,6, 39,21, 15,45.

25 DRO, 123M/E/1018–9, discussed in H.P.R. Finberg, 'Supplement to the Early Charters of Devon and Cornwall', in W.G. Hoskins, *The Westward Expansion of Wessex*, Department of English Local History Occasional Papers, 13 (Leicester, 1960), pp. 23–25.

26 For the text of the charter, see the references in n. 35 on p. 244. Attempts to follow the bounds on the ground have been made many times, beginning in the sixteenth century when John Hooker of Exeter mistook them for the bounds of the whole of Dartmoor: BL, Harl. Ms 5827, fol. 93v. For other attempts, see n. 36 on p. 244, and also S. Pearce, 'Early medieval land use on Dartmoor and its flanks', *Devon Archaeology* 3 (1985), pp. 17–19; Hooke, *Pre-Conquest Charter-Bounds*, pp. 217–24; S. Hands, *The Book of Bickington: From Moor to Shore* (Tiverton, 2000), pp. 37–39; Brewer, *Dartmoor Boundary Markers*, pp. 299–307; B. Ransom, 'Ilsington parish and the landscape of Peadington', *Devon Historian* 65 (2002), pp. 16–20. Publication of a new discussion by Dr Charles Insley is imminent; Professor Fox was very grateful to him for giving him a lengthy tutorial on it.

27 *PnD*, p. 482. The circle is actually of 22 stones. They stand at the southern edge of Soussons Plantation and surround a cist burial; Butler, *Dartmoor Atlas of Antiquities*, vol. I, p. 19 and Fig. 24.3.

28 *PnD*, p. 462; S. Pearce. 'Early medieval land use', pp. 13–19; and other commentaries mentioned in n. 26 above.

29 J.H. Kemble, *Codex Diplomaticus Aevi Saxonici* (London, 1839–48), no. 744; Sawyer, *Anglo-Saxon Charters*, no. 963; Finberg, *Early Charters of Devon and Cornwall*, no. 58; Hooke, *Pre-Conquest Charter-Bounds*, pp. 196–200.

30 *DB*, 17,79–82, 29,9; *PnD*, p. 229; Pearce, 'Early medieval land use', pp 16–17.

31 (Elford) *PnD*, p. 225; (highway) The bounds are discussed in W.G. Hoskins, *The Westward Expansion of Wessex*, Department of English Local History Occasional Papers 13 (Leicester, 1960), pp. 30–33, a contribution by D.F. Farmer: who correctly gives 'highway' for *hig wege*. Rose-Troup and Hooke give 'hay wagon way': Rose-Troup, 'Anglo-Saxon charters of Devon', p. 126; Hooke, *Pre-Conquest Charter-Bounds*, p. 199.

32 T. Greeves, 'Placenames of Dartmoor—lost and found', *Dartmoor Magazine*, 35(1994), pp. 6–8, at p. 8.

33 (Ine) Ine, 46, 57; Whitelock (ed.), *English Historical Documents I*, p. 404. Alfred's laws also dealt with cattle theft, in Alf. 16; F.L. Attenborough (ed.), *The Laws of the Earliest English Kings* (Cambridge, 1922); (Edward the Elder) II Edw, 4:

Attenborough (ed.), *Laws of the Earliest English Kings*, pp. 120–21; (Fonthill) Whitelock (ed.), *English Historical Documents I*, p. 545.

34 V Athelstan, 2; Whitelock (ed.), *English Historical Documents I*, p. 424; Attenborough (ed.), *Laws of the Earliest English Kings*, pp. 154–55.

35 (Loyn) H.R. Loyn, *The Governance of Anglo-Saxon England 500–1087* (London, 1984), p. 142; (Cnut and Edward the Elder) II Cnut, 20, and II Edw, 8: A.J. Robertson (ed.), *Laws of the Kings of England from Edmund to Henry I* (Cambridge, 1925), pp. 184–85, and Attenborough (ed.), *Laws of the Earliest English Kings*, pp. 120–21; and see H.R. Loyn, 'The hundred in England in the tenth and early eleventh centuries', in H. Hearder and H.R. Loyn (eds), *British Government and Administration: Studies presented to S.B. Chrimes* (Cardiff, 1974), pp. 1–15.

36 (Cambs., Essex) H.C. Darby, *The Domesday Geography of Eastern England* (Cambridge, 1952), pp. 241–45, 303–4; (Molland) *DB*, 1,41.

37 (Leics. Wolds) Fox, 'The people of the Wolds in English settlement history', pp. 77–101, at p. 88, Fig. 5.2(a); *idem*, 'The Wolds: before c.1500', pp. 50–61, at p. 55, Fig. (a); (Brown Clee) A.J.L. Winchester, 'Moorland forests of medieval England', in J.D. Whyte and A.J.L. Winchester (eds), *Society, Landscape and Environment in Upland Britain*, Society for Landscape Studies 2 (2004), pp. 21–34, Fig. 3.2b, based on T. Rowley, *The Shropshire Landscape* (London, 1972), p. 50, Fig. 3; (Rymer and Goonhilly/Dry Tree) Winchester, *Discovering Parish Boundaries*, p. 61, Fig. 17, based on (Rymer) O. Rackham, *The History of the Countryside* (London, 1986), pp. 355–56, Fig. 16.5, and (Goonhilly) D. Hooke, *The Landscape of Anglo-Saxon England* (London, 1988), pp. 76–77, Fig. 29 (where other examples of convergence can be found). The Rymer and Goonhilly maps are also in H.J.G. Pound, *A History of the English Parish* (Cambridge, 2000), pp. 69–70, Figs 3.2, 3.3, and Rymer map is also in J.C. Holt (ed.), *Domesday Studies* (Woodbridge, 1987), p. 187, Fig. 2; (Dartmoor) above, Fig. 1.5. Reepham in Norfolk is another example of spokes converging on a hub, in this case no larger than a churchyard in which three parishes' churches stood side by side: Pound, *History of the English Parish*, pp. 70–71, Fig. 3.4

38 Winchester, *Discovering Parish Boundaries*, pp. 61–70 and Fig. 3.3. See also Pound, *History of the English Parish*, pp. 69–71 and Figs 3.2–3.4.

39 Brimpts is first recorded in 1199 (as *Birmestestowe, Brimestow*); S. Pearce, *South-western Britain in the Early Middle Ages* (London, 2004), p. 144; Fox, 'Medieval Dartmoor as seen through the account rolls', pp. 149–72, at pp. 152–54. For Dunnabridge, TNA:PRO, E 132/152B (an account of 1305–6), abstracted in *Short History*, p. 12, and discussed in Fox, 'Medieval Dartmoor as seen through the account rolls', p. 152.

40 (Babeny, Runnage) *PnD*, p. 197; (Wallabrook) *PnD*, p. 16; F. Wilkinson, 'The Dartmoor husbandman', *Devon Historian* 14 (1977), pp. 5–10.

41 A. Winchester, 'Vaccaries and agistment: upland medieval forests as grazing grounds', in J. Langton and G. Jones (eds), *Forests and Chases of England and Wales, c. 1000 to c. 1500* (Oxford, 2010), pp. 109–24.

42 Thorn, 'Hundreds and wapentakes', pp. 26–39, at pp. 36–37.

43 (Third penny) *DB*, 1,45 (on fol. 101b); (fourteenth-century list) *Inquisitions and Assessments relating to Feudal Aids, with other Analogous Documents preserved in the Public Record Office, A.D. 1284–1431. Vol.1: Bedfordshire to Devonshire* (London, 1899), p. 391—but see Thorn, 'Hundreds and wapentakes', p. 38, note 5.

44 (Geld roll) Thorn, 'Hundreds and wapentakes', p. 38; (Stanborough/Halwell) Barlow and Thorn, *Devonshire Domesday*, pp. 11 and 27, n. 15; Haslam, 'The towns of Devon', pp. 262–65. Halwell and Stanborough are both close to Moreleigh, within living memory one of the traditional collecting points for summer cattle being taken to Dartmoor; T. Greeves, 'Red tide: the summer pasturage of cattle on Dartmoor', *Dartmoor Magazine* 43 (1996), pp. 6–8.

Notes to Chapter Seven

1 This chapter was only partly written when Professor Fox died. The first section, on droveways, was the most complete, but none of the envisaged seven maps depicting droveways leading to Dartmoor had been drawn. Some rough preliminary workings for Figs 7.2 and 7.3 were found and the editors have used them to produce the maps which appear below. They have not attempted to produce five maps which were also envisaged, however (see notes 14 and 15). A first draft of the second section, on pastoral husbandry, was found and the editors have filled in the few gaps it contained and produced the illustrative Tables 7.1–7.3 (based on workings found in Professor Fox's papers). The third section, on arable husbandry, existed only as an outline and fragments of text, which the editors have linked into a coherent account consistent with the outline, though sadly it is not as lengthy and detailed as Professor Fox seems to have intended.

2 M. Oppenheim, *The Maritime History of Devon* (Exeter, 1968); M. Duffy (ed.), *A New Maritime History of Devon*, 2 vols (London, 1993–94).

3 I.D. Margary, *Roman Roads in Britain* (London, 1973). For saltways, see F.T.S. Houghton, 'Saltways', *Transactions of the Birmingham and Warwickshire Archaeological Society*, 54 (1932), pp. 1–17; Hooke, *The Landscape of Anglo-Saxon England*, pp. 2–9; eadem, *The Anglo-Saxon Landscape: The Kingdom of the Hwicce* (Manchester, 1985), pp. 122–26.

4 Prominent works are: A. Haldane, *The Drove Roads of Scotland* (London, 1952); K.J. Bonser, *The Drovers: Who they were and where they went* (London, 1970); P.G. Hughes, *Wales and the Drovers* (London, 1943); R.J. Colyer, *The Welsh Cattle Drovers* (Cardiff, 1976); C. Skeel, 'The cattle trade between Wales and England from the fifteenth to the nineteenth centuries', *Transactions of the Royal Historical Society*, 4th ser. 9 (1926), pp. 135–58; H.P.R. Finberg, 'An early reference to the Welsh cattle trade', *AHR* 2 (1954), pp. 12–14; C. Dyer, 'Farming Practice and techniques: The West Midlands', *AHE&W III*, pp. 222–37, at p. 234; D.L. Farmer, 'Marketing the produce of the countryside, 1200–1500, *AHE&W III*, pp. 378–85; D. Moss, 'The economic development of a Middlesex village', *AHR* 28 (1980), pp. 104–14, at p. 114. For references to droving in the south west, Gerard (mid seventeenth-century), cited in Trow-Smith, *History of British Livestock Husbandry*, p. 179; Halliday (ed.), *Richard Carew of Anthony*, p. 107. See also Everitt, 'The marketing of agricultural produce', pp. 539–42.

5 Hooke, *Anglo-Saxon Landscape: Kingdom of the Hwicce*, pp. 120–26, 145–49; R. Muir, *The New Reading the Landscape: Fieldwork in Landscape History* (Exeter, 2000), p. 106; Rackham, *The History of the Countryside*, p. 276, Fig. 12.13.

6 See, for example, Klein, *The Mesta*; Braudel, *The Mediterranean*, pp. 89, 95; M.J. Walker, 'Laying a mega-myth: Dolmens and drovers in prehistoric Spain', *World Archaeology* 15, no. 1, *Transhumance and Pastoralism* (June, 1983), pp. 37–50, and Barker and Grant (eds), 'Ancient and modern pastoralism in Central Italy', pp. 15–88.

7   Witney, *The Jutish Forest*; Everitt, *Continuity and Colonisation*; Fox, 'The people of the Wolds in English settlement history', pp. 77–101; Hooke, 'Pre-conquest woodland: Its distribution and usage', pp. 113–29.

8   For example, C. Taylor, *Roads and Tracks of Britain* (London, 1979), pp. 148–49, 163–4; or B. Hindle, *Roads, Tracks and their Interpretation* (London, 1993), ch. 6, which does not distinguish between transhumance and droving to market.

9   Witney, *The Jutish Forest*, p. 132. Andrew Fleming discusses the *directionality* of prehistoric Dartmoor reaves, seeing their 'lowland-upland axis' as reflecting journeys and 'the biennial movement of flocks and herds and those who tended them'; Fleming, *The Dartmoor Reaves*, pp. 197–98.

10 Everitt, *Continuity and Colonisation*, p. 269.

11 Colyer, *Welsh Cattle Drovers*, pp. 92, 105–9, Hindle, *Roads, Tracks and their Interpretation*, ch. 6; Hughes, *Wales and the Drovers*, pp. 59–63; Skeel, 'Cattle trade between Wales and England', pp. 146–48; Bonser, *The Drovers*, p. 45.

12 Everitt, *Continuity and Colonisation*, pp. 17, 36, 39.

13 Beresford and Finberg, *English Medieval Boroughs*, p. 90.

14 Everitt, *Continuity and Colonisation*, p. 36.

15 No draft map of the Northlew to Dartmoor droveway could be found. Fig. 7.3 has been prepared by the editors on the basis of the above description and annotations made by Professor Fox on an O.S. map found among his papers.

16 (*Chauelesweye*) PnD, pp. 475, 524.; (Buckland) Hooke, *Pre-Conquest Charter-Bounds*, p. 199.

17 Maitland, *Domesday Book and Beyond*, p. 16; (Thorverton) W.G. Hoskins, *Devon and its People* (Exeter, 1959), pp. 30, 31.

18 Hughes, *Wales and the Drovers*, p. 48, suggests 14–16 miles per day; Colyer, *Welsh Cattle Drovers*, p. 60, suggests 15–20 miles.

19 DRO, Denbury tithe map; (Shute Lake) DRO, CR 1401–1404; (Watershoot) PnD, p. 104. Tom Greeves has used oral recollections to describe the use of Denbury Green as a collecting point for animals being taken to Dartmoor for summer pasture within living memory; Greeves, 'Red Tide: The summer pasturage of cattle on Dartmoor', pp. 6–8; *idem*, '"Mr Coaker is riding today"', *Devon Life* 6, no. 1 (July 2001), pp. 76–77.

20 A.H. Smith, *English Place-name Elements: Jafn-Ytri*, English Place-name Society 26 (Cambridge, 1956).

21 D.N. Parsons and T. Styles, *Vocabulary of English Place-names: A–Box* (Nottingham, 1997), p. 7.

22 Hoskins, 'Cholwich', pp. 78–94, at p. 88.

23 (Shoeing for the drove) Colyer, *Welsh Cattle Drovers*, pp. 59–60, 94–104, Plate I; Bonser, *The Drovers*, ch. 5; Skeel, 'Cattle trade between Wales and England'; (shoeing working oxen) M. Watts, *Working Oxen* (Princes Risborough, 1999), pp. 26–28. Oxen were shod on Dartmoor in the nineteenth century, at least, as the shoes survive; personal communication from Tom Greeves.

24 (North Bovey) DRO, 1508M/Moger/357; (map of Owlacombe Common, 1808) DRO, 1311M/3/4.

25 (Boroughs) Beresford and Finberg, *English Medieval Boroughs*, s.n.; (South Zeal) DRO, South Tawton tithe map, c.1840; (Gough) E.J.S. Parsons, *The Map of Great Britain, c. AD 1360, known as the Gough Map* (Oxford, 1958).

26 (Crediton) Hooke, *Pre-Conquest Charter-Bounds*, pp. 86–90; (Harford) PnD, p. 275.

Notes to pages 207–14   **255**

27 B. Donn, *A Map of the County of Devon 1765*, DCRS and University of Exeter facsimile reprint (1965).

28 J. Ogilby, *Britannia . . . a Geographical and Historical Description of the Principal Roads thereof . . .* (1675), plate 29, 'Road From London to the Lands End'; DRO, Ashburton tithe map.

29 DRO, Staverton Tithe apportionment; (*Yeoldelonde*) PnD, p. 148; (*eald*) PnD, pp. lviii, 677.

30 (Staverton) Exeter Cathedral Archive, D&C Ch. Comm. 6034/6/1a-b; (charter) Hooke, *Pre-Conquest Charter Bounds*, p. 97, *ealdan herepath*; (Oldway) PnD, p. 289 (Doccombe) Canterbury Cathedral Archives, CCA-U15/14/5, court held on the feast of St Edmund, 7 Hen. VII, m. 2.

31 The exercise is concerned with cattle only, but the manuscript indicates that Professor Fox had intended to write a further section on other livestock. Even the section modelling two cattle rearing farms was incomplete, but the calculations were sufficiently far advanced for the editors to have been able to complete them and to produce the two illustrative Tables—but any errors remain theirs alone.

32 (Holding sizes) Fox, 'Tenant farming and tenant farmers: Devon and Cornwall', pp. 722–43; (Stokenham) TNA:PRO, SC 11/168; (Woodbury) TNA:PRO, E 315/385; (Uplyme) BM, Eg. Ms 3134.

33 (Oxen) J. Langdon, *Horses, Oxen and Technological Innovation: The Use of Draught Animals in English Farming from 1066 to 1500* (Cambridge, 1986); (1525 survey) TNA:PRO, E315/385; (50a. ploughed by 8-ox team) B.M.S. Campbell, *English Seigniorial Agriculture, 1250–1450* (Cambridge, 2000), p. 133.

34 (50–60% arable) Fox, 'Occupation of the land: Devon and Cornwall', pp. 154–58; (convertible husbandry) Finberg, *Tavistock Abbey*, pp. 104–8; Fox, 'Farming practices and techniques: Devon and Cornwall', pp. 303–23; H.S.A. Fox and O.J. Padel (eds), *The Cornish Lands of the Arundels of Lanherne, Fourteenth to Sixteenth Centuries*, DCNS, new ser. 41 (2000), p. lxxi; S.J. Rippon, R.M. Fyfe and A.G. Browne, 'Beyond villages and open fields: The origins and development of a historic landscape characterised by dispersed settlement in south-west England', *Medieval Archaeology* 50 (2006), pp. 31–70. For a nineteenth-century comment, see Thomas Tonkin's gloss on Richard Carew's well-known description of convertible husbandry: *Carew's Survey of Cornwall to which are added notes by . . . Thomas Tonkin* (London, 1811), p. 63, note 1.

35 Fox, 'Farming practices and techniques: Devon and Cornwall', pp. 303–9; Campbell, *English Seigniorial Agriculture*, pp. 330–34; C. Dyer, *Standards of Living in the Later Middle Ages: Social Change in England c. 1200–1520* (1989; Cambridge, 1998), p. 117.

36 Fox, 'Occupation of the land: Devon and Cornwall', pp. 153–57.

37 (fertility rate) In 1316–17 each of ten cows on the demesne at Cuxham, Oxon, produced a calf, though few other demesnes could match that; Trow-Smith, *History of British Livestock Husbandry*, p. 117, n.3, and see Campbell, *English Seigniorial Agriculture*, p. 145, where a 60–73% reproduction rate is reckoned more typical; (acreage to support 1 cow) Vancouver, *General View of the Agriculture of the County of Devon*, pp. 212–13; J. Billingsley, *General View of the Agriculture of the County of Somerset* (Bath, 1795), pp. 122, 144; (south western practice) J.L. Langdon, 'The economics of horses and oxen in medieval England', *AHR* 30 (1982), pp. 31–40, at p. 33.

38 Campbell, *English Seigniorial Agriculture*, pp. 104–6, where other ratios are also discussed.

39 Campbell, *English Seigniorial Agriculture*, p. 143; Finberg, *Tavistock Abbey*, Tab. XVIII, pp. 133–35, contains a price series which suggests that in south-west Devon the average price for mature cattle may have been a little higher than 11s.

40 Campbell, *English Seigniorial Agriculture*, p. 143.

41 The fee for a summer's pasturage, under the guardianship of the Crown's herdsmen, was 1½d. per beast, and the rate charged on the privately owned outer moors is likely to have been the same (to avoid being undercut by the central moor). However, as has been discussed in chapter 2, many farmers did not commit their stock directly into the Crown's hands but instead took them to middlemen, who paid the 1½d. fee themselves but no doubt charged a higher fee to the farmer. This fee cannot have been a great deal higher than 1½d. because farmers always had the option of placing cattle directly onto the moor, but no direct evidence of it exists. The 6d. proposed here may be too high.

42 TNA:PRO, SC 6/826/21–3, *Cal Inq Misc IV: 1387–1393*, pp. 44–45.

43 In demesnes across England reproduction rates were usually 60–73%, and a single cow's dairy produce was typically worth 4s. in the early fourteenth century, though output may have been lower in the south west; Campbell, *English Seigniorial Agriculture*, pp. 144–46. Finberg, *Tavistock Abbey*, pp. 135–37, describes the terms of employment of Tavistock Abbey's dairywomen.

44 (1393 inventory) DRO, 410Z/F/1, printed in H.M. Peskett, 'The probate inventory of Sire John Daumarle, 1393', *DCNQ* 32 (1971), pp. 79–82, where Sir John Daumarle's career and estates are briefly summarised; (1366 account) DRO, 158M/M/11.

45 At this point the manuscript becomes fragmentary. It seems that Professor Fox intended to add a third example of a demesne which depended on Dartmoor's pastures for its livestock; Tavistock Abbey's manor of Hurdwick, which was distinguished for the great number of livestock which were kept (in the fifteenth century more than on any other Devonshire demesne for which accounts or inventories survive—and its name, meaning 'herd farm', suggests this must also have been the case in the Saxon period). The manorial accounts contain references to demesne livestock depastured on Dartmoor; for example, Devon RO, W1258M/D/52/2, and see Finberg, *Tavistock Abbey*, p. 131.

46 Fox, 'A Geographical Study of the Field Systems of Devon and Cornwall'; *idem*, 'The chronology of enclosure and economic development in medieval Devon', pp. 181–202; *idem*, 'Peasant farmers, patterns of settlement and *pays*', pp. 41–74, at pp. 55–57. The county's enclosure was so complete at such an early date that until the middle of the twentieth century some scholars denied that it had ever contained any open fields—for example, C.S. and C.S. Orwin, the *Open Fields* (Oxford, 1938), p. 61.

47 DRO, 1508M/manor/Halstock/2.

48 DRO, W1258M/D/41/2.

49 (Borcombe) DRO, 123M/TB/263; (Uplyme) A. Watkin (ed.), *The Great Chartulary of Glastonbury*, Somerset Rec. Soc. (1947–56), iii, p. 586.

50 Written by Christopher Dyer.

Notes to Conclusion

1 M. Kowaleski, *Local Markets and Regional Trade in Medieval Exeter* (Cambridge, 1995), pp. 45–46.

2 Fox, 'Farming practice and techniques: Devon and Cornwall', pp. 319–20.

3 Kowaleski, *Local Markets and Regional Trade in Medieval Exeter*, pp. 322–23.

4 Finberg, *Tavistock Abbey*, pp. 133–35.

5 Kowaleski, *Local Markets and Regional Trade in Medieval Exeter*, pp. 247–48.

6 K. Smith, J. Coppen, G.J. Wainwright and S. Beckett, 'The Shaugh Moor project: Third report, settlement and environmental investigations', *Proceedings of the Prehistoric Society*, 47 (1981), pp. 205–73; R. Fyfe, 'Paleoenvironmental perspectives on medieval landscape development', in S. Turner (ed.) *Medieval Devon and Cornwall: Shaping an Ancient Countryside* (Macclesfield, 2006), pp. 10–23.

7 See, for example, Fig. 51 in Siraut, *Exmoor: The Making of an English Upland*, p. 88, which shows the wide swathe of north Devon from which sheep were sent to Exmoor in 1736. The system of agistment, on a central royal forest and an outer ring of manorial commons, seems to have been remarkably similar to that of Dartmoor: *ibid.*, pp. 36–37, 53–56, 61, 69–76, 87–90.

Bibliography

Unprinted Primary Sources

The National Archives: Public Record Office

C 132, 133, 134, 135, 139 (Inquisitions post Mortem).
C 145 (Inquisitions Miscellaneous).
E 134 (Exchequer Depositions).
E142 (Extents, Inquisitions and Valors).
E 164 (King's Remembrancer, Miscellaneous Books).
E179 (Lay Subsidies).
E 315 (Court of Augmentations).
SC 2 (Court Rolls).
SC 6 (Ministers' and Receivers' Accounts).
SC 11, 12 (Rentals and Surveys).
STAC 2 (Star Chamber Proceedings).

Devon Record Office

Bedford Estates Collection—1258M.
Cary of Torre Abbey Collection—4088M.
Courtenay of Powderham Collection—1508M.
CR Collection (Manorial records formerly held by Exeter City Library).
DD Collection (Records formerly Exeter City Library).
Exeter Diocese.
Exeter Diocese Records—Glebe terriers.
Luxmoore of Oakhampton Collection—314M.
Mallett Family Collection—Z13.
Mallock of Cockington Collection—48/13.
Petre Collection—123M.
Seymour of Berry Pomeroy Collection—1392M.
Short Family Collection—1311M.
Tithe maps.
Torquay Natural History Society Collection—43/14.
Tremayne of Collacombe Collection—158M, 410Z.
Z17 Collection (Manorial and estate records formerly held by Exeter City
    Library).

North Devon Record Office
Chichester of Arlington Collection.

West Devon Record Office
Roborough Estate Collection.

Exeter Cathedral Archive
Dean and Chapter estate archive.

Powderham Archive
1787 Estate Atlas.

Cornwall Record Office
Arundel & Lanherne and Trerice Collection.

Royal Institution of Cornwall
Henderson Collection (Grylls Archive).

Devon & Cornwall Record Society
Pole's Charters.

Duchy of Cornwall Office
Ministers' Accounts.

British Library
Additional MSS.
Additional Charters.
Egerton MSS.
Harleian MSS.

Canterbury Cathedral Archives
Dean and Chapter Archive.
Church Commissioners' Manorial Court Rolls.

Staffordshire Record Office
Sutherland Papers, Lilleshall Abbey deeds.

Printed Primary Sources

Attenborough, F.L. (ed.), *The Laws of the Earliest English Kings* (Cambridge, 1922).
Barlow, F. (ed.), *English Episcopal Acta; 11 & 12: Exeter, 1046–1184 & 1168–1257* (Oxford, 1996).

Barlow, F. and F.R. Thorn (ed.), *The Devonshire Domesday*, Alecto edition (London, 1991).

Bearman, R. (ed.), *Charters of the Redvers Family and the Earldom of Devon 1090–1217*, DCRS new ser. 37 (1994).

Birch, W. de G. (ed.), *Cartularium Saxonicum: A Collection of Charters relating to Anglo-Saxon History* (London, 1885–93).

Calendar of Inquisitions Miscellaneous.

Calendar of Inquisitions post Mortem.

Calendar of the Close Rolls.

Calendar of the Patent Rolls.

Caley, J. and J. Hunter (eds), *Valor Ecclesiasticus*, 6 vols, Record Commission (1810–41).

Crossley-Holland, K. (ed.), *The Exeter Riddle Book* (London, 1978).

Curia Regis Rolls, 3–4 Hen. III (London, 1938).

Dawes, M.C.B. (ed.), *The Black Prince's Register*, ii (London, 1931).

Deedes, C. (ed.), *Registrum Johannis de Pontissara, Episcopi Wyntoniensis AD MCCLXXXII–MCCCIV*, vol. i, Canterbury and York Society 19 (1915).

Domesday Book, vol. 4, *Libri Censualis Vocati Domesday Book, Additamenta ex Codic. Antiquiss.*, Record Commission (London, 1816), fols 83–494b [the Exon Domesday].

Donn, B., *A Map of the County of Devon 1765*, DCRS and University of Exeter facsimile reprint (1965).

Dunstan, G.R. (ed.), *Register of Edmund Lacy, Bishop of Exeter, 1420–1455*, vol. ii, DCRS, new ser. 10 (1966).

Erskine, A.M. (ed.), *The Devonshire Lay Subsidy of 1332*, DCRS, new ser. 14 (1969).

Furnivall, F.J. (ed.), A. Borde, *The First Boke of the Introduction of Knowledge*, EETS extra ser. 10 (London, 1870).

Hanham, A. (ed.), *Churchwardens' Accounts of Ashburton, 1479–1580*, DCRS, new ser. 15 (1970).

Hingeston-Randolph, F.C. (ed.), *Bishop Grandisson's Registers* 3 (London, 1899).

Hingeston-Randolph, F.C. (ed.), *The Registers of Walter Bromescombe and Peter Quivil* (London, 1889).

Hobhouse, E. and C.I. Elton (eds), *Rentalia et Custumaria Michaelis de Ambresbury, 1235–1252, et Rogeri de Ford, 1252–1261*, Somerset Record Society 5 (Taunton, 1891).

Inquisitions and Assessments relating to Feudal Aids, with other Analogous Documents preserved in the Public Record Office, A.D. 1284–1431. Vol. 1: Bedfordshire to Devonshire (London, 1899).

Kemble, J.H. (ed.), *Codex Diplomaticus Aevi Saxonici* (London, 1839–48).

Kingsford, C.L. (ed.), *The Stonor Letters and Papers, 1290–1483*, vol. i, Camden Society 3rd ser. 29 (1919).

Lacroix, P. (ed.), Jehan de Brie, *Le Bon Berger ou le Vray Régime et Gouvernement de Bergers et Bergères* (Paris, 1879).

London, V.C.M. (ed.), *The Cartulary of Canonsleigh Abbey (Harleian Ms. No. 3660): A Calendar*, DCRS, new ser. 8 (Exeter, 1965).

Midgley, L.M. (ed.), *Ministers' Accounts of the Earldom of Cornwall 1296–97*, ii, Camden Society 3rd ser. 68 (1945).

Napier, A.S. and W.H. Stevenson (eds), *The Crawford Collection of Early Charters and Documents now in the Bodleian Library* (Oxford, 1895).

Neilson, N. (ed.), *A Terrier of Fleet, Lincolnshire*, British Academy Records of the Social Economic History of England and Wales 4 (1920).

Nicolas, Sir H. (ed.), *Privy Council of England, Proceedings and Ordinances, 10 Richard II–33 Henry VII (1386–1542)*, 7, Record Commission (1837).

Ogilby, J., *Britannia . . . a Geographical and Historical Description of the Principal Roads thereof . . .* (1675).

Oschinsky, D. (ed.), *Walter of Henley and other Treatises on Estate Management and Accounting* (Oxford, 1971).

Parsons, E.J.S., *The Map of Great Britain, c. AD 1360, known as the Gough Map* (Oxford, 1958).

Powicke, F.M. and C.R. Cheney (eds), *Councils and Synods, with other Documents relating to the English Church, II: AD 1205–1313* (Oxford, 1964).

Robertson, A.J. (ed.), *Laws of the Kings of England from Edmund to Henry I* (Cambridge, 1925).

Rotuli Chartarum in Turri Londoniensis Asservati, i, Pt 1, Record Commission (London, 1837).

Rotuli Hundredorum, I, Record Commission (London, 1812).

Round, J.H. (ed.), *Calendar of Documents preserved in France illustrative of the History of Great Britain and Ireland* (London, 1899).

Rumble, A. (ed.), *Domesday Book: Cambridgeshire* (Chichester, 1981).

Stoate, T.L. (ed.), *Devon Lay Subsidy Rolls, 1524–27* (Bristol, 1979).

Stratton, C.R. (ed.), *Survey of the Lands of William, First Earl of Pembroke*, Roxburghe Club, vol. 2 (Oxford, 1909).

Stubbs, W. (ed.), William of Malmesbury, *De Gestis Regum Anglorum*, I, Rolls Series (London, 1887).

Taxatio Ecclesiastica Angliae et Walliae Auctoritate P. Nicholas IV (London: Record Commission, 1802).

Thorn, C. and F. Thorn, *Domesday Book: Devon*, Phillimore edition (Chichester, 1985). [*DB*]

Torr, C. (ed.), *Wreyland Documents* (Cambridge, 1910).

Whitelock, D. (ed.), *English Historical Documents; I: c.500–1042* (London, 1955; 2nd edn 1979).

White's History, Gazetteer and Directory of Devonshire 1850.

Secondary Works

Aalen, F., 'Clochans as transhumance dwellings in the Dingle Peninsula', *Journal of the Royal Society of Antiquaries of Ireland* 94 (1964), pp. 39–45.

Acheson, E., *A Gentry Community: Leicestershire in the Fifteenth Century, c.1422–c.1485* (Cambridge, 1992).

Adams, A., *Zeal Monachorum: A Devon Rural Parish 1086–1801* (Zeal Monachorum, 2002).

Albarella, U. and S.J.M. Davis, 'Mammals and birds from Launceston Castle, Cornwall: decline in status and the rise of agriculture', *Circaea: The Journal of the Association of Environmental Archaeology* 12 (1996 for 1994).

Alcock, N.W., P. Child and M. Laithwaite, 'Sanders, Lettaford: A Devon
    longhouse', *PDAS* 30 (1972), pp. 227–33.

Alexander, J.J., 'The beginnings of Lifton', *Trans. Devon. Assoc.* 63 (1931),
    pp. 349–58.

Allan, J., 'Medieval pottery and the dating of deserted medieval settlements on
    Dartmoor', *PDAS* 52 (1994), pp. 141–48.

Atkin, M.A., 'Land use and management of the upland demesne of the de Lacy
    family of Blackburnshire *c*.1300', *AHR* 42 (1994), pp. 1–19.

Ault, W.O., *Open-field Farming in Medieval England* (London, 1972).

Austin, D., 'Excavations in Okehampton Deer Park, Devon 1976–1978', *PDAS* 36
    (1978), pp. 191–239.

Austin, D., 'Dartmoor and the upland village of the southwest of England', in
    D. Hooke, *The Medieval Village* (Oxford, 1985), pp. 71–80.

Austin, D. and M.J.C. Walker, 'A new landscape context for Hound Tor',
    Medieval Archaeology 29 (1985), pp. 132–52.

Austin, D., G.A.M. Gerrard and T.A.P. Greeves, 'Tin and agriculture in
    the Middle Ages and beyond: Landscape archaeology in St Neot parish,
    Cornwall', *Cornish Archaeology* 28 (1989), pp. 5–251.

Austin, D., and J. Thomas, 'The "proper study" of medieval archaeology: A case
    study', in D. Austin and L. Alcock (eds), *From the Baltic to the Black Sea:
    Studies in Medieval Archaeology* (London, 1997), pp. 43–78.

Bainbridge, T.H., 'A note on transhumance in Cumbria', *Geography* 25 (1940),
    pp. 35–36.

Barker, G. and A. Grant (eds), 'Ancient and modern pastoralism in Central Italy:
    an interdisciplinary study in the Cicolano mountains', *Papers of the British
    School at Rome* 59 (1991), pp. 15–88.

Baring-Gould, S., *A Book of the West, I: Devon* (London, 1899).

Beacham, P., 'Rural building: 1400–1800', in N. Pevsner and B. Cherry, *The
    Buildings of England: Devon* (London, 1989).

Beresford, G., 'The medieval manor of Penhallam, Jacobstow, Cornwall',
    Medieval Archaeology 18 (1974), pp. 90–145.

Beresford, G., 'Three deserted medieval settlements on Dartmoor: A report
    on the late E. Marie Minter's excavations', *Medieval Archaeology* 23 (1979),
    pp. 98–158.

Beresford, M.W., *The Lost Villages of England* (London, 1954).

Beresford, M.W. and H.P.R. Finberg, *English Medieval Boroughs: A Hand-list*
    (Newton Abbot, 1973).

Beresford, M.W. and J.K.S. St Joseph, *Medieval England: An Aerial Survey*
    (Cambridge, 1979).

Biddick, K., *The Other Economy: Pastoral Husbandry on a Medieval Estate*
    (Berkeley, CA, 1989).

Bil, A., *The Sheiling, 1600–1840: The Case of the Central Scottish Highlands*
    (Edinburgh, 1990).

Billingsley, J., *General View of the Agriculture of the County of Somerset* (Bath,
    1795).

Birrell, J., 'Who poached the king's deer?', *Midland History* 7 (1982), pp. 9–25.

Birrell, J., 'Deer and deer farming in medieval England', *AHR* 40, pt 2 (1992),
    pp. 112–26.

Birrell, J., 'A great thirteenth-century hunter: John Giffard of Brimpsfield', *Medieval Prosopography* 3 (1994), pp. 37–66.

Birrell, J., 'Peasant deer poachers in the medieval forest', in R. Britnell and J. Hatcher (eds), *Progress and Problems in Medieval England* (Cambridge, 1996), pp. 68–88.

Blake, M.J., 'Hooker's Synopsis Chorographical of Devonshire', *Trans. Devon. Assoc.* 47 (1915), pp. 334–48.

Blair, J. (ed.), *Minsters and Parish Churches: The Local Church in Transition 950–1250* (Oxford, 1988).

Blanchard, I., 'Labour productivity and work psychology in the English mining industry', *EHR* 2nd ser. 31 (1978), pp. 1–24.

Bloch, M., *Les Caractères Originaux de l'Histoire Rurale Française* (Oslo, 1931).

Bonser, K.J., *The Drovers: Who They Were and Where They Went* (London, 1970).

du Boulay, F.R.H., 'Denns, droving and danger', *Archaeologia Cantiana* 76 (1961), pp. 75–87.

du Boulay, F.R.H., *The Lordship of Canterbury: An Essay on Medieval Society* (London, 1966).

Braudel, F., *The Mediterranean and the Mediterranean World in the Age of Philip II*, vol. 1 (London, 1972).

Bray, A.E., *A Description of the Part of Devonshire bordering on the Tamar and the Tavy . . .*, vol. 1 (London, 1836).

Bray, G. (ed.), *Tudor Church Reform: The Henrician Canons of 1535 and the Reformatio legum ecclesiasticarum*, Church of England Record Society 8 (2000).

Brewer, D., *Dartmoor Boundary Markers* (Tiverton, 2002).

Britnell, R., *The Commercialisation of English Society 1000–1500* (Cambridge, 1993).

Britnell, R. and B.M.S. Campbell (eds), *A Commercialising Economy: England 1086–c.1300* (Manchester, 1995).

Brunsden, D., *Dartmoor*, British Landscapes Through Maps 12 (Sheffield, 1968).

Buckley, J.A. (ed.), *Thomas Beare's The Bailiff of Blackmore 1586* (Camborne, 1994).

Burt, W. (ed.), *Dartmoor: A Descriptive Poem*, by N.T. Carrington (London, 1826).

Butler, J., *Dartmoor Atlas of Antiquities*, Vols I–V (Exeter, 1991–1997).

Camden, W., *Britannia*, ed. P. Holland (London, 1610).

Cameron, K., *English Place-names* (1961; 3rd edn, London, 1977).

Campbell, B.M.S., *English Seigniorial Agriculture, 1250–1450* (Cambridge, 2000).

Campbell, E.M.J., 'Kent', in H.C. Darby and E.M.J. Campbell (eds), *The Domesday Geography of South-East England* (Cambridge, 1962), pp. 527–32.

Carrier, E.H., *Water and Grass: A Study of the Pastoral Economy of Southern Europe* (London, 1932).

Carrington, N.T., *Dartmoor: A Descriptive Poem, with a Preface and Notes by W. Burt, esq.* (London, 1826).

Chang, C., 'Archaeological landscapes: The ethnoarchaeology of pastoral land use in the Grevena province of Greece', in J. Rossignol and L. Wandsnider (eds), *Space, Time and Archaeological Landscapes* (New York, 1992), pp. 65–89.

Cherry, B., and N. Pevsner, *The Buildings of England—Devon* (London, 2nd edn, 1989).

Chope, R.P., *The Book of Hartland* (Torquay, 1940).

Christie, P., and P. Rose, 'Davidstow Moor, Cornwall: The medieval and later sites. Wartime excavations by C.K. Croft Andrew 1941–42', *Cornish Archaeology*, 26 (1987), pp. 163–94.

Coates, R., 'New light from old wicks: The progeny of Latin *vicus*', *Nomina* 22 (1999).

Coker, J., *A Survey of Dorsetshire* (London, 1732).

Colgrave, B. (ed.), *Two Lives of St Cuthbert* (Cambridge, 1940).

Colyer, R.J., *The Welsh Cattle Drovers* (Cardiff, 1976).

Cox, B., 'Place-names of the earliest English records', *English Place-name Society* 8 (1975–76), pp. 12–66.

Cracknell, B., *Canvey Island: The History of a Marshland Community* (Leicester, 1959).

Crossing, W., *A Hundred Years on Dartmoor* (Plymouth, 1901).

Crossing, W., *Guide to Dartmoor* (Plymouth, 1912).

Crossing, W., *Crossing's Dartmoor Worker*, ed. B. Le Messurier (Newton Abbot, 1966).

Darby, H.C., *The Domesday Geography of Eastern England* (Cambridge, 1952).

Darby, H.C., *Domesday Geography of South West England* (Cambridge, 1967).

Darby, H.C., *Domesday England* (Cambridge, 1977).

Davidson, J.B., 'Some Anglo-Saxon boundaries now deposited at the Albert Museum, Exeter', *Trans. Devon. Assoc.* 8 (1876), pp. 396–419.

Davies, E., 'The patterns of transhumance in Europe', *Geography* 25 (1940), pp. 155–68.

Dobson, M., '"Marsh fever": The geography of malaria in England', *Journal of Historical Geography* 6 (1980), pp. 357–89.

Donkin, R.A., *The Cistercians: Studies in the Geography of Medieval England and Wales* (Toronto, 1978).

Drewett, P., *et al.*, 'The excavation of a Saxon sunken building at North Marden, West Sussex, 1982', *Sussex Archaeological Collections* 124 (1986), pp. 109–18.

Duffy, M. (ed.), *A New Maritime History of Devon*, 2 vols (London, 1993–94).

Dugdale, W., *Antiquities of Warwickshire* (London, 1656).

Dugdale, W., *Monasticon Anglicanum*, ii (1819).

Dyer, C., 'Seasonal settlement in medieval Gloucestershire: Sheepcotes', in H.S.A. Fox (ed.), *Seasonal Settlement*, Vaughan Paper No. 39 (Leicester, 1996), pp. 25–34.

Dyer, C., *Warwickshire Farming 1349–c1520: Preparations for Agricultural Revolution*, Dugdale Society Occasional Paper (1981).

Dyer, C., *Standards of Living in the Middle Ages: Social Change in England c.1200–1520* (Cambridge, 1989; revised edition, 1998).

Dyer, C., 'Farming practice and techniques: The West Midlands', in E. Miller (ed.), *Agrarian History of England and Wales; III 1348–1500* (Cambridge, 1991), pp. 222–37.

Dyer, C., 'Sheepcotes: Evidence for medieval sheep farming', *Medieval Archaeology* 39 (1995), pp. 136–64.

Dyer, C., *Making a Living in the Middle Ages: The People of Britain 850–1520* (London, 2003).

Dyer, C., 'Alternative agriculture: Goats in medieval England', in *People, Landscape and Alternative Agriculture. Essays for Joan Thirsk*, ed. R. Hoyle (*AHR* supplement series 3, 2004), pp. 20–38.

Dyer, C., *An Age of Transition? Economy and Society in England in the Later Middle Ages* (Oxford, 2005).

Ekwall, E., *The Concise Oxford Dictionary of English Place-names* (3rd edn, Oxford, 1947).

Elliott, G., 'Field systems of northwest England', in A.R.H. Baker and R.A. Butlin (eds), *Studies of Field Systems in the British Isles* (Cambridge, 1973), pp. 41–92.

Epstein, S., *Freedom and Growth: The Rise of States and Markets in Europe, 1300–1750* (London, 2000).

Evans, E.E., *Irish Heritage* (Dundalk, 1942).

Evans, E.E., *Irish Folk Ways* (London, 1957).

Evans, R, *Home Scenes; or Tavistock and its Vicinity* (Tavistock, 1846).

Everitt, A.M., 'Country, county and town: Patterns of regional evolution in England', *Journal of Historical Geography* 3 (1977), pp. 1–19.

Everitt, A.M., *Landscape and Community in England* (London, 1985).

Everitt, A.M., *Continuity and Colonisation: the Evolution of Kentish Settlement* (Leicester, 1986).

Everitt, A.M., 'The marketing of agricultural produce', in J. Thirsk (ed.), *Agrarian History of England and Wales; IV 1500–1640* (Cambridge, 1997), pp. 466–592.

Everitt, A., 'River and wold: reflections on the historical origins of region and pays', *Journal of Historical Geography*, 3 (1977), pp. 1–19.

Everson, P., 'An excavated Anglo-Saxon sunken-featured building and settlement site at Salmonby, Lincolnshire', *Lincolnshire Hist. Archaeol.* 8 (1973), pp. 61–72.

Farmer, D.L., 'Marketing the produce of the countryside, 1200–1500', in E. Miller (ed.), *Agrarian History of England and Wales; III 1348–1500* (Cambridge, 1991), pp. 324–430.

Fellows-Jensen, G., 'A Gaelic-Scandinavian loan-word in English place-names', *Journal of the English Place-name Society* 10 (1977–8), pp. 18–25.

Field, J., *English Field-names: A Dictionary* (Newton Abbot, 1972).

Finberg, H.P.R., 'The early history of Werrington', *EHR* 59, no. 234 (May, 1944), pp. 237–51.

Finberg, H.P.R., 'The Stannary of Tavistock', *Trans. Devon. Assoc.* 81 (1949), pp. 155–84.

Finberg, H.P.R., *Tavistock Abbey: A Study in the Social and Economic History of Devon* (Cambridge, 1951).

Finberg, H.P.R., *The Early Charters of Devon and Cornwall* (Leicester, 1953).

Finberg, H.P.R., 'An early reference to the Welsh cattle trade', *AHR* 2 (1954), pp. 12–14.

Finberg, H.P.R., 'Supplement to the Early Charters of Devon and Cornwall', in W.G. Hoskins, *The Westward Expansion of Wessex*, Department of English Local History Occasional Papers 13 (Leicester, 1960), pp. 23–25.

Finberg, H.P.R., 'Anglo-Saxon England to 1042', in *idem* (ed.), *The Agrarian History of England and Wales, I, ii, AD 43–1042* (Cambridge, 1972).

Fleming, A., *The Dartmoor Reaves: Investigating Prehistoric Land Divisions* (London, 1988; 2nd edn, Bollington, 2007).

Fleming, A., 'The reaves reviewed', *PDAS* 52 (1994), pp. 63–74.

Fleming, A. and N. Ralph, 'Medieval settlement and land use on Holne Moor, Dartmoor: The landscape evidence', *Medieval Archaeology* 26 (1982), pp. 101–37.

Ford, W.J., 'Pattern of Settlement in the Central Region of the Warwickshire Avon', unpubl. MA thesis, University of Leicester (1973).

Ford, W.J., 'Some settlement patterns in the central region of the Warwickshire Avon', in P.H. Sawyer (ed.), *Medieval Settlement: Continuity and Change* (London, 1976), pp. 274–94.

Fox, A., 'A monastic homestead on Dean Moor, S. Devon', *Medieval Archaeology* 2 (1958), pp. 141–57.

Fox, H.S.A., 'A Geographical Study of the Field Systems of Devon and Cornwall', unpubl. Ph.D. thesis, University of Cambridge (1971).

Fox, H.S.A., 'The chronology of enclosure and economic development in medieval Devon', *EHR* 28 (1975), pp. 181–202.

Fox, H.S.A., 'Peasant farmers, patterns of settlement and *pays*: Transformations of the landscapes of Devon and Cornwall during the later Middle Ages', in R. Higham (ed.), *Landscape and Townscape in the South West*, Exeter Studies in History 22 (Exeter, 1989), pp. 41–74.

Fox, H.S.A., 'The people of the Wolds in English settlement history', in M. Aston, D. Austin and C. Dyer (eds), *The Rural Settlements of Medieval England* (Oxford, 1989), pp. 77–101.

Fox, H.S.A., 'Occupation of the land: Devon and Cornwall', in E. Miller (ed.), *Agrarian History of England and Wales; III 1348–1500* (Cambridge, 1991), pp. 152–74.

Fox, H.S.A., 'Farming practices and techniques: Devon and Cornwall', in E. Miller (ed.), *Agrarian History of England and Wales; III 1348–1500* (Cambridge, 1991), pp. 303–23.

Fox, H.S.A., 'Tenant farming and farmers: Devon and Cornwall', in E. Miller (ed.), *Agrarian History of England and Wales; III 1348–1500* (Cambridge, 1991), pp. 722–43.

Fox, H.S.A., 'Medieval Dartmoor as seen through the account rolls', *PDAS* 52 (1994), pp. 149–72.

Fox, H.S.A., 'The millstone makers of medieval Dartmoor', *DCNQ* 37, pt 5 (1994), pp. 153–57.

Fox, H.S.A. (ed.), *Seasonal Settlement*, Vaughan Paper No. 39 (Leicester, 1996).

Fox, H.S.A., 'The Wolds before c1500', in J. Thirsk (ed.), *Rural England: an Illustrated History of the Landscape* (Oxford, 2000), pp. 50–61.

Fox, H.S.A., *The Evolution of the Fishing Village: Landscape and Society along the South Devon Coast, 1086–1550* (Oxford, 2001).

Fox, H.S.A., 'Taxation and settlement in medieval Devon', in M. Prestwich, R. Britnell and R. Frame (eds), *Thirteenth century England X: Proceedings of the Durham Conference 2003* (Woodbridge, 2005), pp. 168–85.

Fox, H.S.A., 'Fragmented manors and the customs of the Anglo-Saxons', in
    S. Keynes and A. Smyth (eds), *Anglo-Saxons: Studies presented to Cyril Roy
    Hart* (Dublin, 2005), pp. 78–97.
Fox, H.S.A., 'Butter place-names and transhumance', in O.J. Padel and
    N. Parsons (eds), *A Commodity of Good Names: Essays in Honour of
    Margaret Gelling* (Donnington, 2008), pp. 252–64.
Fox, H.S.A., 'Lords and wastes', in R. Goddard, J. Langdon, M. Muller, *Survival
    and Discord in Medieval Society: Essays in Honour of Chris Dyer* (Turnhout,
    2010), pp. 29–48.
Fox, H.S.A. and O.J. Padel (eds), *The Cornish Lands of the Arundels of
    Lanherne, Fourteenth to Sixteenth Centuries*, Devon and Cornwall Record
    Society, new ser. 41 (2000).
Fyfe, R., 'Paleoenvironmental perspectives on medieval landscape development',
    in S. Turner (ed.), *Medieval Devon and Cornwall: Shaping an Ancient
    Countryside* (Macclesfield, 2006), pp. 10–23.
Gardiner, M., 'A seasonal fishermen's settlement at Dungeness, Kent', *Medieval
    Settlement Research Group Annual Report* 11 (1996), pp. 18–20.
Gawne, E., 'Field patterns in Widecombe Parish and the Forest of Dartmoor',
    Trans. Devon. Assoc. 102 (1970), pp. 49–69.
Gawne, E., and J. Sanders, *Early Dartmoor Farmhouses: Longhouses in
    Widecombe and some Surrounding Parishes* (Chudleigh, 1998).
Gelling, M., *Place-names in the Landscape* (London, 1984).
Gelling, M., *The Landscape of Place-names* (Stamford, 2000).
Gerrard, S., *Book of Dartmoor Landscapes Through Time* (London, 1997).
Gerrard, S., *The Early British Tin Industry* (Stroud, 2000).
Gibson, E. (ed.), William Camden, *Britannia, or, a Chorographical Description
    of Great Britain and Ireland, together with the Ancient Islands / written in
    Latin by William Camden and translated into English with additions and
    improvements by Edmund Gibson* (4th edn, London, 1772).
Gill, C. (ed.), *Dartmoor: A New Study* (Newton Abbot, 1970).
Goodacre, J., *The Transformation of a Peasant Economy: Townspeople and
    Villagers in the Lutterworth Area, 1500–1700* (Aldershot, 1994).
Gover, J.E.B., A. Mawer and F.M. Stenton, *The Place-names of Devon*, 2 vols
    (Cambridge, 1931–32).
Gover, J.E.B., *The Place-names of Warwickshire* (Cambridge, 1936).
Gray, H.L., *English Field Systems* (Cambridge, 1915).
Greeves, T., 'The Devon Tin Industry 1450–1750: an Archaeological and
    Historical Survey', unpubl. Ph.D. thesis, University of Exeter (1981).
Greeves, T., 'Placenames of Dartmoor—lost and found', *Dartmoor Magazine* 35
    (1994), pp. 6–8.
Greeves, T., 'Red tide: The summer pasturage of cattle on Dartmoor', *Dartmoor
    Magazine* 43 (1996), pp. 6–8.
Greeves, T., '"Mr Coaker is riding today"', *Devon Life* 6, no. 1 (July 2001),
    pp. 76–77.
Greeves, T., 'Was Brentor a Dark Age Centre', *Dartmoor Magazine* 71 (2003),
    pp. 8–10.
Greeves, T., 'The beamworks of Dartmoor—a remarkable heritage of the tinners',
    Dartmoor Magazine 75 (2004), pp. 9–11.

Greeves, T., 'The start of history—two inscribed stones from western Dartmoor', *Dartmoor Magazine* 91 (2008), pp. 8–10.

Greig, O. and W. Rankine, 'A stone-age settlement system near East Week, Dartmoor: Mesolithic and Post-Mesolithic Industries', *PDAS* 5 (1953), pp. 8–26.

Haldane, A., *The Drove Roads of Scotland* (London, 1952).

Halliday, F.E. (ed.), *Richard Carew of Anthony: The Survey of Cornwall etc.* (London, 1953).

Hamerow, H., *Early Medieval Settlements: The Archaeology of Rural Communities in Northwest Europe, 400–900* (Oxford, 2002).

Hands, S., *The Book of Bickington: from Moor to Shore* (Tiverton, 2000).

Haslam, J., 'The towns of Devon', in J. Haslam (ed.), *Anglo-Saxon Towns in Southern England* (Chichester, 1984).

Hasted, E., *History and Topographical Survey of the County of Kent*, 2nd edn (Canterbury, 1797–1801).

Hatcher, J., *Rural Economy and Society in the Duchy of Cornwall 1300–1500* (Cambridge, 1970).

Havinden, M. and F. Wilkinson, 'Farming', in C. Gill (ed.), *Dartmoor: A New Study* (Newton Abbot, 1970), pp. 139–82.

Hemery, E., *High Dartmoor: Land and People* (London, 1983).

Henderson, C.G. and P.J. Weddell, 'Medieval settlements on Dartmoor and in west Devon: The evidence from excavations', *PDAS* 52 (1994), pp. 119–40.

Herring, P., 'An Exercise in Landscape History: Pre-Norman and Medieval Brown Willy and Bodmin Moor', unpubl. M.Phil thesis: University of Sheffield (1986).

Herring, P., 'Transhumance in medieval Cornwall', in H.S.A. Fox (ed.), *Seasonal Settlement*, Vaughan Paper No. 39 (Leicester, 1996), pp. 35–44.

Herring, P., 'Cornish uplands: Medieval, post-medieval and modern extents', in I.D. Whyte and A.J.L. Winchester (eds), *Society, Landscape and Environment in Upland Britain*, Society for Landscape Studies 2 (2004), pp. 37–51.

Herring, P., 'Medieval fields at Brown Willy, Bodmin Moor', in S. Turner (ed.), *Medieval Devon and Cornwall: Shaping an Ancient Countryside* (Macclesfield, 2006), pp. 78–103.

Herring, P., and J. Nowakowski, 'Beehive huts', in N. Johnson and P. Rose, *Bodmin Moor: An Archaeological Survey*, vol. 1 (London, 1994), pp. 98–100.

Higham, M.C., 'Aergi place-names as indicators of transhumance: problems of the evidence', in H.S.A. Fox (ed.), *Seasonal Settlement*, Vaughan Paper No. 39 (Leicester, 1996), pp. 55–60.

Hill, D. and A.R. Rumble, *The Defence of Wessex: The Burghal Hidage and Anglo-Saxon Fortifications* (Manchester, 1996).

Hindle, B., *Roads, Tracks and their Interpretation* (London, 1993).

Hipkin, S., 'The structure of landownership and land occupation in the Romney Marsh region, 1646–1834', *AHR* 51, pt 1 (2003), pp. 69–94.

Holt, J.C. (ed.), *Domesday Studies* (Woodbridge, 1987).

Hooke, D., *The Anglo-Saxon Landscape: The Kingdom of the Hwicce* (Manchester, 1985).

Hooke, D., *The Landscape of Anglo-Saxon England* (London, 1988).

Hooke, D., 'Pre-Conquest woodland: Its distribution and usage', *AHR* 37 (1989), pp. 113–29.

Hooke, D., *Pre-Conquest Charter-Bounds of Devon and Cornwall* (Woodbridge, 1994).

Hoskins, W.G., *Devon* (London, 1954).

Hoskins, W.G., *Dartmoor*, National Park Guide no. 1 (London, 1957).

Hoskins, W.G., *Devon and its People* (Exeter, 1959).

Hoskins, W.G., *Provincial England* (London, 1963).

Hoskins, W.G. and H.P.R. Finberg (eds), *Devonshire Studies* (London, 1952).

Hoskins, W.G. and L. Dudley, *The Common Lands of England and Wales* (London, 1963).

Houghton, F.T.S., 'Saltways', *Transactions of the Birmingham and Warwickshire Archaeological Society* 54 (1932), pp. 1–17.

Hughes, P.G., *Wales and the Drovers* (London, 1943).

Johnson, M. and P. Rose, *Bodmin Moor: An Archaeological Survey*, I, *The Human Landscape to c.1800* (London, 1994).

Jones, A.M., 'The excavation of a multi-period site at Stencoose, Cornwall', *Cornish Archaeology* 39–40 (2000–1), pp. 45–94.

Jones, G., *Saints in the Landscape* (Stroud, 2007).

Jope, E.M., 'Cornish houses', in *idem* (ed.), *Studies in Building History* (London, 1961), pp. 214–22.

Kettle, A.J., 'Agriculture, 1300–1540', in *VCH Shropshire* 4 (Oxford, 1989).

Keynes, S., *The Diplomas of King Æthelred 'the Unready' 978–1016: A Study in their use as Historical Evidence* (Cambridge, 1980).

Klein, J., *The Mesta: A Study in Spanish Economic History, 1273–1836* (Harvard, 1920).

Knoop, D. and G.P. Jones, *The Medieval Mason* (Manchester, 1949).

Kowaleski, M., *Local Markets and Regional Trade in Medieval Exeter* (Cambridge, 1995).

Le Roy Ladurie, E., *Montaillou: Cathars and Catholics in a French Village 1294–1324* (1978; English trans. London, 1980).

Langdon, J.L., *Horses, Oxen and Technological Innovation: The Use of Draught Animals in English Farming from 1066 to 1500* (Cambridge, 1986).

Langdon, J.L., 'The economics of horses and oxen in medieval England', *AHR* 30 (1982), pp. 31–40.

Le Messurier, B., 'The post-prehistoric structures of central north Dartmoor: A field survey', *Trans. Devon. Assoc.* 111 (1979), pp. 59–73.

Linehan, C.D., 'A forgotten manor in Widecombe-in-the-Moor', *Trans. Devon Assoc.* 94 (1962), pp. 463–92.

Linehan, C.D., 'Deserted sites and rabbit-warrens on Dartmoor, Devon', *Medieval Archaeology* 10 (1966), pp. 113–44.

Lopez, R., 'The origin of the Merino sheep', *The Joshua Starr Memorial Volume: Studies in History and Philology*, Jewish Social Studies 5 (New York, 1953), pp. 151–68.

Loyn, H.R., 'The hundred in England in the tenth and early eleventh centuries', in H. Hearder and H.R. Loyn (eds), *British Government and Administration: Studies presented to S.B. Chrimes* (Cardiff, 1974), pp. 1–15.

Loyn, H.R., *The Governance of Anglo-Saxon England 500–1087* (London, 1984).

Margary, I.D., *Roman Roads in Britain* (London, 1973).

Marshall, W., *The Rural Economy of the West of England, including Devonshire . . .*, 2 vols. (1796, reprinted Newton Abbot, 1970).

MacDermot, E.T., *The History of the Forest of Exmoor* (Newton Abbot, 1973 edn).

McDonnell, J., 'The role of transhumance in northern England', *Northern History* 24 (1988), pp. 1–17.

Maitland, F.W., *Domesday Book and Beyond: Three Essays in the Early History of England* (Cambridge, 1897).

Mee, A., *Devon* (London, 1938).

Miles, H. and T. Miles, 'Pilton, North Devon: Excavations within a medieval village', *PDAS* 33 (1975), pp. 268–70.

Miller, E. (ed.), *Agrarian History of England and Wales; III 1348–1500* (Cambridge, 1991).

Mills, A.D., *A Dictionary of English Place Names* (Oxford, 1991).

Moore, S. and P. Birkett, *A Short History of the Rights of Common upon the Forest of Dartmoor and the Commons of Devon* (Plymouth, 1890).

Morris, R., *Churches in the Landscape* (1989; London, 1997).

Moss, D., 'The economic development of a Middlesex village', *AHR* 28 (1980), pp. 104–14.

Muir, R., *The New Reading the Landscape: Fieldwork in Landscape History* (Exeter, 2000).

Nall, W., 'Alston', *Transactions of the Cumberland and Westmorland Antiquarian and Archaeological Society* 7 (1886).

Newbiggin, M.I., *Modern Geography* (London, 1911).

Newman, P., *The Dartmoor Tin Industry: A Field Guide* (Newton Abbot, 1998).

Newman, P., 'Tinworking and the landscape of medieval Devon, c.1150–1700', in S. Turner (ed.), *Medieval Devon and Cornwall: Shaping an Ancient Countryside* (Macclesfield, 2006), pp. 123–43.

Nowakowski, J. and P. Herring, 'The beehive huts on Bodmin Moor', *Cornish Archaeology* 24 (1985), pp. 185–96.

O'Dubhthaigh, N., 'Summer pasture in Donegal', *Folk Life* 22 (1983–84), pp. 42–54.

Okasha, E., *Corpus of Early Christian Inscribed Stones of South-west Britain* (London, 1993).

O'Donovan, M.A. (ed.), *Charters of Sherborne* (Oxford, 1988).

Oppenheim, M., *The Maritime History of Devon* (Exeter, 1968).

Orwin, C.S. and C.S., *The Open Fields* (Oxford, 1938).

Oxford English Dictionary. [OED]

Padel, O.J., *Cornish Place-name Elements* (Nottingham, 1985).

Page, F., '*Bidentes Hoylandiae*: A medieval sheep farm', *EHR* 1 (1926–9), pp. 603–13.

Page, M., 'The technology of medieval sheep farming: Some evidence from Crawley, Hampshire, 1208–1349', *AHR* 51, pt 2 (2003), pp. 137–54.

Parsons, D.N. and T. Styles, *The Vocabulary of English Place-names*, 3 vols (Nottingham, 1997–2004).

Pearce, S., 'Early medieval land use on Dartmoor and its flanks', *Devon Archaeology* 3 (1985), pp. 13–19.

Pearce, S., *South-western Britain in the Early Middle Ages* (London, 2004).

Pearse, C., 'Sheep creeps and holes', *Dartmoor Magazine* 61 (2000), pp. 34–35.

Peskett, H.M., 'The probate inventory of Sire John Daumarle, 1393', *DCNQ* 32 (1971), pp. 79–82.

Pollard, A. (ed.), *Works of Robert Herrick*, i (London, 1891).

Polwhele, R., *The History of Devon*, ii (London, 1793).

Postan, M.M., 'Medieval agrarian society in its prime: England', in M.M. Postan (ed.), *The Cambridge Economic History of Europe, I: The Agrarian Life of the Middle Ages* (Cambridge, 1966), pp. 548–632.

Postan, M.M., *The Medieval Economy and Society. An Economic History of Britain 1100–1500* (London, 1972).

Postan, M.M., 'Village livestock in the thirteenth century', in *idem, Essays on Medieval Agriculture and General Problems of the Medieval Economy* (Cambridge, 1973), pp. 214–48.

Postles, D., 'The Oseney Abbey flock', *Oxoniensia* 49 (1984), pp. 141–52.

Postles, D., *The Surnames of Devon* (Oxford, 1995).

Postles, D., *Naming the People of England, c.1100–1350* (Cambridge, 2006).

Pound, H.J.G., *A History of the English Parish* (Cambridge, 2000).

Pounds, N.J.G. (ed.), *The Parliamentary Survey of the Duchy of Cornwall*, DCRS, new ser. 25 and 27 (1982, 1984).

Powell, R., *Depopulation Arraigned* (London, 1636; reprinted Amsterdam, 1976).

Power, E., 'Peasant life and rural conditions', in J.R. Tanner, C.W. Previte-Orton and Z.N. Brooke (eds), *The Cambridge Medieval History*, vii (Cambridge, 1932), pp. 716–50.

Preston-Jones, A. and P. Rose, 'Medieval Cornwall', *Cornish Archaeology* 25 (1986), pp. 135–85.

Rackham, O., *The History of the Countryside* (London, 1986).

Ramm, H.G., R.W. McDowall and E. Mercer, *Shielings and Bastles* (London, 1970).

Ransom, B., 'Ilsington parish and the landscape of Peadington', *Devon Historian* 65 (2002), pp. 16–20.

Reaney, P.H., *Dictionary of English Surnames* (Oxford, 1958).

Reichel, O.J., 'The Devonshire Domesday. V. The Hundreds of Devon', *Trans. Devon. Assoc.* 33 (1901), pp. 554–639, and a series of articles on individual hundreds, in *Trans. Devon. Assoc.* scattered between vols 26 (1894) and 54 (1922), and its *Supplements* 1–10 (1928–38).

Rippon, S.J., R.M. Fyfe and A.G. Browne, 'Beyond villages and open fields: The origins and development of a historic landscape characterised by dispersed settlement in south-west England', *Medieval Archaeology* 50 (2006), pp. 31–70.

Risdon, T., *The Chorographical Description: or, Survey of the County of Devon* (1714, edition of 1811).

Roberts, B.K., 'A study of medieval colonisation in the forest of Arden, Warwickshire', *AHR* 16 (1968), pp. 101–13.

Roberts, B.K., 'Field systems of the west midlands', in A.R.H. Baker and R.A. Butlin (ed.), *Studies of Field Systems in the British Isles* (Cambridge, 1973), pp. 188–231.

Rose-Troup, F., 'Anglo-Saxon charters of Devon', *DCNQ* 17 (1932–3), pp. 124–26.

Round, J.H., 'Domesday survey', in *VCH Essex*, vol. 1 (Westminster, 1903), pp. 368–74.

Rowe, S., *A Perambulation of the Antient & Royal Forest of Dartmoor & the Venville Precincts* (Plymouth, 1848).

Rowley, T., *The Shropshire Landscape* (London, 1972).

Sawyer, P.H., 'The "Original Returns" and Domesday Book', *EHR* 70 (1955), pp. 177–97.

Sawyer, P.H. (ed.), *Anglo-Saxon Charters: An Annotated List and Bibliography*, R. Hist. Soc. Guides and Handbooks, 8 (London, 1968).

Seymour, D., *Torre Abbey* (Exeter, 1977).

Siraut, M., *Exmoor: The Making of an English Upland* (Chichester, 2009).

Skeel, C., 'The cattle trade between Wales and England from the fifteenth to the nineteenth centuries', *Transactions of the Royal Historical Society*, 4th ser. 9 (1926), pp. 135–58.

Skipp, V.H.T., *Discovering Sheldon* (Birmingham, 1963).

Skipp, V.H.T., *Discovering Bickenhill* (Birmingham, 1963).

Skipp, V.H.T., *Medieval Yardley: The Origins and Growth of a West Midlands Community* (London, 1970).

Smith, A.H., *English Place-name Elements* 2 vols, English Place-name Society, 25, 26 (Cambridge, 1956).

Smith, A.H., *The Place-names of Gloucestershire*, vol. 3 (Cambridge, 1965).

Smith, K., J. Coppen, G.J. Wainwright and S. Beckett, 'The Shaugh Moor project: Third report, settlement and environmental investigations', *Proceedings of the Prehistoric Society* 47 (1981), pp. 205–73.

Somers Cocks, J., 'Dartmoor and Domesday Book', *DCNQ* 30 (1965–67), pp. 290–93.

Somers Cocks, J., 'Saxon and early medieval times' and 'Exploitation', in C. Gill (ed.), *Dartmoor: A New Study* (Newton Abbot, 1970), pp. 245–75.

Somers Cocks, J., 'The Stannary bounds of Plympton & Tavistock', *DCNQ* 32, pt 3 (1971), pp. 76–79.

Somers Cocks, J., and T. Greeves, *A Dartmoor Century 1883–1983: One Hundred Years of the Dartmoor Preservation Association* (Postbridge, 1983).

Spooner, G. and F. Russell (eds), *Worth's Dartmoor* (Newton Abbot, 1953; 1967 edn).

Stanbrook, E., *Dartmoor Forest Farms: A Social History from Enclosure to Abandonment* (Tiverton, 1994).

Stanes, R., *The Old Farm: A History of Farming Life in the West Country* (Exeter, 1990).

Stenton, F.M., *Anglo-Saxon England* (Oxford, 1943).

Stephenson, M., 'Wool yields in the medieval economy', *EHR* 2nd ser. 41, no. 3 (1988), pp. 368–91.

Stone, D., 'The productivity and management of sheep in late medieval England', *AHR* 51, pt 1 (2003), pp. 1–22.

Stone, D., *Decision Making in Medieval Agriculture* (Oxford, 2005).

Swanson, R., 'Economic change and spiritual profits: Receipts from the peculiar jurisdiction of the Peak District in the fourteenth century', in N. Rogers (ed.), *Harlaxton Medieval Studies, III: England in the Fifteenth Century, Proceedings of the 1991 Colloqium* (Stamford, 1993).

Swanton, M. and S. Pearce, 'Lustleigh, south Devon: Its inscribed stone, its churchyard and its parish', in S. Pearce (ed.), *The Early Church in Western Britain and Ireland: Studies Presented to C.A. Ralegh Radford*, British Archaeological Reports (Oxford, 1982).

Tanner, H., *Essay on the Cultivation of Dartmoor* (London, 1854).

Taylor, C., *Roads and Tracks of Britain* (London, 1979).

Thirsk, J. (ed.), *Rural England: An Illustrated History of the Landscape* (Oxford, 2000).

Thirsk, J., 'Farming techniques: Grassland and stock', in *eadem* (ed.), *Agrarian History of England and Wales; IV 1500–1640* (Cambridge, 1967), pp. 179–95.

Thorn, F.R., 'Hundreds and wapentakes' in F. Barlow and *idem*, *The Devonshire Domesday*, Alecto edition (London, 1991), pp. 26–42.

Thomas, F.W.L., 'Beehive houses in Harris and Lewis', *Proceedings of the Society of Antiquaries of Scotland* 3 (1857–60), pp. 127–29.

Thoresby's *Excursions in Leicestershire* (1790).

Tonkin, T., *Carew's Survey of Cornwall to which are added notes by . . . Thomas Tonkin* (London, 1811).

Trow-Smith, R., *A History of British Livestock Husbandry to 1700* (London, 1957).

Turner, S., *Ancient Country: The Historic Character of Rural Devon*, Devon Archaeological Society Occasional Paper 20 (2007).

Underdown, D., *Revel, Riot and Rebellion: Popular Politics and Culture in England, 1603–1660* (Oxford, 1985).

Vancouver, C., *General View of the Agriculture of the County of Devon* (London, 1808).

VCH Cumberland (London, 1905).

Vidal de la Blache, P., *Principles of Human Geography* (1926 trans. of French edn of 1922).

Walker, M.J., 'Laying a mega-myth: Dolmens and drovers in prehistoric Spain', *World Archaeology* 15, no. 1, *Transhumance and Pastoralism* (June, 1983), pp. 37–50.

Ward, A., 'Transhumance and place-names: An aspect of early Ordnance Survey mapping on the Black Mountain commons, Carmarthenshire', *Studia Celtica*, 33 (1999), pp. 335–48.

Watkin, A. (ed.), *The Great Chartulary of Glastonbury*, 3 vols, Somerset Record Society 59, 63–64 (1947–56).

Watts, M.A., *Archaeological and Historical Survey at Gomerock, Kingswear, Devon* (Exeter, 1997).

Watts, M., *Working Oxen* (Princes Risborough, 1999).

Weddell, P.J. and S.J. Reed, 'Excavations at Sourton Down, Okehampton, 1986–1991', *PDAS* 55 (1997), pp. 35–147.

Welldon Finn, R., 'The making of the Devonshire Domesdays', *Trans. Devon. Assoc.* 87 (1957), pp. 93–123.

Whetter, J., *Cornwall in the 17th Century* (Padstow, 1974).

Wickham, C., *Land and Power: Studies in Italian and European Social History, 400–1200* (London, 1994).

Wilkinson, F., 'The Dartmoor husbandman', *Devon Historian* 14 (1977), pp. 5–10.

Williams, M., *The Draining of the Somerset Levels* (Cambridge, 1970).

Williamson, T., *The Norfolk Broads: A Landscape History* (Manchester, 1997).

Winchester, A.J.L., 'Shielings in upper Eskdale', *Transactions of the Cumberland and Westmorland Antiquarian and Archaeological Society* 84 (1984), pp. 267–68.

Winchester, A.J.L., *Landscape and Society in Medieval Cumbria* (Edinburgh, 1987).

Winchester, A.J.L., *The Harvest of the Hills: Rural Life in Northern England and the Scottish Borders, 1400–1700* (Edinburgh, 2000).

Winchester, A.J.L., *Discovering Parish Boundaries* (Princes Risborough, 2000).

Winchester, A.J.L., 'Moorland forests of medieval England', in J.D. Whyte and A.J.L. Winchester (eds), *Society, Landscape and Environment in Upland Britain*, Society for Landscape Studies 2 (2004), pp. 21–34.

Winchester, A.J.L., 'Vaccaries and agistment: Upland medieval forests as grazing grounds', in J. Langton and G. Jones (eds), *Forests and Chases of England and Wales, c.1000 to c.1500* (Oxford, 2010), pp. 109–24.

Witney, K.P., *The Jutish Forest: A Study of the Weald of Kent from 450 to 1380 AD* (London, 1976).

Woods, S., *Uncle Tom Cobley and All—Widecombe-in-the-Moor* (Tiverton, 2000).

Woolner, D., 'Peat charcoal', *DCNQ* 30 (1965–67), pp. 118–20.

Worth, R.H., 'Presidential address', *Trans. Devon. Assoc.* 62 (1930), pp. 49–115.

Worth, R.H., 'Dartmoor 1788–1808', *Trans. Devon. Assoc.* 73 (1941), pp. 203–25.

Worth, R.H., 'The tenants and commoners of Dartmoor', *Trans. Devon. Assoc.* 76 (1944), pp. 187–214.

Young, A., *Annals of Agriculture and other Useful Arts*, 45 vols. (1784–1809).

Index

Cockingford 110–11, 130, 154, 195, 198, 201, 207–8
Cockington 108–11, 116–19, 130, 133–4, 154, 195, 197, 200–2, 207–8
Codelip, John 56
Coldestone, in Shaugh Prior parish 171
Coldridge 211
Cole, John 58
Colesworthy, in Ilsington parish 154
Collishull, Richard 102
Combe, in Throwleigh parish 78
Combebowe, in Bridestowe parish 168
common rights (of pasture) 35–6, 48–61, 84–8, 161–2, 222, 226–7, 239 n. 44
  by day only 52, 73, 91
  limited to winter stock 52, 54, 72, 85, 87
  restrictions on outsiders 36
  stints 86
Commons of Devon 48–61, 168
Compostella (Spain) 206
convertible husbandry 119, 212
Coombe Cellars, in Combeinteignhead parish 28
Corndon, in Widecombe parish 166
Cornwall 30, 40, 41, 44, 77–8, 101, 104
Cornwall, earls and dukes of 27, 47, and see Duchy of Cornwall
Cornwood 10, 44, 54, 73, 82, 84, 88–9, 96, 105, 161–2, 171, 205
coroner 104
Corringdon Ball, in South Brent parish 10, 84–5
Coryton 79
Cosdon, in South Tawton parish 22, plates 1, 2
Cossick, in Moretonhampstead parish 249 n. 36
Cotswolds 34, 36, 170
Courtenay family 88–90
Courtenay, Hugh 84–5
Coventry and Lichfield, bishop of 35
Cowick 151–2

Cowsen, in Sourton parish 200
Creaber Green pound, in Gidleigh parish 67
Crediton 73, 88, 207, 208
Crocker, Richard 78
crosses 95, 97, 169, 200
Crossing, William 23, 65, 77, 78
Crowland Abbey (Lincs) 3, 35
Crow Tor, in Lydford parish 65
Cudlipp[town], in Peter Tavy parish 56, 81, 126–7, 146–8, 156
Culm Measures 123, 142, 200
Cumberland 28, 31, 78, 142–3, 150
Cusancia, William de 20

Dabernoun, John 50
Dainton 112–14
dairying 73, 86, 123, 127, 145–57, 161, 214, 218–20
Dart, river, valley 19, 44, 65, 104, 121, 176, and see West Dart
Dartmoor,
  colonisation of 20, 22, 129, 158–69, 181–90
  distinctive identity of residents 14–18
  manorial moors in 24, 50, 67, 81–6, 88–91, 131–81, 166–81
Dartmoor, manor of Lydford or,
  account rolls 57–9, 61, 63–8, 71–2, 74, 75, 88, 89–90
  agistment lists 57–68, 70–1, 74–6
  bailiwicks or quarters of 19, 24, 64, 67–8, 185
  courts, court rolls 47, 56–9, 61, 69, 70, 72–4, 76
  officials 50–1, 61–4, 75, 182, and see herdsmen
  surveys, rentals 20, 57, 72
Dartmoor Preservation Society 20
Dartmouth 225
Daumarle, Sir John 13, 219–20
Dauncy, Sibyl 82
Deancombe, in Dean Prior parish 104
Dean Prior, Dean Moor 10, 13, 79, 81, 92–3, 95, 102, 104, 171, 207